THE NATURE OF INQUISITORIAL PROCESSES IN ADMINISTRATIVE REGIMES

The Nature of Inquisitorial Processes in Administrative Regimes

Global Perspectives

Edited by

LAVERNE JACOBS

University of Windsor, Canada

SASHA BAGLAY

University of Ontario Institute of Technology, Canada

Routledge

Taylor & Francis Group

LONDON AND NEW YORK

First published 2013 by Ashgate Publishing

2 Park Square, Milton Park, Abingdon, Oxfordshire OX14 4RN
52 Vanderbilt Avenue, New York, NY 10017

Routledge is an imprint of the Taylor & Francis Group, an informa business

First issued in paperback 2020

British Library Cataloguing in Publication Data
A catalogue record for this book is available from the British Library

The Library of Congress has cataloged the printed edition as follows:
Jacobs, Laverne A.
The nature of inquisitorial processes in administrative regimes : global perspectives / By Laverne Jacobs and Sasha Baglay.
pages cm
Includes bibliographical references and index.
ISBN 978-1-4094-6947-6 (hardback) 1. Abuse of administrative power. 2. Judicial review of administrative acts. 3. Administrative procedure. 4. Administrative law. 5. Judicial power. I. Baglay, Sasha, 1978- II. Title.
K3416.J33 2013
347'.012--dc23

2013004541

ISBN 978-1-4094-6947-6 (hbk)
ISBN 978-0-367-60131-7 (pbk)

Contents

PART 2 EU ADMINISTRATIVE LAW AND POLYJURAL DECISION-MAKING

PART 3 TRUTH COMMISSIONS AND PUBLIC INQUIRIES I – VIEWS OF COMMISSIONERS

PART 4 TRUTH COMMISSIONS AND PUBLIC INQUIRIES II – OBSERVERS' REFLECTIONS

List of Tables

List of Contributors

Professor Michael Asimow, Visiting Professor, Stanford Law School, Stanford University, and Professor of Law Emeritus, UCLA School of Law, USA

Professor Jean-Bernard Auby, Director of the Center on Changes in Governance and Public Law, Sciences Po (Institut d'Etudes Politiques de Paris), France

Professor Sasha Baglay, Faculty of Social Science and Humanities, University of Ontario Institute of Technology, Canada

Hon. Thomas R. Braidwood, Q.C., retired Justice of the British Columbia Court of Appeal and Commissioner of the Commissions of Inquiry into the Use of Conducted Energy Weapons in British Columbia, Canada

Professor Robin Creyke, College of Law, Australian National University and Senior Member, Administrative Appeals Tribunal, Australia

Professor Giacinto della Cananea, Professor of Administrative Law and EU Administrative Law, University of Rome "Tor Vergata", Italy

Dr. Nora J. Farrell, Ombudsperson, Ryerson University, Canada

Justice Stephen T. Goudge, Court of Appeal for Ontario, Canada and Commissioner of the Inquiry into Pediatric Forensic Pathology

Ms. Samantha Green, J.D. 2012 (University of Toronto), Toronto, Canada

Professor Gerald Heckman, Faculty of Law, University of Manitoba, Canada

Professor Herwig C. H. Hofmann, Professor of European and Transnational Public Law and Jean Monnet Chair at the University of Luxembourg, Luxembourg

Professor Jula Hughes, Faculty of Law, University of New Brunswick, Canada

Professor Laverne Jacobs, Faculty of Law, University of Windsor, Canada

Professor Mary Liston, Faculty of Law, University of British Columbia, Canada

Professor Scott Prasser, Public Policy Institute, Australian Catholic University, Australia

Professor Lorne Sossin, Dean, Osgoode Hall Law School, York University, Canada

Dr. Robert Thomas, Professor of Public Law, School of Law, University of Manchester, UK

Professor Gus Van Harten, Osgoode Hall Law School, York University, Canada

Acknowledgments

There are many people whom we would like to thank and without whom this project would not have been realized. The Social Sciences and Humanities Research Council of Canada, the Faculty of Law of the University of Windsor, the University of Windsor, the Ontario Ministry of the Attorney General, and the Law Foundation of Ontario all provided generous support.

We are grateful to the contributors to this collection, who were also participants at the international research workshop, "The Nature of Inquisitorial Processes in Administrative Regimes: Global Perspectives," which was held at the University of Windsor, Faculty of Law on May 26–27, 2011. They traveled, at times very far distances, to participate in the workshop and took the time to carefully revise their papers for this edited collection.

We thank the discussants at the workshop for their knowledgeable insights: Michael Gottheil, Ian Greene, Audrey Macklin, Marcia Valiante, Christopher Waters, and David Wright. A number of University of Windsor law students have assisted in the preparatory phases through to the editing of this volume. These students include the Comparative Administrative Law Fellows of the summer of 2011: Melissa Kwok, Maria Mavrikkou and Ki Lin Tay; and research assistants John Brennan, Lauri Daitchman, Navjot Grewal, Krina Mahaisuria, Heather McMahon, Alicia Maiuri, and Cynthia Morgan. We are grateful to them also. Finally we thank the anonymous reviewers and the editors at Ashgate for their invaluable feedback and assistance in the publication of this book.

Chapter 1
Introduction

Laverne Jacobs and Sasha Baglay

The inquisitorial process originates in the Civil Law tradition. Yet, in some adversarial jurisdictions, including Canada and Australia, administrative law decision-making has been enhanced by procedures that involve more active participation by decision-makers themselves. Called "inquisitorial process", "activist adjudication", an "inquiry decision-making model", "investigatory process" and various similar terms, these approaches show a dynamic embrace of inquisitorial sensibilities. The inverse is also true – adversarial processes have been brought in by policy-makers in a number of jurisdictions to enhance traditional inquisitorial decision-making. While the existence of multi-traditional decision-making is not new, in recent years, polyjural approaches have emerged most notably in the administrative state.

The "administrative state" occupies a growing place in the regulation of people's daily affairs. The administrative state is typically understood as the web of social and economic regulation that touches on individuals and corporations through the decisions made by a variety of governmental administrative actors. The range of administrative law contexts in which inquisitorial processes are used runs from routine hearings held to determine essential welfare benefits for citizens, to investigations to assist in enforcing economic regulation, procedures for deciding who will enter and remain within a country's borders, and inquiries to establish the truth after a population has experienced what are often unique, but tragic, events. Administrative actors have traditionally emanated from national or sub-national government, though, with the changing nature of governance, supranational administrative decision-making plays a burgeoning and vital role. In some jurisdictions, individuals rely on administrative decision-making to resolve more everyday disputes than traditional courts of law.[1]

"Inquisitorial processes" is the expression that we have adopted to designate the inquiry powers of administrative governance. We have chosen the term to denote both the narrow sense of the rules of procedure that find their roots in

1 In Canada, this idea has been stated explicitly by the Supreme Court in *Nova Scotia (Workers' Compensation Board) v Martin; Nova Scotia (Workers' Compensation Board) v Laseur,* [2003] 2 SCR 504. The idea arises indirectly, with both positive and negative connotation, through studies examining the growth of executive power. See, for example, Paul Craig & Adam Tomkins, eds, *The Executive and Public Law: Power and Accountability in Comparative Perspective* (New York: Oxford University Press, 2006).

the Civil Law tradition of litigation, as well as the terminology used in several common law jurisdictions to reference, broadly, administrative action that is non-adversarial. As academics in the field of administrative law, we were intrigued by the growing use of active inquiry powers within administrative processes in our home country of Canada. In Canada, the implementation of inquisitorial processes garnered mixed responses from both administrative adjudicators and the public. We were aware that inquisitorial processes had been adopted in other traditionally adversarial jurisdictions to assist in administrative decision-making, and sought to explore the reasons for their adoption, the challenges to their implementation, and their effectiveness. Similarly, in Civil Law jurisdictions, where there is a tradition of inquisitorial legal process, we wondered about the use of mixed inquisitorial–adversarial processes and lessons to be learned about their success. Overall, we saw merit in bringing together recent developments in mixed-model administrative decision-making, here and elsewhere, in order to contribute to a neglected but developing literature on comparative administrative process and institutional design. As demonstrated by the nature and number of participants at the research workshop that formed the initial meeting of the contributors to this book,[2] this is a literature that is of value to government policy-makers, administrative law decision-makers, lawyers, academics and the public. The present collection of essays represents the response of 16 individuals – academics, members of the administrative justice community, judges, and others – from seven jurisdictions who also found this phenomenon worthy of study. They represent jurisdictions that are traditionally adversarial and which have imported an inquisitorial approach, as well the reverse. While we cannot purport to represent the globe, we believe that the contributors to this collection reach important conclusions about their own jurisdictions, and raise questions which may valuably be explored in others.

This book analyzes the use of inquisitorial processes in administrative law. It does so by considering three distinct contexts, and four key themes that cut across the use of inquiry powers within them. As for the three contexts, in many jurisdictions across the globe, inquisitorial processes in administrative law exist within hearing procedures, public inquiries and other similar institutions used to investigate the cause of a public event, and investigations conducted by oversight bodies and regulators. It is around these contexts that this collection's chapters are structured: they form the backbone of the book's table of contents. Four central themes emerge from the chapters in this volume: i) terminology and scope of the

2 Entitled *The Nature of Inquisitorial Processes in Administrative Regimes: Global Perspectives*, this international research workshop was held on May 26 and 27, 2011 at the Faculty of Law, University of Windsor, Canada. The participants were invited from academia, government, the tribunal community and the judiciary. The number of participants exceeded, with permission, the 30 person maximum prescribed by the conditions of the generous Social Sciences and Humanities Research Council of Canada Aid to Research Workshops Grant that funded us. Detailed information about the workshop may be found on its website: http://www.uwindsor.ca/law/inquisitorial-processes.

concept of inquisitorial process; ii) justifications for the use of inquiry powers; iii) the effectiveness of inquisitorial processes; and iv) implications of adopting such powers. We explore the contours and depth of these themes in this Introduction.

Administrative law covers a wide field of diverse subject matter which may not be the same in any two territorial jurisdictions. One element that tends to be common to the administrative state in every jurisdiction, however, is a need to balance the elements of fairness, efficiency, thoroughness, effectiveness, and respect for human rights within the administrator's fact-gathering and decision-making procedures. National and supranational states have moved towards developing methods that are flexible as a central response to this requirement of administrative governance. Although the degree of attribution to fairness, efficiency, thoroughness, and respect for human rights varies according to context, these flexible methods aim to allocate an appropriate weight to each factor in performing this balancing act. The chapters in this book illustrate that hearing processes within administrative agencies and tribunals are one, if not the most, evident place where this balancing act has taken place. Can a desired level of flexibility be obtained to meet the goal of efficiency while providing the public with adequate fairness and access to justice? How, if at all, can an approach of active adjudication assist in achieving this objective? The authors in this volume grapple with these questions from a variety of perspectives and within the context of seven jurisdictions. Their answers and the debate that they raise are enlightening. In the final analysis, one may conclude from their studies that whether one is dealing with a national or supranational state, clearly defined policy goals and a commitment to fairness and human rights in achieving them should ultimately be the foundation for any administrative process chosen. In an era where it is not unusual to find lack of resources advanced by governments as a reason to justify processes that privilege efficiency over thoroughness and fairness, the collective voice of this volume suggests that paying more attention to substance can result in more satisfactory formal procedures.

Administrative decision-making has traditionally fallen within the province of the executive branch of government of the nation state. However, this book also presents a timely moment to reconsider who is at the helm of rendering such decisions as changes around the globe broaden our understanding of the nature of the actors who undertake the decision-making required to implement public programs. In the UK, for example, administrative decision-making has moved from being the responsibility of tribunals connected to executive branch departments to members of the judiciary.[3] Similarly, with the rise of globalization, we see a shift from public policies and programs executed solely by the domestic executive to a role for supranational executive-like power. The questions of who is responsible for putting in place policies and how accountability can be ensured is a new challenge arising in the European Union, as discussed by Giacinto della

3 See Lord Justice Carnwath, "Tribunals and the Courts – the UK Model" (2011) 24 Can J Admin L & Prac 5.

Cananea and Herwig Hofmann in their respective chapters. They explore the extent to which inquiry powers alleviate burdens and pose challenges to decision-making and individual rights.

Public inquiries[4] are perhaps the quintessential means by which inquisitorial processes are used by an executive branch of government. They are usually struck by the executive branch of government and run by a present or former member of the judiciary, with powers of investigation and coercion. For example, in 2011, the UK government established an inquiry into the culture, practices and ethics of the press, after incidents that suggested that members of the press had intercepted voicemail.[5] In 2010, the Government of Israel established an independent public commission chaired by retired Supreme Court judge Jacob Türkel. The purpose of the commission was to examine the actions of the Israeli military during an operation in May, 2010 which was designed to enforce a naval blockade against

---

4 Scott Prasser offers a useful set of criteria to define public inquiries:

- they are non-permanent, ad hoc organizational forms;
- they are appointed by government and exist at whim of the government;
- they are not part of any existing agency or department;
- the majority of inquiry's membership is drawn from outside the public sector and does not include sitting ministers or backbenchers;
- their terms of reference should be clearly stated and information about a given inquiry should be actively promoted;
- they should actively seek public participation;
- their findings should be made public.

See Scott Prasser, "Royal Commissions and Public Inquiries: Scope and Uses" in Patrick Weller, ed, *Royal Commissions and the Making of Public Policy* (Melbourne: McMillan Education Australia, 1994) 1 at 4.

Public inquiries may have different titles, including "Commissions of Inquiry", "Royal Commissions" and "Task Forces." In practice, there is often little difference, in terms of importance and functions, between royal commissions and other types of inquiry. However, depending on jurisdiction, some differences may exist with respect to their powers. For example, in Australia, royal commissions have a statutory basis and possess coercive powers, unlike other types of inquiry which do not always have statutory backing and, consequently, may have weaker information-gathering powers and protections. See Scott Prasser's chapter in this volume. In Canada, however, no significant difference in terms of actual powers is drawn between royal commissions and commissions of inquiry, although it is generally accepted that a title "royal" conveys a particular sense of prestige.

Generally, commissions of inquiry can be of two types: (1) advisory or policy inquiries – to research policy issues and advise the government on policy development; (2) investigative – to find out the facts and causes of a given event.

5 The Inquiry, which was chaired by Lord Justice Leveson, published Part 1 of its report in November, 2012. See *An Inquiry into the Culture, Practices and Ethics of the Press* at http://www.official-documents.gov.uk/document/hc1213/hc07/0780/0780.pdf .

the Gaza Strip and which resulted in death and injuries.[6] In Canada, some of the recent federal inquiries have looked into the role of Canadian officials in renditions to torture[7] and the sponsorship program intended to publicize certain government programs and make federal presence more visible across Canada.[8] In Australia, recent federal inquiries have dealt with the role of certain Australian companies in the UN Oil-for-Food Program (2005–06) and equine influenza (2007–08).[9]

However, inquisitorial processes may equally be exercised by legislative oversight bodies and institutions based on the ombudsman.[10] In this volume, we examine not only public inquiries but also legislative oversight bodies, and ombuds institutions, to explore the nature and effectiveness of their investigatory powers. Recent events around the world show a proliferation of independent accountability agencies, including ombuds institutions, created to investigate a variety of societal issues. Specific examples include the Lokpal Bill in India, a civil society initiative to establish an anticorruption ombudsman. The latest iteration of this bill is currently being debated in the Indian Parliament.[11] The veritable

---

6 The incident that gave rise to the inquiry was as follows. On May 31, 2010, a flotilla of six vessels organized by the Humanitarian Relief Foundation and Free Gaza Movement approached the coast of Israel intending to break Israel's naval blockade of the Gaza Strip. The Israeli military sent several warnings to the ships, requesting them to turn back. When the ships did not stop or turn back, the military commenced boarding and takeover. The takeover of one ship – *Mavi Marmara* – turned violent resulting in nine ship passengers dead and over sixty persons injured. See the Türkel Committee at http://www.turkel-committee.com/index-eng.html.

7 Commission of Inquiry into the Actions of Canadian Officials in Relation to Maher Arar (2006): http://www.pch.gc.ca/cs-kc/arar/Arar_e.pdf.

8 Commission of Inquiry into the Sponsorship Program and Advertising Activities (2005–06): http://epe.lac-bac.gc.ca/100/206/301/pco-bcp/commissions/sponsorship-ef/06-03-06/www.gomery.ca/en/phase1report/index.asp.

9 Austl, Commonwealth, Royal Commissions and Commissions of Inquiry: http://www.aph.gov.au/About_Parliament/Parliamentary_Departments/Parliamentary_Library/Browse_by_Topic/Key_Internet_Links/Copy_of_law/royalcommissions.

10 Throughout this book, the following terminology has been adopted in order to promote gender neutrality while also respecting the names of ombuds institutions. The capitalized expression "Ombudsman" has been used for specific names (for example, the Swedish Ombudsman, the Ombudsman of Ontario). The lowercase words "ombudsman", "ombudsperson" and "ombuds" have been used, as nouns and adjectives, to represent general institutions, with preference for the use of the gender-neutral forms of "ombudsperson" and "ombuds" wherever possible.

11 For general information about the history and controversy of the Lokpal Bill see: Mark T Kozlowski, "A Monsoon in Delhi Anna Hazare, the Lokpal Bill, and the Future of India" (2011) 8:1 Pitt Political Review 1, online: http://ppr.pitt.edu/ojs/index.php/ppr/article/view/11/14; see also "India: Ombudsman Law Talks deadlocked", *BBC News*: http://www.bbc.co.uk/news/world-south-asia-13787876. A copy of the bill may be found online: http://www.docstoc.com/docs/76989664/Janlokpal-Bill-Version-22.

explosion of freedom of information oversight agencies, particularly in countries experiencing transitional justice is yet another example.[12]

The first part of this Introduction defines the key notions of adversarial, inquisitorial and ombuds processes. The second part of the Introduction explores the four theoretical themes that emerge from the work of the authors of this volume on inquisitorial processes in administrative law.

Part I

Inquisitorial, Adversarial & Ombuds Dispute Resolution Processes

Inquisitorial and adversarial decision-making paradigms present ideal-types of decision-making processes. Presently, around the world, the existence of pure adversarial or pure inquisitorial decision-making systems is rare, and such pure systems are generally said not to exist at all.[13] Most jurisdictions that were either traditionally adversarial or traditionally inquisitorial have shown some degree of merging of the two traditions.[14] Nevertheless, there is value in keeping in mind these two ideal-types. They are useful in placing in perspective the derivation of many of the tools, ideas and debates presented in this volume. The ombuds is a third distinct model of dispute resolution whose features share similarities with traditional inquisitorial processes.

Adversarial processes

Adversarial and inquisitorial models distinguish themselves according to whether the parties or the decision-making body has control over: i) the ability to initiate the action or application with which the decision-maker is seized, ii) the gathering of evidence, and iii) the determination of the sequence and nature of

---

12 See generally John M Ackerman & Irma E Sandoval-Ballestros, "The Global Explosion of Freedom of Information Laws" (2006) 58 Admin L Rev 85. Although not all countries have adopted an ombuds approach, the number of countries with freedom of information legislation has grown ninefold over the past three decades since 1982. An archived history of the emergence of freedom of information laws around the world may be found online: freedominfo.org.

13 Modern day scholars who have posited this idea include Amalia D Kessler, "Our Inquisitorial Tradition: Equity Procedure, Due Process, and the Search for an Alternative to the Adversarial" (2005) 90 Cornell L Rev 1181 at 1187 [Kessler]; Leroy Certoma, "The Non Adversarial Administrative Process and the Immigration Review Tribunal" (1993) 4 Public Law Review 4 [Certoma]; Janet Walker & Oscar Chase, *Common Law, Civil Law and the Future of Categories* (Markham, Ont: LexisNexis, 2010).

14 *Ibid.*

the proceedings.[15] Adversarial processes have the distinct characteristic of leaving carriage of the case to the parties in opposition. As Amalia Kessler writes:

> In the adversarial model, the parties are responsible for initiating and conducting the litigation. They gather all the evidence and present it orally, in open court, subjecting witnesses to examination and cross-examination, and the court serves as a neutral umpire, deciding the questions of fact and law raised by the parties. In addition, the parties bear primary responsibility for determining the sequence and manner in which evidence is presented and legal issues are argued.[16]

Kessler's commentary evokes several additional underlying ideas that animate the adversarial tradition. First, with respect to the gathering of evidence and its presentation in court, the notion of a judge keeping a distance from the collection of evidence that may be used to prove the case of either party is a tenet of the adversarial tradition. Judges are to stay away from descending into the fray of fact gathering as such a "descent" could lead to a perception of bias in favor of or against one of the parties. In the adversarial system, the judge's role is to weigh relevant evidence that has been brought to him or her and to draw conclusions from this evidence within the confines of the law. The result of the judicial analysis is normally a legally binding order.

Second, strict rules of evidence, procedure and ethics constitute another distinguishing mark of the adversarial system.[17] Rules of evidence and procedure are designed to shield the decision-maker "from evidence regarded as unfair or prejudicial to one of the parties."[18] Rules of ethics fulfill a complementary function by protecting the parties from being subjected to a competitive arena in which any type of maneuver or behavior can be used by a party in order to "win." All of these rules collectively aim to ensure that the contest between parties is fair. While the parties may bear primary responsibility for determining the sequence and manner in which evidence is presented and issues are argued, there must still be some boundary between what is and is not acceptable behavior in gathering and presenting evidence.

Finally, an important idea to which Kessler's comments allude is that argumentation is of primordial importance to reaching an outcome. In an adversarial system, however, it is possible that using admitted evidentiary material to produce persuasive arguments may not necessarily present a full factual picture of what occurred. This is because, as Certoma writes, "the truth is the product of

---

15 Kessler, *supra* note 13 at 1187. See also generally, JA Jolowicz, "Adversarial and Inquisitorial Models of Civil Procedure" (2003) 52 International and Comparative Law Quarterly 281 and more broadly, the classic article by Mirjan Damaska, "Structures of Authority and Comparative Criminal Procedure" (1975) 84 Yale LJ 480.

16 Kessler, *supra* note 13 at 1188 (footnotes omitted).

17 Certoma, *supra* note 13.

18 *Ibid* at 6.

a collaboration between the parties rather than the product of a complete factual judicial inquiry."[19] If determining truth, a full set of facts, or a complete record is the object of the inquiry, then these objectives may not be most easily attained using an adversarial system. The system has also proved costly for litigants (especially self-represented ones) who must gather their own evidence, master the rules and acquire expertise in presentation in order to be successful.

Inquisitorial processes

One of the central distinguishing features of the inquisitorial tradition is the active participation of the decision-maker. In inquisitorial systems, the decision-maker participates in the investigation and collection of evidence and controls the proceedings. As with the discussion of adversarial processes above, inquisitorial processes can be examined with respect to the same three features: i) the decision-maker's ability to initiate the action or application; ii) the gathering of evidence and iii) the determination of the sequence and nature of the proceedings.[20] Kessler describes the archetype of the inquisitorial process in the following way:

> [I]n the inquisitorial model, the court itself initiates the litigation and undertakes significant responsibility for gathering evidence, not just for ruling on the conclusions that should be drawn from it. Such evidence, including witness testimony, is taken outside the courtroom by a judge or court-appointed commissioner, and a written record is then submitted to the court as the basis for its judgment. Furthermore, the court is largely responsible for determining the sequence and manner in which issues of fact and law are considered and decided.[21]

Although the inquisitorial model historically featured court-initiated trials, bringing actions to the court by the parties is much more common today in jurisdictions that were traditionally inquisitorial.[22] As for the gathering of evidence, evidence was historically collected by both the court and the parties with the court playing a primary role. Speaking of the nineteenth-century inquisitorial tradition that had migrated to the courts of equity in the United States, Kessler asserts that evidence was taken primarily through *ex parte* examination before court-appointed

19 Certoma, *supra* note 13.

20 Kessler, *supra* note 13 at 1187.

21 *Ibid* at 1187 (footnotes omitted).

22 French civil procedure, for example, indicates that as a general principle, only the parties may initiate a proceeding. See Article 1 of Book One of the French Code of Civil Procedure which reads: "Only the parties may institute proceedings, save where the law shall provide otherwise. They shall have the right to terminate the same prior to them being disposed of by way of a judgment or by virtue of the law" in the *French Code of Civil Procedure in English 2008*, translated by Nicolas Brooke (New York: Oxford University Press, 2009) at 1.

officials.[23] It was also taken outside of the courtroom and without the presence of the parties.[24] The procedure allowed for the party seeking testimony to file written interrogatories with the court. The court would then appoint an officer to present the interrogatory to the witness and record the testimony of the witness in a narrative (as opposed to verbatim transcript) form. This written narrative was transmitted to the court as an official record of testimony.[25] Notably, those appointed to collect the evidence would typically also be given authority to determine whatever fact-finding was required in the case. As such, they could order the parties and witnesses to produce documents and subject them to examination under oath. They also played an active role in determining which evidence should be heard and the questions that should be asked.[26]

Beyond the evidence being taken in a written, narrative form, outside of the courtroom, it was also taken in secret. The secret nature meant that witness testimony recorded by a court-appointed official would not be revealed by the court until all of the witnesses had been examined. Strict rules governed how those commissioned to take the evidence were to seal and deliver it to the court. The reasons for secrecy were twofold. First, it aimed to prevent a party from seeking out the weak parts of their own case in order to quickly find or fabricate testimony that would buttress their position.[27] Secondly, safeguarding secrecy required each witness to testify entirely from memory. By not hearing the evidence of others, there was a lesser chance that their own testimony would be affected, either intentionally or inadvertently.[28]

Today, in jurisdictions that use processes derived from the inquisitorial tradition, oral evidence may be taken from witnesses, including expert witnesses called by the parties or appointed by the court from a list of experts that the court has compiled. There is no cross-examination although the parties may ask the court to put certain matters to the witnesses.[29] The parties may also produce additional evidence.[30]

Those from the adversarial tradition sometimes question the ability of the inquisitorial decision-maker to guarantee procedural fairness. The involvement of the decision-maker in gathering evidence is sometimes perceived as an avenue to the loss of the court's impartiality. Moreover, if the idea of a party-driven, open court process is to act as a check on government institutions, then this too, seems lost with the inquisitorial system which is largely driven by the court.

---

23 Kessler, *supra* note 13 at 1204–7.

24 *Ibid.*

25 *Ibid* at 1207.

26 *Ibid* at 1209.

27 *Ibid* at 1219.

28 *Ibid* at 1216.

29 Certoma, *supra* note 13 at 8.

30 *Ibid* at 7.

Certoma argues that it would be inappropriate to say that fact-finding compromises a court's neutrality. The main concern of the inquisitorial judge is "the collection of all of the relevant and significant evidence irrespective of whether it is in favor of or against either party."[31] Furthermore, the evidence gathered by the decision-maker should be considered as being used to supplement that produced by the parties.[32]

Due to the adversarial tradition's reliance on the parties to produce the evidence, sufficient evidence dealing with the wider public interest in public law matters may be neglected. Some, including Certoma, suggest that a non-adversarial system is better suited for matters in which there is a significant public interest component. More specifically, with the inquisitorial process' emphasis on full factual inquiry, the broader public interest may be better served. The validity of this argument rests, however, on the ability of public interest evidence to be brought to the decision-maker, regardless of the process used. There may be mechanisms designed to ensure that public interest issues are considered even within adversarial systems.

Ombuds

The "ombudsman"[33] is traditionally a neutral appointed actor who investigates allegations of maladministration in the executive branch of government[34] (and in

31 Certoma, *supra* note 13 at 7.

32 *Ibid.*

33 For an explanation of the terminology relating to ombuds roles that is used in this volume, please see *supra* note 10.

34 The concept of the ombuds is generally said to date back to the initial Swedish Ombudsman of 1809 (The *SwedishJustitieombudsman*) although there was an earlier version of it in Sweden in the eighteenth century, and accounts can be found of a much earlier incarnation of an integrity branch of government that existed in sixteenth-century China (see Hon James J Spigelman AC, "The Integrity Branch of Government – the First Lecture in the 2004 National Lecture Series for the Australian Institute of Administrative Law" (Speeches of Supreme Court of New South Wales, Sydney, Australia, April 29, 2004), online: http://www.lawlink.nsw.gov.au/lawlink/supreme_court/ll_sc.nsf/pages/SCO_speech_spigelman_290404 (last accessed April 15, 2012)); see also Ray Huang, *1587, A Year of No Significance: The Ming Dynasty in Decline* (New Haven: Yale University Press, 1981) at 53–54). Finland and Denmark each established a national Ombudsman in 1950 and 1953 respectively. The institution began to spread outside of Scandinavia in the 1960s including to the United Kingdom in 1967 and to Canada in the province of Alberta the same year. See generally Linda C Reif, *The Ombudsman, Good Governance and the International Human Rights System* (Boston: Martinus Nijhoff Publishers, 2004) at 1 [Reif, *Ombudsman, Good Governance*] (for the history and nature of the ombudsman). See also, Donald C Rowat, ed, *The Ombudsman: Citizen's Defender* (Toronto: University of Toronto Press, 1966) [Rowat]. See also Linda C Reif, ed, *The International Ombudsman Anthology: Selected Writings from the International Ombudsman Institute* (Boston: Kluwer Law, 1999) [Reif, *Selected Writings*]. See also Stephen Owen, "The Ombudsman: Essential Elements & Common Challenges" in Linda C Reif, Mary A Marshall & Charles Ferris, eds, *The Ombudsman: Diversity and Development* (Edmonton: International Ombudsman Institute, 1993) 1. See

the judiciary in some jurisdictions[35]). An ombuds' main powers are to investigate and recommend[36] although in some jurisdictions, they may also prosecute officials for dereliction of their duties.[37] An ombudsperson's investigation is generally launched through citizen complaint; however, ombuds may also have the power to initiate investigations themselves. In order to remain independent from the executive branch of government which the office is to oversee, a classic ombuds is usually an officer of the legislative branch of government who reports directly to parliament or the legislature instead of to the executive. As a result, some have chosen to use the neutral term classic parliamentary "ombuds-officer" to describe them.[38]

The office of the classic ombuds serves two purposes. It is simultaneously a means of helping the public to resolve disputes with government and a vehicle for providing accountability to the public from within the machinery of government. As Linda Reif has described, "the general objectives of the ombudsman are the improvement of the performance of the public administration and the enhancement of government accountability to the public."[39] The powers of the classic parliamentary ombuds-officer are established by statute. Reif summarizes the general functions of these officers as follows:

- to investigate complaints and allegations;
- to secure redress in cases where the complaint is found to be justified; and
- to help bring about improvements in administrative systems and procedures generally.[40]

One of the first established ombuds institutions, the Swedish Ombudsman could explore the question of whether an official had authority to make a decision and

---

Roy Gregory & Peter Hutchesson, *Parliamentary Ombudsman: A Study in the Control of Administrative Action* (London: Allen and Unwin for the Royal Institute of Public Administration, 1975) [Gregory] (on the establishment of the ombudsman in the United Kingdom, in particular, Chapter 2 "From Ombudsman to Parliamentary Commissioner"). Finally, see also, on the modern, variegated role of the ombuds institution, the contribution by Nora Farrell in this volume.

35 See Sten Rudholm, "The Chancellor of Justice" in Rowat, *ibid* at c. 1 -"Sweden's Guardians of the Law" [Rudholm].

36 See "Introduction" in Rowat, *ibid* at 7.

37 See Rudholm, *supra* note 35 at 18–19. In Sweden, the Ombudsman was initially also vested with the position of being the crown prosecutor. In 1948, court procedure in Sweden redesigned the Ombudsman office so that all prosecutorial functions were removed other than those for prosecuting higher government officials for offenses stemming from a dereliction of duty or abuse of authority.

38 We use the two terms interchangeably throughout this chapter.

39 See Reif, *Ombudsman, Good Governance*, *supra* note 34 at 2.

40 *Ibid* at 218.

whether a decision was materially justified by the facts of the case.[41] The Swedish Ombudsman investigated broad issues of maladministration and was understood to be "the guardian of the people's common and individual rights."[42] Issues of administrative discretion were examined in the context of courts, prosecutors, police and prisons. The Swedish Ombudsman could investigate complaints or simply investigate matters that he discovered on his own. The scope of his investigation included questions relating to neglected procedural rules and failure to give information regarding administrative decisions taken.

The Swedish Ombudsman's office was not limited to interfering in situations where there were faults. His presence alone worked to prevent faults by aiming to improve the administration. As Bexelius has asserted with respect to the nineteenth- and early twentieth-century Swedish Ombudsman for Civil Affairs: "the foremost object of the office has always been … to work for a better protection of rights and to try to prevent faults by directing attention to the true substance of the law and to improvements in practice and in the statutes for the benefit of the general public."[43] One still sees today, in the version of the classic ombuds that has developed in Canada, a broad scope of issues that may be investigated.[44]

In terms of evidence gathering, the main tool that an ombuds employs is investigation. Currently, ombuds generally have statutorily granted ancillary powers which assist with their investigations. Traditionally, the Swedish Ombudsman was provided the power to inspect public offices, attend discussions

---

41 It is important to note that, in the nineteenth and early twentieth centuries, the Swedish Ombudsman was tasked more and more with surveillance of public administration in part because of administrative expansion but also because of the absence of administrative law precedent, the absence of political responsibility on the part of ministers for administrative officials, and the jurisdiction of the Supreme Administrative Court which did not look beyond the legality of decisions rendered. See Alfred Bexelius, "The Ombudsman for Civil Affairs" in Rowat, *supra* note 34 at c. 1 -"Sweden's Guardians of the Law" at 23, 26 [Bexelius].

42 *Ibid* at 40.

43 *Ibid* at 42.

44 See, for example, Ontario's *Ombudsman Act*, RSO 1990, c O.6, which allows the Ontario Ombudsman discretion to investigate in the following circumstances:

> Function of Ombudsman
>
> 14. (1) The function of the Ombudsman is to investigate any decision or recommendation made or any act done or omitted in the course of the administration of a governmental organization and affecting any person or body of persons in his, her or its personal capacity.
>
> Investigation on complaint
>
> (2) The Ombudsman may make any such investigation on a complaint made to him or her by any person affected or by any member of the Assembly to whom a complaint is made by any person affected, or of the Ombudsman's own motion.

The statute further allows the Ombudsman to act in the following broad discretionary circumstances:

and deliberations, and to examine the records and files. There was an obligation on every official to furnish the Ombudsman with any information that he may request.[45] Today, in Canada, statutory ombuds are endowed with similar strong investigatory powers such as the power to subpoena evidence and enter premises.[46] Similar to the inquisitorial process, investigations are usually done in private. However, unlike the inquisitorial and adversarial systems, which lead ultimately to binding decisions, the outcome of an investigation by an ombuds is normally a recommendation. The ombuds recommends to government, if it is wrong, that it change its position. This recommendation is accompanied by a report to the parties involved and to Parliament or the legislature.[47] In addition, powers of negotiation and persuasion are often used to convince the government to rectify its actions.

Over the past few decades, variations on the classic ombuds model have developed around the world. These variations have emerged in an attempt to address the specific problems that members of the public have had in their interaction with state bureaucracy.[48] One type of newer ombuds model that is particularly germane to the present collection is the specialty or single-purpose ombuds institution. As Marshall and Reif define it, a single-purpose ombuds has "jurisdiction over a particular or specialized subject-matter only."[49] They note that specialty ombuds have come to exist in many diverse areas including health services, armed services, the police, correctional services access to information and child protection. They note also that specialty ombuds are also often endowed with functions and powers that go beyond the classic ombuds profile. For example, these ombuds may possess tools such as order-making powers, they may have additional statutory obligations such as educating the public and they may move away from the traditional model with respect to appointments.[50]

Cross-fertilization among the adversarial, inquisitorial and, to a lesser extent, the ombuds models has led to a rich set of tools for administrative institutional

---

Procedure after investigation

21. (1) This section applies in every case where, after making an investigation under this Act, the Ombudsman is of opinion that the decision, recommendation, act or omission which was the subject-matter of the investigation,

(a) appears to have been contrary to law;

(b) was unreasonable, unjust, oppressive, or improperly discriminatory, or was in accordance with a rule of law or a provision of any Act or a practice that is or may be unreasonable, unjust, oppressive, or improperly discriminatory;

(c) was based wholly or partly on a mistake of law or fact; or

(d) was wrong.

45 See Rudholm *supra* note 35 at 20. See also generally, Bexelius *supra* note 41, at 25.

46 See for example, Ontario's *Ombudsman Act, supra* note 44.

47 Reif, *Ombudsman, Good Governance, supra* note 34 at 222.

48 *Ibid* at 225.

49 *Ibid* at 230.

50 *Ibid.*

design. Nevertheless, the chapters in this collection illustrate that as these traditions borrow from each other, issues relating to terminology, justification, effectiveness, and implication arise. It is to these issues that we next turn.

Part II[51]

Themes of this Edited Volume

Inquisitorial process: terminology and scope of the concept

As the works of this volume demonstrate, it is widely accepted that administrative hearing processes are hybridized. They manifest attributes that stem from both adversarial and inquisitorial legal traditions. The larger looming and overarching questions are what to call these hybridized processes and what the tools and procedures are that define them.

In the three chapters by Robin Creyke, Robert Thomas, and Samantha Green and Lorne Sossin, the authors address the adequacy and scope of the term "inquisitorial" in relation to administrative decision-making in Australia, the UK and Canada. As Robin Creyke asserts, Australian tribunals were designed to operate in an inquisitorial manner by statute, yet courts and tribunals have been reluctant to set up, sanction or even promote alternative modes of process beyond those with which they are most familiar. Creyke notes that the inquisitorial features of Australian tribunals do not represent the traditional European notion of inquisitorial. Inquisitorial features of Australian tribunals include being able to inform themselves on any matter, compel the appearance of witnesses, and compel the production of documents. The inquisitorial process also allows tribunals the discretion to determine their own procedure. Australian tribunals fall on a spectrum ranging from those that are heavily investigative to those that are adversarial. Ultimately, Creyke raises the very compelling idea that any term we may adopt to replace "inquisitorial" should embrace more than what occurs in the hearing and extend to pre-hearing processes as well. She argues that it is in these "subterranean elements of tribunal processes" that the most active intervention takes place, interventions such as the narrowing of issues, the identification of whether there is a sustainable case, the issuing of non-binding opinions on law or facts, and attempted mediation and other dispute resolution methods used to reach settlement.

Robert Thomas asserts that tribunals in the UK need to develop a vision of their procedural approach. Thomas argues that neither the adversarial nor the inquisitorial label adequately captures the distinct nature of administrative decision-making in the UK. Instead, he argues for a third method, which he terms

51 Parts of this subsection draw inspiration from L Jacobs, S Baglay et al, "The Nature of Inquisitorial Processes in Administrative Regimes: Global Perspectives – Research Workshop Report" (2011) 24 CJALP 261–83.

"an active, enabling, and investigative approach", and which has been advanced generally by tribunals. The approach has been used, in particular, in relation to unrepresented claimants who appeal against government decisions. Although UK tribunals have become more active, this development has been piecemeal, with no exact guidelines.

Green and Sossin start from the perspective that a new paradigm is emerging in the Commonwealth in which active adjudicators are the norm and not the exception. They take issue, however, with the parallel phenomenon of any administrative proceeding that is non-adversarial simply being termed "inquisitorial." Green and Sossin argue that most administrative proceedings in the Commonwealth may be located somewhere between the court room model and an inquiry model and argue that these hybridized approaches deserve more attention. "Active adjudication" is the term that they adopt for the expansive, hybridized, middle ground between adversarial and inquisitorial administrative models. The approach of active adjudication employs tools such as the obtaining of early disclosure by the tribunal, tribunal-led focusing of issues, and tribunal facilitation in eliciting and testing the parties' evidence. Green and Sossin suggest that this approach is particularly well-suited to settings where an administrative tribunal deals with parties marked by power imbalances, manages polycentric issues or complex statutory mandates, for it may enhance efficiency, fairness and effectiveness.

Outside of the Commonwealth, the challenge of naming and defining non-adversarial administrative processes is equally relevant. In the United States, Michael Asimow observes that, from reading the administrative procedure acts, which are enacted in every state, one "would conclude that American administrative adjudication is a world of judicialized and highly adversarial proceedings." However, through close examination of "mass benefit distribution" agencies, he demonstrates that administrative adjudication is much less adversarial and judicialized than it appears. Inquisitorial procedures, as they have been named by the US Supreme Court,[52] are used in mass justice benefit distribution agencies, such as those concerned with veterans' appeals and Social Security disability. Asimow examines the structure and functioning of these agencies, highlighting their inquisitorial features and the benefits and drawbacks that they present.

In France, administrative law litigation is traditionally inquisitorial. In his chapter, Jean-Bernard Auby outlines the features of France's inquisitorial administrative process. These features include the judge's sole authority to conduct the adjudication, his or her ability to request documents and witnesses, and the power to modulate the burden of proof. Auby asserts that the most interesting aspects of inquisitorial procedure are related to evidence. French administrative judges are not bound by the official list of types of evidence they can admit. They can admit what they consider relevant. However, the inquisitorial character is not without limitations: judges are not fully in command of framing of the case – they

52 See, for example, *Sims v Apfel*, 530 US 103 (2000) (in which the US Supreme Court remarks on the inquisitorial structure of Social Security proceedings).

may not initiate the case. Auby discusses the current evolution taking place in French administrative law litigation procedure in which administrative litigation is less judge-driven and more party-driven. In his chapter, Auby discusses the adoption of adversarialism to render more flexible France's traditional inquisitorial administrative litigation. Recent reforms in litigation procedure in France, relating to the issuing of injunctions and the ability to obtain urgent relief, have allowed parties to gain more control over proceedings. These reforms do not diminish the power given to judges, but judges can now more often adopt the position of "mere referee looking at the parties in battle." Auby's contribution serves to emphasize the pervasiveness of hybridized decision-making in administrative law.

Finally, Herwig Hofmann adds an additional twist to the issues of terminology and scope by discussing the concept of the "duty of care" in EU administrative law decision-making. The duty of care is a concept distinct from the duty of care found in the private law of torts. In EU administrative law, the "duty of care" imposes an obligation to inquire on administrative actors. Also referred to as the "duty of diligent and impartial examination", the duty applies to all aspects of administrative activity, from rule-making to adjudication. It "sets the standard for the amount and detail of information to be established prior to taking a decision, and the way in which information is then processed." Its principles guide decision-makers in determining such procedural elements as whether to follow up on a complaint, whether to pursue a preliminary investigation, and the extent and depth to which an investigation should be taken prior to making a final decision. In some cases, an administrative body will need to examine scientific evidence and expertise. The duty of care would require administrative bodies in those circumstances to check that all scientific evaluation, both favorable and unfavorable, has been made available to them. In the end, Hofmann illustrates how EU law has developed a largely inquisitorial approach to information gathering for administrative decision-making, and has done so primarily through principles developed through the jurisprudence of the Court of Justice of the European Union. At the same time, he is clear in underscoring that decision-making by an EU authority rests ultimately on information gathered by a range of actors who have both the right to request information and an obligation to provide it namely, the decision-making authority itself, and other public and private actors (such as a member state or a private party).

Nora Farrell discusses the difference in scope of the inquiry powers that exist under three ombuds models in Canada: classical, hybrid and organizational. On the one side of the spectrum is the classical model, which envisions the broadest scope of inquisitorial powers, including coercive powers to compel testimony and production of records. On the opposite side are organizational ombuds, often found in the private sector, which do not have authority to investigate, but usually have access to all records and can make recommendations to address systemic issues. Farrell's piece raises an issue as to what terminology would most accurately reflect the powers and procedures under each model: are all of them properly inquisitorial, even in the absence of the power to investigate?

Laverne Jacobs examines the concept of investigation in the administrative law context of access to information regulation. Access to information is a relatively unique regulatory context in which the administrative actors, the information commissioners, retain key features of the ombuds institution while also adopting adversarial and inquisitorial adjudicative elements. Her chapter goes further to interrogate the broader notion of a "specialty ombuds" model in which investigatory and adjudicative powers are endowed on a classical ombuds, illustrating that such models are best understood as independent accountability agencies.

Mary Liston's chapter on the hybrid model of oversight represented by British Columbia's Representative for Children and Youth (RCY) provides yet another challenging example from the point of view of terminology. Briefly reviewing the history of approaches to child welfare, she notes a shift from the adversarial model towards an ombudsman-like approach and finally towards a new hybrid model of the RCY, which is "a legislative officer, has the powers of a commissioner of inquiry, retains many of the functions of an ombuds, and possesses the structural independence of a provincial auditor general." The RCY combines a variety of functions and powers including systemic advocacy, investigation of deaths and critical injuries to children, policy development, monitoring and reporting, multidisciplinary coordination across government departments and promotion of public accountability. The underlying objective is to provide a mechanism of consultative problem-solving, although in the context of investigation of children's critical injuries and deaths the RCY may serve a more adversarial and confrontational function. Clearly, neither adversarial nor inquisitorial terms would properly characterize hybrid models of oversight, underscoring the need for new terminology.

Justifications for the use of an "inquisitorial" process

ENTITLEMENT, DELAY, COSTS, (UN)FAIRNESS AND REPRESENTATION

What motivates government to promote or design a more enabling role for administrative tribunals? As Robert Thomas observes in his chapter on the UK: "[o]ne reason why the appropriate mode of tribunal procedure seems so unclear is largely because of the multiplicity of pressures motivating and restraining tribunal procedure and the complex and disparate situations in which the issues arise." In exploring the pressures for and against active adjudication, Thomas argues that it is not rare for high-profile issues in government to engulf the question of tribunal procedure. In the UK, tribunals generally exist to address social areas of law where litigants may not be able to afford representation. However, governmental attempts to reduce the cost of publicly funded legal aid has put pressure on administrative tribunals to level the playing field by assisting claimants. Thomas asserts, "[i]f a claimant is unrepresented, then the tribunal should bridge the gap between itself and the claimant by adopting an enabling approach." The orthodox view that representation enhances the chances of an applicant's success is being challenged by tribunals becoming better able at handling unrepresented appellants.

The enabling techniques are used both prior and during the hearing and include effectively drawing out relevant evidence.

Are there any inherent justifications for the use of active adjudication in an administrative process? To what extent should the nature of the parties to an administrative process or the issues involved influence whether an active approach to adjudication is appropriate? The paradigm of individual versus state is the dominant one in the contexts of administrative action in the subject matter and territorial jurisdictions that we have studied in this volume. In Australia, the United Kingdom and the United States, for example, social benefit distribution is a key area in which an active adjudication processes has been instigated. Michael Asimow asserts that when dealing with issues that arise under a governmental benefit scheme, the central notion of entitlement to the benefit justifies the use of an inquisitorial process. The state has an obligation to assist its residents to obtain the benefits to which they are entitled.

Asimow's moral claim to the legitimate use of an inquisitorial process rings true on a commonsense level. At the same time, one sees that governments in many jurisdictions have adopted active adjudication for reasons that are more pragmatic and have done so in subject areas that have little to do with public entitlement to a governmental benefit. As discussed by Robin Creyke, Australia's Law Reform Commission devoted itself to studying the problems of cost, delay and unfairness prevailing in the adversarial justice system which had led to "a crisis in civil litigation in Australia." Addressing these challenges led to Australia's interest in adopting inquisitorial methods in both civil litigation and administrative action. As pointed out by Heckman, in the refugee protection context, an inquisitorial approach is considered well suited for reasons of efficiency, fairness (refugee claimants are likely to be unrepresented and, thus, might be disadvantaged in adversarial proceedings), as well as the nature of refugee protection obligations (whereby there is no truly adversarial relationship between the claimant and the state). Cuts to legal aid are often a motivating factor for the development of inquisitorial administrative procedure. The increased numbers of unrepresented claimants occasioned by diminished legal aid may necessitate more active adjudication by decision-makers to ensure fair and full examination of relevant issues. First raised by Robert Thomas, this point is equally noted by Gerald Heckman for its relevance to the changing Canadian government policy on refugee protection. However, when it comes to assessing whether such an approach will meet success, as Heckman observes, "... much will depend on the members' experience and training in inquisitorial procedures and likely on the resources and time available to members to perform their function adequately."

The challenges of delay, costs, fairness and representation collectively feed into the ability of an individual to access a potential right, benefit or privilege offered through a governmental program. Viewed in this light, active adjudication does not necessarily have to be confined to the realm of individual-state disagreements. In Canada, for example, administrative law spreads beyond the individual-state realm to any area, including discrimination and rental housing, where a public policy has been put in place to regulate activities or where tribunals have been created to reduce court backlog and apply their expertise in a specialized area of law. Active approaches to administrative hearing processes have similarly extended beyond citizen-state subject areas to areas where private parties often counter each other. For instance, the province of Ontario, Canada introduced an active approach to adjudication in the context of determining claims of discrimination under the provincial human rights code to avoid earlier problems of delay in the system.[53]

ATTAINING THE TRUTH

Attaining the truth is another major rationale for the use of inquisitorial processes. Yet, in her discussion of inquisitorial process in Australia's administrative law context, Robin Creyke reflects critically on how the challenge of attaining the truth fits uncomfortably within the many, and sometimes, conflicting goals of administrative law. As Creyke observes, in Australia, administrative law is designed to be simultaneously fair, just, informal, economic and quick. She is skeptical that a system designed to operate "in a manner which is both economical and quick" can also "allow for the thorough analysis that is implied in a system designed to identify the truth." There is an innate contradiction in these goals which renders questionable attempts by policy-makers to introduce inquisitorial methods within an adversarial administrative law context to further the ability of administrative actors to decide matters on the fullest evidentiary record possible.

Jula Hughes similarly questions the ability of both inquisitorial and adversarial proceedings to fulfill a truth-seeking function and raises the salient point that "knowing the truth" is determined, *inter alia*, by who controls the discovery of the truth, and by the ability of witnesses to effectively participate in the process and be heard. Hughes speaks, for example, of the participatory barriers faced by vulnerable and marginalized persons as well as "testimonial muteness of trauma victims" who are frequently disbelieved and, as a consequence, disenfranchised in the legal process. Due to trauma, such witnesses may not be able to present their stories in a coherent, precise and detailed fashion, thereby failing to meet the mainstream indicators of credibility. The process that eliminates the voices

53 See Ontario, Legislative Assembly, Ontario Hansard, 38:2 (April 26, 2006) at 1340 (Hon. Michael Bryant), available online: http://www.ontla.on.ca/house-proceedings/transcripts/files_html/2006-04-26_L066A.htm#PARA189 (last accessed on April 15, 2012). There, the Minister of Justice introduced the bill that occasioned major amendments to the Ontario *Human Rights Code*, RSO 1990, c H.19 after it came into force in 2008. Minister Bryant emphasized that the proposed changes would shorten the 4 to 5 year delay that was plaguing the average human rights complaint as it moved from its initial stages, through witness interviews and other fact-gathering, and on to resolution. He noted that the new human rights regime would allow applicants for remedies to apply directly to the human rights tribunal and that the tribunal would have powers to "engage in a fact-gathering process to assist the parties to resolve their dispute", the capacity to "ensure that all relevant evidence is before it and ... to compel parties to provide this information."

of marginalized groups may not only distort the finding of the truth, but also undermine the legitimacy of the truth-seeking process.

Hughes suggests that the procedural innovations adopted by the Canadian Truth and Reconciliation Commission on Indian Residential Schools (TRC) may offer inspiration for devising more inclusive processes in the regular justice system. Given that most witnesses appearing before the Commission represent marginalized and vulnerable groups (many are indigenous, elderly, with a history of abuse, including sexual abuse, and "a fraught relationship with settler society justice institutions"), the TRC has taken a victim-centered approach "to pursue a form of truth-seeking that is designed to facilitate participation in its process with a view to contributing to the broader goal of reconciliation between indigenous and settler society Canadians." Following neither adversarial nor inquisitorial model, this approach seeks to increase participation of witnesses by, for example, providing various types of space for survivors to share their stories (for instance, in a survivor sharing circle or in a one-on-one meeting with a TRC volunteer), providing emotional support throughout the statement-taking events, and generally flexible terms of statement-taking (for instance, no strict time-keeping for statements, no involvement of legal representatives, absence of cross-examination and oaths).

Hughes' point about the knowability of truth finds useful connection to Heckman's chapter, which raises a question about the relationship between truth-seeking and the duty to inquire in the refugee protection context, where claimants are often asked to testify about their traumatic experiences. The narrowly constructed duty to inquire, which does not require a decision-maker to seek clarification of the claimant's testimony or ascertain the impact of a claimant's psychiatric condition on his/her ability to give evidence may distort the tribunal's findings as to whether the claimant is telling the truth or whether a described event has occurred.

The truth-seeking function is also central to public inquiries and is fundamental to their ability to restore public confidence in public institutions, especially following a tragic event. Key to carrying out these tasks is the ability of a commission to choose how to conduct its proceedings – formally or informally, with or without hearings, using inquisitorial or adversarial model – while ensuring fair and efficient process. The design of the inquiry procedure plays an important role in the truth-seeking function: who should be heard? How can they reach prospective participants, especially in cases where there is a broad range of stakeholders or affected individuals? How and when are we to determine that the truth has been found?

The effectiveness of inquiry powers

How can we ensure that inquiry powers work optimally? Two authors address the question of effectiveness directly.

Gerald Heckman's chapter raises an interesting question with respect to the interpretation of inquisitorial powers in the context of asylum adjudication in

Australia. Although the Australian Refugee Review Tribunal (RRT) possesses broad inquisitorial powers, Australian courts have held that, except in limited circumstances, the RRT is under no statutory duty to inquire. The meaning of the "inquisitorial" function has been interpreted more narrowly than envisioned by the classical inquisitorial model, arguably reflecting the importance of promoting expediency and cost-effectiveness in adjudication. Heckman asks: "Can a tribunal which is not required to exercise its responsibility for the gathering of evidence properly be called inquisitorial?" Is it appropriate to give efficiency considerations so much weight in defining the content of the inquisitorial function?

Laverne Jacobs' contribution speaks to the fundamental but overlooked issue of ensuring that public policy goals are met through choice of procedure. She reports on the results of a qualitative empirical study that examines how the investigatory approach of the federal ombuds-officer in charge of regulating access to information in Canada succeeds in meeting its legislated policy goal of promoting a culture of government transparency. The research project, which surveyed access to information officials in the federal government, shows how, if at all, the results of investigations relating to freedom of information are translated into longer-term effects, policies, and practices that ensure a culture of transparency within government departments. Analyzing her findings through the central theoretical values of institutional competence, access to justice, efficiency and effectiveness, Jacobs concludes that with greater resources such as training, and with wider powers of education and research, the federal Office of the Information Commissioner's investigatory oversight could play a significant role in helping government achieve the aim of the access legislation – namely, engendering a stronger culture of transparency. Her study speaks to a larger debate within the freedom of information context relating to whether investigative or adjudicative regulatory oversight is more effective in promoting government accountability in the keeping and sharing of records.

The question of effectiveness indirectly comes through many of the other chapters, particularly those relating to commissions of inquiry. How are we to evaluate the effectiveness of a commission of inquiry? Is it by its final report, by the process it adopts (how it balances various interests; how independent and transparent it is), by its impact on policy-makers or by all these factors? Whether effectiveness has been achieved may also depend on who is conducting the evaluation.

The chapters by Van Harten and Prasser highlight the importance of independence of inquiries and of the purposes for which they are established, which in turn may serve as markers of a commission's effectiveness. Since, as demonstrated by the Goudge and Braidwood inquiries, restoring public confidence in public institutions is often one of the key tasks of an inquiry, it is important that the inquiry itself is seen as independent and as established for a legitimate investigative purpose rather than for reasons of political expediency. Prasser's chapter usefully illustrates the latter point by examining both the legitimate uses of public inquiries and their abuse for political gain in Australia. Van Harten focuses on the importance of independence at each stage of the inquiry's work not only for its ability to carry out its mandate, but also for being seen by the public as a truth-seeking undertaking that has conducted a fair, open and thorough investigation. Both chapters draw attention to the potential threats to inquiries' independence and their vulnerability to abuse, depending on how their powers and terms of reference are defined, who is appointed as a commissioner, what are the reporting timeframes, and what is the post-inquiry reaction by government.

In the context of a discussion of various ombuds models, Farrell draws attention to the importance of commitment to procedural values in ensuring effectiveness of these bodies. She argues that regardless of how a specific ombuds has been established, it can provide a high level of administrative fairness "as long as the prerequisites of independence, impartiality and a commitment to contributing to an ethos of fairness are explicit in its design and in its implementation."

Implications of adopting inquiry powers

Several authors in this volume discuss the practical implications of incorporating active inquiry powers into administrative hearing processes. They primarily identify the need to train adjudicators in inquisitorial processes, and for institutional resources to support administrative investigations. However, an interesting confluence of additional repercussions flow from the use of inquiry powers within the administrative state. These include the positive and negative impacts of judicial review on administrative inquiry powers: judicial review may either have a denaturing effect or provide an avenue of reinforcement. A further implication that comes with using inquiry powers within the administrative state is the need to design inquisitorial procedures that respect procedural fairness and human rights. The impact of judicial review and rights-respecting procedures are discussed in this section.

HAVING THE DUTY TO INQUIRE ENFORCED BY REVIEWING COURTS

In Australia's refugee adjudication, courts have been reluctant to impose an extensive duty to inquire on the Refugee Review Tribunal, signaling that considerable importance is attached to the fact that the tribunal needs to deal with a high volume of claims in an expedient and cost-effective manner. While such a minimalist approach allows tribunals flexibility in the exercise of its discretionary powers, it, as highlighted by Heckman, also creates concerns about the ability of claimants to have a fair and full hearing. Heckman argues that in any context where a claimant has a constitutional right to a hearing, as in Canada, courts should step in to ensure that refugee adjudicators are subject to a "robust constitutional duty to inquire." But, ironically, it is the degree to which a given jurisdiction adheres to a constitutional doctrine of the separation of powers that may influence the courts' attitude to the procedure of administrative bodies, as Robin Creyke discusses in her chapter. In Australia, a strong constitutional separation of powers doctrine has prevented courts from imposing the duty to inquire if that duty relates, as it most often does, to factual or policy issues. Judicial review in Australia focuses only on the legality of administrative decisions. Separation of powers is a deterring factor that is not as prevalent in Canada.

DENATURING AND EDIFYING EFFECTS OF JUDICIAL REVIEW

When exercised, what impact does judicial review have on inquisitorial administrative processes? The ability to design its procedure and conduct information gathering in an efficient and often less formal way than in judicial proceedings is seen as an important advantage of commissions of inquiry. Therefore, subjecting commissions of inquiry to judicial review raises a concern that this will make the process more rigid and complex, thereby constraining the ability of commissions to effectively investigate a given matter. Not surprisingly, it was traditionally considered that commissions of inquiry should not be subjected to extensive control by the courts. Prasser, for example, notes that in the past, Australian royal commissions faced limited external review and tended to operate outside the legal system with its checks and balances. There is, however, growing acceptance in Australia that due to the effect that public inquiries can have on private interests, judicial review should not be precluded.

In the Canadian context, as Justice Braidwood's chapter illustrates, study commissions are viewed as recommending bodies that provide opinions to the government, not decisions or determinations of rights. Where a commission has the power to make a finding of misconduct or to otherwise affect procedural or substantive rights, administrative law standards of fairness are applied. However, in reviewing whether a commission has complied with its duty of procedural fairness, courts have to be careful not to modify public inquiry powers.[54]

Within the context of administrative agency hearings that provide mass distributive justice of governmental benefits, Asimow notes that once these agencies became subjected to judicial review, the requirement of keeping an appropriate record (including detailed reasons) in case of judicial review led to much less efficiency at the agency level and eventually backlogs.

By contrast, Liston demonstrates the complementary role that adversarial courts can play through judicial review by protecting investigative bodies against threats to their ability to carry out their mandates. Drawing on a recent case where the Office of the British Columbia Representative for Children and Youth sought to enforce its right to information and disclosure, she notes the positive power of judicial review for a body with inquiry powers.

DESIGNING FAIR PROCEDURES WITHIN ADMINISTRATIVE CONTEXTS THAT RELY ON INQUIRY POWERS

Although public inquiries are usually associated with an inquisitorial process, considerations of fairness may prompt the injection of adversarial elements into

54 See *Chrétien v Canada (Commission of Inquiry into the Sponsorship Program and Advertising Activities, Gomery Commission)*, 2008 FC 802 (aff'd by 2010 FCA 283) for a useful review of relevant principles and case law on the issue.

the proceedings. In the Australian context, Prasser notes the tension between coercive powers of royal commissions, which are necessary to conduct effective investigation, and the protection of civil liberties of those who may be subject to such powers. The reflections of Canadian Commissioners Goudge and Braidwood echo a similar point and demonstrate that the degree of procedural fairness that should be accorded to affected parties depends on the nature of a commission of inquiry. For example, Braidwood's study commission into the use of conducted energy weapons by provincially regulated law enforcement agencies was not required to provide a high degree of procedural fairness. Fairness was accomplished by the ability of interested parties to give evidence and suggest witnesses to be called, but with no cross-examination. By contrast, the investigatory commission, which inquired into the death of Mr Dziekanski (which occurred after a conducted energy weapon was employed against him) and also had the power to make findings of misconduct, was structured as an adversarial process, resembling a full trial. In comparison, the Goudge Inquiry into pediatric forensic psychology in Ontario combined elements of inquisitorial and adversarial process, particularly during the hearing process. The preparatory stage and the development of policy recommendations stage were largely inquisitorial seeking to collect necessary information and identify relevant issues. The hearing process, which dealt with contested facts and had public reputations at stake, was adversarial, but with imposed times on examination and cross-examination. The use of various techniques of fact-finding in the Goudge Inquiry ultimately sought to provide a balance between fairness and efficiency.

The need to protect rights within the context of inquisitive administrative action arises even more forcefully in the context of EU inspections. By virtue of regulatory and jurisprudential developments arising in the past decade alone, EU administrative actors possess wide powers of inspection within the realm of investigation for anticompetitive commercial behavior. The European Commission may inspect not only business premises, but also the homes of managers, directors and secretaries whenever it has a reasonable suspicion that relevant evidence is being held there. In his chapter, Gacinto della Cananea raises the fundamental question of the limits that exist on the Commission's inspection powers and the safeguards against their abuse. He explores three theoretical limits to the exercise of these powers. First, there is the constitutional principle of the inviolability of the home found in the European Convention of Human Rights. Second, there are the procedural constraints placed on the Commission. Third is the principle of "legality" which would circumscribe the power to what is necessary.

della Cananea notes that the jurisprudence of the Court of First Instance,[55] along with recently enacted regulations,[56] suggest that legal conceptualizations of both the Commission's power and the power of member states now permit multiple sites of authority for coercive power. The validity of the Commission's

55 See, for example, *Minoan v Commission*, Case T-66/99(2003) (CFI).

56 Regulation n.1/2003.

coercive powers calls into question the traditional realist paradigm that only states have a monopoly on the legitimate use of force.

Conclusion

After reviewing the exciting work of the contributors to this volume, we arrange our concluding comments around four principal ideas. Most fundamentally, the nature of inquisitorial processes is informed by the changing nature of administrative bodies themselves. There is clearly cross-fertilization amongst legal traditions: adversarial, inquisitorial, ombuds, and others. The resulting hybrids are themselves at times *sui generis* and at times able to adapt and grow according to the defining elements of their originating processes. At bottom, regardless of labels, flexible processes are respected in the administrative state as governments seek to develop processes that are efficient, effective and expedient without sacrificing fairness or violating fundamental rights.

Beyond cross-fertilization, there is also growing flexibility within specific bodies themselves. We see this through the diverse nature of public inquiries, ombudsman and specialized legislative officers such as access to information commissions and commissions designed for the protection of children. This intra-institutional flexibility promises the potential of mandates and procedures that can be tailored to better respond to the needs of various environments.

Secondly, regardless of the administrative process we adopt, inquisitorial or adversarial, its ultimate effectiveness and fairness may very well depend on the knowledge and expertise of the decision-maker. Adjudicator training should occupy a central role, given the impact that an administrative decision may have on an individual. Governments would do well to place highly within their allocation of funding, resources for continuing adjudicator education. Models of education may be shaped along grand lines relating to performing the duty to inquire, fairness, and respecting rights. It would also be wise for adjudicators to be informed of the types of academic debates that underlie the challenge of providing inquisitorial adjudication, such as the academic debates that arise in this volume.

There are additional areas of exploration which would profit from further independent research. In particular, what are participants' experiences with inquisitorial processes? Do litigants find active adjudication useful for getting out the truth? And if so, why? A few of the chapters touch on this issue by highlighting the particular challenges faced by vulnerable and marginalized groups in the hearing process. They suggest that an important aspect of institutional design is the need to create administrative bodies and processes that facilitate the voice of the vulnerable. Indeed, a process or institution that is poorly designed may make the vulnerable even more vulnerable. Finally, it is not only the vulnerability of those who are appearing before administrative bodies that should concern us but also the vulnerability of the institutions themselves.

Ultimately, in the spirit of collaborative learning and learning across jurisdictions, we believe that one of the most important lessons is that it may be useful to do away with the ideologies behind both "inquisitorial" and "adversarial" procedures. Instead of focusing on institutional design and process that privilege a place for the adversary or the inquisitor, creating a space in which truth is found efficiently and effectively, rights are respected and one can access a just result, means making room for central policy goals and sensitivity to all involved to guide the discussion. We suggest that reconceiving administrative process and institutional design to avoid the adversary and inquisitor, twinned with opening the door to constructive dialogue however labeled or designed, is the most valuable lesson shared across jurisdictions.

PART 1
Inquisitorial Hearing Processes in Administrative Law – Comparative Perspectives

Chapter 2

Pragmatism v Policy: Attitude of Australian Courts and Tribunals to Inquisitorial Process

Robin Creyke*

No court in Australia has given unequivocal support to adoption of inquisitorial processes. Underpinning this reluctance are multiple factors. Historically, bodies like the English Star Chamber bred suspicion of inquisitorial notions. Lawyers and judges in common law countries, trained in the adversarial method, have been reluctant to embrace different roles, or to impose the additional burdens of an inquiry process on an executive charged with being efficient. That resistance has been fuelled by awareness of the additional resources required to undertake the investigative role. Finally, there is institutional dissonance in a country where appeals go from inquisitorial tribunals to courts operating in an adversarial mode. Nonetheless, there are circumstances when the duty arises. Some are sanctioned by the courts; some are legislative; and others are practical responses by tribunals.

The Inquisitorial / Adversarial Distinction in Australian Courts and Tribunals

In the Australian context, inquisitorial procedures have traditionally conjured up notions of European-based civil law procedures, and have been used in contradistinction to the common law's adversarial system. In an examination in 2000 of the civil justice system in Australia, the Australian Law Reform Commission (ALRC) summarized the distinction: "… the common law system [is one] of conducting proceedings in which the parties, and not the judge, have the primary responsibility for defining the issues in dispute and for investigating and advancing the case."[1]

---

* Sincere thanks to Mark Smyth for his assistance in development of this chapter, and to Caitlin Baillee for her help with the final proofing of the material.

1 Austl, Commonwealth, Australian Law Reform Commission, *Managing Justice: A Review of the Federal Civil Justice System*, Report No 89 (Canberra: Australian Government Publishing Service, 2000) at 102 [ALRC].

By contrast:

> The term "inquisitorial" refers to civil code systems in which the judge has such primary responsibility. "Inquisitorial" also connotes an inquiry where the decision-maker investigates a matter. Civil code proceedings represent, in procedural theory, "judicial prosecution" of the parties' dispute, as opposed to "party prosecution" of the dispute under the common law system.[2]

At the same time as the ALRC pointed out "in civil matters at least, there is a significant degree of convergence of the practices in common law and civil code countries."[3] In other words: "It is the combination of these elements within each of the two families of common law and civil law and their respective court procedures and practices which permit the short-hand descriptors of 'adversarial' and 'inquisitorial' to be used."[4]

This interest in inquisitorial process was due to a crisis in civil litigation in Australia. Problems of cost, delay and unfairness in the prevailing adversarial civil justice system were of concern to government and led to the request for the ALRC to explore the possibility of adoption of inquisitorial process.[5] The tribunals covered by the ALRC's survey were the principal federal tribunals: the Administrative Appeals Tribunal (AAT), a multi-jurisdiction tribunal with power to review decisions across government,[6] and the specialist tribunals, the Social Security Appeals Tribunal (SSAT), the Veterans' Review Board (VRB), and the Migration, and Refugee, Review Tribunals (MRT and RRT). Each of these tribunals was established to operate in a manner which possessed inquisitorial features.

In the result, the ALRC did not recommend adoption of the European civil law model, preferring to opt for improvements to the existing system. The Commission was undoubtedly conscious of the difficulties of grafting foreign tissue on to a body with particular constitutional, institutional and political characteristics.[7] In addition, and ironically, given the statutory indicators that they operate in an

---

2 Austl, Commonwealth, Australian Law Reform Commission, *Review of the Federal Civil Justice System*, Discussion Paper 62 (Canberra: Australian Government Publishing Service 1999) at para 2.25 [Review of the federal civil justice system].

3 *Ibid* at para 2.26. Antoine J Bullier, "How the French Understand the Inquisitorial System" (2001) 29 AIAL Forum 47.

4 Austl, Commonwealth, Australian Law Reform Commission, *Review of the Adversarial System of Litigation: Rethinking the Federal Civil Litigation System*, Issues Paper 20 (Canberra: Australian Government Publishing Service 1997) at paras 2.6–2.8 [Review of the Adversarial System of Litigation]. See also Gerard Brennan, "Key Issues in Judicial Administration" (1997) 6 Journal of Judicial Administration 138.

5 Review of the Adversarial System of Litigation, *supra* note 4 at para 15.1.

6 The AAT has been granted jurisdiction in over 400 pieces of legislation.

7 Cheryl Saunders "Lessons and Insights from Other Common Law Countries" (1991) Admin Review 2 at 3.

inquisitorial manner, the ALRC noted that there was "no support from tribunals for the imposition of a general duty to investigate case facts and issues."[8]

At the same time, with a nod to the intention that federal tribunals should not operate like courts, the ALRC did suggest tribunals' "legislation and practice should emphasize the administrative and investigative character of tribunal processes" and their procedures should "permit enhanced and independent inquiry into case facts and a process that does not rely primarily on a single hearing, but on a mixture of oral hearings and decisions on the papers."[9]

Taxonomy

The description of the processes of these tribunals is not settled. In the course of its inquiry, the ALRC described the functions of federal tribunals as "investigative."[10] In other words, they were not inquisitorial, nor adversarial but a hybrid of the two. However, "investigative" has not won universal acceptance. A former Justice of the High Court of Australia, Michael Kirby, described "investigative", along with "adjudicative" and "inquisitorial" as having a tendency to mislead.[11] He was not alone on the Court in holding that view as its exploration of how to describe the RRT indicates:[12]

> It has been said in this Court on more than one occasion that proceedings before the Tribunal are inquisitorial, rather than adversarial in their general character. ... The word "inquisitorial" has been used to indicate that the Tribunal, which can exercise all the powers and discretions of the primary decision-maker, is not itself a contradictor to the cause of the applicant for review. Nor does the primary decision-maker appear before the Tribunal as a contradictor. The relevant ordinary meaning of "inquisitorial" is "having or exercising the function of an inquisitor", that is to say "one whose official duty it is to inquire, examine or investigate." As applied to the Tribunal "inquisitorial" does not carry that full ordinary meaning. It merely delimits the nature of the Tribunal's functions.

---

8 Review of the federal civil justice system, *supra* note 2 at para 12.147.

9 Austl, Commonwealth, Australian Law Reform Commission, *Managing Justice: A Review of the Federal Civil Justice System*, Report 89 (2000) at 21.

10 *Ibid.*

11 *Re Minister for Immigration and Multicultural Affairs, Ex parte Epeabaka* (2001) HCA 23, 206 CLR 128 at para 63.

12 *Minister for Immigration v SZIAI*, [2009] HCA 39, (2009) 259 ALR 429 at 434 [*SZIAI*].

Instead, the Court opted for "non-adversarial",[13] to differentiate tribunal procedures from those associated with courts.[14] Such a description, based on what features tribunals lack, rather than identifying what they share, is unhelpful. Other attempts to suggest an alternative descriptor for tribunals' processes, such as "interventionist",[15] "enabling",[16] "cooperative", "facilitated", "dialogue-based",[17] have proved equally unappealing. Whether the expression favored at this conference – an "active engagement" approach – will be adopted, is as yet unknown.

Australian commentary on the meaning of "inquisitorial" has focused on the objective of truth finding in inquisitorial review and the permissive powers of tribunals to distinguish their mode of operations. But this too can be misleading. A common objective of Australian tribunals is that they operate in a manner described as: "fair, just, informal, economic and quick."[18] Leaving aside the obvious tension between these requirements, operating in a manner which is "economical and quick" does not allow for the thorough analysis that is implied in a system designed to identify the truth.

Permissive powers of Australian tribunals such as removal of the requirement that they comply with rules of evidence have also been motivated more by a desire to reduce formality and delay in proceedings, and facilitate comparatively inexpensive and efficient adjudication, than a rejection of adversarial process.[19] On neither count do these features of Australian tribunals suggest a strongly inquisitorial mode of operations.

---

13 *Minister for Immigration v Wang*, [2003] HCA 11, 215 CLR 518 at 541, per majority (Gleeson CJ, McHugh, Gummow and Hayne JJ).

14 *Minister for Immigration and Citizenship v SZGUR*, [2011] HCA 1, (2011) 273 ALR 223 at para 23 [*SZGUR*].

15 Rosemary Balmford, "The Life of the Administrative Appeals Tribunal: Logic or Experience" in R Creyke, ed, *Administrative Tribunals: Taking Stock* (Canberra: Centre for International and Public Law, Australian National University, 1992) at 50 [Creyke, *Taking Stock*].

16 Andrew Leggatt, *Tribunals for Users: One System, One Service. The Report of the Review of Tribunals* (London: Tribunals Review Programme, 2001) at para 7.4.

17 Letter from Bernadette Rogers (Conference Registrar, Administrative Appeals Tribunal) to the author (2004).

18 *Administrative Appeals Tribunal Act 1975* (Cth), s 2A [*AAT Act*]; *Migration Act 1958* (Cth), ss 353, 420 [*Migration Act*]; *Social Security (Administration) Act 1991* (Cth), s 141 [*SS Admin Act*]. See also *ACT Civil and Administrative Tribunal Act 2008* (ACT), ss 6, 7 [*ACAT Act*]; *Administrative Decisions Tribunal Act 1997* (NSW), ss 3(b), 73 [*NSWADT Act*]; *Queensland Civil and Administrative Tribunal Act 2009* (Qld), s 3; *State Administrative Tribunal Act 2004* (WA), s 9 [*SAT Act*]; *Victorian Civil and Administrative Tribunal Act 1998* (Vic), ss 97, 98 [*VCAT Act*].

19 Narelle Bedford & Robin Creyke, *Inquisitorial Process in Australian Tribunals* (Melbourne: Australian Institute of Judicial Administration, 2006) at 8–9 [Bedford & Creyke].

The extent to which Australian merits review tribunals can properly be called "inquisitorial" has taken place within this definitional debate. At present, the most that can be concluded is that, as the High Court indicated: "the term "inquisitorial" has been applied to tribunal proceedings to distinguish them from adversarial proceedings and to characterize the Tribunal's statutory functions."[20] In other words, to say in Australia that tribunals are inquisitorial is to say no more than that they are non-adversarial. The upshot is that the taxonomic task in Australia remains unfulfilled. What is needed is a descriptor for the unique characteristics which capture the fact that Australian tribunals are neither inquisitorial, nor adversarial in the true senses of those words. In particular, it should be recognized that applying a label solely to tribunal hearings is misleading. A feature of tribunal (and increasingly court) processes is that a descriptor is needed to characterise the bulk of tribunal dispute settlement procedures which occur prior to and at times after a hearing. In the meantime, tribunals are still labeled inquisitorial or investigative and these adjectives will be used in this chapter.

Australian Adjudicative System

Settlement of disputes within Australia takes place within a judicial framework which reflects the fact that Australia is a federation with a relatively homogenous political and legal system. There is a national federal court system comprising at its lowest level a magistrates court, followed next in the hierarchy by the federal (and family) courts, with the High Court of Australia at the apex of the system. Each state and territory – the sub-national units of the polity – has an indigenous court system which largely replicates the tiers of the federal system. Homogeneity of the law is effected by what has been called the "autochthonous expedient",[21] that is, there is a right of appeal from the state and territory court systems to the federal court system and ultimately the High Court, and which permits under the Constitution the conferral of federal judicial power on the state courts.

Complicating this picture is the nature of "federal judicial power." The Australian Constitution, like its United States counterpart, reflects the political doctrine of separation of powers. That doctrine has inhibited federal court judges from exercising non-judicial functions, and confines the federal courts' role to decision-making within the narrow band of what is "judicial." These features of the constitutional landscape in Australia have impacted on federal tribunals.

The remit of merit review tribunals is to make decisions about executive issues, according to law, fact and policy. This has an impact on both courts and tribunals. Since regard to policy, for example exceeds the strict ambit of judicial power, federal courts are prohibited from reviewing aspects of decision-making

20 *SZGUR*, *supra* note 14 at para 23.

21 *R v Kirby; Ex parte Boilermakers' Society of Australia*, [1956] HCA 10, 94 CLR 254 at 268.

by federal tribunals. The courts hear appeals from these tribunals, usually on a question of law, and the courts supervise federal tribunals' exercise of authority through judicial review. But they cannot go further. At the same time since federal tribunals are prohibited from exercising federal judicial power, tribunals are incapable of making decisions which are definitive pronouncements of law, and of enforcing their judgments, these being indicia of judicial power. In summary, constitutionally, Australian courts are not in a position to reassess the merits, as opposed to the legality of decisions, due to the strict separation of powers doctrine. A duty to inquire on the part of tribunals could properly extend into factual or policy matters, and it is beyond the jurisdiction of the federal judiciary to review such matters.

The position is at first sight different in the states. By way of background, state and territory tribunals – particularly the so-called "super tribunals" – have a combined civil and administrative jurisdiction. That is, they adjudicate on private disputes, such as consumer and tenancy claims, as well as government decisions. Nonetheless, they too have been set up, in varying degrees, to operate in an inquisitorial fashion. A difference, however, is that in these jurisdictions, separation of powers notions have less influence.[22] As a consequence, the major state tribunals, at least in theory, are capable of making final decisions and exercising powers akin to those of the judiciary. However, the theory has not been matched by the practice. There has been controversy about whether tribunals do have, or should have, the same functions and powers as courts.[23] The result is that in practice, apart from their combined civil and administrative jurisdiction, state and territory tribunals are generally subject to the same limitations as their federal counterparts, particularly in light of the potential conferral on them of federal judicial power.[24]

The consequence is that throughout Australia courts operating according to adversarial process hear appeals or review decisions by tribunals operating in the investigative or inquisitorial spectrum. Inevitably there is a tendency for courts to expect tribunals to comply with procedures aligned to the adversarial processes with which the courts are familiar. This means that the system of review of tribunal decisions by courts has tended to dampen the development by tribunals of the distinctive characteristics which could better enable them to differentiate themselves from their judicial cousins.

22 *Kable v Director of Public Prosecutions for NSW*, [1996] HCA 24, 138 ALR 577.

23 *State Rail Authority of NSW v Consumer Claims Tribunal* (1988), 14 NSWLR 473; cf *Fuentes v Standard Knitting Mill Pty Ltd*, [2003] NSWCA 146.

24 *Kirk v Industrial Relations Court of New South Wales*, (2010) 239 CLR 531.

Australian Tribunals: Inquisitorial Features

Tribunals were deliberately established to operate informally and according to inquisitorial features. A key finding of the Kerr Committee's foundational report on administrative law in Australia was that "the code of procedure for the Tribunals should clearly spell out that they are not bound to follow adversary procedures … [I]n most cases, the investigative or inquisitorial process would be most apposite."[25] These recommendations were implemented for the federal tribunals,[26] and were the model for the major state and territory multi-purpose tribunals.[27]

Nonetheless, the extent of investigative features varies significantly between tribunals. The ALRC, in its inquiry into the federal civil justice system, identified four investigative models within the federal tribunal system: in models 1 and 2 only the applicant appeared at the hearing, with or without a pre-hearing process;[28] model 3 involved both parties appearing, with no prehearing process; model 4, the model in practice in the Administrative Appeals Tribunal, has both parties appearing and there is a prehearing process to assist with preparation and presentation of the application.[29] An equally varied set of models applies within the states and territories. Accordingly, to describe Australian tribunals as inquisitorial must be seen against this spectrum of procedural styles.

Inquisitorial indicators in their statutes are that Australian tribunals:

- have no burden of proof;
- are to be "satisfied" in reaching their decision;
- may inform themselves on any matter;
- can compel the appearance of witnesses;
- can compel the production of documents;
- have discretion to determine their own procedure;
- can have informal proceedings;

25 Austl, Commonwealth, *Commonwealth Administrative Review Committee Report*, Paper No 144 (1971) at paras 295(g), (h), and 334 [Kerr Committee Report] as modified by Austl, Commonwealth, *Final Report of the Committee on Administrative Discretions*, Paper No 316 (1973) at paras 172(j), 136, 173 [Bland Committee Report].

26 Austl, Commonwealth, Administrative Review Council, *The Structure and Form of Social Security Appeals*, Report No 21 (Barton: Australian Government,1984) at paras 141, 142, 147; Austl, Commonwealth, Committee for the Review of the System for Review of Migration Decisions, *Non-Adversarial Review of Migration Decisions: The Way Forward* (Canberra: The Committee, 1992) at paras 7.1.1–7.1.4 [CROSROMD]; Gillian Osborne, "Inquisitorial Procedure in the Administrative Appeals Tribunal – A Comparative Perspective" (1982–3) 13 Federal Law Review 150 at 150 [Osborne].

27 Explanatory Memoranda for the Civil and Administrative Tribunal Bill 2009 (Qld) 4, 34–6 and the Civil and Administrative Tribunal Bill 2008 (ACT) 4, 7–8.

28 For example, SSAT or MRT.

29 Review of the federal civil justice system, *supra* note 2 at paras 12.113–12.114.

- are not bound to abide by the rules of evidence;
- can make decisions on written submissions alone; and
- can hear matters without parties being legally represented.[30]

No single tribunal possesses all these inquisitorial attributes. Rather, Australian tribunals appear on "a spectrum ranging from the heavily investigative to the adversarial."[31]

Toward the inquisitorial end of the spectrum, the Migration Review Tribunal (MRT)[32] and the Refugee Review Tribunal (RRT) were "overtly designed as 'inquisitorial'."[33] A report described the inquisitorial features of the Immigration Review Tribunal (IRT), the forerunner of the MRT, in these terms:

> ... it is usually only the applicant who attends any "hearings", and he or she is often not represented by anyone else, whether a lawyer or otherwise. Tribunal members themselves are responsible for actively assisting the applicant to present his or her case, identifying all the relevant issues, thoroughly testing the evidence and protecting the interests of both applicant and the Department or Minister.[34]

These features meant their members take greater control of the proceeding and have little choice about taking a more proactive approach.

At the same time, the statutes for the major Australian tribunals such as the federal Administrative Appeals Tribunal (AAT), the NSW Administrative Decisions Tribunal (NSWADT) and the Victorian Civil and Administrative Tribunal (VCAT), also contain adversarial features illustrated by:

- references to "parties", "disputes" and "hearings";[35]
- parties' right to have legal representation;[36]
- parties' right to have a reasonable opportunity to present their case;[37]
- the tribunal deciding on the evidence it admits;[38]
- in some instances, the awarding of costs;[39] and

---

30 Bedford & Creyke, *supra* note 19 at 14–15.

31 *Ibid* at 18.

32 Including its predecessor, the Immigration Review Tribunal (IRT).

33 Bedford & Creyke, *supra* note 19 at 5.

34 CROSROMD, *supra* note 26 at para 7.1.2. Creyke notes that this procedure has been retained by the MRT: Bedford & Creyke, *ibid* at 77, 92.

35 *AAT Act*, *supra* note 18, ss 34J, 35; *NSWADT Act*, *supra* note 18, ss 67, 70, 75(1); *VCAT Act*, *supra* note 18, Pt 4 Div 2, ss 3, 101.

36 *AAT Act*, *ibid*, s 32; *NSWADT Act*, *ibid*, s 71; *VCAT Act*, *ibid*, s 62.

37 *AAT Act*, *ibid*, s 39.

38 *AAT Act*, *ibid*, ss 34E, 40(5), 43(2B).

39 *NSWADT Act*, *supra* note 18, s 88; *VCAT Act*, *supra* note 18 at s 109(2).

- judicial membership or leadership.[40]

However, even at the adversarial end of this spectrum, Australian tribunals share key minimum inquisitorial features. They have discretion as to their procedures, are not bound by the rules of evidence, may proceed with minimal formality or technicality, may inform themselves on any matter they deem appropriate, and may summon witnesses, documents or other evidence.[41] This amalgamation of adversarial and inquisitorial features in Australian tribunals has prevented their development of a classic inquisitorial model and opened the way for identification of a distinct model of procedure, which is flexible, expert, user-friendly, and employs case management powers to achieve the overriding objectives of tribunals, that is, to be accessible and to adopt an enabling role.[42]

Judicial and Tribunal Attitudes to Inquisitorial Process in Australia

The response of Australian courts and tribunals to this mixture of features has been equally ambivalent. In 1985 in *Prasad v Minister for Immigration*[43] the Federal Court devised general principles to guide tribunals about when to investigate, subject only to a specific contrary statutory intention. The starting point was that

---

40 *AAT Act, supra* note 18 at s 7(1); *NSWADT Act, supra* note 18 at ss 4, 7, 78; *VCAT Act, supra* note 18, at ss 9–13, 64(2), 64(3), 65. Justice Garry Downes, "Introduction: The Obligation to Assist" (Welcome address delivered at the seminar "The Obligation to Assist Model Litigants in Administrative Appeals Tribunal Proceedings", Canberra, 26 August 2009) at 2–3; Robin Creyke, "Tribunals: Divergence and Loss" (2001) 29 Federal Law Review 403 at 416–7 [Creyke, "Tribunals: Divergence and Loss"]; Margaret Allars, "Neutrality, The Judicial Paradigm and Tribunal Procedure" (1991) 13 Sydney Law Review 377 at 405 and 410 [Allars, "Tribunal Procedure"]; Mark Aronson & Nicola Franklin, *Review of Administrative Action* (Law Book Company, 1987) at 237–8; Bland Committee Report, *supra* note 25 at paras 136, 295(d), 324.

41 *AAT Act, supra* note 18, ss 33, 37, 38, 40; *Civil and Administrative Tribunal Act 2009* (ACT), s 8, Pts 5, 6 [*ACAT Act*]; *NSWADT Act, supra* note 18, s 73(3); *VCAT Act, supra* note 18, s 98(1)(d); *SAT Act, supra* note 18, s 32(2); *Migration Act, supra* note 18, ss 353, 359; *SS Admin Act, supra* note 18, ss 151, 158, 165, 165A, 166, 167, 175, 192, 195; *Veterans' Entitlement Act 1986* (Cth), s 138; Allars, "Tribunal Procedure"; Scott Henchcliffe, "Theory, Practice and Procedural Fairness at Administrative Appeals Tribunal Hearings" (1995) 13 Australian Bar Review 243 at 243 [Henchcliffe]; Robin Creyke, "Administrative Tribunals" in Matthew Groves & HP Lee, eds, *Australian Administrative Law: Fundamentals, Principles and Doctrines* (Port Melbourne Australia: Cambridge University Press, 2007) 77 at 90 [Creyke "Administrative Tribunals"]; Gerard Brennan, "Comment: the Anatomy of an Administrative Decision" (1990) 9 Sydney Law Review 1 at 1–8.

42 Kenny Mullan, "Editorial" in *Tribunals Spring 2011* (UK Judicial College, 2011) 1.

43 *Prasad v Minister for Immigration*, [1985] FCA 47, 6 FCR 155.

administrative tribunals are under "no general obligation to initiate inquiries or to make out an applicant's case."[44] Tribunals are generally entitled to be guided by the submissions of the parties and the materials before them.[45]

Nonetheless, there are exceptions to the duty to inquire, as it became known. The exceptions were framed in *Prasad* in these terms, and have been accepted widely since:

> ... where it is obvious that material is readily available which is centrally relevant to the decision to be made ... to proceed to a decision without making any attempt to obtain that information may properly be described as an exercise of the decision-making power in a manner so unreasonable that no reasonable person would have so exercised it.[46]

Subsequent Developments

Since that first pronouncement the courts have been prepared to find there was a duty of inquiry where:

- an applicant was disadvantaged in presenting their case because unrepresented,[47] disabled,[48] lacked education,[49] had language or cultural difficulties,[50] was of advanced age,[51] in detention,[52] under stress,[53] or had suffered a recent tragedy;[54]
- personal liberty was at stake;[55]

---

44 *Minister for Immigration v Le*, [2007] FCA 1318, 242 ALR 455 at para 60 (Kenny J).

45 *Emiantor v Minister for Immigration*, [1997] FCA 1356, 48 ALD 635, at pg 653 (Merkel J); *Re Norman Edwin Tuite v Administrative Appeals Tribunal Veterans' Appeals Division and Repatriation Commission*, [1993] FCA 71, 40 FCR 483 at 487–9; *Chen v Minister for Immigration*, (2000) 106 FCR 157 [114]; *Scott v Human Rights and Equal Opportunity Commission*, [2010] FCA 1323 at para 53 and 63 (no duty sounding in damages to advise of potential welfare pensions or benefits); *SZJBA v Minister for Immigration*, [2007] FCA 1592 at para 60.

46 *Prasad v Minister for Immigration*, [1985] FCA 47, 6 FCR 155 at 169 (Wilcox J) (emphasis added).

47 *Mustafay v Secretary, Department of Family and Community Services*, [2004] AATA 819 at para 5.

48 *Grant v Repatriation Commission*, [1999] FCA 1629, (1999) 57 ALD 1 [*Grant*].

49 *Joseph v Health Insurance Commission*, [2005] FCA 1042.

50 *SZMWQ v Minister for Immigration*, [2010] FCAFC 97 at para 141.

51 *Minister for Immigration v Le*, [2007] FCA 1318, 164 FCR 151 at 176.

52 *Videto v Minister for Immigration*, [1985] FCA 326, (1985) 8 FCR 167.

53 *Re Patricia Hudson and Child Support Registrar*, [1998] AATA 863.

54 *Re Katrina Marie Akers v Minister for Immigration, Local Government and Ethnic Affairs*, [1988] FCA 459, 20 FCR 363.

55 *Goldie v Commonwealth*, [2002] FCA 261, 117 FCR 566 at 569.

- the applicant was a war veteran, entitled to the special treatment accorded this group;[56]
- the applicant had specifically requested the tribunal to undertake inquiries;[57]
- the missing information was obvious and administratively simple to acquire, for example, the attachments to a facsimile which transmitted only the cover sheet;[58]
- the decision-maker was in a unique position to acquire the information;[59]
- the decision-makers actively discouraged the applicant from raising issues which would have assisted the application;[60]
- the evidence clearly lacked a probative basis,[61] or was obviously outdated;[62] and
- the decision-maker did not disclose the existence of centrally relevant information.[63]

Factors militating against a duty included circumstances where:

- an inquiry would have prevented the tribunal from operating economically or quickly,[64] unduly prolonged the hearing,[65] or would have nullified the remedial effect of the decision when time was of the essence;[66]
- the party requesting the inquiry was unwilling to bear the cost;[67]
- the applicant was sufficiently well educated to make their own submissions,[68] or was legally represented, particularly by counsel;[69] or
- the matter related to something of monetary value, or from which the

---

56 For example, *Grant, supra* note 48; *Brew v Repatriation Commission* (1999) 94 FCR 80; *McKerlie v Repatriation Commission*, [2010] FCA 1127, 52 AAR 535 at 546.

57 *Sun Zhan Qui v Minister for Immigration & Ethnic Affairs*, (1997) 81 FCR 71 at 91, 119. cf *SZLGP v Minister for Immigration and Citizenship*, [2009] FCA 1470, (2009)112 ALD 501 at 515.

58 *SZJBA v Minister for Immigration*, [2007] FCA 1592, 164 FCR 14.

59 *Lek v Minister for Immigration*, [1993] FCA 493, (1993) 117 ALR 455 1; doubted in *Minister for Immigration v QAAH of 2004*, (2006) 231 CLR at 17.

60 *Videto v Minister for Immigration*, [1985] FCA 326, (1985) 8 FCR 167 at 178–9.

61 *SZGRK v Minister for Immigration*, [2010] FCA 153.

62 *Tickner v Bropho*, [1993] FCA 208, (1993) 40 FCR 183 at 197–9.

63 *Detsongjarus v Minister for Immigration*, [1990] FCA 364, (1990) 21 ALD 139.

64 *Re Hargreaves and Australian Community Pharmacy [No 2]*, (1995) 41 ALD 147.

65 *Battenberg v The Union Club*, (December 9, 2004), [2004] NSWADT 285 at para 23.

66 *Re J Wattie Canneries Limited v Thomas Plunkett Hayes, Comptroller-General of Customs; Petersvile Industries Limited and Mccain Foods (Australia) Pty Limited*, [1987] FCA 240 (21 July 1987), (1987) 74 ALR 202.

67 *Re Achurch and Comcare*, (2003) 77 ALD 531.

68 *Joseph* (applicant a doctor); *Emiantor v Minister for Immigration*, (1997) 48 ALD 635.

69 *Re Golem and Transport Accident Commission [No 1]*, [2002] VCAT 319, (2002) 19 VAR 265; *SZMWQ v Minister for Immigration*, (2010) 187 FCR 109 at 149.

> applicant stood to gain a financial windfall, such as a development application.[70]

The cases over the years following *Prasad* which accepted a duty to inquire were initially relatively infrequent[71] but have increased. Nonetheless, many Federal Court and tribunal decisions have denied any such obligation.[72] The conflicting findings ensured that the issue would need High Court attention. In 2009 in *Minister for Immigration v SZIAI*[73] *(SZIAI),* the opportunity arose.

SZIAI involved a claim by a Bangladeshi citizen for refugee status on the ground that he had a well-founded fear of persecution due to his conversion from being a Sunni, to an Ahmadi, Muslim. SZIAI's supporting documents were certificates said to be signed by those associated with the Ahmadiyya Muslim Jamaat at Khulna in Bangladesh. The RRT wrote to the Ahmadiyya Muslim Association of Australia which responded, following an inquiry, that it believed the certificates were forged. The issue was whether the tribunal should then have tried to contact the authors of the documents in Bangladesh, their telephone numbers being on the certificates. The tribunal sought the views of SZIAI and his solicitor on the Association's views. They declined to comment, other than saying that SZIAI maintained his story and could not otherwise prove his claims.

The Court dismissed the application finding that there was no obligation on the tribunal to inquire further since telephoning the numbers would not resolve the critical fact, namely, the authenticity of the documents, and SZIAI had indicated he had no other way of proving his claim. The Court upheld the narrow range of factors attracting the duty of inquiry and, in the context of legislative restrictions on claims under the *Migration Act 1958* (Cth) confined such circumstances to a jurisdictional, that is, serious error for failure to exercise the tribunal's review jurisdiction.[74] Beyond that the Justices were not prepared to go.[75] The Court's reluctance exercised a chilling effect on the further expansion of any duty to

---

70 *Campbell v Port Phillip City Council*, [1999] VCAT 128 (30 June 1999).

71 For an overview of that case law: Robin Creyke & John McMillan, *Control of Government Action: Text, Cases and Commentary*, 2nd ed (Chatswood, NSW: LexisNexis Butterworths, 2009) at 986–9; Mark Smyth "Inquisitorial Adjudication: The Duty to Inquire in Merits Review Tribunals" (2010) 34 Melbourne University Law Review 230 at 247–260; Matthew Groves, "The Duty to Inquire in Tribunal Proceedings" (2011) 33 Sydney Law Review 179.

72 Collected by Kenny J in *Minister for Immigration v Le*, [2007] FCA 1318, (2007) 164 FCR 151 at 174–5.

73 *SZIAI, supra* note 12.

74 *Ibid* at 436.

75 For a discussion of *SZIAI*, see: Smyth, *supra* note 71; Rebecca Heath & Anna Johnson, "Casenote: *Minister for Immigration v SZIAI*" (2010) 17 Australian Journal of Administrative Law 66.

inquire and courts since then have been careful to ensure that any material sought is centrally relevant,[76] and readily available.[77]

A second opportunity arose in 2011 for High Court consideration of the issue. In *Minister for Immigration v SZGUR*[78] *(SZGUR)* the High Court confirmed its approach in *SZIAI*. The RRT had rejected SZGUR's claim on credibility grounds. The agent for SZGUR had written to the tribunal asking for an independent assessment of SZGUR's mental health. This was to support the view of SZGUR's treating psychiatrist that his depression and bipolar mood disorder had had an effect on his memory.[79] The contention was that the inconsistencies in SZGUR's stories were not due to him lying but rather to his psychiatric conditions. A provision in the *Migration Act 1958* (Cth) permits the Secretary of the department to arrange for a medical examination.[80] SZGUR had offered to pay for the assessment. The tribunal rejected the application, a decision overturned on appeal to the Federal Court. Special leave to appeal to the High Court was granted which upheld the principles relating to the duty enunciated in *SZIAI*, and confirmed that the discretionary power imposed no obligation to inquire, or even to consider whether to do so.[81] As the Court noted, "there is nothing to suggest that SZGUR could

76 *Minister for Immigration and Citizenship v Dhanoa*, [2009] FCAFC 153, (2009) 180 FCR 510 (not centrally relevant to advise of a scheme which would have given applicant more points towards visa since scheme not in existence at time of application); *SZNYI v Minister for Immigration and Citizenship*, [2010] FCA 221, (2010) 114 ALD 220 (information not centrally relevant as would not have changed outcome); *SZLGP v Minister for Immigration and Citizenship*, [2009] FCA 1470 (inquiry re employment status of applicant's former employer in China was an obvious inquiry about a critical fact); *Khant v Minister for Immigration and Citizenship*, [2009] FCA 1247, (2009) 112 ALD 241 (failure to contact applicant invited to make a submission was failure in "duty to review" since without information tribunal could not make proper decision).

77 *Lai v Minister for Immigration and Citizenship*, [2010] FCA 540 (no requirement to obtain information about hairdressing course in Vietnam since comparison not easily made given variety of courses in Australia); *Brown v Minister for Immigration and Citisenship*, [2009] FCA 1098 (no obligation to get sentencing remarks relating to applicant when transcript not readily available); *SZNMJ v Minister for Immigration and Citizenship*, [2009] FCA 1345 (no obligation to seek information from psychologist who diagnosed post-traumatic stress disorder given obligation of confidentiality on psychologist); *SZNBX v Minister for Immigration and Citizenship*, [2009] FCA 1403 (no obligation to contact Latvian lawyer likely to be uncooperative especially as no contact details provided); *SZMJM v Minister for Immigration and Citizenship*, [2010] FCA 309 (department on behalf of tribunal not required to make inquiries of a hospital in Pakistan since information not readily available); *SZOER v Minister for Immigration and Citizenship*, [2010] FCA 1100 and *Minister for Immigration and Citizenship v MZYCE*, [2010] FCA 767 (no obligation on tribunal when applicant able to make inquiry).

78 *SZGUR*, *supra* note 14.

79 *Ibid* at 230.

80 *Migration Act*, *supra* note 18, s 427(1)(d).

81 *SZGUR*, *supra* note 14 at para 22.

not have obtained from his psychiatrist a more expansive report than the bare certificates which were provided."[82] The Court confirmed it was for the applicant to present evidence to support his case.

Following *SZGUR* it may now be said that unless a failure to investigate or inquire is so egregious as to amount to a failure properly to exercise review powers, no obligation is imposed on tribunals to be inquisitorial. Beyond that the courts have provided little guidance.

Policies behind Reluctance to Impose Duty to Inquire

Judicial reluctance towards the duty to inquire can be explained from a constitutional, a pragmatic and a doctrinal perspective. As the constitutional structure discussed earlier indicates, the separation of powers doctrine prevents Australian courts from reassessing the merits, as opposed to the legality, of a decision. Since a duty to inquire may relate to factual or policy matters which lie outside federal judicial power, it is for the tribunals not the courts, to decide to what extent they should take an interventionist role. Tribunals have not been proactive in responding to this challenge.

For pragmatic reasons, courts have been reluctant to expect tribunals to operate in an inquisitorial manner. Tribunals are underfunded, and were intended to be a cheaper means of settling disputes than courts. Saddling them with inquiry burdens would undermine this objective. The need for efficiency to deal with large caseload, enjoined by the "economical and quick" elements of their objects, underscores this requirement and is frequently referred to as an answer to a complaint that the tribunal should take a more interventionist approach.[83]

Although procedurally classified as "inquisitorial", Australian parliaments have modified the European model to suit the Australian tribunal landscape.[84] Requiring tribunals to undertake inquiries would impinge on tribunals' statutory injunction to operate in a flexible manner. The following extract exemplifies the courts' reluctance to require tribunals to be more interventionist:

> [a]lthough s 33(1)(c) of the AAT Act permits the Tribunal to ignore the rules of evidence and procedure and inform itself of any matters in any way it thinks appropriate, the section does not envisage the Tribunal calling the evidence itself or taking over the conduct of cases. It must always respect the rights of the

82 *Ibid* at 232–3 per French CJ; Kiefel J, Gummow J at 246; Heydon and Crennan JJ agreeing with both judgments.

83 Bedford & Creyke, *supra* note 19 at 62.

84 See too UK Administrative Justice & Tribunals Council, *Principles for Administrative Justice* (2010), Principle 2 at 21.

> parties and the perceptions of others about the system. It ought also to pause long before substituting itself as the actual or possible adversary.[85]

The court's caution about exploring what are the indicia of an inquisitorial model has been fuelled by the systemic and cultural entrenchment of adversarialism, and is exacerbated by legal training, tribunal leadership and the hierarchy of review.[86] This reluctance is perpetuated in those tribunals, like the AAT, in which parties are commonly represented.[87]

The equating of active intervention with bias[88] has also been at the forefront of factors inhibiting a more interventionist approach by tribunals in Australia.[89] The argument is that the more decision-makers enter into the "dust of conflict",[90] the more predisposed they are toward a certain outcome and the less capable of objectively adjudicating a dispute.[91] The risk of taking an active role in proceedings has been noted by the ALRC,[92] and the Administrative Review Council (ARC),[93] and encourages the reticence of tribunal members to adopt inquisitorial procedures.[94]

The cultural bias is also manifest in the pragmatic application of the rules of evidence. While not bound by the formal rules of evidence, in practice tribunals use the rules since "[s]ome procedure, some order of receiving evidence, must be established or we will simply sit looking at each other in silence."[95] Aside from this necessity, rules of evidence are applied because they are "the attempt made, through many generations, to evolve a method of inquiry best calculated to prevent

---

85 *Grace Hannah Perring v Australian Postal Corp*, [1993] FCA 192, (1993) 31 ALD 693 at 697.

86 Joan Dwyer, "Fair Play the Inquisitorial Way: A Review of the Administrative Appeals Tribunal's Use of Inquisitorial Procedures" (1997) 5 Australian Journal of Administrative Law 5 at 6 [Dwyer].

87 *AAT Act*, *supra* note 18, s 34. Also the case in the state equivalents, for example *NSWADT Act*, *supra* note 18, s 71.

88 Bedford & Creyke, *supra* note 19 at 35–8.

89 *R v War Pensions Entitlement Appeal Tribunal; Ex parte Bott*, [1933] HCA 30, (1933) 50 CLR 228, at 256 [*Bott*]; *S395/2002 v Minister for Immigration*, (2003) 216 CLR 473, at 488–9; *R v Full Industrial Court of South Australia; Ex parte Gameau* (1982) 31 SASR 62 at 72–3; *Perring v Australian Postal Corp* (1993) 31 ALD 693.

90 *Yuill v Yuill*, (1945) 1 All ER 183 at 189.

91 Osborne, *supra* note 26 at 150, 172; PD Connolly, "The Adversary System – Is It Any Longer Appropriate?" (1975) 49 Australian Law Journal 439 at 441.

92 Austl, Commonwealth, Australian Law Reform Commission, *Federal Tribunal Proceedings*, Issue Paper 24 (Canberra: Australian Government Publishing Service, 1999) at para 6.82; Bedford & Creyke, *supra* note 19 at 35.

93 Austl, Commonwealth, Administrative Review Council, *Social Security Appeals*, Report No 8 (1980) at para 5.035.

94 Bedford & Creyke, *supra* note 19 at 25.

95 *Golem v Transport Accident Commission*, (1984) 1 FCR 354.

error and elicit truth."[96] The slowness of tribunals to substitute an alternative set of procedural rules has contributed to this default situation.[97]

The organizational leadership of Australian tribunals too has exacerbated the cultural bias of common lawyers against the inquisitorial system. This risk was alluded to by the Bland Committee which recommended that the presidential members of the proposed AAT "must not be addicted to the adversary process and desirably they need wide experience of administration or of administrative law."[98] Despite these warnings, judicial leadership of tribunals[99] has meant "a more judicial flavor [has] percolate[d]"[100] through tribunals, especially those which hear non-administrative law matters. Even leadership by senior lawyers of the specialist tribunals has contributed to the formalization of tribunal practice.[101]

Finally, Australian tribunals operate in a system in which ultimate review is by a court, generally following a formal and adversarial approach, rather than a tribunal with informal and inquisitorial practices. The "dissonance between the processes of the review body and the tribunal being reviewed"[102] in Australia is non-existent in the European civil law system which separates its administrative review from its civil and criminal system.[103] This procedural disconnect has encouraged a tendency towards adversarial procedures and reinforced the unwillingness to find a duty to inquire.[104]

Policies Favoring Duty to Inquire

However, there are policies encouraging the duty. The view that intervention can lead tribunals to breach procedural fairness is not universal. For example, in *Weinstein v Medical Practitioners Board of Victoria*,[105] the Victorian Court of Appeal rejected a finding that the provision requiring VCAT to inform itself "in any way it thinks fit" did not authorize the Board to make inquiries. Rather, the Court said, the expression had work to do, defined the character of the tribunal's

---

96 *Bott*, *supra* note 89 at 256; *Re Gee and Director-General of Social Services* (1981) 3 ALD 132.

97 Dwyer, *supra* note 86 at 5, 6.

98 Bland Committee Report, *supra* note 25 at para 136.

99 The state and territory multi-purpose tribunals, other than ACAT, have judicial presidential members: Creyke, "Tribunals: Divergence and Loss", *supra* note 40 at 403, 413.

100 *Ibid* at 403, 413.

101 RA Macdonald, "Judicial Review and Procedural Fairness in Admin Law: II" (1980) 26 McGill L J 1 at 12; Allars, "Tribunal Procedure", *supra* note 40 at 377, 393.

102 Bedford & Creyke, *supra* note 19 at 6.

103 *Ibid* at 4, 6.

104 *Ibid* at 43.

105 *Weinstein v Medical Practitioners Board of Victoria*, [2008] VSCA 193 [*Weinstein*].

hearing, and authorized it "to 'inform itself' ... subject always to the overriding obligation to accord procedural fairness."[106] As the Court said:

> Parliament [through use of the expression] has clearly differentiated the panel's conduct of a formal hearing from the judicial paradigm. Whereas the judicial function is essentially passive ... the panel's work is thus stamped with an inquisitorial character ... the panel's role as investigator is envisaged as being active, not passive.[107]

Supporting this approach is the principle that procedural fairness takes its color from the particular statute and the circumstances of the case.[108] These necessarily involve consideration of the tribunal's function and inquisitorial powers.[109] In this context the Court noted that the fair-minded observer can be taken to know of the investigative role of the tribunal,[110] and as Dwyer pointed out, "[t]o achieve a fair outcome it may be necessary for the Tribunal to direct the inquiry, to adopt an inquisitorial mode."[111]

Another factor favoring intervention is that tribunal members are generally experts and, under the doctrine of "official notice",[112] are better equipped than judges to decide the tribunal's level of inquiry and capacity to investigate. Their expertise also permits tribunal members, when informing themselves, to rely on their own knowledge and to check the facts.[113]

More generally, administrative law is not a contest. The right of access to tribunals is to enable citizens to obtain a correct or preferable decision by government. There should be no contest as demonstrated by the absence of any legal onus of proof. These features of the process are reinforced by Model Litigant Policies[114] that impose obligations on government agencies federally and elsewhere[115] to handle litigation honestly and fairly, and to avoid litigation where possible. They also require the government party at a hearing to act promptly, not

---

106 *Ibid* at para 28.

107 *Ibid* at para 30.

108 *Kioa v West*, [1985] HCA 81, (1985) 159 CLR 550.

109 *Applicant VEAL of 2002 v Minister for Immigration*, [2005] HCA 72, (2005) 80 ALJR 228 at paras 26–7.

110 *Weinstein v Medical Practitioners Board of Victoria*, [2008] VSCA 193 at para 36.

111 Dwyer, *supra* note 86 at 5, 34.

112 "Official notice" is the tribunal analogue of "judicial notice": *Commonwealth Shipping Representative v P & O Branch Service*, [1923] AC 191 at 212; Austl, Commonwealth, Australian Law Reform Commission, *Uniform Evidence*, Issue Report 102 (Canberra: Australian Government Publishing Service, 2006).

113 *Weinstein v Medical Practitioners Board of Victoria, supra* note 105 at 28.

114 For example, *Judiciary Act 1903* (Cth), s 55ZF(1); *Legal Services Directions 2005* App B.

115 Available in NSW, Queensland, South Australia, Victoria and the ACT.

to take forensic points, nor advantage of an applicant's lack of experience or funds. Breaches of the policies attract costs sanctions.[116]

Such policies have produced criticisms of an agency which simply filed a submitting appearance, thus depriving the court of the assistance of the executive,[117] and commendations to the solicitor for an agency when the solicitor's associate informed the presiding judge that the Court had overlooked one of the appellant's grounds of appeal.[118] In the result, the Court set aside its orders, and reversed the decision.

Recent legislative and policy exhortations to the courts at both federal and state level also encourage dispute resolution by means other than formal hearings.[119] An object of the *Civil Dispute Resolution Act 2011* (Cth) is to ensure, as far as possible, that people "take genuine steps to resolve disputes before certain civil proceedings are instituted." "Genuine steps" enjoin the settlement, or the narrowing the scope, of the matter by means other than a hearing, including pre-conference processes.[120] Although the Act does not apply to the major federal tribunals,[121] their exclusion may have been due to the fact that the Act specifically applies to civil, not administrative disputes, and the legislation of the tribunals already enjoins use of alternative dispute resolution processes. Undoubtedly, however, the introduction of the legislative exhortation will encourage greater attention to solving or narrowing disputes prior to any formal hearing.

In this vein an amendment to the AAT Act encourages less adversarial hearings. Section 33(1AA) provides: "In a proceeding before the Tribunal for a review of a decision, the person who made the decision must use ... *best endeavours* to assist the Tribunal to make its decision in relation to the proceeding" (emphasis added).[122] Although unenforceable, the provision is an incentive not to delay matters

---

116 *Western City Developments Pty Ltd v Chief Commissioner of State Revenue (No 2)*, [2010] NSWADTAP 72; *Australian Competition and Consumer Commission v Australia and New Zealand Banking Group Ltd (No 2)*, [2010] FCA 567.

117 *Mahenthirasasa v State Rail Authority of New South Wales (No 2)*, (2008) 72 NSWLR 273.

118 *SZLPO v Minister for Immigration (No 2)*, [2009] FCAFC 60, (2009) 255 ALR 435.

119 *Civil Dispute Resolution Act 2011* (Cth) [*Civil Dispute Resolution Act*]. The Act came into effect on 1 August 2011. Initially Victoria and New South Wales have also made moves towards a similar approach in civil claims. (See Robert McLellan, "Early Resolution, Better Outcomes", *The Australian* (July 29) 29–30). However, the state protocols, which required parties to take "reasonable steps" rather than "genuine steps" had the potential to cause confusion and have been postponed for 18 months in NSW and repealed in Victoria in March 2011. (Samantha Bowers, "Pre-action Protocols Put on Hold", *The Australian Financial Review* (26 August 2011) 21).

120 *Civil Dispute Resolution Act*, *ibid*, ss 3, 4.

121 *Ibid* Part 4.

122 *AAT Act*, *supra* note 18, s 33(1AA).

unnecessarily,[123] and reinforces the Model Litigant Policy. Costs orders, where applicable, can be used for compliance. These developments signal the heightened emphasis on non-adjudicative processes which is being fostered in Australia.

Practical Steps to Achieve Non-Adversarial Process in Australian Tribunals

Despite the courts' reluctance to encourage more interventionist approaches, tribunals, to varying degrees and with different levels of legislative support, have adopted inquisitorial practices. Migration tribunals, the most proactive,[124] summons persons to give evidence or produce documents,[125] require the department to arrange investigations or medical examinations,[126] and examine witnesses.[127] The SSAT holds pre-hearing processes,[128] requires the agency to provide information or documents including an applicant's file,[129] and asks questions or seeks clarification from witnesses.[130] The AAT requires receipt of relevant agency material and may require documents to be lodged by anyone,[131] may summons documents or witnesses itself, and members actively question parties at hearings.[132] More commonly tribunals direct parties to provide further evidence, such as medical or tax records held by government agencies, which are not practicable for the tribunal to acquire.[133]

Tribunals also actively engage in a range of prehearing processes,[134] including conferencing, case management, and forms of alternative dispute resolution, to encourage parties to identify or narrow the issues in dispute or achieve settlement.[135] Some engage private sector bodies or employees to perform investigative functions.[136] The success of these processes is indicated, for example, by the AAT, where between 83 and 85 per cent of matters do not progress to a hearing.[137]

---

123 *Re James Robinson and Repatriation Commission* [2010] AATA 617 (unreported).

124 Bedford & Creyke, *supra* note 19 at 8.

125 *Migration Act*, *supra* note 18, ss 363(3), 427(3).

126 *Ibid*, ss 363(1)(d), 427(1)(d).

127 *Ibid*, ss 366D, 427(6).

128 *SS Admin Act*, *supra* note 18, ss 166A, 166B.

129 *Ibid*, ss 157, 165.

130 *Ibid*, ss 165A, 167.

131 *AAT Act*, *supra* note 18, s 37.

132 *Ibid*, s 40(1A).

133 ALRC, *supra* note 1 at para 12.159.

134 For example, *AAT Act*, *supra* note 18, s 3(1), Part IV, Div 3.

135 *Ibid*, ss 32, 34; Allars, "Tribunal Procedure", *supra* note 40 at 377, 410; Henchcliffe, *supra* note 41 at 243, 243.

136 For example, in the veterans' jurisdiction; and the MRT/RRT engage their own staff and rely on departments for country information: Bedford & Creyke, *supra* note 19.

137 AAT *Annual Report 2009–2010* at 24, online: http://www.aat.gov.au/Publications/AnnualReport.htm.

The percentage of applications to the AAT which do not proceed to a hearing is significant. As mentioned earlier, there is a tendency in the discussion on whether a tribunal is operating in an adversarial or an inquisitorial manner to focus on the hearing as the sole forum in which identification is made of the predominant style of operations of the body. This is misguided and misleading.

Undoubtedly, the issue does arise in relation to the tribunals' hearing processes. The jurisprudence cited in this chapter relate solely to this aspect of the tribunals' processes. Whether and when it is appropriate for members at a hearing to adopt a more active or interventionist approach is a necessary element of the training of tribunal members. The need to balance fairness with an interventionist style of operation raises legal issues in relation to fair process of which members must be constantly aware. Breaching natural justice is a fate facing those who transgress the legal limits. Nonetheless, encouraging active participation of members in tribunal hearings is a desirable objective if the goals of tribunal operations being "fair, just, economical, informal and quick" are to be reached.

However, the reality is that most opportunities for the intervention or engagement processes within tribunals occur prior to a hearing. The practice indicates that in relation to tribunals case management and the use of pre-hearing dispute resolution processes are responsible for settlement in the preponderance of cases. The figures for the AAT which are replicated in other tribunals is approaching the same percentage. The spotlight should, therefore, be turned to the subterranean elements of tribunal processes since that is where most active intervention occurs. It is there that the narrowing of issues, the identification of whether there is a sustainable case, opinions in the form of non-binding opinions on law or facts, and attempted mediation or conciliation to reach a settlement occurs. It is there in the less formal meetings that discussion occurs which leads frequently to use of a pre-hearing dispute resolution procedure which results in the dispute resolving, or at the least a narrowing of the issues which do go forward to a hearing. Too little attention has to date been paid to these critical elements of the procedures of tribunals.

Recognition of the locus of tribunals' workload particularly prior to a hearing has been slow, principally because tribunals themselves have not made due allowance for them, because governments have an expectation that tribunals will be less costly than courts, and because of a failure to acknowledge the upfront financial burden of tribunals taking an active role in dispute settlement. As a consequence, use of inquisitorial procedures is limited by inadequate resources to fund a needed medical report, or investigation into a missing but essential element of a hearing. In Australia only the migration tribunals were funded for research staff, although a number of tribunals do have legally trained staff to conduct preliminary conferences and undertake mediation and conciliation.

At the hearing interventionist processes are restricted by legal counsel, and inhibited by concerns from tribunal members, not trained in investigation methodology, or fearful of the risk of apprehended bias. It is no accident that the least adversarial tribunals[138] are those where only the applicant appears or rarely has legal representation,[139] or where lawyers are barred from or subject to restrictions in appearing.[140]

Conclusion

Inquisitorial processes have had a chequered history in Australian tribunals. Despite ostensibly being created to be different from courts, tribunals have not wholeheartedly embraced alternative forms of procedure. Since it is in procedural, not functional terms, that tribunals differ from courts, this reluctance is disappointing. What it reflects is the strength of the prevailing adversarial legal culture, and a timidity by tribunals and their members to venture into novel territory.

Nonetheless, there are signs, both legislative and practical, that this position is changing. Perhaps the most encouraging example is the rallying call from the High Court in *SZGUR* for tribunals to spell out what are their unique characteristics and how best they should operate within their specific statutory frameworks. In other words, in asking them to define what it is to be "non-adversarial", the Court has signaled that it is time for tribunals "to carve out a philosophy of their own existence."[141] That is the challenge that lies ahead.

138 Bedford & Creyke, *supra* note 19 at 8.

139 SSAT.

140 For example, QCAT, VRB, MRT/RRT.

141 John McMillan, "Merit Review and the AAT: A Concept Develops" in J McMillan, ed, *The AAT – Twenty Years Forward* (Canberra: AAT et al, 1998) at 33.

Chapter 3

From "Adversarial v Inquisitorial" to "Active, Enabling, and Investigative": Developments in UK Administrative Tribunals

Robert Thomas

Introduction

When designing an adjudication system, there are normally a number of procedural choices to be considered. A principal design issue concerns the role of the adjudicator and that of the parties. Should the adjudicator be passive or proactive? What should be the role of the parties and their contribution? This chapter explores these questions in the context of administrative tribunals in the United Kingdom.

As a common law jurisdiction, court hearings in the UK are generally conducted on an adversarial basis: each litigant will present his or her own case and attack that of the opponent.[1] The adjudicator is an impartial referee whose role is primarily to hold the ring between the parties and to decide the case solely on the basis of the evidence and arguments that the parties have chosen to present. Given the long history of adversarial process, this approach is adopted in virtually all civil and criminal litigation in the UK.[2]

By contrast, in inquisitorial proceedings, the judge assumes a proactive role of identifying issues and gathering evidence and also takes full control of the proceedings and governs the participation of the parties. The term "inquisitorial" is though nebulous and can carry a range of possible meanings. A soft inquisitorial approach may mean that the judge can make inquiries by asking questions or, with the assistance of the parties, investigate the issues. By contrast, a fully inquisitorial procedure denotes a more wide-ranging role for the judge from

1 These definitions draw upon M Allars, "Neutrality, the Judicial Paradigm and Tribunal Procedure" (1991) 13 Sydney Law Review 377 at 381–5; Andrew Leggatt, *Tribunals for Users: One System, One Service* (London: Tribunals Review Programme, 2001) at paras 7.2–7.5 [Leggatt].

2 The principal exceptions are the small claims court (which deals with low-value civil claims) and the Family and Children's Courts. Both these courts tend to operate in a more informal way than other civil litigation.

the pre- to post-hearing stage; the judge takes charge of the case and of case management, issues directions as to which particular matters and evidence require examination; the judge may also commission expert evidence.

The labels – adversarial and inquisitorial – are commonly used in discussions of judicial procedure. However, it is arguable that they do not adequately capture, either descriptively or normatively, the distinctive nature of administrative adjudication. An alternative way of expressing the underlying idea is to consider what degree of intervention – ranging from a passive, reactive stance to a more proactive or intrusive one – is required to ensure that appeals are decided properly.[3]

Over recent years, a third method – the enabling approach – has been advanced specifically in relation to unrepresented claimants who appeal against decisions of a "repeat-player" government agency. In the enabling approach, the tribunal gives an unrepresented appellant every possible assistance to enable her to participate and to compensate for her lack of skills or knowledge.[4] This is achieved through a combination of creating the right atmosphere and assisting the appellant by bringing out relevant facts.

The question of judicial procedure in administrative tribunals is vexed and a perennial area of discussion – usually without clear conclusions. It can also be a difficult matter upon which to generalise because the issues are so complex and wide-ranging. The differences between the institutions vary enormously and there has been little cross-jurisdictional investigation. Nonetheless, a common theme emerges: tribunals have been relatively successful in moving more toward an active, enabling, and investigative approach. Major challenges remain of course. Tribunals have yet to articulate a fuller vision of what type of active approach they aspire to undertake. The need to develop this vision will become more insistent if proposed restrictions to publicly funded representation are implemented.

The structure of the chapter is as follows. After an overview of recent reforms to the UK's tribunal system, the chapter considers the general position and debate over tribunal procedure and the pressures for and against active adjudication. The chapter then considers the practice in the largest two tribunal jurisdictions – social security and immigration adjudication.

Tribunal Adjudication in the UK

In the UK, administrative tribunals are the standard mechanism for legal control over administrative decision-making. They determine appeals against various administrative decisions and are staffed predominantly by legally-qualified

3 Peter Cane, *Administrative Tribunals and Adjudication* (Oxford: Hart Publishing, 2009) at 239–244.

4 K Bell, *Research Study on Supplementary Benefit Appeal Tribunals – Review of Main Findings: Conclusions and Recommendations* (1975) at 18; Leggatt, *supra* note 1 at paras 7.4–7.5.

tribunal judges who are accompanied by non-legal members. Tribunals are separate statutory adjudicative bodies and are viewed as part of the judicial rather than administrative arm of the state. They specialise in deciding appeals across a wide-ranging of administrative decision-making, from high volume jurisdictions such as social security, immigration, and employment to lower volume jurisdictions such as education, mental health, and criminal injuries compensation. The Tribunals Service consists of 36 separate jurisdictions, yet over 90 per cent of the caseload is concentrated in just three jurisdiction: social security, employment, and immigration.[5] In 2009–10, tribunals received 793,900 appeals; in 2010–11, there will be over 1 million appeals.[6]

Individual tribunal jurisdictions have been in existence for decades and have developed on an ad hoc and unsystematic basis as isolated adjudication systems without any sense that they comprised an overall tribunal *system*.[7] Each tribunal adopted its own procedure without any joined-up approach. However, with the landmark Tribunals, Courts and Enforcement Act (TCEA) 2007, most of the major tribunals have been brought together into a single structure: the two-tier system of the First-tier and Upper Tribunals, each of which are comprised of distinct chambers. The First-tier Tribunal is currently organised into 7 chambers: War Pensions and Armed Forces Chamber; Social Entitlement Chamber; Health, Education and Social Care Chamber; General Regulatory Chamber; Tax Chamber; Immigration and Asylum Chamber; Land, Property and Housing Chamber. The Upper Tribunal has 4 chambers: Administrative Appeal Chamber; Tax and Chancery Chamber; Immigration and Asylum Chamber; and the Lands Chamber.

The First-tier Tribunal hears initial fact-based appeals while the Upper Tribunal determines onward challenges on error of law grounds. If the Upper Tribunal finds that there is an error of law, then it can either correct that error and determine the appeal itself, or it can send the appeal back for rehearing by the First-tier Tribunal.[8] The system of onward challenges used to be incoherent with onward challenges either by way of judicial review or to a specialist second-tier tribunal and then judicial review. The intention behind the TCEA 2007 has been to create a new, simplified statutory framework for tribunals which provides coherence and will enable future reform. Two particular features are worth highlighting. First, the

---

5 Tribunals Service, *Annual Statistics for the Tribunals Service 2009–10* (2010) at 4, online: http://www.tribunals.gov.uk/Tribunals/Documents/Publications/TS_AnnualStatisticsReport0910.pdf. Most tribunals deal with "individual and state" disputes. Employment Tribunals, which decide with "party and party" disputes and are not *administrative* tribunals, are not discussed here.

6 For an overview of the UK tribunal system, see M Elliott & R Thomas, *Public Law* (Oxford: Oxford University Press, 2011), ch 17.

7 RE Wraith & PG Hutchesson, *Administrative Tribunals* (London: Allen & Unwin, 1974).

8 *Tribunals, Courts and Enforcement Act 2007* (UK), c 15, s 11.

Upper Tribunal is a superior court of record, that is, it has a status akin to that of the higher courts and it has a role in providing leadership for the various chambers of the First-tier Tribunal.[9] Second, the Upper Tribunal is increasingly taking over the routine judicial review work of the higher courts.[10] The TCEA 2007 has also meant a wide-ranging unification of the tribunals system across multiple areas of work: a statutory guarantee of the independence of the tribunal judiciary; bringing tribunals more clearly within the judicial rather than the administrative system; a Tribunal Procedure Committee to write tribunal procedure rules; greater administrative coherence; and cross-ticketing of judges between different tribunal jurisdictions.

Tribunal Procedures

Where do UK tribunals sit on the adversarial–inquisitorial spectrum? It is widely acknowledged that the complexity and fragmentation of the administrative justice "landscape" (including the plurality of approaches: adversarial versus inquisitorial or investigative; legally qualified judges or lay people; legal representation or self-representation, with or without advice and guidance) precludes easy generalisation. The nature of tribunals, the issues they deal with, and their caseloads vary enormously. Some tribunals (for instance, social security and criminal injuries compensation) adopt a relatively active approach.[11] Other tribunals (immigration and employment tribunals) tend to be more adversarial and court-like in nature. By contrast, other tribunals, such as special educational needs and mental health, have been described as hybrid or quasi-inquisitorial.

Despite the difficulties of generalising, the following points can be made. First, tribunals have long been viewed as less adversarial than formal court litigation. Part of the rationale for tribunals is that they can determine cases in a less formal way than the courts. Nonetheless, tribunals have developed against the backdrop of a court-focused adversarial process. No tribunal in the UK adopts a completely inquisitorial approach. They may often adopt a user-friendly approach, but tribunals are unable to step outside of their judicial role by assisting a party to prepare his case or to gather evidence. By contrast, other institutions, in particular, ombudsmen and the Independent Review Service which reviews social fund decisions, do not have oral hearings but do have a specific mandate to investigate cases themselves. No tribunal operates in this way. The basic obligation to prepare and present a case rests with the parties concerned. Tribunals have been established by their parent government department, but government has seldom paid much attention to the issue of procedure. Instead, the matter has normally been left to

9 *Tribunals, Courts and Enforcement Act*, *supra* note 8, s 3(5).

10 *Ibid*, ss 15–21. See in particular *R. (Cart) v Upper Tribunal* [2011] UKSC 28.

11 Criminal Injuries Compensation Appeal Panel, *Annual Report and Accounts* (2005–06 HC 1428) at 14, online: http://www.official-documents.gov.uk.

the tribunals themselves to determine. The relevant legislation is almost always silent on the issue, though specific provisions often give an indirect steer.[12] In the absence of a direct mandate to adopt an inquisitorial approach, tribunals have habitually assumed that they should proceed more or less like courts by adopting an adversarial approach, though without some of the more trappings of formal court litigation.

The type of procedure a tribunal uses is the result of a wide range of factors. For instance, Mental Health Review Tribunals are "to a significant extent inquisitorial" in large part because the medical member must undertake a medical examination of the patient to form an opinion of the patient's mental condition.[13] Other tribunals have been occasionally prodded by the courts to be more active. For instance, the courts have noted that the Special Educational Needs Tribunal "cannot proceed on a purely adversarial basis, but has a duty to act inquisitorially when the occasion arises by making sure it has the necessary basic information on which to decide the appeal before them, rather than rely entirely on evidence adduced by the parties. The tribunal will usually have much greater relevant expertise than the parents who appear before them".[14]

Other factors which influence tribunal procedures include: the particular adjudicative context and culture that a tribunal has developed; the emphasis placed upon the burden of proof; the inapplicability of the normal rules of evidence; guidance from the courts and the second-tier tribunal; the preferences of individual judges; operational factors, such as time targets for clearing cases; and whether the parties are represented and, if so, then how effectively.

The presence of all of these factors can make it difficult to identify any general trends. Nonetheless, it is possible to discern a wider change over recent years away from a traditional adversarial approach. Often seen as court-substitutes, tribunals have adopted the default position of the adversarial process.[15] However, with the TCEA 2007, there is a general acceptance that the model of tribunals has shifted, and with it the appropriate procedure. The 2007 Act does not impose any particular procedural model on tribunals. Nonetheless, there is an implicit assumption that court procedures are not necessarily applicable. For instance, the Act explicitly

12 There is no statute which explicitly enables a tribunal to adopt an adversarial or inquisitorial approach. The nearest – and a rare – instance is the Employment Tribunals (Constitution and Rules of Procedure) Regulations, SI 2001/1171, Schedule 1, para 11: "The tribunal shall make such enquiries of persons appearing before it and witnesses as it considers appropriate and shall otherwise conduct the hearing in such manner as it considers most appropriate for the clarification of the issues before it and generally to the just handling of the proceedings."

13 *R. (Ashworth Hospital Authority) v Mental Health Review Tribunal for West Midlands* [2001] EWHC Admin 901 at para 16; The Tribunal Procedure (First-tier Tribunal) (Health, Education and Social Care Chamber) Rules, SI 2008/2699, r 34.

14 *W v Gloucestershire County Council* [2001] EWHC Admin 901 at para 15.

15 Gabriele Ganz, *Administrative Procedures* (London: Sweet & Maxwell, 1974) at 29–35.

emphasises the accessibility and expertise of tribunals (as opposed to courts) and the development of innovative dispute resolution methods.[16]

The traditional model of tribunals rested upon the following basis that they were essentially court-substitutes and part of the machinery for adjudication rather than administration. As tribunals operated under the shadow of the courts, the assumption was that they were adversarial rather than inquisitorial.[17] By contrast, the new model of tribunals, which has emerged over recent years, views tribunals as the adjudicative segment of a broader administrative process for implementing policy, the purpose of which is to achieve right decisions efficiently. A key feature is that tribunals possess special expertise and can, if need be, adopt an active approach to ensure that all those issues which have a bearing on the outcome of an appeal are investigated irrespective of whether or not they have been raised by the parties.[18]This new model is reflected in the overriding objective of the tribunal procedure rules: the need to ensure that appeals are dealt with fairly and justly in a manner proportionate to their importance, complexity, anticipated costs and the resources of the parties.[19] Tribunals should avoid unnecessary formality and seek flexibility, enable the parties to participate, use any special expertise effectively, and avoid delay. The parties are obliged to co-operate with the Tribunal in this objective. While this broader trend does not explicitly address the issue of whether adversarial or inquisitorial approaches are appropriate, the wider themes are that tribunals should be flexible and not tied down by an adversarial procedure but adopt an active approach if this is justified by the overriding objective. In short, the reform of tribunals has provided a new context for considering and analysing issues of tribunal procedure.

Pressures For and Against Active Adjudication

One reason why the appropriate mode of tribunal procedure seems so unclear is largely because of the multiplicity of pressures motivating and restraining tribunal procedure and the complex and disparate situations in which the issues arise. The debate is also linked to wider issues such as the role of tribunals within the broader administrative process, the use of oral hearings and the role, and especially the funding of representation for tribunal appellants.

One of the principal forces for a more active approach arises from the position and function of tribunals as judicial institutions taking administrative decisions

---

16 See *Tribunals, Courts and Enforcement Act*, *supra* note 8, s 2(3).

17 This model is closely associated with the *Franks Report of the Committee on Administrative Tribunals and Enquiries* (Cmnd 218, 1957).

18 This model is associated with a variety of recent developments summarised and developed in R Carnwath, "Tribunal Justice – A New Start" (2009) Public Law 48.

19 *Tribunals, Courts and Enforcement Act*, *supra* note 8, s 22(4); Tribunal Procedure (First-tier Tribunal) (Social Entitlement Chamber) Rules, SI 2008/2685, r 2.

that implement public policy. Given the fundamental difference between ordinary civil proceedings and administrative adjudication because of the wider public interest at stake over and above the interests of the competing parties in achieving correct decisions, tribunals form part of a wider administrative process for implementing policy.[20] If tribunals are to take decisions that best implement policy goals, then they should rely upon the best available information rather than just the evidence presented by the parties, which requires an active style of adjudication.

An active approach often arises naturally from the issues upon which tribunals adjudicate. In some contexts, there can be a complex interrelationship between the nature of the decision exercise to be taken, the tribunal's expertise, and the (partial) inapplicability of "adversarial" concepts, such as the burden of proof.[21] Tribunals are often concerned not so much with finding facts which are capable of exact demonstration, but with assessing future risk and/or engaging in a process of judgment or evaluation. For instance, different tribunals have to decide various matters such as whether it would be unduly harsh for an asylum applicant at risk of persecution in one part of a country to relocate internally to another part of the same country where he would not be at risk, or whether the illness of a mental health patient is of a nature and degree that it justifies detention, or whether agreements between businesses distort competition contrary to competition law.[22] Determining such issues properly is perhaps not best characterised as ascertaining whether the facts have been proved to the requisite standard of proof. Instead, it can involve an holistic approach to adjudication in which an expert tribunal engages in varying degrees of active investigation to ensure that the best decision is made because there is an important underlying public interest at stake. A related point, but one not yet fully developed in the UK, is that the lessons tribunals draw from an active approach can be utilised by agencies to improve initial decision-making.

On the other hand, there is the still the strong influence of the court-based model, especially in relation to procedure. Oral hearings seem closely connected with representation and an adversarial process. However, recent government policy on tribunals has been to reduce the need for hearings before tribunals through better decisions and innovative proportionate dispute resolution (PDR)

---

20 Robert Thomas, *Administrative Justice and Asylum Appeals: A Study of Tribunal Adjudication* (Oxford: Hart, 2011) at 5–11 [Thomas].

21 The applicability of the burden of proof in such proceedings is problematic and contested. I say "partial" because a modified burden of proof – the burden of persuasion – remains relevant in much adjudication.

22 See *Karanakaran v Secretary of State for the Home Department* [2000] 3 All ER 449 (asylum); *JJB Sports PLC v Office of Fair Trading* [2004] CAT 17 (competition law); *R (DB) v Mental Health Review Tribunal* [2005] EWHC Admin 587 (mental health).

methods.[23] This in turn will reduce the need and cost of representation. As it is, tribunals have increased the number of paper-only appeals, but still remain tied to oral hearings as the norm.

Perhaps the most high-profile issue is the funding of representation. Indeed, it is no exaggeration to say that the debate over tribunal procedure is usually subsumed within the debate over legal aid funding. Representation is intrinsically connected to diametrically opposed factors: effective access to justice and its cost (and the government's wish to reduce it). The functions of representatives are to assist the tribunal and to advise and represent claimants. In this way, representation bridges the gap between the tribunal and the lay claimant in which the claimant knows the facts, but not the law, while the tribunal knows the law, but not the facts. If a claimant is unrepresented, then the tribunal should bridge the gap between itself and the claimant by adopting an enabling approach. However, tribunals mostly operate in those areas of social law in which the individuals concerned may not be able to afford to pay a representative. Hence the need for publicly funded representation. The general position until 2011 was that while legal aid was unavailable before tribunals, it was available for advice and assistance in some areas (for example, social security) and representation was funded in other areas (mental health and immigration).

The orthodox view has been that representation significantly enhances appellants' successful outcomes.[24] As tribunals have not been that adept at adopting an adequate enabling approach and the risk is that an unrepresented appellant will be disadvantaged, it has often argued that the resources must be found to provide publicly funded representation before all tribunals. But for reasons of cost, the government has always been reluctant to expand legal aid and is currently trying to restrict it. However, recent empirical research suggests that the orthodox view requires revision. Tribunals have become better at handling unrepresented appeals by assisting appellants. An unrepresented appellant who receives good advice before a tribunal hearing is just as likely to achieve a favourable outcome as a represented appellant.[25] Represented parties do not always do better than unrepresented parties, especially if they have received pre-hearing advice. Of course, represented appellants clearly benefit from representation in a variety of ways – providing technical or legal knowledge, giving moral support, speaking for the appellant and providing general support). Nonetheless, the evidence indicates

---

23 Department for Constitutional Affairs, *Transforming Public Services: Complaints, Redress and Tribunals* (Cm 6243, 2004) at para 10.11 [Department for Constitutional Affairs].

24 H Genn & Y Genn, *The Effects of Representation in Tribunals* (London: Lord Chancellor's Department, 1989).

25 M Adler, "Can Tribunals Deliver Justice in the Absence of Representation?" (ESRC Paper, 2007). See also M Adler, "Tribunal Reform: Proportionate Dispute Resolution and the Pursuit of Administrative Justice" (2006) 69 Modern Law Review 958 at 980–2.

that the success rates of unrepresented appellants can be attributed to the active and enabling approach adopted by tribunals.[26]

The overall picture may then be a more nuanced than it was previously thought to be, but it is not a perfect one. The extent to which a tribunal is able to provide an effective enabling approach will depend upon the individual judge and his or her experience in being able to draw out the evidence effectively. Research into asylum appeal hearings found that unrepresented appellants tended to experience lower rates of success than represented appellants and that there were significant differences of approach between different judges. Some judges provided the unrepresented appellants with assistance; others did not.[27]

However, policy developments have been moving quickly and the UK's current Conservative–Liberal Democrat coalition government elected in May 2010 is intent on severely reducing publicly funded assistance and representation as part of its fiscal deficit reduction plan. The government's plan is to remove legal aid entitlement completely from certain areas of law. Funding for advice for social security, advice and representation for immigration and other appeals (for example, education) would be removed altogether; only legal aid for asylum, immigration detention, and mental health cases would be retained.[28]

While normally indifferent to tribunal procedure, the government's invocation of the inquisitorial nature of tribunals has often gone together with the view that tribunals are able to handle unrepresented appeals adequately (and therefore government need not fund representation).[29] From the government's perspective, the adversarial tradition is seen as a major contributory factor to high legal aid costs.[30] Accessible, active, and user-friendly tribunals enable appellants to their cases without assistance.[31] However, the proposals have been criticised as highly problematic. As a Parliamentary Committee has noted, the proposals require considerable further refinement, assume a major change in the way the

26 See Adler, *supra* note 25.

27 Thomas, *supra* note 20 at 116–7, 125–8.

28 Ministry of Justice, *Proposals for the Reform of Legal Aid in England and Wales* (Cm 7967, 2010) [Ministry of Justice]. From the government's perspective, the UK's legal aid system is one of the world's most expensive – currently over £2 billion per annum – and it intends to restrict legal aid as part of the Ministry of Justice's commitment to reducing the deficit. Most of this is criminal and civil legal aid rather than legal aid for tribunals. In 2009–10, legal aid costs in relation to social security appeals were £28.3 million; immigration appeals £88.8 million; and education appeals £3 million. The government wants to cut the legal aid budget by £350 million a year.

29 Leggatt, *supra* note 1 at para 4.21; Department of Constitutional Affairs, *supra* note 23 at para 10.11.

30 R Bowles & A Perry, *International Comparison of Publicly Funded Legal Services and Justice Systems* (Ministry of Justice Research Series 14/09, 2009) at 36.

31 Ministry of Justice, *supra* note 28. The government's other two arguments are that the issues involved are of lower importance than fundamental ones concerning safety and that help and advice are available from a number of other sources.

accessibility of the justice system has come to be viewed, and many concerned (including tribunals) are quite unprepared.[32] Nonetheless, the government is intent upon implementing its proposals.[33]

Despite the clear progress tribunals have made, it remains to be seen how they will cope with the near-wholesale withdrawal of legal aid. Tribunals need to do more to be more user-friendly and less legalistic. Judicial concerns have focused upon the limits of active tribunal procedure and the role of advisors and welfare organisations in explaining decisions and assisting claimants with hearings. Withdrawing assistance may mean good cases do not come before tribunals; conversely, those with hopeless cases may appeal and end up wasting both their own and the tribunal's time. The lack of pre-hearing assistance and preparation may also increase the length of hearings.[34]

Restricting legal aid is not the whole story though. Another issue, addressed below, is government representation. While government departments can be represented by a presenting officer, such officers rarely attend appeal hearings because of staff shortages. The absence of a government representative to defend the initial decision and cross-examine clearly changes the dynamics of the appeal hearing.

Another pressure for an active approach arises from the need for an efficient adjudication process. The risk is that an adversarial process increases delay and costs. By contrast, by adopting an active approach, the tribunal can focus the hearing on the issues that matter. Given the increasingly managerial contexts in which many tribunals operate, this has assumed some importance. Many tribunals operate within key performance indicator targets, typically to ensure that they determine a certain percentage of their caseload within a stated period of time.[35] Tribunals also have case-management powers and are expected to manage cases as efficiently as possible. It may be that, over time, the greater pressure for an active approach comes from this rather than other sources.

Opposing the pressures for an active approach are various counter-doctrines. First of all is the potential threat to judicial neutrality. To maintain the perception of impartiality, tribunals should not descend into the arena between the parties. This counter-doctrine is sometimes seen as over-blown. Nonetheless, it is not altogether invalid. UK tribunals place great store not just by their constitutionally independent position, but also by the perception of their neutrality in the context of day to day hearings. Some tribunals may be cautious about intervening for

32 House of Commons Justice Committee, *Government's Proposed Reform of Legal Aid* (2010–11 HC 681).

33 Legal Aid, Sentencing and Punishment of Offenders Bill 2011.

34 Senior President of Tribunals, *Senior President of Tribunals' Annual Report* (February 2011) at 9, online: http://www.judiciary.gov.uk/publications-and-reports/reports/Tribunals/spt-annual-report-2011 [Senior President of Tribunals].

35 See Tribunals Service, *Annual Report* (2009–10 HC239), appendix C, online: http://www.official-documents.gov.uk/document/hc1011/hc02/0239/0239.pdf.

fear of criticism that they are biased. An active approach may be justified by the power-disparities, but there is also the need for fairness to the relevant government department. Furthermore, there can sometimes be a conflict of goals. For instance, tribunals often experience difficulty in seeking to investigate a case thoroughly and to ensure that the best aspects of an individual's case are brought out as fully as possible, while at the same time seeking to raise those points which might be unfavourable to an individual's case because, for instance, the relevant government department is either poorly represented or not represented at all. Trying to tread this delicate line while also remaining independent and impartial poses a real challenge for even the most experienced tribunal judges. By contrast, a traditional adversarial approach is safer, more conservative, and less likely to result in claims that the tribunal has acted unfairly.

Other counter-doctrines include the concern that too active an approach risks placing excessive trust in the tribunal and that it can lead to prejudgment of the issues. A general view is that a tribunal aided by representation on both sides is more likely to arrive at better decisions than a tribunal acting alone. There is also the influence of adversarial bias: the adversary process is habitually seen as the "gold standard" process for producing and testing evidence.

Practical obstacles to an active approach can arise if tribunals lack adequate powers and resources with which to case-manage appeals proactively from start to finish or with which to collect their own reports or evidence. While judges can ask their own questions at hearings and help unrepresented appellants, tribunals cannot normally build and develop a case from its start by taking overall responsibility for investigating the issues. Any procedure that emerges is then likely to be seen as a compromise position in which much of the responsibility rests with the parties, but which also enables the tribunal to undertake important though limited investigation.

There is also the issue of judicial competence and training. To ask carefully phrased and neutral questions into sensitive matters which may sometimes appear detrimental to an individual's case requires training, skill, and experience. Many tribunal judges are part-time and not necessarily equally competent to do this. Finally, there is the risk that a more active approach might relieve the parties of their responsibilities of presenting and scrutinising the evidence and somehow shift the applicable burden of proof from the appellant to the tribunal.

To summarise: tribunals have developed a more inquisitorial approach, but they have not totally rejected the adversarial approach; rather, they have applied an inquisitorial gloss to a basically adversarial process.[36] This suggests that the adversarial–inquisitorial dichotomy is no longer an insightful way to understand the role of tribunals. The practice of tribunals will often seem inadequate in some way because it can rarely be described as fully adversarial or inquisitorial. Instead, a new model – active, investigative, or intrusive adjudication – is required, one

36 T Mullen, "A Holistic Approach to Administrative Justice?" in M Adler, ed, *Administrative Justice in Context* (Oxford: Hart 2010) at 391 [Mullen].

which recognises the need for tribunals to adopt varying degrees of intervention and activism depending upon a wide variety of different factors which will fluctuate from one case to the next. It is therefore to the practice in individual tribunal systems to which we now turn.

Social Security Adjudication

Like other welfare states, the UK spends a considerable proportion of total government spending on social security and benefit programmes. There are annually 5.9 million benefit claimants. Social security is a highly complex, intricate, and fast-changing area of law. Claims for benefits are made initially to one of the various decision-making agencies of the Department for Work and Pensions. If refused, then a claimant may appeal. Social security adjudication has a low appeal rate (less than 2 per cent of claimants who could appeal do so), but is the largest appeal system. In 2008–09, the tribunal decided 245,500 appeals. In 2009–10, it received 339,000 appeals and is forecast to receive 436,000 appeals by 2011–12.[37] In 2007–08, the tribunal overturned the department's decision in 47 per cent of appeals.[38]

Social security tribunals are strongly predisposed toward active adjudication. The department and the claimant are not supposed to be locked into adversarial combat, but engaged in a co-operative process of investigation in which both parties play their part. The adjudication process is viewed as part of a wider decision-making process which is designed to ensure that claimants receive neither more nor less than the amount of social security benefit to which they are properly entitled (as opposed to the benefits to which the parties may be contending that they are entitled). Tribunals' investigatory function is to decide cases correctly; they are not limited to the issues raised by the parties. As the Supreme Court has put it, the adjudication process is "inquisitorial rather than adversarial".[39]

The active or investigatory nature of the adjudication process arises in large part because of the legitimate public interest in ensuring that policy is being implemented; the tribunals form part of the statutory machinery for investigating claims.[40] But there are other factors.[41] Social security law is highly complex.

37 Senior President of Tribunals, *supra* note 34 at 39.

38 President of Appeal Tribunals, *Report by the President of Appeal Tribunals on the Standards of Decision-making by the Secretary of State 2007–08* (Tribunal Service, 2008) at 12 [Report by the President of Appeals Tribunals 2007–08].

39 *Kerr v Department for Social Development* [2004] 1 WLR 1372 at paras 61–62 (Lady Hale); *R v Medical Appeal Tribunal (North Midland Region), ex parte Hubble* [1958] 2 QB 338, 240.

40 *R v Deputy Industrial Injuries Commissioner, ex parte Moore* [1965] 1 QB 456, 486.

41 R (IS) 11/99 [1998] UKSSCSC CIB 4189 1997 (01 October 1998) [31].

It is extremely unlikely that a claimant will be able to navigate the regulations and decision-making process unaided. Many claimants may be poorly educated. Given this, tribunals are under a duty to consider and determine relevant questions irrespective of whether they have been expressly raised by a claimant.[42]

There is also the distinctive role of the appeals stage within the wider decision-making process. Indeed, the tribunal's active approach can partly be understood as a response to changes in initial decision-making. Initial claims are paper- and form-based; the claimant will not meet the decision-maker until the appeal hearing. The hearing then provides the sole opportunity for establishing the facts of the case by enabling the decision-maker to engage directly with the claimant. Many appeals are allowed because the tribunal elicits additional information from the claimant through face-to-face engagement at the hearing.[43]

As regards representation, claimants may qualify for publicly funded advice and assistance before hearings, but not for representation at them. The degree of representation varies – 72 per cent of appellants are currently unrepresented – its provision depends upon local government, *pro bono* funding, and welfare organisations.

In such circumstances, social security tribunals have long adopted an enabling approach.[44] Likewise, the courts have emphasised that tribunals need to have particular regard to the presence of representation. Nonetheless, representation should not relieve a tribunal of adopting an active approach; a poorly represented claimant should not be placed at any greater disadvantage than an unrepresented party.[45] According to the Tribunal President, an active role by a tribunal may reduce the "added value" of having representation; nonetheless, representation remains of immense benefit to claimants.[46]

While the Department is entitled to be represented at hearings, the actual levels of attendance by departmental presenting officers has declined substantially. In 2000–01, the Department was represented at some 40 per cent of hearings. Since then, levels of government representation have dropped to 16 per cent.[47] The explanation is simply that it is too expensive for the department to be represented in every case, so it focuses upon its resources upon the most important cases. Without

---

42 Decision of the Social Security Commissioners (now the Upper Tribunal (Administrative Appeals Chamber), Decision CIB/4751/2002, CDLA/4753/2002, CDLA/4939/2002, and CDLA/5141/2002 (21 January 2004) at para 32; *Mongan v Department for Social Development* [2004] NICA 16 [14]–[17]; *Hooper v Secretary of State for Work and Pensions* [2007] EWCA Civ 495.

43 Report by the President of Appeals Tribunals 2007–08, *supra* note 38 at 6.

44 See House of Commons Social Services Committee, *Social Security: Changes Implemented in April 1988* (1988–89 HC 437-ii) at paras 26–37.

45 *Mongan v Department for Social Development* [2004] NICA 16 at 18.

46 House of Commons Work and Pensions Committee, *Decision-making and Appeals in the Benefits System* (2009–10 HC 313), Ev 118 (evidence of Judge Robert Martin, President of the First-tier Tribunal (Social Entitlement Chamber)).

47 *Ibid* at para 164.

government representation, the tribunal will explain the department's decision to the appellant, prompting concerns of undermining tribunal neutrality. The absence of a presenting officer should not necessarily be problematic. However, what the tribunals' unease illustrates is that they have not fully changed their mind-set.

There are limits to the degree of active adjudication by social security tribunals. Claimants must opt in for an oral hearing; those who do not have their appeals determined on the papers, which limits an active approach.[48] While the tribunals investigate at the hearing, the responsibility for gathering evidence, such as medical reports, rests with the claimant. Tribunals cannot assist a claimant in the way an advisor might by advising a claimant to appeal, or collecting evidence in the preparation of an appeal. Consequently, the Tribunal has criticised proposed legal aid restrictions, but their concerns have been largely ignored by the government.[49] When claimants are represented, tribunals are not obliged to adopt an active approach.[50] Furthermore, it is important to appreciate that an active approach is not limited to assisting the claimant; it can equally extend to investigating those issues which may ultimately be detrimental to the outcome of an individual's appeal. For instance, tribunals may, but are not obliged to, investigate when there are positive aspects of an initial decision not in issue before the tribunal, but which were possibly invalid (that is, the tribunal might make a less favourable decision than the one under appeal) so long as it acts fairly and is not seen as both prosecutor and judge.[51] Finally, the substantial increases in caseload combined with an increasingly managerial approach risk undermining an active approach; the risk is that the pressure to process appeals quickly will undermine efforts to investigate.

Immigration and Asylum Adjudication

By contrast with social security adjudication, the immigration appeals system starts from the premise that the process is and ought to be primarily adversarial. The burden of proof is on the appellant; it is for the parties to present the evidence that they wish to rely upon and to advance whatever contradictions they wish;

48 N Wikeley, "Burying Bell: Managing the Judicialisation of Social Security Tribunals" (2000) 63 Modern Law Review 475 at 496.

49 *Proposals for the Reform of Legal Aid in England and Wales: Response by President of the Social Entitlement Chamber* (February 2011), online: http://www.judiciary.gov.uk/media/media-releases/2011/responses-proposals-for-the-reform-of-legal-aid.

50 [2000] UKSSCSC CSDLA_336_2000 (27 December 2000).

51 [2008] UKSSCSC CDLA 884/2008 (7 July 2008); *AP-H v Secretary of State for Work and Pensions* (DLA) [2010] UKUT 183 (AAC). For instance, a welfare claimant may have received a decision that he is entitled to a certain level of benefit because of disability needs and may challenge the decision on the basis that the benefits awarded are too low. However, the tribunal may investigate the matter and hold that the claimant is not entitled to any benefit at all if it finds that the individual's disability is insufficiently serious.

and, to maintain its independence, the Tribunal should not descend into the arena. The Immigration Judge acts as an impartial assessor of the evidence presented rather than as an investigator who takes the lead in ascertaining the evidence. Nonetheless, there is an ongoing debate over the issue. The views of the higher courts on the matter have oscillated wildly.[52] Many Immigration Judges recognise that the adversarial process does not necessarily work well in practice and engage in varying degrees of active adjudication.

The immigration appeals process is the second largest tribunal after social security. Initial decisions are taken by the UK Border Agency. In 2009, the agency made some 2.45 million visa decisions in addition to 297,780 after-entry decisions and 24,285 initial asylum decisions. Some categories of refusal decisions can be appealed to the First-tier Tribunal (Immigration and Asylum Chamber) (FTTIAC), which in 2009 decided 198,505 appeals.[53] The caseload is diverse: asylum represents approximately 10.8 per cent of all receipts, managed migration 24.8 per cent, entry clearance appeals 24 per cent, and family visit appeals 39.7 per cent.[54]

It has been said that the degree to which the process can engage in active adjudication depends on which issues are being dealt with, moment to moment, in an appeal.[55] There are various factors which motivate and constrain an active approach in immigration appeals.

First, there is the particular prominence of human rights issues in immigration appeals, especially in refugee cases. The Tribunal has doubted whether the terms adversarial or inquisitorial accurately explain the nature of the asylum jurisdiction because of its distinctive features: the lower standard of proof (reasonable degree of likelihood); the shared duty of co-operation between the parties; the fact that the appellant will be possessed alone of almost all the relevant personal knowledge while the Home Office will be better placed to deal with general country conditions;

52 See *R v Special Adjudicator, ex parte Demeter* [2000] Imm AR 424 at 430 (Moses J noting that "the appeal should be, and is, adversarial. It is important that the special adjudicator should avoid, if possible, giving any appearance of entering into the arena by challenging the account that the applicant gives himself"); *Shirazi v Secretary of State for the Home Department* [2003] EWCA Civ 1562; [2004] 2 All ER 602 at 611 (Sedley LJ noting that the asylum jurisdiction is "as much inquisitorial as it is adversarial"); *HK v Secretary of State for the Home Department* [2006] EWCA Civ 1037 at para 27 (Neuberger LJ noting that "an Immigration Judge has an almost inquisitorial function, although he has none of the evidence-gathering or other investigatory powers of an inquisitorial Judge").

53 Home Office, *Control of Immigration: Statistics United Kingdom 2009* (Home Office Statistical Bulletin 15/10, 2010).

54 Senior President of Tribunals, *supra* note 34 at 50. Some appeals (for example, asylum and managed migration) are conducted in-country; in entry clearance appeals, the appellant will not attend their appeal hearing because the appeal is being pursued from overseas, but his or her sponsor may attend.

55 Interview with the Vice-President of the Upper Tribunal (Immigration and Asylum Chamber).

and the overriding duty that cases receive anxious scrutiny.[56] Given the error costs, decisions should be made on the best available material.

Again, the role and presence of representation is crucial. Given concerns over the variable quality of immigration representatives, only regulated persons can act as an immigration representative. Legal aid is available for both advice and representation, but is shrinking and likely to be withdrawn altogether except for asylum and detained cases. The difficulties may be especially acute in the immigration context given the importance of the issues at stake, the complexity of the extensive rules and case-law, and the fact that the tribunal system is principally viewed and operated as an adversarial process. Judges are expected to adopt an enabling approach in unrepresented appeals.

On the other side, non-attendance by the agency at appeal hearings has been a persistent problem. In 2009–10, 30 per cent of appeals proceeded without the Home Office.[57] The lack of a government representative to cross-examine appellants raises obvious difficulties for judges when testing an appellant's account is essentially to fact-finding, but who want to remain neutral.[58] Critical of the absence of presenting officers, the Tribunal has issued guidance so that judges can ask questions for clarification purposes while remaining neutral.

However, the difficulty of treading the fine line between acceptable questioning of an appellant to clarify certain issues and unfair and acceptable cross-examination combined with opportunistic claims of judicial misconduct has prompted many challenges against "biased" judges, with different responses from the Tribunal and the courts.[59] The Tribunal's view has been that the public interest requires that matters are properly investigated; it would be wrong for an asylum appellant either to succeed or fail because of no or inadequate representation of the Home Office.[60] As the purpose is to ascertain the true position, the proceedings

56 United Nations High Commissioner for Refugees (UNHCR), *Handbook on Determining Refugee Status* (Geneva, UNHCR, 1992) at 196; *Gimedhin v Secretary of State for the Home Department* (1464), date notified 23 August 1996; *RK v Secretary of State for the Home Department (Obligation to investigate) Democratic Republic of Congo*, [2004] UKIAT00129 at para 46.

57 UK, HC, *Parliamentary Debates*, vol 511, col 551W (17 June 2010). This prompted headlines such as "Home Office Surrenders to Migrants", *The Sunday Times* (25 April 2010).

58 As one Immigration Judge has explained, "theoretically, we are conducting an adversarial hearing. It is bad enough when the appellant is unrepresented. It becomes even worse when there is no presenting officer as well."

59 This jurisdiction is well-known for producing such a plethora of cases which can be used to support any proposition or view.

60 *LK v Secretary of State for the Home Department (Adjudicators: "anxious scrutiny" – public interest) Democratic Republic of Congo* [2004] UKIAT 00308; *M (Chad) v Secretary of State for the Home Department* [2004] UKIAT 00044.

are not purely adversarial.[61] By contrast, the courts have emphasised that extensive questioning would undermine the tribunal's neutrality and the adversarial nature of the process.[62]

The degree of activism is also affected by wider issues of tribunal procedure. Consider, for instance, the pressure on the tribunal to determine appeals quickly. The adoption of active adjudication often presupposes a hearing in the first place, but this will often not be the case. Paper-only appeals illustrate the tensions between justice and managerial pressures: they impose lower transaction costs and enable quicker processing, but afford little opportunity for an active approach and leave appellants with lower success rates.[63]

Other factors might militate against an active approach at appeal hearings. Judges normally only have access to the appeal file on the day of the hearing and there is little opportunity to undertake pre-hearing research. In asylum cases, Immigration Judges may often have a difficult task in dealing with all of the factual issues raised in an appeal. Evidence in chief is usually given by a written statement and representatives are relied upon to draw the judge's attention to those points specifically relied on to justify asylum. Judges are discouraged from undertaking post-hearing research.[64] As appeals can only be determined on the basis of evidence disclosed to both parties, any such research would require the hearing to be re-convened, which risks delay. Furthermore, the Tribunal has no ability to commission expert evidence; this rests with the appellant.

Statutory rules as to which facts can be taken into account – either expanding or limiting the evidence that the tribunal can consider – also give an indirect steer in terms how active the tribunal can be. For instance, in asylum cases, the fundamental issue is a forward-looking one – assessing future risk of persecution or torture. The tribunal can take account of new evidence,[65] and this forward-looking approach is more amenable to active investigation, especially given the issues at stake in refugee and human rights appeals.

61 *SH v Secretary of State for the Home Department (Subsequent decision: how far relevant?) Turkey* [2005] UKIAT 00068 at 20: "it is a strange reflection on the ways of thinking that have been allowed to grow up around a judicial system that it should be possible for counsel seriously to criticise an adjudicator for trying to get at the truth."

62 *JK (Democratic Republic of Congo) v Secretary of State for the Home Department* [2007] EWCA Civ 831.

63 Robert Thomas, "Immigration Appeals for Family Visitors Refused Entry Clearance" (2004) Public Law 612; H Genn & G Richardson, "Tribunals in Transition: Resolution or Adjudication?" (2007) Public Law 116.

64 *EG v Entry Clearance Officer, Lagos (post-hearing internet research) Nigeria* [2008] UKAIT000015. For instance, in asylum cases a common issue is whether or not the conditions in the claimant's country of origin are such that he may be at risk on return. A judge who feels that the country information presented at the hearing is inadequate may be tempted to undertake research after the hearing.

65 *Nationality, Immigration and Asylum Act 2002*, (UK), c 41, s 85(4) [*Nationality, Immigration and Asylum Act*].

By contrast, in ordinary immigration appeals, the tribunal can only consider those facts in existence at the date of the initial decision.[66] The appeal process is viewed as a means of appealing against the assessment of evidence rather than an extension of the original administrative decision-making process with new facts being introduced along the way.[67] Even here, though, there is some leeway as the tribunal can consider evidence that was in existence but not submitted to the initial decision-maker. However, concerns have been expressed at the high number of appeals that succeed because of new evidence and the associated costs; allowing new evidence to be submitted on appeal encourages inadequate applications and leads to unnecessary and expensive appeals: applicants should make a new application rather than use the appeal process.[68] This in turn has prompted government either to prohibit the Tribunal from considering evidence not previously submitted or to consider abolishing some appeal rights altogether.[69]

Over recent years, the jurisdiction has made important steps toward an active approach. This has mainly taken the form of judges questioning appellants at hearings. However, the Tribunal has always avoided making any general statement of principle. As immigration is the most highly contested area of public law, there is clear concern within the Tribunal that hardening a discretionary active approach into a positive duty to investigate would raise acute problems. Given the difficult factual basis (for example, in asylum cases), such an obligation could in many cases never be fully discharged; it could always be open to the losing party to argue that he had lost not because he failed on the facts, but because the judge had failed to investigate fully. It could also result in perverse behavioural consequences: representatives might give up preparing appeals and off-load the work onto the Tribunal. In practice, the risk would be this would shift the burden of proof away from the appellant to the Tribunal.

Particular considerations arise in relation to the Upper Tribunal. In considering onward challenges, the second-tier tribunal is not necessarily limited to the arguments advanced by the claimant. If there is an obvious point of asylum law clearly apparent from the evidence but which has not been raised, then the tribunal should investigate.[70] Second, the Upper Tribunal has a special responsibility to

---

66 *Nationality, Immigration and Asylum Act, supra* note 65, s 85(5). For similar provisions in other tribunal systems, see, for example, the Education (Prohibition from Teaching or Working with Children) Regulations, SI 2003/1184, reg 13(2)(b); *Social Security Act 1998*, s 12(8)(b).

67 *R v Immigration Appeal Tribunal, ex parte Weerasuriya* [1983] 1 All ER 195.

68 House of Commons Home Affairs Committee, *Immigration Control* (2006–05 HC 775) at para 339.

69 *Nationality, Immigration and Asylum Act, supra* note 65, s 85A (Tribunal prevented from considering evidence not submitted at the time of making the original application); A Travis & O Bowcott, "Overseas relatives of British families to lose visit visa appeal rights", *The Guardian* (9 May 2011).

70 *R v Secretary of State for the Home Department, Ex parte Robinson* [1998] QB 929.

assist first-tier judges, primary decision-makers, and appellants, by giving general guidance through lead cases. In the asylum context, this takes the form of factual country guidance on the risks facing a generic category of asylum applicant, which is to be followed in subsequent individual appeals.[71] This enterprise requires an investigative approach to ensure all relevant evidence is considered.[72]

Third, country guidance can sometimes involve the Tribunal overriding the wishes of a party who does not wish to continue with an appeal. For instance, fearful that the Tribunal may issue country guidance beneficial to many asylum claimants, the Home Office has sometimes conceded the individual case thereby preventing the appeal from proceeding further.[73] A major problem for the Tribunal, the solution has been to require the Tribunal's consent thereby taking the conduct of litigation out of the litigants' hands. For the Upper Tribunal, the public interest in engaging in up to date assessments of risks in countries giving rise to commonly occurring situations (for example, whether there is a risk of indiscriminate violence arising from armed conflict in Iraq) and in using its expertise to assist Immigration Judges, primary decision-makers and many hundred other appellants can override the wishes of the parties.[74] Overall, despite its predisposition toward adversarial processes, the immigration and asylum tribunal system has made significant steps toward active adjudication.

Conclusion

This brief exploration and analysis suggests three main conclusions. One is that despite its significance, the question of tribunal procedure has rarely been consciously addressed by policy-makers. No tribunal in the UK has been deliberately established as an inquisitorial or adversarial tribunal. Tribunal procedure has not been imposed, but has developed incrementally and interstitially as a result of a wide range of factors. A second conclusion is that the language of "adversarial" and "inquisitorial" can safely be set aside: it does not capture the distinctive nature of variable active or intrusive administrative adjudication. Under this model, the role of tribunals fluctuates in accordance with the nature of the issues being considered, the presence and ability of the parties to contribute, the broader public interest in implementing policy goals, and other factors. UK tribunals are already a fair

71 See generally Thomas, *supra* note 20, ch 7.

72 As Laws LJ noted in *S & Others v Secretary of State for the Home Department* [2002] EWCA Civ 539; [2002] INLR 416 (CA) 436, 431 (Laws LJ), the enterprise assumes "something of an inquisitorial quality, although the adversarial structure of the appeal procedure of course remains".

73 *MA v Secretary of State for the Home Department (Operational Guidance, prison conditions, significance) Sudan* [2005] UKAIT00149 at paras 27–8.

74 *HM and Others v Secretary of State for the Home Department (Article 15(c)) Iraq CG* [2010] UKUT 331 (IAC).

way down this road of carving out for themselves a distinctive active role. Many commentators would like tribunals to proceed further.[75] However, what is lacking is a coherent articulation of a model of variable active or intrusive adjudication which applies across all tribunals. Given its role in providing judicial leadership to first-tier tribunals, this is clearly a task for the Upper Tribunal. Thirdly, looking to the future, tribunals are likely to face a number of challenges, not least possible reductions in publicly funded representation. Tribunal procedure has not attracted the sustained research it deserves. More study is required to discover how tribunals can best perform the role of active adjudication to deliver individual justice and to implement policy.

75 C Harlow & R Rawlings, *Law and Administration* (Cambridge: Cambridge University Press, 2009) at 526–7; Mullen, *supra* note 36 at 411.

Chapter 4
Administrative Justice and Innovation: Beyond the Adversarial/Inquisitorial Dichotomy

Samantha Green[1] and Lorne Sossin[2]

Introduction

The purpose of this chapter is to explore the various mechanisms and processes through which tribunals can assume a greater role in hearings than they have in the traditional adversarial process. As the chapters in this collection by Robin Creyke and Robert Thomas illustrate, the idea that tribunals should be understood in terms of their similarity to (or deviation from) a court hearing, in which the judge is a neutral and passive arbiter, is giving way to a new paradigm in the Commonwealth in which an accessible administrative hearing featuring active adjudicators is a norm, not the exception. At the same time, any administrative proceeding which is not adversarial is too often simply lumped together as "inquisitorial." An inquisitorial proceeding is generally one where the decision-maker engages in fact finding. We suggest most administrative proceedings may be located somewhere between the model of the courtroom and the model of the inquiry and that these hybrids and halfway houses merit more attention.

Traditionally, the academic literature on this topic has focused on the adversarial–inquisitorial dichotomy. While the distinctions made in this discourse are useful, and will be referenced in this chapter, our analysis focuses on the experiences of what we term "active adjudication" – a model which occupies a broad swath between the adversarial and inquisitorial norms. Active adjudication has no single, universally accepted definition. While a potentially expansive sphere, active adjudication as we employ the term includes the following aspects:

---

1 Portions of this research were completed while working as a summer student with Environment and Land Tribunals of Ontario (ELTO). I am grateful to Doug Ewart and Michael Gottheil, ELTO's then Executive Chair, for their input and guidance on this research.

2 I am also a member of the Health Professions Appeal and Review Board and the Health Services Appeal and Review Board. The views expressed in this study are my own and do not reflect the views of either Board or its members.

- obtaining early disclosure to the tribunal (including by suggesting, *without* directing, additional areas to be covered or witnesses who might be called);
- tribunal-led focusing of the issues for determination using the information supplied by the parties and its own expertise;
- tribunals facilitating the eliciting and testing of the parties' evidence at a hearing;
- tribunals adapting to the needs of the parties who come before it to ensure meaningful access, including accessible procedures, rules and practices in the conduct of hearings; and
- tribunals approaching the goal of the hearing as the exercise of statutory jurisdiction through fair and reasonable decisions – which includes but is not limited to submissions from parties who may (or may not be) opposed in interest.

We argue that the move to adopt active adjudication may enhance the efficiency, fairness and effectiveness for many administrative tribunals and that the benefits of this model are distinct both from adversarial and inquisitorial models of legal process.

This chapter examines what we have found to be an increasing preference for active adjudication in Canada. We do so by discussing recent Canadian jurisprudence on administrative law. We also expand our research to Commonwealth countries including the United Kingdom and Australia, to help elucidate the potential applications of active adjudication.

This chapter is divided into three sections which include the rationales and mechanisms for an active role for tribunals in adjudication, and its implications. The first section of this chapter will introduce the various examples of active adjudication, and the distinction between this model and adversarial and inquisitorial models. The second section examines the various mechanisms by which a more active hearing model may be achieved by a tribunal. Finally, the third section explores the implications of active tribunals, for the decision-makers, for the parties and for advocacy.

Rationales for An Active Tribunal Role in the Hearing Process

Adversarial, Non-Adversarial, and Active Adjudication

"Adversarial" and "non-adversarial" processes are frequently contrasted as competing procedural models in legal systems. However, most Commonwealth adjudicative tribunals will employ a mixture of these elements. This procedural mix makes it particularly difficult to place any given body, or even a specific proceeding, on one end of the spectrum or the other. That said, it is generally accurate to characterize a particular tribunal as closer to either the adversarial or non-adversarial end of the spectrum.

The Law Reform Commission of Australia attempted to define some of the attributes normally associated with adversarial and non-inquisitorial models in its 1998 review of federal tribunals and the adversarial system.

Adversarial processes may include the following general characteristics:[3]

- minimal intervention by the decision-maker, whose role is to ensure fairness of the proceedings, meaning that each party is able to present their case without oppression or undue interference by the other party;
- the absence of independent fact-finding undertaken by the decision-making body;
- party control of the proceedings, particularly in (i) defining the issues and (ii) deciding which factual material is considered by the decision-maker;
- an emphasis on "winning" the contested issues, with each party trying to secure a favourable outcome rather than a decision considered correct by reference to some external standard;
- an emphasis on a single determinative hearing with oral argument and case presentation.

Non-adversarial processes, by contrast, may include:[4]

- tribunal control over the proceedings, including any hearings, wherein tribunal members define issues and decide which factual material will be considered;
- tribunal engagement in independent fact-finding through requests for additional information from the parties or by calling witnesses on its own motion;
- statutory direction to arrive at the correct or preferable decision;
- less emphasis on a single determinative hearing with oral arguments and case presentation – submissions by the parties may more frequently be written rather than oral;
- absence of legal representation in the hearing;
- restrictions on witnesses to answer questions only from tribunal members, with parties having no right to cross-examine or address the tribunal.

There are at least two additional ways in which tribunal procedures are sometimes described as "non-adversarial." First, the term might be applied to proceedings "where the government party involved does not seek to put its view separately from the documentary material it provides to the tribunal and the tribunal is willing to rely to a greater extent on the government party's documents, research

---

3 Australasian Law Reform Commission, *Issue Paper 24: Review of the Adversarial System of Adjudication (Federal Tribunals and the Adversarial System* (Sydney: Australasian Law Reform Commission,1998) at para 2.13 [Australasian Law Reform Commission].

4 *Ibid* at para 2.15.

and written submissions."[5] Secondly, models of alternative/assisted dispute resolution (ADR) such as mediation, conciliation and arbitration are sometimes included in references to "non-adversarial" processes.[6] These two approaches to "non-adversarial" proceedings are not explored further in this chapter but merit attention in relation to the active adjudication model which is explored.

In Australia the enabling legislation for tribunals has begun to reflect the need for improved flexibility by providing for the tribunals to determine their own procedures.[7] Tribunals have begun to emerge as "hybrid hearing" models where "the process steps look more like the adversarial model, but with characteristics of an inquiry-based model such as the tribunal leading the questioning process."[8]

In addition to context-specific procedural fairness requirements recognized at common law in Canada, several practical factors may influence the actual processes that a tribunal will select in each case. The Law Reform Commission of Australia observes that these might include:[9]

- the resources available to tribunals and their decision makers (for example, whether a tribunal has the resources to conduct its own investigations, the number of tribunal members and the tribunal's caseload);
- the personal preferences of tribunal decision makers and the membership and "culture" of the tribunal (for example, lawyer members may be more comfortable with courtroom based procedure);
- the nature of the case (for example, the complexity of the questions of fact, law or credit raised by the case and whether there is a further level of review available);
- factors relevant to the parties (for example, their level of relevant knowledge and experience and the nature and extent of their representation in the proceedings, if any);
- decisions or dicta of appeal or review courts concerning alternative adjudicative or dispute resolution processes.

Both inquisitorial and active adjudication may fit within this broader non-adversarial category. However, there are important distinctions between the non-adversarial adjudication and active adjudication. Inquisitorial processes may include some of the "non-adversarial" characteristics alluded to above, but also generally include an express "truth-seeking" function. The classic inquisitorial

5 Australasian Law Reform Commission, *supra* note 3 at para 2.16.

6 *Ibid.*

7 As the Commission notes, the Australian Social Security and Appeals Tribunal and the Australian Refugee Review Tribunal were established to explicitly use "informal and non-adversarial processes". *Ibid* at para 2.14.

8 Ombudsman Saskatchewan, *Practice Essentials for Administrative Justice*, (Saskatchewan: Saskatchewan Ministry of the Attorney General 2009) at 35.

9 Australasian Law Reform Commission, *supra* note 3 at para 2.17.

settings in the Canadian context are commissions of public inquiry and Coroner's Inquests. In each case, a decision-maker has statutory authority to investigate and report on matters which are specified in the terms of reference. An inquisitorial process in this context is less concerned with adjudication and more with investigation and findings. These inquisitorial decision-makers are provided with a range of compulsory powers to obtain evidence, testimony or other information relevant to the investigation.

Adjudicative tribunals, the subject of this study, are suited neither to the adversarial model nor the inquisitorial model. Adjudicative tribunals in Canada are most often agencies, boards, commissions, which exercise decision-making authority on cases within statutorily defined subject matters. The adversarial/inquisitorial dichotomy appears to set up black and white options – either the adjudicator is passive or is directing the hearing. Increasingly, this dichotomy itself is coming under criticism. Adjudicators are seeking a "third way" that is non-adversarial, but also non-inquisitorial. These tribunals aim at "problem-solving"[10] and fulfilling their statutory mandate rather than "truth-seeking." We believe active adjudication captures this third way.

There are many convincing reasons to enhance a tribunal's role in the hearing process through active adjudication. At one time, it may have been important to maintain the legitimacy of tribunal proceedings through a court-like, adversarial proceeding. The reference to such adjudicative tribunals as "quasi-judicial" in Canada's administrative law jurisprudence is testament to the era when tribunals were defined largely by their similarity to or difference from the judicial norm. However, this era is passing.[11] Increasingly administrative justice is being recognized as a norm of its own. We will discuss the personal impact of administrative adjudication on participants in the implications of active adjudication section of this chapter. The following sections of this chapter will discuss the willingness of Canadian courts to refrain from interfering in tribunal adjudication, particularly in the area of immigration law. We see this deference as an important step in avoiding the creep of legalism that threatens the distinctiveness of administrative justice.

Canadian Context

This issue has arisen notably in the context of the recent affirmation of tribunal jurisdiction over human rights legislation and the *Canadian Charter of Rights*

---

10 Arie Freiberg writes about the development of problem-solving courts in the context of criminal justice in the United States, Canada and the United Kingdom. In describing the shift towards problem-solved, Frieberg notes that courts have shifted to non-adversarial justice. Arie Freiberg, "Post-Adversarial and Post-Inquisitorial Justice: Transcending Traditional Penological Paradigms" (2010) at 8, online: http://papers.ssrn.com/sol3/papers.cfm?abstract_id=1609468.

11 For discussion, see Lorne Sossin, "The Ambivalence of Administrative Justice in Canada: Does Canada Need a Fourth Branch?" Adam Dodek & Daniel Jutras, eds, *The Sacred Fire: The Legacy of Antonio Lamer* (Lexis Nexis, 2009) 51.

and Freedoms.[12] The fact that many tribunals see parties who are not represented by counsel and may have adjudicators without legal training, has created anxiety about how tribunals can adapt to their *Charter* jurisdiction in Canada. The question is whether tribunals should become more like courts to facilitate the hearing of human rights or *Charter* issues, or whether the process of hearing such claims should be adapted to the realities of diverse tribunal settings?

Even before the *Charter* debate concerns about procedural fairness and fettering the discretion of adjudicative tribunals have fuelled the argument that tribunals should act more like courts.[13] Attempts by tribunals to shift to a less judicial model have, ironically, led to litigation before the courts. Perhaps it is an even greater irony that, for the most part, courts have expressed support for such an evolution and affirmed that less adversarial process should not be equated with less fairness.[14]

Notably, the Federal Court of Appeal's recent decision in *Thamotharem v Canada (Minister of Citizenship and Immigration)*[15] has confirmed that tribunals may adopt a wider range of active adjudication practices. In *Thamotharem* the Court considered the validity of Guideline 7 Concerning Preparation and Conduct of a Hearing in the Refugee Protection Division. As noted in the introduction of the Guideline the "Refugee Protection Division (RPD) is the largest division of Canada's largest administrative tribunal" and the guidelines set out the obligations of the RPD and its participants.[16] At issue in *Thamotharem* was the guideline which governed the conduct of Refugee Protection Officers (RPOs) who work for the RPD and are responsible for carrying out the "activities necessary for a full and proper examination of a claim."[17] The provision stipulated that:

> In a claim for refugee protection, the standard practice will be for the RPO to start questioning the claimant. If there is no RPO participating in the hearing, the

---

12 In *Nova Scotia (Workers' Compensation Board) v Martin*, [2003] 2 SCR 504, *Paul v British Columbia (Forest Appeals Commission)*, [2003] 2 SCR 585 and *R v Conway*, [2010] 1 SCR 765 the Supreme Court confirmed an expansive jurisdiction for administrative decision-makers to apply *Charter* remedies so long as the decision-maker has a general statutory power to determine questions of law and where that jurisdiction is not removed from the decision-maker by statute. In *Tranchmontagne*, the Supreme Court separately affirmed the jurisdiction of tribunals in Ontario over human rights disputes.

13 David Mullan, "Tribunals Imitating Courts – Foolish Flattery or Sound Policy" (2005) 21 Dalhousie LJ 1 at 3.

14 *Thamotharem v Canada (Minister of Citizenship and Immigration)*, 2007 FCA 198 [*Thamotharem*].

15 *Ibid*.

16 Immigration and Refugee Board Canada, *Guidelines Issued by the Chairperson Pursuant to Section 159(1)(h) of the Immigration and Refugee Protection Act, Concerning Preparation and Conduct of a Hearing in the Refugee Protection Division*, December 15 2006, online http://www.irb-cisr.gc.ca/eng/brdcom/references/pol/guidir/Pages/GuideDir7.aspx [IRB, Guideline 7]. Note from the editors: Guideline 7 was revised in 2012 to reflect legislative changes to the refugee determination system.

17 *Ibid*.

> member will begin, followed by counsel for the claimant. Beginning the hearing in this way allows the claimant to quickly understand what evidence the member needs from the claimant in order for the claimant to prove his or her case.[18]

This guideline meant that standard practice would be for the Refugee Protection Officer to begin questioning a refugee claimant – rather than the claimant starting by presenting his or her case. *Thamotharem* argued that this procedural ordering, which prevented him from being questioned first by his own counsel, violated his right to a fair hearing. This argument implied that only a traditional adversarial-type Board hearing could ensure the level of procedural fairness required at common law.

The Court considered whether Guideline 7 violated the fairness of proceedings before the Immigration and Refugee Board. In *Baker v Canada (Minister of Citizenship and Immigration)* the Supreme Court had found that "[t]he more the process provided for, the function of the tribunal, the nature of the decision-making body, and the determinations that must be made to reach a decision resemble judicial decision making, the more likely it is that procedural protections closer to the trial model will be required by the duty of fairness."[19] Applying the contextual factors laid out in *Baker*,[20] the Federal Court of Appeal in *Thamotharem* held that the nature of the Board's hearings were closer to that of a formal judicial model, requiring trial-like procedures.[21] However, the Court went on to say that because Parliament specifically chose an inquisitorial model for the Board, not all elements of conventional adversarial procedure were required to meet common law standards of procedural fairness.[22] The direct implication of this finding is that

18 IRB, Guideline 7, *supra* note 16.

19 *Baker v Canada (Minister of Citizenship and Immigration)*, [1999] 2 SCR 817 para 23 [*Baker*].

20 The *Baker* factors include (paras 23–27): (1) the nature of the decision being made and the process followed in making it; (2) the nature of the statutory scheme and the terms of the statute pursuant to which the body operates; (3) the importance of the decision to the individual or individuals affected; (4) the legitimate expectations of the person challenging the decision; (5) the choices of procedure made by the agency itself.

21 *Thamotharem, supra* note 14 at 41.

22 *Ibid* at para 35. The FCA upheld Justice Blanchard's reasoning in the Federal Court 2006 FC 16. Justice Blanchard based his reasoning on the *Immigration and Refugee Protection Act*, SC 2001, c 27 [IRPA]. Section 170 of the IRPA states:

> The Refugee Protection Division, in any proceedings before it,
> may inquire into any matter that is considers relevant to establishing whether a claim is well-founded;
> ...
> (g) is not bound by any legal or technical rules of evidence,
> ...
> (i) may take notice of any facts that may be judicially noticed, any other generally recognized facts and any information or opinion that that is within its specialized knowledge.

– at least where tribunals' enabling statutes demand or suggest it – a more active process is not inconsistent with a fair hearing. According to the Court:[23]

> A relatively inquisitorial procedural form may reduce the degree of control over the process often exercisable by counsel in adversarial proceedings, especially before inexperienced tribunal members or those who lack the confidence that legal training can give. Nonetheless, *the fair adjudication of individual rights is perfectly compatible with an inquisitorial process*, where the order of questioning is not as obvious as it generally is in an adversarial hearing. [emphasis added]

The Court went on to note more generally that the procedural protections necessary to meet the level of fairness required by *Baker* must be tailored to fit the model of adjudication chosen by the legislature.[24] The Court also observed that "[i]nquisitorial processes of adjudication are not unfair simply because they are relatively unfamiliar to common lawyers."[25]

The Court emphasized the knowledge and training of Board members in assessing whether Thamotharem's procedural rights were violated. Board members received limited training in the appropriate ways to question vulnerable refugee claimants. This training in active questioning was viewed by the Court as an important procedural protection.[26] Active hearings clearly have limits. For example, the Court observed that duty of fairness forbids members from questioning in an overly aggressive and badgering manner, or in a way that otherwise gives a reasonable apprehension of bias.[27]

The Court in *Thamotharem* also noted that in most cases before the Board there was no party opposing the claim being made. While RPOs were often present, their role was – at least according to the Court – one of assisting the Board member rather than arguing against the claimant's case. Under these circumstances, members will be required to make all of the inquiries necessary to come to a fair decision.[28] In *Restrepo Benitez v Canada (Minister of Citizenship and Immigration)*, a case where Guideline 7 was also at issue, the Federal Court found that tribunal members must act fairly, impartially and judiciously, but this

---

Justice Blanchard reasoned that the Board was not adversarial because of the above provisions of its legislation and despite the "aggressive and probing nature of the questioning conducted at hearing before the Board by RPOs and Board members" (at paras 72–75).

23 *Ibid* at para 44. The Australian Law Reform Commission notes that indications from High Court in Australia are that they are suspicious of any move to an inquisitorial approach as being sufficient to meet constitutional protections for procedural fairness: Australian Law Reform Commission, *supra* note 3 at para 2.42.

24 *Ibid* at para 41.

25 *Ibid* at para 48.

26 *Ibid* at para 38.

27 *Ibid* at para 39.

28 *Ibid* at para 46.

does not mean that "a member should not question a claimant or, indeed, that a member may not question in advance of the claimant's counsel."[29]

In the case of *Badalyan v Canada (Minister of Citizenship and Immigration)*[30] the Federal Court applied similar reasoning to an issue about the order of questioning. In this case a mother and daughter applied for refugee protection in Canada after they were allegedly stalked, threatened and assaulted by men in connection with the work of Ms. Badalyan's late husband in their country of origin. The women fled to Canada and applied for refugee protection in 2006. Their claim was rejected by a member of the Refugee Protection Division (RPD) of the Immigration and Refugee Board (IRB) and they appealed that decision.

In their appeal the appellants' main issue was an alleged lack of procedural fairness. At the RPD hearing, Ms. Badalyan made an application to have her son-in-law testify first since he apparently knew more about Ms. Badalyan's husband's past. A psychologist's report stated that not requiring Ms. Badalyan to testify first was important because of her nervousness in testifying, triggered by post-traumatic stress.

At issue in *Badalyan* was the interpretation of the same provision of Guideline No. 7, as in the *Thamotharem* case, in combination with another provision that states, "[t]he member may vary the order of questioning in exceptional circumstances."[31] In this case, the applicants suggested that the applicant should have the right to choose the order of questioning, at least in special circumstance cases. The applicants contended that since the burden of proof rested with them, they should be able to choose the order of questioning. However, the Board and the Federal Court agreed that the Board member should choose the order of questioning. In its decision the Court noted that RPD hearings are "inquisitorial rather than adversarial"[32] and that "the Board is master of its own procedure, provided that the principles of natural justice are upheld."[33]

The courts' respect for boards and tribunals as mater of their procedure extends to how statutory obligations are interpreted. For example, in *Vancouver Pile Driving Ltd. (VPDL) v British Columbia (Assessor of Area No. 8 – Vancouver Sea to Sky Region)* (2008), the BC Supreme Court considered an appeal by VPDL from a decision of the Property Assessment Appeal Board that its rules allowed

---

29 *Restrepo Benitez v Canada (Minister of Citizenship and Immigration)*, 2006 FC 461 at para 124. The Federal Court in *Rajaratnam v Canada*, [2005] FCJ No 2037, had a similar view when it found that procedural fairness had not been violated by the Immigration Appeal Division member asking supplementary questions of the applicant during his testimony. The Court chose to characterize the member's questions as "energetic" rather than a violation of procedural fairness (at para 11).

30 *Badalyan v Canada (Minister of Citizenship and Immigration)*, [2010] FCJ No 66 [*Badalyan*].

31 *Ibid* at para 10.

32 *Ibid* at para 16; see Guideline 7 at note 16.

33 *Ibid* at para 15.

it to improperly refuse the appellant's request for an adjournment.[34] In this case, the Court found the Board had not violated the appellant's right to procedural fairness. The Court found that even though the Board has an inquisitorial function, the permissive language in the *Assessment Act* gives the Board flexibility in determining its procedures.[35]

The case of *Thamotharem* dealt with the amount of discretion given to the Board to determine the order of those questioning a witness, whereas the *Badalyan* case dealt with the issue of who determines the ordering of witness testimony. In both cases the reviewing Courts chose to defer to the Boards' decisions because of the Board's inquisitorial, rather than adversarial model, therefore allowing the Board to be master of its own procedures. Similarly, the Court in *Vancouver Pile Driving* gave deference to the Board in determining when to apply its procedural rules in a way that could limit its inquisitorial function. These cases demonstrate that courts will defer to Boards in applying active procedures, where Parliament has framed the Board's enabling legislation as permitting such discretion.

The move away from adversarial adjudication in administrative settings and toward a more active approach is not confined to Canada.[36] Canadian courts have been increasingly willing to allow tribunals flexibility in determining their own hearing procedures even when the procedures divert from the court-like adversarial rules.

Mechanisms for and Challenges to Creating an Active Tribunal Role in the Hearing Process

In Canada, it appears that the line between inquisitorial and adversarial models has become blurred in administrative adjudication. As tribunals attempt to meet

---

34 *Vancouver Pile Driving Ltd. (VPDL) v British Columbia (Assessor of Area No. 8 – Vancouver Sea to Sky Region)*, 2008 BCSC 810, [2008] BCJ No 1171 at para 90 [*Vancouver Pile Driving*].

35 *Ibid* at para 110. The finding of an inquisitorial function was based on the wording of s 57 (1) of the *Assessment Act*, RSBC 1996, c 20 which provides:

57(1) In an appeal under this Part, the board *may* reopen the whole question of the property's assessment to *ensure* accuracy and that assessments are at actual value applied in a consistent manner in the municipality or rural area, and… The Board notes that the word ensure in 57(1)(a) connotes an inquisitorial function however, the word "may" does not impose a necessary obligation on the Board to reopen the whole question of the property's assessment. [emphasis added]

36 In this connection, please see the papers in this collection which discuss the development of a more active approach in jurisdictions traditionally characterized by an adversarial tradition. Robert Thomas examines this phenomenon as it relates to the United Kingdom, Robin Creyke similarly analyzes a form of active adjudication in Australia and Michael Asimow describes the value of an inquisitorial approach in matters of administrative law justice, such as Social Security adjudication, in the United States.

the important goals of flexible adjudication and enhanced access to justice, active adjudication, as we have termed it, appears to provide some answers. However, to enable the implementation of active adjudication we believe it is important for both tribunals and legislators to consider how best to integrate an active approach into daily adjudication.

There are a variety of mechanisms available to tribunals and legislatures that are considering enhancing the role of tribunals in the hearing process. These mechanisms may include the introduction of model codes, adjudicator tone and formality, adjudicators requesting further information, and adjudicator focusing of the issues. Each will be discussed in turn.

Model Codes

Model codes have become the source of much discussion in Canada during the last ten years, particularly with the release of three reports advocating the adoption of model codes for tribunals in Saskatchewan,[37] British Columbia[38] and Alberta.[39] Model codes are guides for tribunal processes which are consistent with the requirements of procedural fairness and efficiency. All these reports, which are discussed below, identified that there is a need to examine the ways in which tribunals can most effectively and efficiently engage in adjudication. In general the idea behind introducing model codes is to provide a coherent set of standards for adjudicative tribunals in particular jurisdiction. We found this goal of efficiency and coherency resulted in the Canadian proposed model codes identifying procedures for tribunals which fit within active adjudication.

For example, provision 3.1 of the proposed Alberta Model Code (2008) would allow tribunals to request more information from the parties concerning any errors or omissions in the application. The code also proposes that non-coercive investigative powers be granted to tribunals. The report notes that the granting of coercive investigative powers should be done on an individual tribunal basis because the need for such powers is rare.[40]

The proposed Saskatchewan Model Code would allow tribunals to opt-in on a case-by-case basis, unlike the Alberta Code which is meant to apply to all tribunals

---

37 The Law Reform Commission of Saskatchewan, *Consultation Paper: A Model Code of Procedure for Administrative Tribunals* (May 2003), online: http://www.lawreformcommission.sk.ca/Admin1.htm.

38 Administrative Justice Office, "British Columbia's New Administrative Tribunals Act" (Paper presented to the Council of Canadian Tribunals 21st Annual Conference, 20 June 2005), online: http://www.ag.gov.bc.ca/ajo/down/paper_on_ata_to_ccat_21st_annual_conference.pdf [Administrative Justice Office].

39 Alberta Law Reform Institute, *Powers and Procedures of Administrative Tribunals*, Consultation Memorandum No. 13 (September 2008), online: http://www.law.ualberta.ca/alri/docs/cm013.pdf.

40 *Ibid* at 59.

in that province. The proposed Saskatchewan Code recommends that tribunals inform applicants of any additional information they will require, prior to the hearing.

The Saskatchewan Code also discusses the need to make the investigatory powers of tribunals explicit. The courts have held that tribunals may conduct investigations as long as they disclose their findings to the parties involved in the case. The report also notes that a recent study of environmental tribunals in Canada found that eight out of twelve environmental tribunals already engage in fact-finding.[41]

In order to encourage the use of investigative procedures the Saskatchewan report recommends the inclusion of the following language in the model code: "A tribunal is authorized to direct any informal enquiry or investigation or otherwise gather information relating to an application in order to determine whether to conduct a hearing, or for consideration at a hearing."[42]

In 2002 the British Columbia administrative justice project released a white paper on administrative justice reform which advocated for the creation of Model Statutory Powers and Procedures for tribunals. This recommendation was implemented in 2004 by the *Administrative Tribunals Act* (ATA). Section 27 of the ATA authorizes tribunal chairs to hire their own investigators, lawyers, and experts as necessary. According to the former Administrative Justice Organisation (AJO),[43] next steps for reform may include the creation of model procedural rules or practice directives for tribunals,[44] though this does not appear to have happened to date. An area for further research may be why model rules have not to date been popular, though the fragmentation of the administrative justice community, and the lack of coordination between boards and tribunals, may suggest one barrier to widespread adoption of model codes.

The non-structural mechanisms which enable active adjudication will be discussed below. Most of these mechanisms are procedures and practices which tribunal members can adopt throughout the course of a hearing.

Formality and Setting the Tone

Formality is something which can be evident in both adversarial and active regimes and should not be associated exclusively with one or the other. Thomas Thawley writes that in the context of the Australia's Administrative Appeals Tribunal the level of formality of a hearing was determined by the behavior of the tribunal members, in particular the presiding member.[45]

41 Law Reform Commission of Saskatchewan, *supra* note 37.

42 *Ibid.*

43 Administrative Justice Office, *supra* note 38. As of June 2009 the Administrative Justice Office was dissolved and most of its responsibilities were assumed by the Dispute Resolution Office of the BC Attorney General.

44 *Ibid.*

45 Tom Thawley, "Adversarial and Inquisitorial Procedures in the Administrative Appeals Tribunal" (1997) 4 Australian Journal of Administrative Law 61 at 75.

When tribunal members communicate with the parties involved in the case in order to obtain more information there may be a need to balance the level of formality employed. There is tension between the need to avoid the appearance of bias and the desire as to avoid intimidating the parties, particularly self-represented claimants. The New Zealand Law Commission recommends that legislatures amend the enabling legislation of tribunals to require "tribunals to conduct hearing with as little formality as is consistent with a fair and efficient process."[46] The Commission hopes this will aid in the development of a "culture of informality."

The role of tribunal members in adjudication was examined by the Canadian Immigration Appeal Division (IAD) which launched its Innovation Plan in 2006. As part of this plan the IAD adopted a proactive approach to adjudication while noting that many of the elements of this approach were already in place at the IAD.[47]

The IAD Innovation Plan highlights that there is a need to avoid the traditional arguments distinguishing between adversarial and inquisitorial models, and a need to focus on the process which will produce the best results.

Requesting More Information

Tribunal members have the ability take a more active role in guiding the hearing participants through the hearing process. Observers of tribunal systems in many countries often comment that tribunal members should not simply be observing proceedings but should be constructively contributing to the progression of the hearing. The need for an active role for tribunal members has been expressed in the context of the UK by Nick Wikeley who commented on how the purely adversarial nature of tribunals often falls short of the ideal.[48] Wikeley quotes a social security tribunal commissioner who explains:

> ...that there is clearly a duty upon a tribunal to ensure that all relevant questions have been asked of a claimant. It could not be otherwise given the complexity of social security law and the fact that few claimants have advisors and that many are poorly educated. The asking of questions is largely achieved by ever-more sophisticated claim forms but even the incomes support claim form, which runs several pages, cannot ask all possibly relevant questions.[49]

---

46 Law Commission of New Zealand, *Tribunal Reform* (Wellington: 2008) at 90 [New Zealand Law Commission].

47 Immigration and Refugee Board of Canada, *Immigration Appeal Division Innovation Initiative* (Ottawa: 2006) at 18.

48 Nick Wikeley, "Future Directions for Tribunals: A United Kingdom Perspective" in Robin Creyke, ed, *Tribunals in the Common Law World* (Sydney: The Federation Press, 2008) 187.

49 *Ibid* at188.

Wikeley notes that the "inquisitorial ethos" is not necessarily the direction in which the pendulum should swing. In particular, over recent years inquisitorial processes have become just as procedurally dense as adversarial systems and also seem to lack the flexibility for the work of tribunals. However, Joan Dwyer has highlighted that there are ways in which tribunal members can play a more active role in asking for more information, while remaining within the adversarial system. We would suggest this characterization of a middle ground between adversarial and inquisitorial extremes is precisely what we seek to carve out as the zone of active adjudication. The examples Dwyer provides include instances where the parties have overlooked an issue that the tribunals require information on (ie, jurisdiction) and where parties have conceded on a matter that appears inconsistent with the evidence.[50]

The New Zealand Law Commission is generally supportive of a more active role for tribunals in that country. In particular, it suggests that all tribunals should have the power to call and examine witnesses, and obtain production of papers, documents and, records for inspection by the tribunal.[51] Further, the Commission notes that many adversarial tribunals in that country already have these powers.

Defining the Issues

One way of ensuring more efficient and effective hearings is for the tribunal to facilitate the identification of key issues. Dwyer offers the example of *Re Nicholls and Secretary to the Department of Primary Industry*[52] where the tribunal had to decide a jurisdictional matter based on whether a boat was foreign or Australian. After ten days of hearings the tribunal found that it did not have enough information to answer the question and wrote a letter to each of the parties requesting their stance on whether the boat was foreign or not. It then held a separate hearing on this issue.[53] Tribunal members can also be more active in the pre-hearing procedures including pre-hearing conferences.[54]

50 Joan Dwyer, "Fair Play the Inquisitorial Way" (2002) 22 Nat'l Ass'n Admin L Judges 100 at 100.

51 New Zealand Law Commission, *supra* note 46 at 93.

52 *Re Nicholls and Secretary to the Department of Primary Industry*, (1988) 22 ALD 596.

53 Joan Dwyer, "Overcoming the Adversarial Bias in Tribunals Procedures" (1991) Fed L Rev 252 at 270.

54 Gary Downes, "Case Management and Tracking at the Administrative Appeals Tribunal" (Speech delivered during a visit to Thailand's Central Administrative Court, February 2006), online: http://www.aat.gov.au/SpeechesPapersAndResearch/speeches/downes/CaseManagementFeb2006.htm.

Implications of Active Adjudication[55]

No two tribunals are alike in the issues they address, the users they serve or in the procedures they select. The above section on model codes in Canada highlights a desire that tribunals not be married to any one process. As discussed in the introductory section of this chapter, active adjudication is not rigidly defined and can be adopted to varying degrees based on the needs of individual tribunals. It appears some Canadian tribunals have begun to apply elements of active adjudication; this chapter has considered the framework of active adjudication and the practical aspects of its implementation. This section reviews some implications of implementing active adjudication which include the need to avoid allegations of bias and to offer training for adjudicators. This section also uses the example of therapeutic jurisprudence to discuss how experiential outcomes for process participants might be better with the use of active adjudication.

Process versus Practice

There is a disconnect which can often be observed between a tribunal's enabling legislation, formal policy statements, and practice directions on the one side, and the actual tribunal practices on the other. It is clear, from experiences elsewhere,

---

55 The research for this section focused on unique active adjudication mechanisms outside of Canada. However within Canada the Ontario Human Rights Tribunal has an active role in its hearings because of its enabling legislation. Section 43 of the Ontario *Human Rights Code*, RSO 1990, c H1, enables this active approach and its provisions include:

> (3) Without limiting the generality of subsection (1), the Tribunal rules may,
> (a) provide for and require the use of hearings or of practices and procedures that are provided for under the *Statutory Powers Procedure Act* or that are alternatives to traditional adjudicative or adversarial procedures;
> (b) authorize the Tribunal to,
> (i) define or narrow the issues required to dispose of an application and limit the evidence and submissions of the parties on such issues, and
> (ii) determine the order in which the issues and evidence in a proceeding will be presented;
> (c) authorize the Tribunal to conduct examinations in chief or cross-examinations of a witness;
> …
> (f) authorize the Tribunal to require a party to a proceeding or another person to,
> (i) produce any document, information or thing and provide such assistance as is reasonably necessary, including using any data storage, processing or retrieval device or system, to produce the information in any form,
> (ii) provide a statement or oral or affidavit evidence, or
> (iii) in the case of a party to the proceeding, adduce evidence or produce witnesses who are reasonably within the party's control; and
> (g) govern any matter prescribed by the regulations.

that providing a process for active adjudication does not ensure that tribunals will operate in a non-adversarial way in practice. There are factors which can pull tribunals "back" toward the adversarial mode.

One example of such a factor is the phenomenon of "adversarial bias" at tribunal proceedings.[56] It is widely assumed that legally trained tribunal members will demonstrate a bias in favor of adversarial proceedings, given their professional background and training in a specific analytical mode. However, Judith McCormack points out that even non-lawyer tribunal members may tend to gravitate toward a particular form of legal analysis if and when their role as adjudicators begins to weaken their connection to the professional communities from which they derive their specific, non-legal expertise. When members' expertise in their subject areas is not actively valued, an analytical vacuum can form that quickly becomes filled with increased legalism. According to McCormack, this general-legal, rather than specialist-expert, mode of adjudication can in turn make tribunal processes noticeably more adversarial.

Participant Experiences

There seems to be a gap in the research by tribunals and scholars on assessing participant experiences with tribunal processes. With a lack of information on how users are experiencing the tribunal system, it is difficult to pinpoint where in the process, a more active tribunal would best assist the user. Some tribunals seem to be living in a false reality because they assess client satisfaction with dispute resolution processes from the perspective of the tribunal and using criteria of settlement rates, time savings and cost effectiveness[57] rather than actually surveying the users. In a needs assessment of BC tribunal dispute resolution, author Craig Darling found that only one out of fifteen tribunals assessed actually used client satisfaction "as a criterion for evaluating effectiveness."[58] To what extent can an active tribunal achieve greater satisfaction for the parties who come before it, and enhance access to justice?

We see therapeutic jurisprudence as an example of the potential positive impact of active adjudication because therapeutic jurisprudence allows the adjudicator to consider a broader spectrum of issues and how they impact individual process participants. Therapeutic jurisprudence is "an approach to law that regards the legal phenomenon…as having therapeutic or anti-therapeutic effects."[59] This

56 Judith McCormack, "Nimble Justice: Revitalizing Administrative Tribunals in a Climate of Rapid Change" (1995) 59 Sask L Rev 385 at 393.

57 Craig Darling, "Initial Research and Preliminary Needs Assessment, BC Dispute Resolution Needs Assessment Project" (Victoria: Accord Canada Dispute Resolution Group, 2006) at 15.

58 *Ibid.*

59 Marilyn McMahon & David Wexler, "Therapeutic Jurisprudence: Developments and Applications in Australia and New Zealand" (2002) 20:2 Law in Context 1 at 1.

approach began in the area of mental health law and has expanded to criminal, family and medical law. Arie Freiberg writes that practically speaking, the therapeutic approach can be seen in the development of problem-oriented courts including, drug courts, mental health courts and domestic violence courts. These courts take a multi-disciplinary collaborative approach where treatment services, judicial intervention and medical monitoring become integrated.[60]

Therapeutic jurisprudence gives the adjudicator flexibility to consider the impact of her decision on the individual participant. The New Zealand Mental Health Review Tribunal has undertaken a therapeutic approach in the handling of its cases which have an active tribunal structure. The Tribunal's decisions are often counter to the outcome sought by the applicants so the tribunal attempts to fulfill its pro-therapeutic intent by providing the applicant with "constructive and positive feedback and encouragement."[61]

Kate Diesfeld and Brian McKenna have conducted a review of that Tribunal's efforts to be pro-therapeutic and some of these practices could likely be applied to tribunals addressing other areas of adjudication. In particular, the authors found that the decisions of the Tribunal often had positive or constructive comments for the applicant. The decisions also demonstrated that the applicant's desires, concerns and well-being had been taken into account.[62] An interesting observation was that the consumer's (applicant's) view was articulated in the Tribunal's decision, in an effort to at least provide validation of the consumer's perspective. Diesfeld and McKenna note, as other authors have, that "those who believe they were able to have their say and are listened to by those making decisions may believe their final decision is more acceptable."[63] The way decisions are written and what they take into account may be a relevant consideration for tribunals with a public interest mandate.

The President of the Victorian Civil and Administrative Tribunal (VCAT), Kevin Bell in his 2008–2009 review of the Tribunal expressed concerns about the adversarial nature of that tribunal.[64] During his review, Bell found that the public perception of VCAT had deteriorated because of an increasingly legalistic adjudication model which allowed lawyers, advocates and experts to dominate proceedings. Because of this perception, VCAT was not living up to its intended purpose which was to provide "quick, cheap and efficient justice for the general public."[65] Bell's report on the VCAT recommends that the tribunal apply

---

60 Arie Freiberg, "Therapeutic Jurisprudence in Australia: Paradigm Shift or Pragmatic Incrementalism" (2003) 20:2 Law in Context 6 at10.

61 Kate Diesfeld & Brian McKenna, "Therapeutic Intent of the New Zealand Mental Health Review Tribunal" (2006) 13 Psychiatry Psychol & L 100 at 101.

62 *Ibid* at 102–104.

63 *Ibid* at 107.

64 Honourable Justice Kevin Bell, *One VCAT President's Review of VCAT* (Melbourne: Victorian Civil and Administrative Tribunal, 2009) at 8 [Bell].

65 *Ibid* at 21.

"therapeutic approaches in the administration of justice."[66] In particular this is meant to address criticism that VCAT has a real or perceived lack of respect for applicants to the tribunal. Bell's interpretation of applying a therapeutic approach is to focus on the wellbeing of the user which, for example means that:

> Self-represented tenants are still evicted by justice institutions … But the way it is done is intended to be dignified and humane. That might involve giving advice about emergency housing assistance. Hence the significance, in therapeutic terms, of the tribunal's recent initiative of making a social assistance database available on the desktop computer of all members.[67]

Notwithstanding such a therapeutic approach (and sometimes because of it) active adjudication may appear to represent a deviation from adjudicative norms and may provoke legal challenge on this basis.

In Narelle Bedford and Robin Creyke's study, concerns of legal challenges were voiced, particularly where the tribunals were composed of single-member panels. These concerns surrounded the potential for allegations of real or apprehended bias which stem from the questions asked by the tribunal member. This was less of an issue for multi-member panels because all the members tended to ask for more information on a host of issues.[68] In response to these comments Bedford and Creyke recommend that "a clear preference should be expressed for having multi-member panels in appropriate matters."[69]

Lori Ferman Disenhouse, legal advisor to the Immigration and Refugee Board of Canada, summarized some of the recent case law (discussed in the first section of this chapter) which points to courts' acceptance of a more active role for tribunals. However, she notes that in order to combat allegations of bias that may stem from this more active role:

> A proactive tribunal member must at all times remain polite, courteous and disinterested in the outcome. A decision-maker can never engage in aggressive questioning or intemperate remarks, but must remain judicious in demeanor even while taking an active role in ensuring that the evidence and the testimony required for an informed and expert decision is before the tribunal.[70]

---

66 Bell, *supra* note 64 at 7.

67 *Ibid* at 83.

68 Narelle Bedford & Robin Creyke, *Inquisitorial Processes in Australian Tribunals* (Melbourne: Australian Institute of Judicial Administration Incorporated, 2006) at 25 [Bedford]. Also see Administrative Review Council, *Better Decisions: Review of the Commonwealth Merits Review Tribunal* (Canberra: Australian Government Publishing Service, 1995) at 35.

69 *Ibid* at 67.

70 Lori Ferman Disenhouse, "Proactive Tribunal Members: Testing the Limits", written for the Immigration and Refugee Board of Canada, at 12.

Training

Very few adjudicators in Canada come to their roles with significant expertise in active hearings. The training bodies which exist, such as the Society of Adjudicators and Regulators in Ontario (SOAR) offer training in the conduct of a hearing, but there is no specialized training (as yet) in active hearings per se. In the Australian context, Bedford and Creyke also found that for tribunals with part-time members there was less confidence in utilizing inquisitorial techniques, because of a lack of experience.[71] Further, Bedford and Cryeke highlight the need for tribunal members to be trained in inquisitorial techniques including "questioning techniques, active listening skills and cross-cultural sensitivity."[72] In an effort to encourage reform, training and education for tribunal members and registrars were issues addressed in the Australian Review of the Adversarial System of Litigation. In its report the Law Reform Commission recommended the following proposals as part of its broader goal of enhancing the administrative justice system and reducing legalism in administrative tribunals.

> Proposal 3.3. Every federal review tribunal should have an effective professional development program with stated goals and objectives. This should include access to induction and orientation programs, mentoring programs, and continuing education and training programs. In particular, legal training in areas relevant to decision making should be made available to members of tribunals who do not have legal qualifications.
>
> Proposal 3.4. The federal review tribunals should establish a Tribunals Council to promote and facilitate the sharing of professional information and experience amongst tribunal members, as well as assisting in education and training for administrative decision makers. This initiative would also have the beneficial effect of providing a reliable source of practical information and advice for government concerning the operation and development of the administrative justice system.[73]

The right to representation is a crucial value in our legal system. However, in the tribunal system the right to representation must be balanced with the need to provide accessible, efficient and effective solutions to disputes.[74] As discussed, there are concerns that the use of representation, particularly lawyers, will increasingly "legalize" the tribunal system. However, it can be difficult to enable self-represented claimants to present their cases given the court-like nature of

71 Bedford, *supra* note 68 at 26.

72 *Ibid* at 27.

73 The Australian Law Reform Commission, *Review of the Adversarial System of Litigation* (Sydney: Australian Law Reform Commission 1998) at 74, online: http://www.austlii.edu.au/au/other/alrc/publications/issues/24/ALRCIP24.html.

74 Bell, *supra* note 68 at 16.

many tribunals. In addition many claimants may lack the capacity to structure an argument, may not be comfortable speaking one of the languages in which the tribunal offers hearings, and may not understand all the process and procedures they are required to follow.

The Health Professions Appeal and Review Board, for example, reviews decisions of the regulated health professional colleges where they decide not to refer complaints to further disciplinary processes. The basis for the review is whether the decision of the college was "reasonable" and its investigation "adequate." Most applicants seeking a review do not have representation and are seeking a finding of wrongdoing against a particular health professional. Without legal training, their approach to ideas like "reasonableness" and "adequacy" tend to be grounded in common sense rather than a legal standard. The dilemma for the Board, roughly half of whose members are legally trained and half of whose members have other backgrounds and expertise, is how to bridge the gap between their obligation to apply their statutory mandate in an impartial and fair fashion, and their commitment to provide an accessible and intelligible (not to mention a fair) hearing. Active hearings have the potential to balance these goals in a way that adversarial models do not.

Active hearing models do not mean departing from the adjudicators' traditional role as a neutral arbiter of a dispute. The first principle of the Canadian Judicial Council's Statement of Principles on Self-Represented Litigants and Accused Persons is that: "Access to justice for self-represented persons requires all aspects of the court process to be, as much as possible, open, transparent, clearly defined, simple, convenient and accommodating."[75]

This notion of "accommodation" in the judicial context is in-line with Sir Andrew Leggatt's report UK report "Tribunals for Users One System, One Service." Leggatt writes, "We are convinced that the tribunal approach must be an enabling one: supporting the parties in ways which give them confidence in their own abilities to participate in the process, and in the tribunal's capacity to compensate for the appellants' lack of skills or knowledge."[76] The more recent UK reforms, and the shift to "enabling" adjudication through tribunals, are explored in this collection by Robert Thomas.[77] Thomas' thoughtful and textured discussion of the tensions accompanying the search for alternatives to the adversarial/inquisitorial dichotomy informs our analysis as well (including the tension that

75 Canadian Judicial Council, *Statement of Principles on Self-represented Litigants and Accused Persons* (2006), online: http://www.cjc-ccm.gc.ca/cmslib/general/news_pub_other_PrinciplesStatement_2006_en.pdf.

76 Sir Andrew Leggatt, *Tribunals for Users: One System, One Service: Report of the Review of Tribunals* (London: Ministry of Justice, 2001) at para 7.5.

77 See Robert Thomas, "From 'Adversarial v Inquisitorial' to 'Active, Enabling and Investigative': Developments in UK Administrative Tribunals" at Chapter 3. See also Lorne Sossin, "Reflections on the U.K. Tribunal Reform: A Canadian Perspective" (2011) 24 CJALP 17.

a less adversarial process implies less impartiality on the part of the decision-maker). Thomas' characterization of tribunal adjudication in the UK as adversarial in nature with an emerging "inquisitorial gloss" captures the evolution which we discuss in the Canadian context below.

The VCAT has statutory limitations on the representation of parties at tribunal hearings. VCAT follows the general rule that parties may only be represented by a professional advocate (legal practitioner or someone with suitable experience) if they are a child, a local council, the government, a credit provider or a home building insurer, if the other party is a professional advocate or is so represented or, finally, if all the parties agree.[78] Further, the tribunal may, at its discretion, allow a party in any case to be represented by anyone, including a professional advocate. Companies and other bodies corporate may be represented by their officers.[79] There are several exceptions to this general rule however, as it stands the majority of the cases that go to VCAT are unrepresented.[80]

As the President of VCAT, Bell heard many complaints about the lack of support given by the tribunal to self-represented parties. Bell notes that tribunal members can better assist self-represented parties in pre-hearing meetings and that members were engaging in training to better understand the problems facing these parties. However, Bell also noted that, in order to fulfill the obligation of a fair hearing, tribunal members may be required to play a more active role, while still remaining impartial, in the following ways:

- To explain to a self-represented party the procedures to be followed;
- To direct the self-represented party positively to the legal and factual issues in the case, helping them to understand what they are;
- To direct the self-represented party negatively away from irrelevant issues, explaining why;
- To assist the self-represented party to present their evidence and to test the evidence of the other party, in that regard asking questions of the self-represented party or the witnesses of the other party to a limited extent where necessary;
- To assist the self-represented party to present his or her submissions in the case by directing his or her attention to the relevant issues and asking for their response.[81]

The point about training should not be glossed over. Active hearing requires, arguably, even more skill and capacity than adversarial hearing. Knowing when and how to intervene in a hearing without becoming an advocate for one side or an adversary of the other is one of the most challenging adjudicative contexts.

78 Bell, *supra* note 64 at 17.

79 *Ibid* at 17.

80 *Ibid.*

81 *Ibid* at 75.

In Canada, the focus of the legal aid system generally is the criminal justice system. To the extent that clinics provide services to those coming before adjudicative tribunals (immigration and refugee board, landlord and tenant boards, social benefits tribunals, etc), typically this is focused on representation in adversarial settings, though there are some important exceptions. One important innovation is the move by many clinics toward public legal information (through services like ClickLaw in British Columbia and CLEONet in Ontario).[82]

The broader implications of an active hearing model affect the model of advocacy which lawyers and paralegals adopt. It is not simply a matter of which parties have representation, in other words, but also what kind of representation they have. Rather than disallowing legal representation, we suggest tribunals adopting an active model work closely with stakeholders and the subject-area specific bar and clinics to provide guidelines on effective advocacy in such settings.

Conclusions

In this study, we have explored the rationale for non-adversarial and more active hearings in administrative adjudication settings. This model attempts to reverse the trend toward more legalized tribunal procedures and the equating of such procedures with fairness to the parties. Where parties are unlikely to be represented, more legalized procedures tend to undermine rather than enhance fairness.

Courts have shown a desire to ensure the requirements of procedural fairness are met, while also allowing tribunals increased flexibility in creating their own procedures where the legislative intent was not to create an exclusively adversarial tribunal. In addition, proposals for the implementation of provincial model codes in Canada, and their acceptance of investigative powers for tribunals indicate a willingness to accept more active roles for tribunals.

Active adjudication may be particularly well-suited to specific kinds of settings. For example, wherever a power imbalance is endemic to a tribunal's process, an active tribunal may "level" the playing field so as to protect the weaker party. An active approach to polycentric issues, such as those regarding the environment, may enable better, more inclusive decisions to be reached. Finally, active hearings are well suited to tribunals with complex statutory mandates, or where the effective and efficient use of resources is a priority. In other words, active adjudication appears to be aligned with the very rationale for establishing many administrative tribunals. Rather than viewing active adjudication by reference to what it is not (adversarial on the one hand, inquisitorial on the other), we hope this chapter contributes to a new vantage on active adjudication for what it is (and how it may enhance administrative justice and the public interest in Canada and beyond).

82 See www.clicklaw.bc.ca and www.cleonet.ca.

Chapter 5
Inquisitorial Adjudication and Mass Justice in American Administrative Law

Michael Asimow*

Adversarial and Inquisitorial Models of Adjudication

The American[1] legal system embraces the adversarial model and rejects the inquisitorial model. By the adversarial model, I mean one largely controlled by contending lawyers rather than by judges and in which the hearing or trial is considered to be separate from the investigation. By the inquisitorial system, I mean one largely controlled by judges rather than by lawyers and in which the hearing or trial is considered to be part of the investigation.

The paradigm case of adversarial adjudication is an American criminal jury trial. The prosecution and defense are each responsible for investigation of the case. At trial, the lawyers frame the issues, choose the witnesses, and control the presentation of evidence. The trial consists mostly of oral testimony and argument and is separate from the previous criminal investigation conducted by the police without judicial supervision. The judge is neutral and relatively passive, exercising such functions as ruling on evidence, keeping order, and instructing the jury. A lay jury decides the facts. It can consider only the information produced at the trial, not its own knowledge. The jury states no reasons for its conclusions. Because of the widespread use of juries, the U. S. criminal justice system may be more adversarial than that of any other country. American civil litigation is, if anything, even more adversarial than criminal litigation, because it is characterized by costly and protracted discovery (controlled solely by lawyers) and extensive motion practice that depends on lawyer initiatives.

By contrast, in a purely inquisitorial proceeding, such as criminal prosecution in many civil law countries, the hearing or trial is the final phase of the investigation. While there are countless variations, most of the evidence is contained in a written dossier assembled by the judge. The judge supervises the investigation

---

* Many thanks to those who assisted me with this chapter, particularly Sasha Baglay, John Crowley, Gene Elrod, Jill Family, David Hill, Laverne Jacobs, Amalia Kessler, James Ridgway, Ron Smith, and Dan Solomon.

1 The term "American" here and in the title refers to the United States of America, not to any other North or South American country. This inexact usage is adopted for convenience.

and interviews the defendant and other witnesses. Before the trial, the judge has concluded that the defendant is likely to be found guilty (otherwise the judge would have dismissed the case prior to trial). The judge controls the presentation of evidence at the trial, the primary purpose of which is to assist the judge in deciding on an appropriate penalty.

Thus one might imagine a spectrum between a purely adversarial approach (like the American criminal jury trial) and a purely inquisitorial approach (like the civil law criminal trial). One might array civil, criminal, or administrative proceedings in any country along the spectrum between purely adversarial and purely inquisitorial. Most proceedings, of course, contain elements of both systems and lie somewhere along the spectrum rather than at the poles.

I doubt whether the American model of adversarial adjudication delivers the best mix of accuracy, efficiency, and acceptability, when compared to the systems of criminal and civil adjudication used in other countries.[2] Partly, I believe that its survival is based on path dependence – it has always been done that way – plus public ignorance of other approaches to justice. How else to explain polling data in which Americans condemn their justice system, but overwhelmingly believe it to be the best in the world?[3] Or data that indicates that the public detests lawyers and trusts judges, but prefers a system in which lawyers rather than judges control the justice system?[4]

Adversarial and Inquisitorial Methods in American Administrative Adjudication

The federal government and every state have enacted administrative procedure acts (APAs). A reader of these APAs would conclude that American administrative adjudication is a world of judicialized and highly adversarial proceedings. Indeed, most formal trial-type hearings mandated by the APA, which are presided over by

2 Michael Asimow, "Popular Culture and the American Adversarial Ideology" in Michael Freeman, ed, *Law and Popular Culture* (Oxford University Press, 2005) at 606 [Adversarial Ideology]; Michael Asimow, "Popular Culture and the Adversary System" (2007) 40 Loyola LA L Rev 653 at 654–68 [Asimow]. For further discussion of the balance of these three factors, see text at note 70.

3 Asimow, *supra* note 2 at 657, citing a 1999 ABA survey in which only 30% of respondents were either extremely or very confident in the U. S. justice system, yet 80% agreed or strongly agreed to the statement "in spite of its problems the American justice system is still the best in the world."

4 Asimow, *supra* note 2 at 654, citing a survey in which only 14% of the public were extremely or very confident in lawyers and 42% were slightly or not at all confident in lawyers. In contrast, 32% were extremely or very confident in judges and only 22% had slight or no confidence in judges. Space limitations preclude further discussion of the reasons why Americans so strongly prefer the adversarial approach to justice, but the topic is pursued in the book chapter and article cited in note 2.

administrative law judges (ALJs), are indeed quite adversarial. However, I intend to argue that the world of administrative adjudication is much less adversarial and judicialized than would first appear.

Judicial and Institutional Approaches to Administrative Adjudication

There is a longtime controversy in American administrative law about the costs and benefits of judicial as opposed to institutional approaches to adjudication. The judicial and institutional approaches are competing ways to think about how an agency should organize its resources in order to make policy or exercise discretion through adjudication. There is a close relationship between the judicial approach and the adversarial model and between the institutional approach and the inquisitorial model. However, the two dichotomies are not entirely congruent.

Someone who favors the judicial model of administrative adjudication draws on the criminal and civil litigation models sketched above. The starting point is that agency adjudication should resemble criminal and civil trials as closely as possible, even when an agency is making policy or exercising discretion. Advocates of judicialized methods are mostly concerned with fairness to private parties, independence and neutrality of the presiding officer, and restricting off-the-record communications to decision-makers. Judicial model supporters are relatively indifferent to efficiency arguments and resist viewing adjudication as a species of policymaking. Thus agency adjudicatory procedures based upon the judicial model are likely to be much closer to the adversarial end of the spectrum than the inquisitorial end.

Advocates of the institutional approach to administrative adjudication do not take criminal or civil trials as their starting point, since such trials usually settle disputes having importance only to specific private parties. Administrative law, on the contrary, is concerned with implementing wide ranging statutory schemes, exercising broad discretion, and vindicating the public interest. While rulemaking may be the preferred modality for agency policymaking, case by case adjudication is often used for that purpose as well. In matters like individualized ratemaking, land use planning, or initial licensing, the agency must use individualized adjudication rather than rulemaking, even though its role is heavily discretionary, future oriented, and policy driven.

Advocates for the institutional approach argue that the entire staff of an agency should be viewed as part of a team working together to produce the best possible result for the public interest.[5] There is no place in the world of institutional

5 See, for example, Richard J Pierce, Jr, *Administrative Law Treatise*, 5th ed (Austin: Wolters Kluwer Law & Business, 2010) at 726. Pierce writes: "The role of a typical agency's staff is much greater than the role of the staff of a trial court or of an appellate court … [When the case reaches the agency head level] staff members may also present their analysis of the case to the agency heads, who are also usually free to consult any staff members except those who have participated in investigating or prosecuting in the

adjudication for restrictions on communications between agency staff and decision-makers or between outsiders and decision-makers. Private litigants should have ample opportunity to furnish inputs into the process, whether in writing or orally, but the process should be viewed as one designed to gather information and analysis from everyone who has something to contribute. Methods of trial (such as cross-examination of experts) may be highly inefficient when used for this purpose. Institutional advocates observe that an agency has many obligations aside from adjudicating specific cases and nearly always suffers from budgetary and staffing constraints. In short, an adjudicatory process based on the institutional approach is likely to be much closer to the inquisitorial end of the spectrum than the adversarial end.

Nevertheless, the judicial/institutional approach and the adversarial/inquisitorial models do not always function together. For example, the decisions of individual cases in the mass justice benefit distribution schemes described in the second half of this chapter do not utilize institutional methods and seldom involve policy-making or discretion, yet they use inquisitorial procedures. Agencies that adjudicate cases involving policy-making or discretion often use adversarial decision-making procedures, although these seem relatively inefficient.

Formal Administrative Hearings – APA and Non-APA

APAs are ubiquitous in U. S. state and federal administrative law.[6] Most of the provisions of the federal APA relate to adjudication (since rulemaking was much less important than adjudication as a policymaking format when the APA was adopted in 1946). The adjudication provisions of the APA tilt strongly in the direction of the judicial approach and the adversarial model. It describes only one form of adjudication, often referred to as "formal adjudication."

---

particular case ... The decision tends to be an amalgam of the views of the agency heads and the staff. The institutional decision often reaches a level that is higher than that attainable by the ablest of administrators or judges who are cut off from sources of expert advice ... The institutional mind has insights that are as profound as those of any individual and may be much more comprehensive, for the appropriate specialists collaborate by considering the judgment of each other, each contributing his or her own particular knowledge and skills." Similarly, see Ralph F Fuchs, "The Hearing Officer Problem – Symptom and Symbol" (1955) 40 Cornell L Q 281 at 289–90.

6 The Federal Administrative Procedure Act was enacted in 1946 and has achieved almost quasi-constitutional status. 5 U.S.C. §551 et. seq. (hereinafter cited as "APA" and without the prefatory 5 U.S.C.) While the APAs of the various states differ, they mostly resemble the federal APA. The National Commissioners on Uniform State Laws recently recommended that the states consider adoption of a new Model State APA of 2010, available at http://www.uniformlaws.org/shared/docs/state%20administrative%20procedure/msapa_final_10.pdf.

Formal hearings under the APA are judicialized and adversarial

An APA formal hearing must be conducted by an Administrative Law Judge (ALJ).[7] ALJs work for the agencies for which they conduct hearings (I refer to this arrangement as "captive ALJs"). Agencies have very little choice in hiring ALJs, since the hiring process is conducted by a separate agency, the Office of Personnel Management, or OPM. OPM does not consider experience in the regulatory scheme administered by the agency but is required to give preference to military veterans. ALJs cannot be assigned to tasks other than judging, are highly compensated, are assigned to cases in rotation, are protected from discharge without cause, and (along with federal employees) are exempt from performance evaluations. Thus ALJs enjoy substantial *de jure* and *de facto* independence from the agencies for which they decide cases.

In APA formal hearings, lawyers (private and staff) tend to control the framing of the issues. Each side offers testimony from its own witnesses and cross-examines the opponent's witnesses.[8] The record is exclusive, meaning that decision-maker is confined to the written record in finding the facts.[9] *Ex parte* contacts with outsiders are forbidden.

State APAs generally follow the federal model on these points. In more than half of the states, ALJs are employed by a central panel, rather than by the agency responsible for the decision. If anything, central panel ALJs are more independent in their outlook than captive-ALJs.

Departures from the default rule of formal agency hearings

However, this account of APA adjudication is radically incomplete. ALJs usually render only proposed decisions; the agency heads (who are responsible for investigation, prosecution, and policy-making) make the final decisions.[10] This arrangement, of course, departs sharply from the judicial approach. Agency heads often receive *ex parte* advice from agency staff members (other than staff members who have played an adversarial role in the particular case). On judicial review, the courts review the decision of the agency heads, not those of the ALJ.

Even in formal hearings, the APA permits substantial deviations from the judicial method. The rules of evidence are not followed.[11] In addition, cross-examination

---

7 There are around 1500 federal ALJs. See generally American Bar Association, *A Guide to Federal Agency Adjudication*, ch. 10, 2nd ed (2012); Russell L Weaver & Linda D Jellum, "Neither Fish Nor Fowl: Administrative Judges in the Modern Administrative State" (2010) 28 Windsor Y B Access Justice 243.

8 The APA guarantees that a party can present its "case or defense by oral or documentary evidence, to submit rebuttal evidence, and to conduct such cross-examination as may be required for a full and true disclosure of the facts." APA, *supra* note 6, § 556(d).

9 *Ibid*, § 556(e). Official notice of non-controversial facts is permitted but the opposing side must have a rebuttal opportunity.

10 *Ibid.*

11 *Ibid*, § 556(d).

is not an absolute right but only if "required for a full and true disclosure of the facts." In certain cases (including claims for benefits and initial licensing), the agency may "when a party will not be prejudiced thereby, adopt procedures for the submission of all or part of the evidence in written form."[12] Separation of functions is not required in determining applications for initial licenses[13] or to proceedings involving the validity or application of rates, facilities, or practices of public utilities or carriers.[14] The members of the agency head can engage personally in investigation and prosecutorial activities, then decide the case, and can engage in ex parte consultations with staff who have not been involved in the prosecution or investigation of the particular case.[15] All of these features seem institutional rather than judicial.

Adjudication outside the APA

The APA does not apply to a huge swatch of cases decided by federal government agencies.[16] In the world of non-APA federal adjudication, it is possible to divide the proceedings between relatively formal and relatively informal. Numerous agencies provide hearings that are just about as formal as those provided under the APA, except that the agency does not use ALJs. There about twice as many non-ALJ federal presiding officers as there are federal ALJs. Agencies that provide adversarial hearings outside the APA include those engaged in adjudication of disputes concerning immigration and deportation, government contracts, civil penalties of various kinds, federal personnel, and many other areas.[17]

---

12 APA, *supra* note 6. However, in determining claims for money or benefits or applications for initial licenses, "an agency may, when a party will not be prejudiced thereby, adopt procedures for the submission of all or part of the evidence in written form." *Ibid.* See *Citizens Awareness Network v United States*, 391 F.3d 338, 354–54 (1st Cir. 2004). The *Citizens Awareness* case upheld procedural rules adopted by the Nuclear Regulatory Commission that dispensed with full rights of cross-examination in nuclear reactor licensing cases. These cases are often quite contentious and involve participation by interveners opposed to granting the licenses. Under the new rules, a party seeking to cross-examine a witness must first seek permission from the hearing officer and must establish that cross is "necessary to ensure the development of an adequate record for decision."

13 *Ibid.*

14 *Ibid*, § 554(d)(B).

15 *Ibid.* See Michael Asimow, "When the Curtain Falls: Separation of Functions in the Federal Administrative Agencies" (1981) 81 Colum L Rev 759 at 765–70.

16 The APA applies only to adjudication "required by statute to be determined on the record after opportunity for an agency hearing ..." APA, *ibid*, § 554(a). Numerous relatively formal hearing schemes do not meet that standard and thus fall outside §554(a). See Michael Asimow, "The Spreading Umbrella: Extending the APA's Adjudication Provisions to All Evidentiary Hearings Required by Statute" (2004) 56 Admin L Rev 1003 at 1004.

17 There are about 83 case-types that fall into the category of non-APA formal adjudication. See Asimow, *ibid* at 1005–08.

There remains a vast universe of non-APA informal agency adjudication. An agency engaged in informal adjudication can structure its decision-making process to suit itself.[18] Informal adjudication is often much closer to the inquisitorial end of the spectrum than the adversarial. Verkuil studied 43 informal adjudication programs in four large cabinet-level agencies to ascertain whether these programs were adversarial or inquisitorial.[19] In each case, he looked for ten indicia of adversarial procedure and counted how many of them were present. Most of the programs had less than half of the adversarial ingredients.[20] In short, the world of federal administrative adjudication is thoroughly mixed between procedures that employ inquisitorial and adversarial methods.

Inquisitorial Methods and Mass Justice – Social Security and Veterans' Benefits

This section considers the decisional process used by the Social Security Administration and Veterans Administration in resolving benefit disputes. The administrative process in these systems is much closer to the inquisitorial end of the scale than the adversarial end. The number of cases resolved by these two immense systems dwarfs the output of agencies that conduct the remainder of federal administrative adjudication.

Social Security Disability

The Social Security disability program is said to be the largest system of adjudication in the western world.[21] In December, 2009, about 10.1 million people were receiving benefits under this system and the annual payments exceeded $100 billion.[22] A related program, Supplemental Security Income (SSI), provides additional payments for disabled persons who meet poverty standards.

---

18 In some cases, the requirement of procedural due process in the 5th and 14th amendments to the U.S. constitution imposes constraints on the decisional process, but due process seldom requires adversarial procedures. Normally it requires only "some kind of hearing" conducted by an impartial adjudicator. *Goss v Lopez*, 419 US 565 (1975).

19 Paul R Verkuil, "A Study of Informal Adjudication Procedures" (1975) 43 U Chi L Rev 739 at 757–79.

20 Courts may not require adversarial procedures such as formal hearings, even if such procedures would facilitate judicial review. *Pension Benefit Guarantee Corp. v LTV Corp.*, 496 U.S. 633 (1990).

21 Jerry L Mashaw, *Bureaucratic Justice* (New Haven: Yale University Press, 1983) at 18.

22 Annual Statistical Report on the Social Security Disability Insurance Program (2009), tables 1, 13, online: http://www.ssa.gov/policy/docs/statcomps/di_asr [Annual Statistical Report].

To qualify for disability benefits, a claimant must be totally and permanently disabled, meaning unable to engage in any gainful activity.[23] This standard calls for a great deal of difficult medical and vocational decision-making. There are four stages in determining eligibility: initial decision, reconsideration, ALJ hearing, and Appeals Council.[24] The initial decision is made by a state-level agency called Disability Determination Services (DDS). In 2008, DDS processed 2,327,000 claims and granted about 56%.[25] A claimant rejected at the DDS level can seek reconsideration by a Federal Reviewing Official (FRO), a staff attorney who must develop the file by obtaining all available evidence.[26] The FRO issues a written decision but does not conduct a hearing. About 12.2% of claims were successful at the FRO level in 2009.

A claimant rejected at the FRO level can request an APA hearing before an ALJ. In 2009, 1057 ALJs worked for Social Security (about 75% of the total number of ALJs on the federal payroll).[27] ALJs received 662,851 new cases in 2009 and had 722,822 pending at year end.[28] About 70% of claimants are represented by attorneys and an additional 18% are assisted by lay representatives.[29]

The final step is an appeal to the Appeals Council.[30] The Appeals Council consists of about 28 judges who are not ALJs. If the appeal fails, the claimant can seek judicial review in a federal district court. Under a set of procedural reforms introduced in 2007, SSA plans to phase out the Appeals Council in favor of a new body called the Decision Review board (DRB) which will review selected ALJ decisions.[31] The DRB is a quality control and management tool, not an appellate remedy for claimants.

The adjudicatory system in Social Security disability cases is deeply troubled. There are lengthy delays in the decision-making process, during which disabled

23 42 U.S.C. §423(d)(1)(A).

24 See Frank S Bloch et al, "Developing a Full and Fair Evidentiary Record in a Nonadversary Setting: Two Proposals for Improving Social Security Disability Adjudications" (2003) 25 Cardozo L Rev 18–28 (describing process) [Bloch et al].

25 Annual Statistical Report, *supra* note 22, Table 59.

26 71 Fed. Reg. 16424, 16432–34 (2007). Social Security recently created the FRO procedure to provide a non-adversarial representative to develop the record prior to the ALJ hearing. See Frank S Bloch, "Representation and Advocacy at Non-Adversary Hearings: The Need for Non-Adversary Representatives at Social Security Disability Hearings" (1981) 59 Wash U L Q 349 at 399–407.

27 Social Security Administration, Key Workload Indicators, Table 2/F8, online: http://www.ssa.gov/policy/docs/statcomps/supplement/2010/2f8-2f11.html [Key Workload Indicators].

28 *Ibid*, Table 2F.9. The average ALJ disposed of 49 cases per month and had 575 cases pending.

29 Bloch et al, *supra* note 24 at 6.

30 The Appeals Council received 106,965 cases in 2009 and had a backlog of 80,040 at the end of the year. Key Workload Indicators, *supra* note 27, Table 2F.11.

31 71 Fed. Reg. 16424, 16437–40 (2007).

and often povertystricken claimants must wait, often for years, to start receiving the benefits to which they are entitled. This backlog will grow worse as the number of claims increases because of retirement of baby boomers and for other reasons.[32] Social Security has experienced great difficulty in managing its ALJ corps. There are serious problems of consistency of decisions as well as productivity.

Many aspects of this immense adjudicatory system are inquisitorial in nature.[33] SSA has an obligation to develop the record once a claimant supplies basic information. It will obtain medical records from the claimant's identified sources and pay for the records it requests. It frequently orders (and pays for) additional medical examinations. The record remains open during the entire administrative process, right through the Appeals Council. Thus a claimant can add additional materials to the file at each of the four administrative stages.[34] The open record approach seems inquisitorial, since an inquisitorial system treats the hearing as phase of the investigation (rather than being sharply separated from the investigation). The ALJ has an affirmative responsibility for developing the record by calling additional witnesses or securing medical reports when the claimant fails to do so. This obligation to assist the claimant applies even if the claimant was represented by a lawyer or a lay advocate.[35]

The most important inquisitorial element in the Social Security adjudicatory scheme is that ALJs are responsible for developing the case both for and against the claimant, then deciding the case. The government is never represented. The Supreme Court upheld this inquisitorial decision-making method under due process in *Richardson v Perales*:

> Neither are we persuaded by the advocate-judge-multiple-hat suggestion. It assumes too much and would bring down too many procedures designed, and working well, for a governmental structure of great and growing complexity. The social security hearing examiner, furthermore, does not act as counsel. He acts as an examiner charged with developing the facts.[36]

---

32 See Bloch et al, *supra* note 24 at 1, 5.

33 See generally Jon C Dubin, "Torquemada Meets Kafka: The Misapplication of the Issue Exhaustion Doctrine to Inquisitorial Administrative Proceedings" (1997) 97 Colum L Rev 1289 at 1300–06.

34 See Bloch et al, *supra* note 24, at 28–36, 59–62. Under reforms introduced in 2007, the claimant must submit evidence no later than 5 business days before the hearing except in unusual circumstances. See 71 Fed. Reg. 16424, 16434–37 (2007).

35 See, for example, *Smolen v Chater*, 80 F.3d 1273, 1288 (9th Cir. 1996).

36 *Richardson v Perales* 402 U.S. 389, 410, 91 S. Ct. 1420, 1432 (1971). From 1982–87, SSA experimented with a system in which SSA was represented in ALJ hearings if the claimant also had representation. The experiment was abandoned after a dubious court decision determined that it violated due process. *Salling v Bowen*, 641 F. Supp. 1046 (W.D. Va. 1986). See Bloch et al, *supra* note 24 at 42–52.

Subsequently, in *Sims v Apfel*,[37] the Supreme Court excused a claimant's failure to exhaust issues before the Appeals Council because of the inquisitorial nature of Social Security hearings. The Court remarked:

> The differences between courts and agencies are nowhere more pronounced than in Social Security proceedings. Although many agency systems of adjudication are based to a significant extent on the judicial model of decision-making … the SSA is perhaps the best example of an agency that is not … The most important of the SSA's modifications of the judicial model is the replacement of normal adversary procedure by … the "investigatory model" … Social Security proceedings are inquisitorial rather than adversarial. It is the ALJ's duty to investigate the facts and develop the arguments both for and against granting benefits … and the [Appeals] Council's review is similarly broad. The Commissioner has no representative before the ALJ to oppose the claim for benefits, and we have found no indication that he opposes claimants before the Council … The Council, not the claimant, has primary responsibility for identifying and developing the issues …[38]

Veterans claims

The sluggish system of Veterans Administration (VA) claims adjudication

The Veterans Administration (VA) decides a vast number of benefit claims. As described in greater detail below,[39] the adjudicatory process begins at a VA regional office (RO) and ends with a decision by the Board of Veterans Appeals (BVA). The caseload is rising steadily because of the aging of Vietnam veterans and changes in evaluation of certain claims, such as Agent Orange injuries or post-traumatic stress disorder (PTSD). In the future, the Iraq and Afghanistan wars will vastly expand the number of claims that the benefit system must resolve. The number of new claims currently exceeds one million per year, but this figure understates the caseload since each "claim" usually seeks several different benefits.[40] There is a crushing backlog of unresolved claims.[41] Nearly everyone is unhappy with the

37 530 U.S. 103 (2000).

38 *Ibid* at 110–12 (citations and internal quotation marks omitted).

39 See text at notes 57–65.

40 See James D Ridgway, "Why So Many Remands? A Comparative Analysis of Appellate Review by the United States Court of Appeals for Veterans Claims" (2009) 1 Vet L Rev 113 at 145–50 [Why So Many Remands]. Each unrelated benefit in a claim is referred to as an "issue." Ridgway observes that 22% of disability claims had at least eight issues. *Ibid* at 146. He estimates that the number of different benefits sought is at least double and probably more than triple the number of claims that VA receives each year.

41 The backlog of unresolved claims is currently around one million and is expected to increase to 2.6 million by 2015. Michael Serota & Michelle Singer, "Veterans Injustice: Unconstitutional Delay at the Department of Veterans Affairs" (2011) 90 Nebr L Rev

sluggish process of veterans' claims processing and adjudication, but there is no consensus on how the system should be reformed.[42] Recently, the Court of Appeals for the Ninth Circuit held that delays in the adjudication of veterans' claims violated the constitutional norm of due process and remanded the case to the trial court to remedy the situation.[43] This far reaching decision harshly criticized the VA decision-making process; it triggered a sharp dissent and will probably be reviewed by the U. S. Supreme Court.

Claims for service-connected disability (by far the most common claims) require complex medical judgments. The claimant must suffer from a current disability that is connected to a disease or injury received during service (the "nexus" requirement). VA must assign a rating (from 10% to 100%) to the

388. The VA takes an average of around 183 days to process a claim at the regional office level. It takes somewhere between three to four and one half additional years to process a claim through the entire administrative process. See James D Ridgway, "The Veterans' Judicial Review Act Twenty Years Later" (2010) 66 NYU Ann Survey of Amer Law 251 [Ridgway, Twenty Years Later]. These are average figures and many claims (particularly those involving PTSD) take much longer to resolve.

42 The fundamental question is whether to modify and improve the veterans' claims system incrementally or scrap it entirely. For a summary of such proposals, see Paul R Verkuil & Jeffrey S Lubbers, "Alternative Approaches to Judicial Review of Social Security Disability Cases" (2003) 55 Admin L Rev 731 at 770–71. Linda Bilmes believes that the VA claims process should be abandoned in favor of one modeled on the IRS – grant all applications and conduct audits to discover errors. Testimony to the House of Representatives Veterans Affairs Committee (March 13, 2007), online: http://www.hks.harvard.edu/fs/lbilmes/CV/VETERANS%20%20Bilmes%202012%20(6).pdf. Others advocate a merger of the VA process with Social Security or the use of ALJs in lieu of the BVA. James T O'Reilly, "Burying Caesar: Replacement of the Veterans Appeals Process Is Needed to Provide Fairness to Claimants" (2001) 53 Admin L Rev 223 (advocating merger of VA claims system with Social Security); William T Fox, "Deconstructing and Reconstructing the Veterans Benefits System" (2003) 18 Kan J Law & Pub Pol 339. But see Rory E Riley, "The Importance of Preserving the Pro-Claimant Policy Underlying the Veterans' Benefits Scheme" (2010) 2 Vet L Rev 77 at 106–14. Riley argues that replacing the system would abandon the pro-veteran bias built into the existing system; in addition, the transition would be costly and would not solve the underlying problems of unmanageable caseload. Reilly argues for modifications such as better incentives and better use of electronic instead of paper-based systems. The VA Claims Processing Task Force recommended abolition of remands by the BVA. Report to the Secretary of Veterans Affairs 34–37 (2001).

43 Recently, the Court of Appeals for the Ninth Circuit held that delays in the adjudication of veterans' claims violated the constitutional norm of due process and remanded the case to the trial court to remedy the situation, but that decision was later set aside on jurisdictional grounds by a Ninth Circuit en banc decision. *Veterans for Common Sense v Shinseki*, 678 F.3d 1013 (9th Cir. 2012), vacating the earlier panel decision reported at 644 F.3d 845 (9th Cir. 2011).

disability.[44] It is estimated that around 88% of claims for disability compensation are granted, at least in part.[45]

The VA claims process is inquisitorial and paternalistic

The adjudicatory process for resolving VA claim disputes is uniquely inquisitorial and paternalistic.[46] There is no statute of limitations on making a claim (which is consistent with the idea that the hearing in an inquisitorial process is simply a phase of an ongoing investigation). The RO (which is responsible for the initial decision on a benefits claim) is subject to elaborate requirements of notice. It must notify claimant of any information or evidence that is necessary to substantiate the claim and furnish all necessary assistance to the claimant in obtaining evidence and obtaining medical opinions.[47] Like the Social Security rule that an ALJ must assist a claimant,[48] the VA's obligation to assist the claimant seems more consistent with inquisitorial than adversarial adjudication. An inquisitorial system is intended to find out the truth rather than to serve as the vehicle for combat between the two sides.[49]

The various procedural rules of VA claims practice are heavily paternalistic and reflect inquisitorial rather than adversarial process. No government official appears at RO or BVA hearings to oppose the granting of benefits. Decision-makers must fully develop any possible claims that arise from documents or testimony even if the claimant has not pressed them. At all levels, the VA must give the veteran

44 Over 4,000,000 veterans and survivors were receiving financial benefits at the end of fiscal year 2010, 87% of which related to service-connected disabilities. See the 2010 Annual Benefits Report of the Veterans Benefits Administration, online: http://www.vba.va.gov/REPORTS/abr/2010_abr.pdf.

45 Ridgway, Twenty Years Later, *supra* note 41 at 116.

46 Historically, veterans' benefits have been considered gratuities rather than entitlements, based on the nation's moral obligation toward its veterans. The system was based on discretion rather than rights and the procedures employed were highly informal and stacked in the claimant's favor. See Richard E Levy, "Of Two Minds: Charitable and Social Insurance Models in the Veterans Benefit System" (2003) 13 Kansas J L & Pub Pol 303 at 304–15 (distinguishing the paternalistic or charitable model from the social insurance model applicable to more modern benefit programs) [Levy].

47 See 38 U.S.C.§§5102(b) and 5103(a) (imposing obligations to notify claimant of any information needed to complete the application or to substantiate the claim); §5103A (imposing on the VA an obligation to exercise reasonable efforts to assist the claimant in obtaining evidence and records and in providing medical examinations and opinions). See *Shinseki v Sanders*, 566 U.S. 396 (2009) (simplifying rules of prejudicial error when VA fails to give notice required by regulations).

48 See text at note 35.

49 The idea that an agency should render assistance to an unrepresented litigant has developed as an element of an enabling or proactive approach to administrative justice in the UK and Canadian administrative justice systems. See the chapters by Thomas and by Green and Sossin in this volume.

the benefit of the doubt if the positive and negative evidence is approximately balanced.[50] This benefit-of-the-doubt rule is highly paternalistic. A veteran may "reopen" a rejected application by presenting "new and material evidence" and some cases are reopened on multiple occasions. The ability to reopen the case is consistent with an inquisitorial approach to adjudication, since the entire process is visualized as a continuing investigation.

VA practice is delawyered. Veterans are usually accompanied at both the RO and BVA levels by lay representatives supplied free by a veteran service organization (VSO) such as the American Legion. Veterans are seldom represented by lawyers because statutes prohibit compensation of lawyers before the judicial review stage.[51]

The VA's inquisitorial system of fact determination and decision-making is rooted in the long and convoluted history of veterans' benefits.[52] These benefits were regarded as gratuities, not entitlements, and the bureaucratic structure that delivered the benefits was wholly paternalistic. In a paternalistic system, there is no place for lawyers or for adversarial procedures like administrative trials. Today, veterans' benefits have become an entitlement rather than a gratuity, but the older paternalistic decision-making process has survived.

Historically, there was no judicial review of VA claims decisions. In 1988, under the Veterans' Judicial Review Act (VJRA),[53] an adversarial system of judicial review in the Court of Appeals for Veterans Claims (CAVC) was superimposed on the VA's inquisitorial fact finding system.[54] CAVC decisions frequently change the

---

50 38 U.S.C. §5107(b).

51 In 2009, 81% of claimants were represented by VSO lay representatives, plus 2% by other lay representatives. Attorneys represented 8% of claimants. 9% had no representation. See The 2009 BVA Annual Report at 21, online: http://www.bva.va.gov/docs/Chairmans_Annual_Rpts/BVA2009AR.pdf [BVA Annual Report]. The ban on compensation of attorneys was upheld by the Supreme Court in *Walters v National Ass'n of Radiation Survivors*, 473 U.S. 305 (1985). The Court believed that the presence of attorneys would be detrimental to the paternalistic and inquisitorial VA claims adjudication system.

52 For a detailed account of the history of veterans' benefits, see James D Ridgway, "The Splendid Isolation Revisited: Lessons from the History of Veterans Benefits Before Judicial Review" (2011) 3 Vet L Rev 135.

53 Pub. L. 100–687, 102 Stat. 4105 (1988) See generally Ridgway, Twenty Years Later, *supra* note 41 at 101.

54 Even the CAVC process has paternalistic elements. By statute a claimant must file an appeal with CAVC within 120 days after mailing of the BVA's decision. This deadline is not "jurisdictional", so it is subject to extension based on equitable considerations. The paternalistic nature of VA benefits was an important factor in the Supreme Court's decision on this point. "What is most telling [of Congress' intent in imposing the 120-day rule] are the singular characteristics of the review scheme that Congress created for the adjudication of veterans' benefit claims. The solicitude of Congress for veterans is of long standing … And that solicitude is plainly reflected in the VJRA, as well as in subsequent laws that place a thumb on the scale in the veteran's favor in the course of administrative and judicial

procedural law of benefit claims, always to increase protection of veterans, not to lessen it (since only veterans, not the VA, can appeal to the CAVC).[55] The addition of judicial review to an informal, inquisitorial system has produced a large number of remands from the CAVC to the VA because of failure to comply with notice requirements or incomplete or inadequate documentation in the record.[56]

The VA claims process

A more detailed account of the VA's adjudicatory system runs as follows. A claim is processed by various teams at the RO, but the decision is the responsibility of a single lay adjudicator (referred to herein as a "ratings specialist").[57] The file includes the detailed medical opinions submitted by the claimant (such as reports of personal physicians) and by the VA medical staff as well as by independent physicians consulted by the VA.

Claimants dissatisfied with the RO decision file a Notice of Disagreement (NOD). The claimant can obtain a review of the case by a Decision Review Officer (DRO), a senior RO adjudicator who has not previously been involved in investigation of the case.[58] The DRO may seek additional evidence. At the veterans' request, the DRO will provide an informal hearing. If the claimant remains dissatisfied with the RO decision after DRO review, the RO prepares a statement of the case (SOC) which contains detailed findings and an explanation of the decision. Within 60 days from the mailing of the SOC, the veteran must file Form VA-9 to perfect the right of appeal to the BVA.

The BVA's decision is based primarily on the written record.[59] Thus it is an appellate process rather than an initial decision. However, claimants frequently seek to introduce new evidence at the BVA level. If the claimant waives remand to the RO to evaluate the new evidence, the BVA judge considers this evidence and decides the case accordingly.[60] BVA has no organized written record from which to decide the case, only a disorganized case file that may run to hundreds or

review of VA decisions ..." *Henderson v Shinseki*, 131 S. Ct. 1197, 1199 (2011) (internal citations and quotation marks deleted). *Henderson* pointed out that the same rule applies to the inquisitorial Social Security disability system – the deadline for obtaining review of SSA benefits decisions in district court is not jurisdictional.

55 Ridgway, Twenty Years Later, *supra* note 41 at 107.

56 See Why So Many Remands, *supra* note 40, which analyzes the problem of CAVC remands in depth.

57 38 CFR §3.103(c)(1).

58 38 C.F.R. §3.2600.

59 38 U.S.C. §7104(a); 38 C.F.R. §19.4.

60 38 C.F.R. §§19.9(b)(3), 20.1304(c) (new evidence can be introduced before BVA if appellant waives the right to have it considered by the RO or if the Board believes that the new evidence will enable it to award benefits). See Ridgway, Twenty Years Later, *supra* note 41, at 125–27. BVA Judge John Crowley told the author that the BVA usually considers the new evidence and that claimants usually waive their right to remand. Telephone conversation, Feb. 25, 2011.

thousands of pages.[61] It is required to consider and decide every possible issue or claim raised by the record.[62]

The BVA has about 60 Veterans Law Judges and about 300 staff counsel.[63] It decides about 48,000 cases per year (about 800 for each judge). BVA hearings are quite informal and are conducted by single Board members either in person or by video-conference.[64] Requesting a hearing considerably prolongs the BVA decisional process, so many claimants waive the hearing.

In 2009, a stunning 37% of BVA cases were decided by remanding the case to the RO (usually because of efforts to introduce new evidence or because of insufficient medical opinions or errors by the RO in giving proper notice or assisting the veteran). Reconsideration of remanded cases is a major contributor to the RO's backlog and delays. Of the remainder, 24% of the appeals were allowed and 36% were denied.[65] Decisions are written by staff members, based on the transcript of the personal hearing, and signed by the member responsible for the case.

Judicial review made the VA process more adversarial

Cases decided by the CAVC after enactment of VJRA in 1988 made the VA process more adversarial. For example, prior to 1988, decisions at the RO level were made by a panel consisting of a physician, a legal specialist, and an occupational specialist. The panel based its decisions on its own expertise or its own research and did not consider itself limited to evaluating the medical data in the files. A claimant was not required to submit medical opinions or other evidence since the panel was able to make its own judgments.

In *Colvin v Derwinski*,[66] the CAVC required RO and BVA decision-makers to base their decision exclusively on the medical evidence in the file or on textbooks, rather than on their own medical judgment. *Colvin* was driven by the court's need

61 The VA is in the process of converting its paper-based system to an electronic data system, but the conversion process has been troubled. Conversion is very costly and far from completed. Ridgway, Twenty Years Later, *supra* note 41 at 129–31.

62 See Why So Many Remands, *supra* note 40 at 136–38.

63 BVA judges have far less independence than ALJs. See Levy, *supra* note 46 at 319–20 (questioning the procedures for appointment and removal of BVA judges).

64 See the BVA's pamphlet "How Do I Appeal?", online: http://www.bva.va.gov/docs/Pamphlets/010202A.pdf. According to the pamphlet, "Personal hearings with a Board Member are informal. They are not like the courtroom hearings you see on TV or in trials … You will be given a chance to make sure any information you think is important is heard by the Board Member … If you have a representative [usually a lay advocate from a VSO] the representative will ask you questions to help you explain your claim. If not, the Board Member will ask you to tell him or her about your claim … You can add evidence to your claim at the hearing … the Board Member will be holding as many as nine other hearings that day!"

65 BVA Annual Report, *supra* note 51 at 21. About 3% were categorized as "other" dispositions.

66 *Colvin v Derwinski*, 1 Vet. App. 171, 175 (CAVC 1991). *Colvin* was overruled on another ground by *Hodge v West*, 155 F.3d 1356 (Fed. Cir. 1999).

to conduct on-the-record review of the VA's decision. As a result, claimants are now required to submit elaborate and complete medical opinions to substantiate their claims. The expert panel was replaced by the lay ratings specialist. Similarly, the BVA judges cannot make decisions based on their own expertise but must confine their decisions to the material in the record. These changes vastly increased the formality of VA decision-making and substantially contributed to VA backlogs.[67]

Prior to 1988, BVA opinions were brief and non-technical, so they could be easily understood by lay people such as the claimant. As a result of the 1988 reforms, BVA's decisions must be lengthy and detailed, so that they can withstand on-the-record judicial review (even though only a tiny percentage of BVA decisions are actually appealed to CAVC). Medical conclusions must be thoroughly explained.[68] In the past, BVA decisions did not comment adversely on the credibility of the claimant or of various witnesses; now the decisions must evaluate the credibility of each witness, including the claimant and his family. In the opinion of the former Chairman of the BVA, Charles Cragin, the net effect of implanting an adversarial judicial review process on top of an inquisitorial, informal and paternalistic claims process, has been quite negative. He believes that it is one of the most important causes of the delays and backlogs in the existing system.[69]

Evaluating Inquisitorial Methods in Mass Justice Adjudication

Inquisitorial System is Appropriate in Many Benefit Schemes

The fundamental point about Social Security and veterans' benefits is that the government's responsibility is not to fight every claim but to make sure that

67 Charles L Cragin, "The Impact of Judicial Review on the Department of Veterans Affairs' Claims Adjudication Process: The Changing Role of the Board of Veterans' Appeals" (1994) 46 Maine L Rev 23 [Cragin].

68 Why So Many Remands, *supra* note 40 at 136–37; Ridgway, Twenty Years Later, *supra* note 41 at 123–25.

69 "Because of the increasing complexity and rapidly evolving state of the law, BVA decisions are lengthier, more complex, and require more time to prepare than ever before. As a consequence, speedy justice in VA claims adjudication has become an elusive target. No decision of the court [CAVC] has yet resulted in an improvement in decision productivity or timeliness anywhere in the entire VA adjudication system. Many decisions have had the exact opposite result." Cragin, *supra* note 67 at 31. Similarly, Ridgway says: "Judicial review has fundamentally reinvented the process in a way that requires many more steps to complete and that demands VA show each step was completed properly ... Increased complexity, such as these new requirements, has become a major issue for the adjudication system ..." Ridgway, Twenty Years Later, *supra* note 41 at 126–27. BVA judge John Crowley told the author that there was virtually no backlog in deciding veterans' claims cases before the 1988 reforms, whereas today there is a crushing backlog. Phone conversation of February 25, 2011.

all claimants receive the benefits for which they are eligible. The programs are entitlements and all approved claims must be paid without regard to budgetary ceilings. For that reason, both programs are deliberately structured to aid and assist claimants, not to make the process more difficult for them. In such systems, inquisitorial methods of dispute resolution seem more appropriate than adversarial combat. In contrast, other federal benefit programs (such as programs providing benefits for victims of black lung disease or for injured longshore workers) involve a clash between an employee and a private employer. Adversarial methods may be more appropriate in these adjudicatory systems.

Balancing Efficiency, Accuracy, and Acceptability

A conventional methodology for evaluation of administrative systems is to balance efficiency, accuracy, and acceptability to participants.[70] Obviously, these criteria point in conflicting directions. Making the process more efficient by speeding it up, for example, may well impair the ability to make accurate determinations and may make the system less acceptable.

In mass justice systems, efficiency is of paramount importance. When literally millions of complex claims must be adjudicated, the procedures should be as cheap as possible to the claimant and to the government and decisions should be rendered as quickly as possible. Inquisitorial processes, involving informal conferences between judges and claimants, can be accomplished quickly and inexpensively. BVA judges often schedule nine hearings a day and usually can get through their docket.[71]

Both the Social Security and VA claims processes are plagued by heavy caseloads and huge backlogs. They cannot afford to slow down for lengthy formal hearings and adversarial combat. Moreover, the extra costs of adding a government representative to argue against the claimant in VA and Social Security hearings would be staggering. These mass justice systems are already laboring under severe personnel shortages and are plagued by delays and backlogs. Indeed, the imposition of an adversarial judicial review system atop the inquisitorial VA system appears to have made the process of claims adjudication slower and less efficient.[72]

Accuracy means determining the correct answer to disputed questions of fact, such as deciding past events or determining a claimant's medical condition. In disability-based benefit systems, most of the evidence comes in the form of medical opinions, but such opinions often conflict. Someone must resolve the conflict. Credibility of the claimant is also important, particularly in cases involving complaints like back pain or psychological disabilities like PTSD.

---

70 See Asimow, Adversarial Ideology, *supra* note 2 at 609–21 for a more detailed balancing of these three factors as between adversarial and inquisitorial approaches to criminal jury trials.

71 Telephone conference with BVA Judge John Crowley, Feb. 25, 2011.

72 See text at notes 66–69.

Many in America believe that adversarial combat (particularly cross-examination) is the best way to reveal the truth. However, for the adversarial system to work, there must be a rough equality between the contending sides in terms of lawyer skills and resources. Often, however, this kind of equality is conspicuous by its absence. One side frequently has more experienced lawyers and much greater financial resources.

In mass justice systems, these disparities are quite significant. Many claimants cannot afford a lawyer or none is available. Social Security claimants may wish to proceed without a lawyer to avoid paying a large contingent fee. Claimants in either system may have a lay representative or represent themselves. They would be at a huge disadvantage if they were pitted against a government lawyer. Thus there are distributional advantages to the inquisitorial approach because the judge can take responsibility for development of the record when a claimant is unrepresented or poorly represented.

Even apart from differences in lawyer skills and resources, few attorneys believe that adversarial combat is an effective way to determine the truth about past events or medical conditions.[73] Lawyers tend to scoff at "the truth" and stress that it is unknowable if such a thing even exists. Finding out and revealing the truth is not their job. Instead, lawyers view the adversarial system as a vehicle to deliver a desired result for a client. Often, that objective requires an attorney to confuse the issues or obscure the truth. In my opinion, a process managed by a competent judge who is responsible for and dedicated to finding the truth seems more likely to deliver accurate results than lawyerly combat.

The third factor in the equation is acceptability of the process to the parties. This factor is intended to be a surrogate for fairness, but acceptability can be measured whereas fairness remains in the eye of the beholder. The conventional wisdom, based on a famous series of experiments by Thibaut and Walker,[74] is that people prefer an adversarial system in which they were represented by their own attorney to an inquisitorial system in which they had no attorney and the proceedings were conducted by a judge. This held true whether the respondent won or lost the case. I do not question the fundamental insight of Thibaut and Walker and many subsequent studies that procedural justice matters greatly. People are deeply concerned that decision-makers seem neutral, unbiased and honest as well as fair, polite and respectful.[75]

However, I do not believe that the Thibaut–Walker findings are easily translated to the administrative process, particularly to mass justice situations. The Social

73 See Jula Hughes, "Home Truths About the Truth Commission Processes – How Victim-Centred Truth and Perpetrator-Focused Adversarial Processes Mutually Challenge Assumptions of Justice and Truth" in this volume.

74 John W Thibaut & Laurens Walker, *Procedural Justice: A Psychological Analysis* (Hillsdale, NJ: L. Erlbaum Associates, 1975), ch. 8 [Thibaut & Walker].

75 See Tom Tyler, *Why People Obey the Law* (New Haven: Yale University Press, 1990), ch. 11.

Security and VA claims processes are inquisitorial, but they are quite different from the Thibaut–Walker experiments. Claimants have the right to be (and usually are) represented by their own advocates – either lawyers or lay representative which was not the case in Thibaut and Walker's experiments. Indeed, a follow-up study by Thibaut and Walker involved a system in which each side could choose its own representative; the variable was whether the judge or the lawyers asked the questions.[76] Here the subjects were equally satisfied with both approaches. This result suggests that an inquisitorial system controlled by the judge is acceptable to litigants provided they can have their own advocate who will articulate their point of view.

Moreover, in real life, people have to pay their lawyers and have a lot at stake. In the Thibaut–Walker experiments, the subjects were students who had nothing at stake; they did not have to pay their lawyers or wait years for a result. The students did not have to contend with depositions or harsh adversarial trials at which they would be cross-examined by their opponent's lawyer. I believe that most normal people (lawyers excepted) are terrified by adversarial process and find an informal inquisitorial proceeding more comfortable. Confronted with these rather unpleasant realities of adversarial litigation, it may be that most people would prefer inquisitorial methods.

Those who oppose the importation of inquisitorial methods into the American justice system stress that European judges are carefully selected right out of law school, are well trained, and pursue judging as a career track. In contrast, American judges are often appointed for political reasons rather than merit. They may be poorly trained, incompetent to decide difficult cases, and subject to an electoral check that may impair independent judgment. However, in administrative law, these arguments are less persuasive. ALJs (who decide Social Security cases) are carefully selected through a merit system and typically devote lengthy careers to administrative judging. They specialize in the type of cases heard by their own agency. Their independence is zealously guarded. In the VA, the BVA judges lack some of the legal protections of independence enjoyed by ALJs, but they are specialized and highly experienced in judging veterans' claims. Most important, they are sympathetic to the claimants and intellectually and legally charged with helping them make their case. For all these reasons, people may be more comfortable with proceedings controlled by administrative judges than by judges in the judicial system.

Conclusion

The U.S. justice system in general and administrative adjudication in particular is generally perceived as adversarial. This chapter has shown that inquisitorial

76 Thibaut & Walker, *supra* note 74, ch. 10.

methods in U.S. administrative adjudication are actually quite common, particularly in Social Security and veterans' claims adjudication.

In those mass justice systems, inquisitorial approaches are consistent with (and perhaps even compelled by) the fundamental idea that the government should assist every eligible beneficiary to receive the benefits to which they are entitled. Moreover, these overburdened systems simply could not afford the inefficiencies associated with adversary trials. Beyond those calculations, however, it may well be that in mass justice, and perhaps in many other administrative and judicial systems as well, inquisitorial methods may be more acceptable to the parties than adversarial methods.

Chapter 6

About the Inquisitorial Character of Administrative Litigation Procedure in French Law

Jean-Bernard Auby

Introduction

This chapter will concentrate on administrative litigation procedure, and its inquisitorial character, and leave aside processes followed by non-adjudicative administrative bodies. Under French law, contrary to what can be found in other systems, there is a clear-cut divide between administrative judicial bodies and "pure" administrative bodies. The kind of intermediate entities which one can find in common law countries under the concept of "tribunals" is not known in French law. A particular body is either an administrative jurisdiction belonging to the same apparatus as the highest administrative courts, or an administrative entity without any judicial power and separated from the administrative justice apparatus. And, if the French system includes some administrative courts specializing in particular fields – litigation concerning social subsidies, for example – these courts belong to the same set of institutions as the "generalist" administrative courts.

At least, the divide remains clear-cut in pure domestic law. European law tends to exercise some blurring influence, though. Functioning of the judiciary in European countries is legally affected by European rules, and in particular some stemming from the European convention on human rights: especially, article 6 of the latter, which contains several principles deriving from a common concept of "fair trial." And case law from the European Court of Human Rights – which is in charge of interpreting the convention – has admitted that some bodies which, under domestic law, could be held as pure administrative bodies, would be considered as administrative judges for the sake of the convention's implementation. This solution is notably applicable to some independent agencies endowed with sanctioning powers.

Nevertheless, we will remain within the limits of adjudicative bodies strictly speaking in national law terms, without ignoring that it would be quite interesting to expand the analysis to procedures followed by "pure" administrative bodies. The issue of their more or less inquisitorial character is one on which there is very little French literature. We will also leave for another day administrative bodies which European law tends to consider as hybridly adjudicative and administrative. There, interesting comparison could certainly be made with the analyses conducted, in this book, by Nora Farrell and Laverne Jacobs.

What we will try to demonstrate is that, while the procedure before the French administrative jurisdictions has always been fundamentally inquisitorial, some recent evolutions are making it evolve, if not towards an adversarial procedural regime, but at least towards one which would certainly be more "parties driven."

Basic Features of Administrative Justice in France

The French judiciary is a typical dualistic one, in which there is a separate set of courts dealing with administrative litigation. This basic statement can be summarily worked out as follows.

First. The main historical root of French administrative law is the creation, in 1799, of what is still the French supreme administrative court: the Conseil d'Etat. It was created, at the very beginning of the Napoleonic period: under the constitutional regime of the Consulat, which immediately preceded the Napoleonic Empire, but during which Napoleon had already taken over. What will be extremely important for the future of national administrative law is the fact that the Conseil d'Etat's position was not only that of a judge. The Conseil d'Etat was, and still is, simultaneously although in different sections, a judge and the central government's advisory body on legal matters.

Further evolution proceeded in two directions. Even if it remained in the intermediate position that has just been mentioned, the Conseil d'Etat acquired eventually a total independence in its adjudicating function, as well as in its advisory one: an important step in that direction was a statute adopted in 1872.[1]

Leaning on their growing independence, the Conseil d'Etat evolved, especially at the end of the nineteenth century, and at the beginning of the twentieth, a large set of judicial review techniques, noticeably the ones which still constitute the "*recours pour excès de pouvoir*", the main action through which an administrative decision can be reviewed by administrative courts.[2]

In 1873, the Tribunal des Conflits (which had been instituted in 1872, with the function of deciding, in cases of uncertainty, whether ordinary courts or the Conseil d'Etat had jurisdiction) issued what is its most famous decision ever, in the case of "*Blanco*."[3] The case was about a young girl who had been knocked

1 Act of 24 May 1872 "*Portant réorganisation du Conseil d'Etat*."

2 The "*recours pour excès de pouvoir*" can be exercised against nearly any kind of administrative decisions, even those which enshrine a large amount of discretion: there is an exception, though, for some highly political decisions taken by the Government or the President – signing a treaty, issuing a bill before the parliament, summoning a national referendum, and so on – which are called "*actes de gouvernement*."

3 Tribunal des Conflits, 8 February 1873.

down by a carriage in a public tobacco plant, and wounded. The Tribunal des Conflits declared two quite important statements.

The first was that, in order to decide whether a case fell under the jurisdiction of the Conseil d'Etat, and not within that of the ordinary court, one had to refer especially to whether it was related to a public service ("*service public*").

The second was that administrative liability was not subject to private law rules, but, at least normally, to special rules, adapted to the service public necessities. The latter aspect was especially important in so far as it consisted in the acceptance of a very large scope for administrative law and the jurisdiction of administrative courts.

Second. The French legal system belongs to the "dualist" tradition, in which there is a special set of courts in charge of administrative litigation (or at least of most of it).

As was mentioned above, this characteristic has historical roots. Leaders of the late eighteenth-century French Revolution were generally not happy with the courts which had had quite a reactionary attitude at the end of the previous period. So, they wished to prevent the courts from interfering with political affairs, even when decided upon by the executive power. This led to the creation, in 1799, of the Conseil d'Etat, the first administrative court, separated from the ordinary courts (which are called in French: "*juridictions judiciaires*", as opposed to "*juridictions administratives*").

As we will see now, other administrative courts were created later. The choice for a separate set of administrative judges was never reversed.

Third. Nowadays, the administrative courts system is organized in the following way.

The core of the system consists of non-specialized courts (in charge of all cases falling under the jurisdiction of administrative courts, and not attributed to a specialized administrative court), and has three layers. At the top, is the Conseil d'Etat. In the middle, eight administrative courts of appeal ("*cours administrative d'appel*").[4] At the bottom, 38 administrative tribunals ("*tribunaux administratifs*").[5]

Judgments issued by administrative tribunals can be challenged before administrative courts of appeal, which are entitled to re-adjudicate completely on the cases submitted to them. Judgments issued by administrative courts can be

4 This layer of administrative jurisdictions has been introduced in 1987 (31 December 1987 Act). "*Cours administrative d'appel*" are not specializing in particular fields: they have jurisdiction on all appeals issued against the judgments made by the "*tribunaux administratifs*" situated within their territorial jurisdictions.

5 The "*tribunaux administratifs*" were created by a 30 September 1953 Decree (something "lighter" existed previously, namely the "*conseils de préfecture*", established in 1800). They are not specialized in particular fields: their jurisdiction has a territorial basis. There is one to four (in the Paris region) "*tribunaux administratifs*" per region; as to its administrative organization, France is divided into 26 regions.

challenged before the Conseil d'Etat by the means of a special proceedings (called "*pourvoi en cassation*") which only entitles the Conseil d'Etat to check if the administrative court of appeal respected the procedural rules they are subject to, and correctly interpreted the law.

Normally, cases are firstly submitted to administrative tribunals, and then, possibly to administrative courts of appeal, and possibly to the Conseil d'Etat. However, there are some cases which have to be submitted directly to the Conseil d'Etat, and which will be definitively disposed of by the latter: mainly cases concerning actions against some prominent regulatory decisions and some other important decisions taken by the Government.

There are also several categories of specialized administrative courts, dealing with litigation arising in areas such as social welfare, discipline of judges and teachers, public accounts monitoring, and so on. Judgments issued by these courts can be challenged before the Conseil d'Etat.

Fourth. The scope of jurisdiction of administrative courts is especially wide, for the two following reasons. The first is that the actions through which administrative judges can be led to review administrative authorities are not only of judicial review in the sense of procedures leading to the review by judges of the legality of administrative decisions: some of them are related to public contracts, others are related to extra contractual liability of public bodies. Contrary to many other legal systems, the French one does not consider that public liability and public contracts are matters for private law – that is, for ordinary law. In French law, both issues are, not totally, but for their main part, subject to special rules of public law, and therefore to special judicial actions before administrative courts.

The second reason derives from the fact that, in reality, French law considers that there are a number of special administrative law rules applicable to every kind of administrative action and entity. There is an administrative law for civil servants ("*droit de la fonction publique*"), for public contracts ("*droit des contrats administratifs*"), for administrative properties ("*droit du domaine public*"), for administrative works ("*droit des travaux publics*"), and so forth. It is not that all administrative acts and entities are always submitted to public law, nor that all public officers, all public contracts, all administrative properties, all administrative works are subject to public law. But they often are, and above all, they always can be if they meet certain criteria:[6] there is no field of administrative activity which is not susceptible to belong in part to public law.[7]

---

6 These criteria have partly been laid down by written legislation, but they mostly derive from case-law.

7 The criteria under which it is admitted that one legal situation falls under public law or not vary. Just to give two examples: assets belonging to public institutions are subject to public law where they are open to the public, or especially adapted for being used in a public service activity (Code of public properties, article L.2111-1); a contract in which a public entity is party is a public law contract if it is externalizing a public service, if it contains provisions which could not be found in an ordinary contract, and in any case

Thus, there is no field of administrative activity in which action falling under the jurisdiction of administrative courts could not arise.

Inquisitorial v Adversarial in General and in the Specific Ambit of Administrative Law

In order to have a clear idea of the criteria under which we will determine that the French administrative litigation system is more or less inquisitorial, let us try and put together some widely admitted ideas about the inquisitorial/ adversarial divide as they are understood in French law.

First. The core idea which governs this divide is certainly that, in an adversarial procedure, the parties are responsible for conducting the litigation, while, in an inquisitorial one, it is the judge who conducts the litigation.

Then, various symptoms associated to the alternative are suggested. Among them, the following ones emerge especially:

- in an adversarial system, the litigation is initiated by the parties, while, in an inquisitorial one, it will sometimes be initiated by the judges themselves;
- in an adversarial system, it is for the parties to determine who will take part to the case (at least, the judges will not initiate the intervention of third parties), while, in an inquisitorial one, judges can have some leeway to associate third parties;
- in an adversarial system, oral hearings will be predominant, while, in an inquisitorial one, the procedure will in general be essentially written;
- in an adversarial system, rules about evidence will be in general, strictly defined, while, in an inquisitorial one, judges will have some latitude as to the types of evidence they can accept;
- in an adversarial system, evidence will be entirely provided by the parties, while, in an inquisitorial one, judges will have a more active role, and can make their own determination about facts to be established, documents to be communicated, witnesses to be summoned, and decide accordingly;
- finally, in an adversarial system, oral evidence will be often taken from witnesses, while, in an inquisitorial one, this will be much less frequent, and there will be no cross examination;

Second. Quite interestingly, comparative law teaches us two mitigating lessons about the divide.

---

where it is public procurement contract (cases of "*Societé des granites porphyrhoides des Vosges*" Conseil d'Etat, 31 July 1912, and "*Epoux Bertin*" Conseil d'Etat, 20 April 1956; Act of 11 December 2001 "*portant mesures urgentes de réforme à caractère économique et financier*" (known as "*Loi MURCEF*").

The first is that, in fact, there exists some grey zone in the middle of the alternative: at least, that, in some cases, judicial procedure will be a mix of inquisitorial elements and adversarial ones. In several chapters of this book, it is suggested that some administrative law adjudicative bodies belonging to systems where judicial procedures are traditionally adversarial, practice some kind of "active", "investigative", "enabling" or "intrusive" procedure, ie a procedure which has a partly inquisitorial character.

The second lesson is that comparative law seems to demonstrate, also, that all systems contain adjudicative bodies before which processes belonging to the dominant type of procedure leaves the way to something which largely borrows the characteristics of the other type. Chapters in this collection show, in particular, that, in some major common law systems – United Kingdom, United States, Australia – one can find one or several groups of jurisdictions, especially in the field of "tribunals", which use an inquisitorial-type procedure.

Third. The reasons leading to opt for a predominantly adversarial procedure or for a predominantly inquisitorial one are, of course, a matter for debate. One can only discern some recurring arguments.

In favor of the adversarial system, the most frequently expressed one is that the judge's neutrality which it entails would be the best possible safeguard for judicial fairness.

In favor of the inquisitorial one, the most regularly proposed argument is that it is the best way of compensating the inequality between parties which can arise out of differences in wealth, knowledge, legal abilities and so on, by allowing the judge to help the weakest party defend her case.

Apart from these two basic positions, which both are respectable, an equally endless debate is possible about which one of the two systems is more susceptible to provide efficiency and accuracy in the establishment of facts, about which one is more susceptible to confer legitimacy to what the judge makes, and so on.

Fourth. The next question is whether the issue of justifications for inquisitorial or adversarial procedures would have specific orientations in the specific ambit of administrative law.

At first glance, the answer is negative, since administrative law litigation is dealt with by predominantly inquisitorial processes in some systems, and by predominantly adversarial processes in some others.

Then, one must be stricken by the fact that, in several common law countries, it is precisely in the field of administrative law litigation that one has departed more or less from the deeply rooted adversarial tradition.

For what reasons? One at least is commonly given by Michael Asimow and Robert Thomas in their chapters, and commonly proposed by them as the rationale for using an inquisitorial oriented procedure in social security adjudication. In this field, as Robert Thomas puts it, "the adjudication process is viewed as part of a wider decision-making process which is designed to ensure that claimants receive neither more nor less than the amount of social security benefit to which they are properly entitled."

A continental lawyer will adhere to this justification, but will probably connect it to a more general idea. It is that, fundamentally, administrative law litigation, at least where it consists of judicial review of administrative decisions, is an "objective" business, an "objective" legal issue: checking if an administrative act abides with the rule of law. This does not mean that the inquisitorial system would, in practice, be more efficient in serving the rule of law, but that, in its vision, administrative litigation is never a matter of "the one who wins is the one who better built her case", but essentially a matter of "making sure that legality is the winner", even sometimes at the expense of the parties entire satisfaction.

As one understands, in this approach, parties are in a sense instruments of the legality. They may win their case, but in the same time they will have been servants of the law. Like the judge herself, the proactive intervention of whom will have, not just complemented, but indeed wrapped and possibly adjusted the ones of the parties.

The Fundamentally Inquisitorial Character of Administrative Litigation Procedure in French Law

First. There is no doubt on the fact that administrative law litigation procedure is, in French Law, fundamentally of an inquisitorial nature.[8]

It is explicitly stated as a principle in several judgments made by the Conseil d'Etat, affirming that it is for the judge to conduct the litigation, and even that is for the judge only to conduct the litigation.[9]

It is worth mentioning that this principle applies to all types of litigation which are submitted to administrative courts, be it judicial review cases, or cases concerning administrative contractual or non-contractual liability.

The inquisitorial character of the procedure is deemed to have a range of consequences, among which one can underline the following ones:

- the action is addressed to the court, which will forward it to the defendant, and not addressed to the defendant;[10]

8 V Lapanne Joinville, "La direction de la procédure devant les Tribunaux Administratifs", (1965) Actualité Juridique Droit Administratif 324; R Denoix de Saint-Marc & D Labetoulle, "Les pouvoirs d'instruction du juge administratif" (1977–1978) Etudes et Documents de Conseil d'Etat 69; Jean-Marie Auby & Roland Drago, "Traité de contentieux administratif" (1984) Librairie Générale de Droit et de Jurisprudence 864; René Chapus, *Contentieux administratif* (Montchrestien, 2006) at 813; Raymond Odent, *Contentieux administratif* (Les Cours de Droit, 1981) at 893.

9 "*Le juge dirige seul l'instruction*": Conseil d'Etat, 16 February 1966, Echernier, Rec. p. 112 – 7 October 1983, Mlle Limoge, Rec. p. 403- 27 November 1985, Société parisienne de matériaux enrobés, Droit Administratif, 1986, n°52.

10 About that aspect, and several others: Tania Enaudi, *L'obligation d'informer dans le procès administratif* (Librairie Générale de Droit et de Jurisprudence, 2002).

- the judge has the power to decide who will be admitted to produce observations in the case (not to decide who will be party in the case: this is determined by the parties themselves, in particular the one who initiates the litigation);
- it is for the judge to communicate to the other parties all documents and writings produced by one party;
- the judge can summon comments, documents, witnesses on her own volition;[11]
- it is for the judge to decide when the case is ready to be heard and to determine the date of the hearing;
- the judge can consider, in her judgment, some kinds of arguments concerning essential aspects of legality ("moyens d'ordre public") even if they have not been invoked by the parties.

The most impressive manifestations of the inquisitorial character of the procedure are probably those which relate to evidence. Firstly, French administrative judges are not the least bound by formal rules concerning the types of evidence they can admit. Secondly, they have always allowed themselves a large possibility of modulating the burden of proof: normally, it falls on the one who initiated the case, but the Conseil d'Etat decided that, in some fields – especially when what is contested is decided by administrative authorities – it would be reversed and borne by the defendant public authority.

Thirdly, administrative judges are often ready to help private parties prove the facts they try to establish provided that they have communicated some minimal convincing argument that what they try to prove could well be the reality. Then, judges can order the administrative authority to produce some pieces of information, or answer questions: and, if the authority shows reluctance or seems to beat around the bush, accept that what has been suggested by the initiating party is established.[12]

Second. These elements characterize undoubtedly a typical inquisitorial procedural regime. However, the inquisitorial character is not without some limitations. Two of them are especially worth indicating.

Even if French administrative judges have important powers which allow them to contribute to framing the case, by inviting some people to join, by summoning

11 For example, Conseil d'Etat, 30 October 2009, Mme Perreux, Revue française de droit administratif, 2009, p. 1125.

12 The seminal judgment, here, is "*Barel*" (Conseil d'Etat, 1954), concerning a case in which the government had not permitted some people to take part in a competition for the selection of top civil servants, because of their political opinions – they belonged to the communist party – but without motivating its decision. The Conseil d'Etat ordered the government to communicate the reasons for the decision; then, the government remaining silent, took for granted that these reasons were effectively related to the acting parties' political opinions.

documents, by referring to some argument not suggested by the parties, and so on, they are not fully in command of that framing. They may not initiate a case on their own. Their judgments may not decide on issues which have not been raised by the parties.

Another limitation to the inquisitorial orientation derives from the submission of the whole litigation procedure to a general principle of "contradiction." This principle means that all pieces of information collected by the judge must be communicated to the parties with some reservations concerning some secrets like the military one. It also means that parties must have been put in position of discussing all the legal arguments on which the judges will base their judgments.

Third. What are the rationales usually relied on in order to justify the predominantly inquisitorial character of administrative law litigation in the French system?

Without any doubt, the one which is constantly referred to is that this inquisitorial character is a necessity for compensating the natural inequality between the state, the administration, and private parties. Judges have always put forward the idea that the administration is in general in possession of most of the information needed in order to establish the facts of a case, and that it is a duty for the judge to compensate the large decisional powers the administration is entrusted with by granting some investigative support to private parties who challenge its decisions.

These are obviously justifications which are attached to the specificities of the administrative law context. Inquisitorial orientations are not a common character of jurisdictional procedures in French law: while criminal procedure is also typically inquisitorial, civil law procedure is, on the contrary, traditionally adversarial.[13]

Some Recent Evolutions Tending to Mitigate the Inquisitorial Orientation in French Administrative Litigation

Administrative law litigation remains, in the French system, fundamentally inquisitorial. However, some recent evolutions are slightly transforming the context, and make administrative adjudication evolve, if not towards an adversarial procedural regime, but at least towards one which would certainly be more "parties driven."

Let us mention, first, that the concept of what administrative litigation and administrative judges are made for has changed a lot, in the sense that their functions is not, in modern times, conceived any more as a mainly "objective" matter, concerning the respect of legality rather than serving the rights of the citizens. It is clear for everyone, now, that administrative litigation has these two

13 Even if, eventually, it has acquired some inquisitorial traits: René Chapus, *De l'office du juge: contentieux administratif et nouvelle procédure civile* (Etudes et Documents du Conseil d'Etat, 1977–1978) at 11.

functions, and even that its primary functions is to protect the rights of the citizens, especially those which can be held as "fundamental."

Secondly, processes before administrative courts have been, in the last decades, subjected to some dramatic reforms which have affected what people can expect when they bring a case before an administrative court, and, relatedly, the type of decisions judges may impose on the administration.

Since 1995,[14] administrative courts have been granted a large power of issuing injunctions addressed to administrative bodies. Since 2000,[15] a range of urgency procedures allow the judges to take, within a very brief period of time, judgments which order the administration to adopt a certain behavior, suspend the implementation of a decision, communicate documents, reconsider a decision, and so on.[16]

These evolutions are a profound change in so far as they permit the citizens to be accorded by the administrative justice decisions which meet more directly their needs than the mere annulment of the administrative decision, which was often the only possible content of judgments previously.

For example, in the past, a civil servant who was unlawfully dismissed could only have the decision quashed by a judge, and possibly have the administration sentenced to pay some compensation: but that is all that she could get from the judge. Nowadays, the same civil servant can obtain, and through a quick procedure, that an injunction be issued and the administration ordered to reintegrate her.

Correspondingly, citizens are now provided with a range of procedural tools, which are, in practice, very much used. And one understands easily that these new procedural rules have strongly increased the possibility for them of influencing the course of cases. They are more evidently in position of building procedural strategies.

In any particular case, private parties can decide to fight against the administration by using urgency procedures. Sometimes, however, they will have an interest in taking the time, by not requiring injunctions: the absence of injunction will then result in the administration being puzzled about what it should do, which may serve their interest.

This does not diminish the directing powers detained by judges in what remains a predominantly inquisitorial system, but makes that the conduct of cases is less fully entrusted to the judges, who can more often adopt the position of a mere referee.

Moreover, it is worth mentioning that the number of lawyers who have been trained in administrative law has increased significantly. This is another factor which determines what can be characterized as a slow departure from the pure inquisitorial model, and a slow move towards a more mitigated one. There are also some indications that neighboring systems sharing the same traditional

14 Act 8 February 1995 "*Relative à l'organisation des juridictions.*"

15 Act 30 June 2000 "*Relative au référé devant les juridictions administratives.*"

16 These procedures do not derive from legislation or case law, but are purely practice.

characteristics – the Spanish one, for example – are following the same path.[17] This might be a symptom of the kind of slow convergence in the citizen's protection against public powers which is encouraged by legal globalization.[18]

17 Eduardo Garcia de Enterria, *Las Transformaciones de la Justicia Administrativa: De excepcion singular a la plenitud jurisdiccional. Un cambio de paradigma?* (Madrid: Thomson Civitas, 2007).

18 Jean-Bernard Auby, *La globalisation, le droit et l'Etat*, 2d ed (Montchrestien, 2010) at 129.

Chapter 7

Inquisitorial Approaches to Refugee Protection Decision-making: The Australian Experience and Possible Lessons for Canada

Gerald Heckman*

Introduction: Refugee Protection and Inquisitorial Systems

Many states around the world, including Canada and Australia, have ratified international conventions that seek to protect non-citizens from the harm they could face if they were returned to their home countries. Under the 1951 Convention Relating to the Status of Refugees[1] and the 1967 Protocol Relating to the Status of Refugees,[2] refugees are defined as persons who "owing to well-founded fear of being persecuted for reasons of race, religion, nationality, membership of a particular social group or political opinion, are outside of the country of their nationality and are unable or, owing to such fear, are unwilling to avail themselves of the protection of that country."[3] Article 33 of the Convention forbids states from returning refugees to countries where their life or freedom would be threatened on one of the Convention grounds. Similarly, the Convention against Torture and Other Cruel, Inhumane or Degrading Treatment or Punishment (CAT)[4] and the International Covenant on Civil and Political Rights[5] protect from *refoulement* persons who, if returned to their home country, would face a danger of torture, a risk to their life or a risk of cruel, inhuman or degrading treatment or punishment.

To fulfill these international responsibilities, many states set up refugee protection systems, which include a procedure to conduct an individualized

---

* I acknowledge the valuable research assistance of Jaime Rosin, LL.B. student, Faculty of Law, University of Manitoba and the financial support of the Manitoba Legal Research Institute. This chapter was originally prepared before extensive 2012 reforms to the Canadian refugee protection system. It has been revised to reflect these statutory modifications. Other aspects of this chapter are current to May 2011.

1 28 July 1951, 189 UNTS 2545, Can TS 1969 No 6, Art 32 [1951 Convention].

2 31 January 1967, 606 UNTS 8791, Can TS 1969 No 29, 6 ILM 386 [1967 Protocol].

3 1951 Convention, *supra* note 1, Article 1A(2).

4 Can TS 1987 No 36 [CAT].

5 19 December 1966, 999 UNTS 171, Can TS 1976 No 47, 6 ILM 368 [ICCPR or the "Covenant"].

assessment of the merits of protection claims. Decision-makers assess whether claimants have a subjective fear of persecution and whether this fear is objectively well-founded – an assessment that can only be based on the claimant's personal narrative of the incidents which motivated their flight and the reasons for which they could not seek their country's protection.[6] Because it is frequently impossible to obtain evidence directly corroborating claimants' statements, the decision-maker must assess their credibility in order to determine whether the events they have described could have occurred in light of the current conditions in their country of origin and whether they are personally believable. These assessments can only occur if claimants are heard by the decision-maker in an interview or formal hearing.

Some states, including Canada and Australia, have opted to build certain inquisitorial or non-adversarial elements into their refugee protection systems,[7] which sit on a decision-making spectrum somewhere between the adversarial model (characterized by a neutral, largely passive umpire who allows the parties to present their cases as they see fit, including the issues to which they confine their dispute as well as the collection and presentation of the evidence, which is subject to strict, well-established rules of evidence and procedures designed to ensure the fairness of the hearing)[8] and the inquisitorial model (where the decision-maker has primary control of and responsibility for the gathering of evidence).[9]

An inquisitorial approach is arguably well tailored to the refugee protection context. First, refugee claimants, who typically lack financial resources and are likely to be unrepresented, might be disadvantaged in adversarial proceedings. As Smyth observes, the informal procedures of an inquisitorial process "are less intimidating for and require less expertise of unrepresented litigants, and inquisitorial powers enable tribunals to assist unrepresented applicants."[10] Enhanced access to justice motivated Australia's choice of a non-adversarial approach to merits review of refugee protection decisions.[11] Secondly, since refugee protection proceedings seek to ensure the state's compliance with international human rights

6 Guy Goodwin-Gill, *The Refugee in International Law*, 2nd ed (Oxford: Clarendon Press, 1996) at 325 [Goodwin-Gill].

7 While the Canadian and Australian refugee protection processes are not strictly speaking "inquisitorial" (see France Houle, "*Thamotharem* and Guideline 7 of the IRB: Rethinking the Scope of the Fettering of Discretion Doctrine" (2008) 25:2 Refuge 103 at 114), I will use the term out of convenience.

8 Margaret Allars, "Administrative Law – Neutrality, the Judicial Paradigm and Tribunal Procedure" (1991) 13 Sydney L Rev 377 at 381.

9 Austl, Commonwealth, Senate Legal and Constitutional References Committee, Sanctuary under Review (28 June 2000) at para 5.23, online: http://parlinfo.aph.gov.au/parlInfo/search/display/display.w3p;query=Id:publications%2Ftabledpapers%2F11774 [Sanctuary].

10 Mark Smyth, "Inquisitorial Adjudication: the Duty to Inquire in Merits Review Tribunals" (2010) 34 Melbourne ULR 380 at 238–9 [Smyth].

11 Sanctuary, *supra* note 9 at para 5.24.

obligations, a goal shared by the state and the claimant, there is no true adversarial relationship.[12] Thirdly, refugee protection systems must deal with large volumes of claims, and the decreased formality of inquisitorial processes relative to their adversarial counterparts, combined with the active control of the proceedings by an expert decision-maker may promote efficiency.[13]

The question of whether, and in what circumstances, inquisitorial systems enhance protection claimants' access to a fair and accurate determination of their claims has become pressing in Canada for two reasons. First, significant amendments to Canada's refugee protection system, implemented in 2012,[14] speed up the determination of protection claims by introducing shorter timelines for various steps in the decision-making process. In the government's view, these changes were needed because it was taking unreasonably long for failed asylum claimants to get a final decision on their claim and be removed from Canada, a delay that encouraged people to make unfounded claims.[15] Though more relaxed than those initially proposed by the government, these timelines will likely constrain refugee claimants' access to representation,[16] especially given the time required to apply for and secure legal aid.[17] Secondly, the availability of legal aid for the representation of refugee claimants in Canada is limited and has been worsening,[18] a situation which will likely lead to an increase in the number of unrepresented or

---

12 Sanctuary, *supra* note 9 at para 5.33. As Smyth, *supra* note 10, observes at 239, administrative decision-making, theoretically, does not involve the parties as adversaries: "The disagreements are between private citizens and the government, and the government, in making its decisions, has a duty to consider the individual citizen's interest."

13 *Ibid* at para 5.24: Smyth, *supra* note 10 at 239.

14 *Protecting Canada's Immigration System Act*, SC 2012, c 17 [*Protecting Canada's Immigration System*]. This statute amended the *Balanced Refugee Reform Act*, SC 2010, c 8 [*BRRA*].

15 Citizenship and Immigration Canada, "Frequently Asked Questions: The refugee system", online: www.cic.gc.ca/english/information/faq/refugees/ref-reform/faq-asp. See also Citizenship and Immigration Canada, News Release, "Balanced Refugee Reform Passes Final Hurdle in Senate, Launches Summer Tour to Promote Refugee Resettlement" (June 29, 2010), online: http://www.cic.gc.ca/english/department/media/ releases/2010/2010-06-29a.asp.

16 See David Matas, "Balancing" (2010) 88 Imm LR (3d) 212 at 218–9 [Matas].

17 Erin Roth, "Is the Proposed Balanced Refugee Reform Act Balanced?" (2010) 86 Imm LR (3d) 168 at 170.

18 Canadian Bar Association, *Canada's Crisis in Access to Justice* (April 2006) at 2; Francois Crépeau & Delphine Nakache, "Controlling Irregular Migration in Canada" (2006) 12 IRPP Choices at 15. See also Canada, Department of Justice, *An Analysis of Immigration and Refugee Law Services in Canada* (2003) at 73–8, online: http://www.justice.gc.ca/eng/rp-pr/other-autre/ir/rr03_la18-rr03_aj18/toc-tdm.htm [DOJ legal aid research]. See generally Sean Rehaag, "The Role of Counsel in Canada's Refugee Determination System: An Empirical Assessment" (2011–2012) 49 Osgoode Hall LJ 71.

poorly represented claimants.[19] To assess the impact of this changing context on Canada's inquisitorial refugee protection system, Australia's experience is highly relevant. Australia's Refugee Review Tribunal (RRT), charged with reviewing the merits of decisions by that country's Department of Immigration and Citizenship (DIAC) to deny claimants protection visas, is statutorily required to function expeditiously by conducting its reviews and recording its decisions within 90 days from the day it receives the necessary documents from DIAC.[20] The RRT also faces challenges regarding legal representation. The proportion of unrepresented claimants appearing before the RRT has averaged just under 52% between 2007–08 and 2011–12.[21] Moreover, the role of representatives at in-person hearings is narrowly circumscribed; the RRT is not required to allow them to participate in the hearing,[22] but usually allows them to speak for the claimant at the close of the hearing.[23]

This chapter reviews some of the challenges that have arisen in the operation of Australia's "inquisitorial" refugee protection system. It then describes the recent changes to Canada's system. Finally, it seeks to identify possible implications of the Australian experience for refugee protection decision-making in Canada.

---

19 Peter Showler, *Fast, Fair and Final: Reforming Canada's Refugee System* (Maytree Foundation, 2009) at 16–17. See also DOJ legal aid research, *ibid* at 79–84.

20 *Migration Act 1958, Act No 62 of 1958 as amended,* s 414A [*Migration Act*]. See Austl, Commonwealth, Migration Review Tribunal–Refugee Review Tribunal, Annual Report 2009–10 at 37, online: http://www.mrt-rrt.gov.au/Forms-and-publications/Annual-Reports.aspx [MRT–RRT Annual Report 2009–10]; in 2009–2010, close to 70% of claims were decided within this timeframe, with an average time to decision of 99 days. In 2010–2011, 71% of cases were finalized within 90 days: MRT–RRT Annual Report 2010–2011 at 27. In 2011–2012, due to a rising caseload and the unavailability of some experienced members, only 32% of cases were finalized within 90 days, with an average time to decision of 149 days: MRT–RRT Annual Report 2011–2012 at 2, 31.

21 The MRT–RRT reports the proportion of cases in which applicants appointed a representative to assist or represent them: Austl, Commonwealth, Migration Review Tribunal–Refugee Review Tribunal, Annual Report 2007–2008 at 31, online: http://www.mrt-rrt.gov.au/Forms-and-publications/Annual-Reports.aspx (45%); MRT–RRT Annual Report 2008–2009 at 40 (45%); MRT–RRT Annual Report 2009–2010 at 7 (55%); MRT–RRT Annual Report 2010–2011 at 39 (53%); MRT–RRT Annual Report 2011–2012 at 28 (61%).

22 *Migration Act*, *supra* note 20, s 427(6).

23 Austl, Commonwealth, Refugee Review Tribunal, *Tribunal Brochure*, May 2010, online: www.mrt-rrt.gov.au/factsheets/default.aspx.

Australia's Experience with Inquisitorial Refugee Protection Decision-making

The Refugee Review Tribunal

In Australia, refugee claimants apply to DIAC for a protection visa. A DIAC case officer, acting as the Minister's delegate, assesses the application usually "on the papers" to determine whether the applicant meets the refugee definition. Unsuccessful applicants may appeal the officer's decision on the merits to the Refugee Review Tribunal.[24] Constituted under the *Migration Act*, the RRT comprises a Principal Member, Deputy Principal Member, senior members and members (full- or part-time) appointed by the Governor-General for a term not exceeding five years.[25] It sits in single member panels appointed by its Principal Member.[26]

Faced with a valid application for review of DIAC's refusal of a protection visa, the RRT "must review the decision."[27] Ordinarily, it must invite the applicant to appear before it at a private hearing[28] to give evidence and present arguments on the issues arising in relation to the decision.[29] The *Migration Act* gives the RRT primary control over and responsibility for the gathering of evidence. In addition to the DIAC case file, submissions from DIAC's secretary and material provided by the applicant,[30] section 424 specifies that "in conducting the review, the Tribunal may get any information that it considers relevant" and "may invite, either orally (including by telephone) or in writing, a person to give information." However, it must disclose to the applicant, orally at a hearing or in writing, particulars of any information it considers would be the reason, or a part of the reason, for affirming DIAC's decision to reject the claim[31] and invite the applicant to comment on or respond to the information. The power to call witnesses rests with the RRT. While applicants may request the RRT to obtain oral evidence from a witness, it is not required to do so. It may take evidence on oath or affirmation, adjourn the review, give information to the applicant and to DIAC, and require DIAC "to arrange for the making of any investigation, or any medical examination, that the Tribunal thinks necessary

24 *Migration Act, supra* note 20, s 412. Detained asylum seekers must apply for review within seven days of notification of the primary decision; other asylum seekers have 28 days to apply.

25 *Ibid*, ss 458–459. Members are eligible for reappointment: s 461.

26 *Ibid*, s 421(1).

27 *Ibid*, s 414.

28 *Ibid*, s 429.

29 *Ibid*, s 425(1).

30 *Ibid*, s 423.

31 *Ibid*, ss 424AA, 424A.

with respect to the review and to give to the Tribunal a report …"[32] It may, in relation to a review, summon a person to appear before it to give evidence and/or to produce documents to the Tribunal.[33] Persons appearing before the Tribunal to give evidence are not entitled to be represented before the Tribunal or to examine or cross-examine any other person appearing before the Tribunal to give evidence.[34]

In keeping with the intent to give the RRT control over the conduct of the hearing and evidence-gathering in particular, these powers are phrased in permissive terms, with liberal use of the word "may", a discretion reinforced in section 420 of the *Migration Act*:

> 420(1) The Tribunal, in carrying out its functions under this Act, is to pursue the objective of providing a mechanism of review that is fair, just, economical, informal and quick.
> (2) The Tribunal, in reviewing a decision:
> (a) is not bound by technicalities, legal forms or rules of evidence; and
> (b) must act according to substantial justice and the merits of the case.

One would expect the RRT to exercise its powers to invite a witness to provide information, to arrange for a medical examination or even to ask questions to elicit specific information from an applicant or witness in a manner consistent with the objective of achieving a fair, just, economical, informal and quick review. However, the objectives of fairness and justice are in tension with those of economy, informality and expedition.[35] A crucial question is whether the RRT appropriately balances these competing objectives, particularly in light of the serious nature of the (often unrepresented) applicants' interests. An equally important question is whether reviewing courts will intervene where balance is not achieved.

The Duty to Inquire

Reviewing courts have reinforced the permissive nature of the RRT's inquisitorial powers. The following principles may be gathered from the case law:

- The term "inquisitorial", as applied to the Tribunal, does not carry the full ordinary meaning of "'having or exercising the function of an inquisitor',

32 *Migration Act, supra* note 20, s 427.

33 *Ibid*, s 427(3).

34 *Ibid*, s 427(6).

35 Robin Creyke, "'Inquisitorial' practice in Australian tribunals" (2006) 57 Admin Review 17 at 17–19. See also *Minister for Immigration and Multicultural Affaires v Eshetu* (1999) 162 ALR 577 (HC) per Gummow J at 600, Gleeson CJ and McHugh J at 588 and Callinan J at 617–618, citing *Sun Zhan Qui v Minister for Immigration and Ethnic Affairs* (1997) 81 FCR 71 (FC).

that is to say 'one whose official duty is to inquire, examine or investigate'."[36] Rather, "it merely delimits the nature of the Tribunal's functions. They are to be found in the provisions of the *Migration Act*. The core function, in the words of s. 414 of the *Act*, is to 'review the decision' which is the subject of a valid application ... under ... the *Act*."[37]

- The Tribunal has an inquisitorial function in the sense that, in the exercise of its review function, it may obtain such information as it considers relevant. That does not "impose upon it a general duty to undertake its own inquiries in addition to information provided to it by the applicant and otherwise under the *Act*."[38]
- The Tribunal's function is "to respond to the case that the applicant advances."[39] Section 425 of the *Act* does not require that it "actively assist the applicant in putting his or her case" or to carry out an inquiry in order to identify what that case might be.[40] A party cannot "simply present the facts and leave it to the Tribunal to search out, and find, any available basis which theoretically the *Act* provides for relief."[41]
- The Tribunal's power to require DIAC to arrange, and report upon, any investigation or medical examination that it thinks necessary does not mean that it is "bound to make particular inquiries or to obtain evidence on medical or other matters."[42] It is neither legally obliged to make an inquiry nor to consider whether it should exercise that power.[43]
- Section 424(1) of the *Migration Act* is not the source of any obligation on the Tribunal to "seek more information that might enhance, detract from or otherwise be relevant to information which it has already received."[44]
- The Tribunal inquiring into a claim is not "an adversarial cross-examiner, but an inquisitor obliged to be fair."[45] It is for the applicant to advance whatever evidence or argument she wishes to advance, and for the Tribunal

---

36 *Minister for Immigration and Citizenship v SZIAI and Anor*, [2009] HCA 39, 259 ALR 429 at para 18 (HC) per French CJ, Gummow, Jayne, Crennan, Kiefel and Bell JJ [*SZIAI*].

37 *SZIAI*, *supra* note 36.

38 *Ibid* at para 1

39 *Dranichnikov v Minister for Immigration and Multicultural Affairs*, [2003] HCA 26, 197 ALR 389 at para 78 (HC) per Kirby J [*Dranichnikov*].

40 *Minister for Immigration and Multicultural and Indigenous Affairs v SCAR* (2003) 128 FCR 553 at para 36 (FC).

41 *Dranichnikov*, *supra* note 39 at para 78.

42 *Minister for Immigration and Multicultural and Indigenous Affairs v SGLB*, [2004] HCA 32, 207 ALR 12 at para 124 (HC) per Callinan J [*SGLB*].

43 *Minister for Immigration and Citizenship v SZGUR and Another*, [2011] HCA 1, 273 ALR 223 at para 22 (HC) per French CJ and Kiefel J [*SZGUR*].

44 *SZGUR*, *supra* note 43 at para 86 per Gummow J.

45 *Re Minister for Immigration and Multicultural Affairs*; *Ex parte Applicant S154/2002*, [2003] HCA 60 at para. 57 (HC) per Gummow J and Heydon JJ [*S154*].

> to decide whether her claim is made out. The Tribunal is not obliged to "prompt and stimulate an elaboration which the applicant chooses not to embark on."[46]

In contrast, Justice Kirby of the High Court of Australia has noted that the inquisitorial nature of the Tribunal "casts obligations upon it that are different from, and in some respects more onerous than" adversarial decision-makers.[47] Indeed, the High Court has recognized that, in some circumstances, the Tribunal may be subject to a limited duty to inquire,[48] described recently as follows:

> The duty imposed upon the Tribunal by the *Migration Act* is a duty to review. It may be that a failure to make an obvious inquiry about a critical fact, the existence of which is easily ascertained, could, in some circumstances, supply a sufficient link to the outcome to constitute a failure to review. If so, such a failure could give rise to jurisdictional error by constructive failure to exercise jurisdiction.[49]

In a comprehensive study of the duty to inquire in Australian merits review tribunals, Smyth observes that courts have raised two threshold requirements to the application of the duty. First, the "further inquiries" must be centrally relevant to the decision to be made – adding to existing evidence and likely to yield centrally relevant information.[50] Smyth argues that by limiting this duty to ascertaining critical facts, courts have balanced the need for merits tribunals to conduct probing merits review of the facts with managerial demands for the expedient and cost-efficient conduct of tribunal proceedings. Secondly, merits tribunals are bound to seek only information that is readily available, an implicit judicial recognition

46 *S154*, *supra* note 45 at para 58.

47 *SGLB*, *supra* note 42 at para 9 per Kirby J.

48 For discussion of the duty to inquire, see also Robin Creyke "Pragmatism v Policy: Attitude of Australian Courts and Tribunals to Inquisitorial Process" at Chapter 2 of this volume.

49 *SZIAI*, *supra* note 35 at para 25. The Court acknowledged that failure to make such an inquiry may result in a decision "being affected in some other way that manifests itself as jurisdictional error." However, it noted at para 24 that it was "difficult to see any basis upon which a failure to inquire could constitute a breach of the requirements of procedural fairness at common law." The need to show jurisdictional error is likely linked to the High Court's ruling, in *Plaintiff S157/2002 v Commonwealth* (2003) 211 CLR 476 that a statutory privative clause did not remove the Court's constitutional authority to grant *certiorari* against protection visa decisions tainted by jurisdictional error, including the denial of procedural fairness. In *SZIAI*, the Court also contemplates, at para 26, that a failure to inquire may be so unreasonable as to found a jurisdictional error. Australian courts first recognized a duty to inquire on this basis in *Prasad v Minister for Immigration and Ethnic Affairs* (1985), 6 FCR 155 at 169–170 (HC).

50 Smyth, *supra* note 10 at 200–252.

of the "managerial imperatives" which constrain them.[51] The courts' emphasis on the discretionary nature of the RRT's inquisitorial powers and their "reluctance to embrace a free-ranging duty to inquire" confirms that they are likely attaching considerable weight to institutional and managerial considerations.[52]

In Smyth's view, reviewing courts, which focus on the legality of decisions, may be loath to invoke the duty to inquire for fear of engaging in disguised merits review by second-guessing the tribunal's use of its fact-finding powers.[53] Merits tribunals are also expected to "inquisitorially manage" hearings in such a way as to achieve their review mandate in a less formal, more accessible, efficient and cost-effective manner.[54] Courts may fear that requiring them to engage in further inquiries could frustrate tribunals' efforts to achieve cost-efficiency.[55] A similar tension between the "legal model" of decision-making processes, where tribunals seek to deliver accurate and independent decisions through fair procedures and the "government model" which privileges tribunals' efficient and cost-effective implementation of government policy, has characterized the context of asylum appeals in the United Kingdom.[56] Smyth concludes that the duty to inquire achieves an appropriate balance between these models:

> [T]he courts have found a duty in only strictly limited circumstances, where the inquiries are centrally relevant and straightforward, and where the statutory structure, circumstances of the hearing and/or position of the applicant necessitate a proactive role for decision-makers. This limited duty to inquire is consistent with ensuring that tribunals carry out their core function of inquisitorial adjudication on the merits, while not unduly infringing flexibility, efficiency, procedural fairness and the legality–merits distinction.[57]

As the next section illustrates, however, the High Court has upheld RRT decisions despite that tribunal's failure to conduct further inquiries, seek additional information or pursue a line of questioning – decisions that, in my view, fail to balance the obligation to conduct fair and accurate merits review with the demands of economy and speed.

---

51 Smyth, *supra* note 10 at 252.

52 *Ibid* at 255.

53 *Ibid* at 235–8.

54 *Ibid* at 245.

55 *Ibid* at 245–6 and 265.

56 Robert Thomas, "Evaluating Tribunal Adjudication: Administrative Justice and Asylum Appeals" (2005) 25 Legal Studies 462 at 472.

57 Smyth, *supra* note 10 at 267.

Judicial Review of RRT Decision-making by the High Court

In this section, I review three cases that illustrate the High Court's approach to the review of the RRT's exercise of its inquisitorial powers. In each case, when it was argued that the Tribunal had failed to exercise one of its inquisitorial powers, the Court determined that there was no legal obligation on it to do so. As a result of such decisions, there is little external incentive on the Tribunal to assist refugee protection claimants through the exercise of its inquisitorial powers, even where procedural fairness or international norms would require it.

The duty to seek clarification of crucial testimony and to put to the claimant the case against her: S154[58]

In *S154*, a Sri Lankan Tamil claimed refugee protection on the basis that she was suspected by authorities of being a member of the LTTE, a Tamil separatist group, and that she feared being recruited by the LTTE. At the RRT hearing, she disclosed, for the first time, that Sri Lankan police officers had taken her into custody, questioned her about LTTE ties and raped her. She stated that she had not revealed the rape to her mother, who had medical problems, or to her husband and added: "I cannot tell this."[59] The RRT member replied that he did not need to ask the applicant "any further question about that particular incident",[60] and continued a prior line of questioning. The claim of rape by Sri Lankan officials was highly relevant to establishing one of the elements of refugeehood – her unwillingness to avail herself of her country's protection.[61] The member dismissed the appeal. He did not accept her rape story, largely because she had not provided that evidence to the Minister's delegate or at a previous abortive RRT hearing and because it was not referred to in a psychologist's report on the applicant.[62] The member noted that his findings regarding the rape claim affected his view of her credibility on other matters.

On judicial review, the applicant argued that the member's response to her story cut her off from an elaboration of the rape that she would otherwise have provided and misled her into believing that the Tribunal needed no further elaboration. She argued that before disbelieving her rape claim based on her failure to raise it in prior proceedings, the member should have put this evidence to her as matters tending to disprove the claim so that she could explain why her previous statements were consistent with the claim. In sum, she claimed that the Tribunal had not discharged its duty to inquire into her claim.

A majority of the Court found that the hearing had fully complied with the requirements of the *Migration Act* and procedural fairness. It emphasized that the

58 *S154*, *supra* note 45.

59 *Ibid* at para 12.

60 *Ibid*.

61 *Ibid* at para 74 per Kirby J, and at para 22 per Gummow J and Heydon JJ.

62 *Ibid* at para 17.

RRT member had returned, albeit obliquely, to the applicant's rape claim, and asked her in general terms whether there was anything she wanted to tell the Tribunal about "these matters." Noting that the Tribunal was not bound by rules of evidence, Gummow and Heydon JJ held that the RRT member was not required to put to the applicant contradictory evidence:

> [H]e was not obliged to … seek a detailed amplification of the prosecutrix's account of the rape including the fullest and most minute particulars she could remember, together with an explanation of her failure to give that account on every earlier occasion when that account might conceivably have been given. The Tribunal conducting an inquisitorial hearing is not obliged to prompt and stimulate an elaboration which the applicant chooses not to embark on.[63]

They neatly summed up the obligations of the Tribunal and applicant: "[I]t was for the prosecutrix to advance whatever evidence or argument she wished to advance, and for the Tribunal to decide whether her claim had been made out."[64]

Justice Kirby, dissenting, would have found that the member's conduct of the hearing breached procedural fairness. First, it was "impermissible to abbreviate the attempt of an applicant to give evidence or to curtail important evidence" relevant to an issue that was clearly important for the decision.[65] Second, the applicant had not known that the records of the earlier proceedings and the psychologist's report would be used against acceptance of her rape claim; she should have been confronted with this apparent flaw in her case and given the opportunity to provide an explanation for her failure to mention the rape earlier, including the risks, within her family and marriage, to the possible stain of defilement, risk of divorce and even expulsion.[66] In his view, the Tribunal's statutory duties to review the claim and to act according to substantial justice imposed on the member an obligation to use inquisitorial techniques, including clarifying points raised by the applicant in the course of answering questions put by the Tribunal:

> … [I]n the case of a vulnerable, anxious applicant, with a poor command of English, little understanding of the procedures and an imperfect appreciation of the law being applied, it would not be enough for the Tribunal simply to leave it to the applicant to prove the case unaided. That would reduce the hearing to a charade.[67]

The majority's narrow view of the obligations resting on the RRT in these circumstances unduly privileges the value of administrative flexibility over that

---

63 *S154*, *supra* note 45 at para 58.
64 *Ibid* at para 57.
65 *Ibid* at para 85.
66 *Ibid* at para 90.
67 *Ibid* at para 88 [footnotes omitted].

of probing merits review and fairness. The applicant's account of rape by police was crucial to establishing her well-founded fear of persecution and of central relevance to the RRT's decision. Rather than encourage the applicant to provide sufficient detail to decide whether her evidence "rang true",[68] the member deprived her of an opportunity to provide important evidence. By not stating that he was inclined to disbelieve the applicant's rape claim because she had not disclosed it earlier, he deprived her of the opportunity to dispel doubts about her credibility that were determinative of the outcome of her claim. Together, these flaws denied her the right to be heard. This will be especially salient for many applicants (approximately 50%) appearing before the RRT without a representative who could recognize gaps or apparent inconsistencies in the evidence and seek to clarify them. Even for represented applicants, effective legal representation at the hearing is at the discretion of the RRT, which decides when it is appropriate for advisers to make submissions.[69]

The duty to ascertain the impact of a claimant's psychiatric condition on her ability to give evidence: SGLB[70] *and SZGUR*[71]

SGLB, another High Court decision on the scope of the RRT's inquisitorial role, concerns the right of vulnerable, mentally disturbed claimants to an accurate and fair merits review. SGLB, an Iranian citizen, travelled to Australia by sea without a visa and was detained pursuant to Australian law. At an initial interview, he stated that he had come for economic reasons and to find a wife. When he applied for a protection visa several months later, he claimed to be fleeing persecution by Iranian authorities based on his Arabic background. The Minister's delegate denied his claim based on inconsistencies in his claims and on country information that contradicted his claim that Arabs were persecuted in Iran.

In a first proceeding, the RRT denied his appeal. After this first decision was quashed on judicial review, the applicant – who remained in detention – was heard again two years later. When he requested that the hearing be adjourned because "he was not psychologically fit to attend", the member sought a written assessment from a detention centre psychologist of the applicant's "general state of mind." The psychologist found that the applicant was emotionally and physically volatile and had engaged in self-harming behavior, but did not appear to have blurred or confused recall. Part-way through the hearing, held via video link, the respondent became highly agitated in response to a question. The member discontinued the hearing and sent the applicant's adviser a letter setting out various inconsistencies in the applicant's testimony and noting that, in light of the psychologist's report,

68 *S154, supra* note 45 at para 95.

69 Austl, Commonwealth, Senate Legal and Constitutional References Committee, *Administration and Operation of the Migration Act: 1958* (March 2006), online: http://www.aph.gov.au, at para 3.110 [Administration].

70 *SGLB, supra* note 42.

71 *SZGUR, supra* note 43.

she could infer that these inconsistencies did not come from "blurred or confused recall." In a lengthy response, which also dealt with the substance of the case, the applicant's adviser requested

> … a further, more independent and expert assessment be undertaken to determine [the applicant's] state of mind and whether there can be justified links to his past claim of trauma and persecution. In other words, an expert assessment to determine the source of such behaviour and whether it stems from serious Post Traumatic Stress Disorder (PTSD). We consider that the Tribunal has a duty to ask the question about [the applicant's] anger and the source of that anger.[72]

The member declined the request, and rejected the applicant's appeal. In evaluating the evidence, she was prepared to accept that SGLB was suffering from PTSD and that this condition affected his ability to give evidence. Though she decided not to draw the conclusion foreshadowed in her earlier letter, she found that the claimant was not credible because of inconsistencies between his oral evidence at the hearing and subsequent written submissions.

On judicial review, the applicant argued that the Tribunal had erred for three reasons. First, there was no evidence upon which it could be satisfied that he was suffering from PTSD. Second, it erred in making findings as to SGLB's credibility where there was no evidence enabling it to assess the effects of PTSD on his credibility. Third, having found that he suffered from PTSD, it failed to satisfy itself that he could take part in the proceedings.[73] A majority of the High Court dismissed all three arguments.

Gummow and Hayne JJ. held that, since the *Migration Act* did not make the question of whether the applicant suffered from PTSD a precondition to the RRT's exercise of jurisdiction, an error regarding this finding did not attract judicial intervention. Moreover, the member could have based her finding of PTSD on her observations of SGLB at the hearing and on extracts from a journal article on the impact of PTSD on asylum seekers' testimony.

They also rejected the applicant's claim that to properly assess the applicant's credibility, the Tribunal was bound to obtain a further psychiatric assessment as requested by the applicant's adviser. While section 427 of the *Act* conferred power on the Tribunal to obtain a medical report, it did not oblige the RRT to do so, nor was the RRT statutorily required to take evidence from a witness if requested to do so by the applicant. Accordingly, the RRT was "under no duty to inquire."[74] The Tribunal had properly decided between inconsistent accounts arising between the applicant's oral evidence at the hearing and his written affidavit evidence.

Finally, the majority rejected the applicant's contention that the Tribunal was bound to ascertain, by seeking expert evidence, that he was mentally competent to

72 *SZGUR, supra* note 43 at para 11.

73 *Ibid* at para 32.

74 *Ibid* at para 43 [footnotes omitted].

take part in the proceeding. The *Act* provided for no such competency requirement. Moreover, it expressly stated that the RRT was not bound by the rules of evidence, including, said the Court, at common law and under the *Evidence Act*. Procedural fairness did not in this case require some "special steps or procedure" to be followed.[75]

Justice Kirby, dissenting, took a broader view of the Tribunal's obligations to inquire into the applicant's psychiatric condition and its incidence on his competence to give evidence and on his initial ability to recall and express events and traumas to which he had been subjected. This, in his view, "was a matter for evidence, not assumption."[76] Procedural fairness required that the Tribunal seek expert medical advice; the applicant's mental condition and its operation upon his competence and conduct "were not matters of general knowledge or matters of which even an expert and experienced body, such as the Tribunal, could take notice without proof."[77] The Tribunal's powers to conduct hearings and to reach conclusions, though broad, were not "completely at large":

> The proceeding must remain a "hearing" as the parliament has provided. It must conform to basic principles of natural justice ... If it does not, there will have been no "hearing" at all. The purported "decision" will not be one such as the Act contemplated.[78]

The High Court rendered a unanimous decision in similar circumstances in *SZGUR, supra*. Relying on *SGLB*, the Court held that the *Migration Act* did not impose upon the Tribunal a duty to obtain a medical report or even to consider whether it should exercise its power to do so.[79] It was the applicant's responsibility to produce a complete psychiatric report which spoke to the connection between his mental condition and his memory in the proceedings.[80] The Tribunal was under no duty to seek information relating to SZGUR's psychological condition in addition to that it had already received.[81] Absent evidence that the applicant's medical conditions impaired his memory, the Tribunal "had no evidence on which it could explain away or put aside the errors and inconsistencies it had found in his evidence."[82]

In *SGLB* and *SZGUR*, the High Court placed on refugee protection claimants the onus to secure independent psychiatric evidence establishing a link between their mental condition and their ability to remember crucial events and otherwise

---

75 *SZGUR, supra* note 43 at para 45.
76 *Ibid* at para 83.
77 *Ibid* at para 90.
78 *Ibid* at para 85.
79 *Ibid* at para 22 per French CJ and Kiefel J.
80 *Ibid* at para 84 per Gummow J; at para 33 per French CJ and Kiefel J.
81 *Ibid* at para 86 per Gummow J.
82 *Ibid* at para 85 per Gummow J; at para 37 per French CJ and Kiefel J.

provide testimony. This may have been a realistic expectation for SZGUR, who was represented and had expressed willingness to meet the costs of a psychiatric assessment.[83] It is not a realistic expectation for unrepresented or detained claimants, like SGLB, suffering from psychiatric disorders.

Can it be said, in light of the High Court's decisions in *Applicant S157* and *SGLB*, that Australia's inquisitorial refugee protection system enhances protection claimants' access to a fair and accurate determination of their claim? The RRT's inquisitorial approach gives Tribunal members "primary control over and responsibility for the gathering of evidence" including information from the applicant and others as well as country conditions information.[84] Its laudable objective is to relieve applicants with limited financial resources and English-language skills and who may have suffered torture or other trauma[85] from the burden of arguing their own case against DIAC or retaining legal counsel to do so.[86] This objective is fully consistent with the principles and methods for fact-finding adopted by the United Nations High Commissioner for Refugees in its Handbook on Procedures and Criteria for Determining Refugee Status.[87] Important secondary sources of international law,[88] they "indicate a practically necessary minimum if refugees are to be identified and accorded protection in accordance with international obligations."[89] The Handbook describes the duties on examiners as follows:

> [W]hile the burden of proof in principle rests on the applicant, *the duty to ascertain and evaluate all the relevant facts is shared between the applicant and the examiner*. Indeed, in some cases, *it may be for the examiner to use all the means at his disposal to produce the necessary evidence* in support of the application. (…)
> While an initial interview should normally suffice to bring an applicant's story to light, it may be necessary *for the examiner to clarify any apparent inconsistencies and to resolve any contradictions in a further interview*, and to

83 Indeed, Gummow J noted that s 427(1)(d) allowed the Tribunal to seek a medical examination that it "thinks *necessary* with respect to the review." As no reason was advanced to explain why the applicant or his agent could not arrange for the examination, it had not been shown that it was necessary for the Tribunal to do so: *ibid* at para 88.

84 Sanctuary, *supra* note 9 at paras 5.23–5.24.

85 *Ibid* at para 5.24.

86 *Ibid* at para 5.27.

87 UNHCR, *Handbook on Procedures and Criteria for Determining Refugee Status*, UNHCR 1979, HCR/IP/4/Eng/REV.1 (Geneva, 1992) [Handbook].

88 The Handbook is evidence of subsequent agreement between the parties on the meaning of the 1951 Convention – part of the treaty's context which guides its interpretation: James C Hathaway, *The Rights of Refugees at International Law* (Cambridge: Cambridge University Press, 2005) at 54.

89 Goodwin-Gill, *supra* note 6 at 328.

> *find an explanation for any misrepresentation or concealment of material facts.*
> (…)
> It will be necessary for the examiner to gain the confidence of the applicant in order *to assist the latter in putting forward his case* and in fully explaining his opinions and feelings.[90]

In sum, examiners should "ensure that the applicant presents his case *as fully as possible* and with *all available evidence*."[91] The Handbook also recognizes that in determining the refugee status of mentally disturbed persons, the first step, wherever possible, should be to obtain expert medical advice on "the nature and degree of mental illness" and "the applicant's ability to fulfill the requirements normally expected of an applicant in presenting his case" which "*will determine the examiner's further approach*."[92]

The UNHCR expects examiners to play an active role in eliciting necessary evidence, clarifying apparent inconsistencies and resolving contradictions to assist the applicant to put forward her case and ensure it is presented as fully as possible and with all available evidence – a role irreconcilable with the High Court's view that the RRT's power to obtain information it considers relevant "is not the source of any obligation to 'seek' more information that might enhance, detract from or otherwise be relevant to information which it has already received."[93]

Observations on the Australian Experience in Inquisitorial Refugee Protection

The RRT's inquisitorial approach, and the limits placed on the role of representatives at the hearing, places applicants at the mercy of tribunal members who must have the necessary skills, experience, competence and resources, including time, to conduct the inquiries required to determine an applicant's status. Far from encouraging members to carry out the function prescribed by the UNHCR as a "necessary minimum" to properly identify refugees, the High Court has narrowly circumscribed the RRT's obligations under the *Migration Act*. It has released members from the obligation to inquire into the plausibility of refugee protection claimants' testimony on a crucial aspect of their claim and their mental capacity to give evidence at their hearing. An inquisitorial system that places on adjudicators no duty to inquire into such basic questions denies claimants their right to be heard, and does not live up to international norms.

In preparing its 2006 report on the administration and operation of the *Migration Act*, the Australian Senate's Legal and Constitutional Affairs Committee received numerous complaints from lawyers and NGOs about the conduct of RRT hearings. Most centered on the broad discretion afforded to members in

90 Handbook, *supra* note 87 at paras 196, 199 and 200 [emphasis added].
91 *Ibid* at 205 [emphasis added].
92 *Ibid* at 208.
93 *SZGUR*, *supra* note 43 at para 86 per Gummow J.

their manner of eliciting evidence from the applicants, including the overuse of "cross-examination techniques" to identify inconsistencies in applicants' evidence and draw adverse credibility findings,[94] and to restrict the role of claimants' representatives.[95] Some complained that members sometimes made conclusions without seeking clarification.[96] The Committee observed that "current provisions allow basic flaws in natural justice, relating to the capacity to respond to adverse evidence, to be properly represented, and to call and challenge witnesses" and concluded that "leaving these matters solely to the arbitrary discretion of Members is not adequate."[97] It recommended that the *Act* be "amended to provide an entitlement to legal representation at Tribunal hearings for applicants and an entitlement to call and examine witnesses at hearings."[98] The Government rejected this recommendation, fearing a return to formal, adversarial adjudication: "The Tribunals are to provide a mechanism for review that is fair, just, economical, informal and quick. The process is intended to be non-adversarial and inquisitorial, and not a formal court hearing."[99]

The Committee also expressed concern that the Migration Review Tribunal (MRT) and RRT be "adequately resourced and funded" to carry out their merits review functions, especially in view of the 90-day target for finalizing reviews on protection visas.[100] Despite the Committee's recommendation that they be reviewed, funding levels remained largely stable in subsequent years, as did the total complement of Tribunal members.[101] In 2012, in response to an increased number of applications to both tribunals and to legislative changes which expanded the RRT's caseload, the number of members has markedly increased.[102] However,

94 Administration, *supra* note 69 at para 3.119 et seq.

95 *Ibid* at para 3.109 et seq.

96 *Ibid* at para 3.119.

97 *Ibid* at para 3.192.

98 *Ibid* at 117 (Recommendation 22).

99 Government Response to Senate Committee Report, Legal and Constitutional References Committee, March 2006, Administration and operation of the *Migration Act* 1958 (May 2007) at 12 [Government response].

100 Administration, *supra* note 69 at para 3.193. It noted, at paras 3.134–3.135, that RRT members' productivity targets were 2.2 cases a week in 2004–05 and commentators had suggested that the challenging nature of their workload could result in pressure to "cut corners." See Australian National Audit Office, Management of Tribunal Operations Migration Review Tribunal and Refugee Review Tribunal Audit Report No. 44 2006–07, 2007.

101 The 2006–2007, 2007–2008, 2008–2009, 2009–2010 and 2010–2011 Annual Reports indicate net cost of services between $38 and 46 million and a total of between 89 and 94 part-time and full-time members: *supra* notes 20 and 21.

102 The 2011–2012 Annual Report indicated an increase to 112 members as of July 2011 and to 145 members as of July 2012. The net cost of services for the MRT–RRT increased to approximately $52 million: MRT–RRT Annual Report 2011–2012, *supra* note 21 at 3, 59.

the MRT–RRT has reported that, to improve efficiency at the tribunals and to reduce the number of unconstituted cases, it has adopted higher annual decision targets for members.[103]

The issues raised by refugee advocates before the Senate Committee and illustrated in *S154* and *SGLB* point to weaknesses in the operation of the RRT's inquisitorial processes. Concerned with their impact on the fairness and accuracy of RRT determinations, the Committee advocated a greater role for legal representatives in RRT hearings, a suggestion rebuffed by the government for reasons of economy, informality and speed. It is questionable whether proceedings before the RRT adequately balance the legal and government models of refugee protection decision-making. The High Court has provided few incentives for RRT members to exercise their inquisitorial powers.[104] Can a tribunal which is not required to exercise its responsibility for the gathering of evidence properly be called inquisitorial? In the following section, I examine Canada's refugee protection system. I argue that recent reforms to the system and failing legal aid coverage may increase the number of unrepresented refugee protection claimants and expose Canada's system to many challenges now faced by Australia.

Canada and Inquisitorial Refugee Protection Decision-making

Canada's Evolving Refugee Protection System

The Refugee Protection Division ("RPD") of the Immigration and Refugee Board ("IRB") is responsible for refugee protection determination. Its members are civil servants appointed in accordance with the *Public Service Employment Act*.[105] Before legislative reforms, implemented in December 2012,[106] RPD members were Governor-in-Council appointees. The RPD has exclusive jurisdiction to hear and determine all questions of law and fact in refugee protection proceedings

103 MRT–RRT Annual Report 2011–2012, *supra* note 21 at 2.

104 The picture is not entirely bleak. The Federal Magistrates Court occasionally quashes RRT decisions where members fail to make inquiries judged necessary by the court: *SZDWF v Minister for Immigration and Multicultural and Indigenous Affairs*, [2005] FMCA 56 (member's failure to secure a copy of the applicant's taped airport interview with immigration officers likely central to his credibility); *SZIWY v Minister for Immigration and Citizenship*, [2007] FMCA 1641 (RRT's failure to consider whether it should exercise its power to obtain an expert psychiatric report); *VWRE v Minister for Immigration and Multicultural Affairs*, [2006] FMCA 430 (failure to call a readily available witness to corroborate the claimant's documentary evidence with which the RRT was not satisfied). The High Court's restrictive reading of the RRT's duty to inquire will likely dampen lower courts' inclination to provide such relief.

105 *Immigration and Refugee Protection Act*, SC 2001, c 27, s 169.1(2) [*IRPA*].

106 *Protecting Canada's Immigration System*, *supra* note 14; *BRRA*, *supra* note 14.

at first instance.[107] Since the reforms, its decisions are subject to a limited right of appeal to the IRB's Refugee Appeal Division ("RAD").[108] The main thrust of the legislative reforms was to speed up the determination of protection claims by introducing stringent timelines for the various stages of this process, described in this section.[109]

Where a person claims refugee protection at a port of entry, an officer with the Canada Border Services Agency ("CBSA") first determines whether the claim is eligible to be referred to the RPD.[110] Eligible claimants are provided with a "Basis of Claim" form requesting information about their identity and about the basis of their protection claim, including a description of the harm they believe they would experience if returned to their country, harm they have experienced, whether they sought protection in their country and the reasons for and details about their flight.[111] Claimants must complete and return the form no later than 15 days after the day their claim is referred to the RPD,[112] failing which an abandonment hearing is scheduled no later than five working days after the due date.[113] A person claiming refugee protection inside Canada other than at a port of entry (making an "inland claim") receives an appointment for an eligibility determination with a Citizenship and Immigration Canada ("CIC") officer and must provide the officer with a completed Basis of Claim form no later than the day of that appointment.[114]

A hearing before the RPD is scheduled no later than 60 days following the date the claim is referred to the RPD.[115] Claims from "designated countries of origin" ("DCO") are singled out for a more expedited process. The Immigration and Refugee Protection Act (*IRPA*) now provides that the Minister of Citizenship and Immigration may, by order, designate countries from which Canada receives

107 *IRPA*, *supra* note 105, s 162(1).

108 *Ibid*, s 110.

109 For a very useful summary of the legislative changes and the access to justice challenges that they have produced for refugee claimants, see University of Ottawa Refugee Assistance Project, "Access to Justice in Canada's New Refugee System: Environmental Scan" (October 2012), online: http://ccrweb.ca/files/uorap_environmental_scan_-_october2012.pdf.

110 *IRPA*, *supra* note 105, s 100. Grounds for ineligibility include where a prior claim by the claimant has been rejected by the RPD or determined to be ineligible, the claimant has come directly from a safe third country designated under regulations (so far, only the United States has been designated) or for grounds of security, violation of human or international rights and serious or organized criminality: *ibid*, s 101.

111 *Refugee Protection Division Rules*, SOR/2012-256, s 1, annex 1 [*RPD Rules*].

112 *IRPA*, *supra* note 105, s 100(4); *Immigration and Refugee Protection Regulations*, SOR/2002-227, s 159.8(2) [*IRP Regulations*]. Where a claim is not referred by the officer to the RPD within three days of receipt, it is deemed to be referred, unless suspended or determined to be ineligible: *IRPA*, *ibid*, s 100(3).

113 *RPD Rules*, *supra* note 111, s 65(2).

114 *IRPA*, *supra* note 105, s 99(3.1); *IRP Regulations*, *supra* note 112, s 159.8(1).

115 *IRP Regulations*, *supra* note 112, s 159.9(1)(b).

more than a threshold number of refugee protection claims a high proportion of which are rejected, withdrawn or abandoned during the same period.[116] The Minister may also designate countries in which, in the Minister's opinion, there is an independent judicial system, basic democratic rights and freedoms are recognized and mechanisms for redress are available if those rights or freedoms are infringed and civil society organizations exist.[117] Hearings of DCO claims must be scheduled 45 days after their referral to the RPD.[118] The time limit for inland DCO claims is 30 days.[119] Time limits may be extended for reasons including fairness and natural justice and "operational limitations of the RPD".[120] Once a hearing date is scheduled, it may be changed only in exceptional circumstances and by no more than 10 working days.[121] Consistent with the legislation's emphasis on timely decision-making, the IRB indicated in pre-reform consultations that postponements (including for non-availability of counsel) would be limited.[122]

Claimants must provide acceptable documents to prove their identity and their claim.[123] They must provide any documentary evidence they wish to rely on in

---

116 *IRPA*, *supra* note 105, s 109(2)(a). The applicable thresholds were established by the Minister of Citizenship and Immigration in the *Order Establishing Quantitative Thresholds for the Designation of Countries of Origin*, (2012) C Gaz I 3378. Countries may be designated if they generated 30 or more claims during any period of 12 consecutive months in the three years preceding the designation and if, over the same period, 75% of determined claims from this country were, in a final determination by the RPD, rejected or determined to have been withdrawn or abandoned or if, over the same period, 60% of determined claims from this country were, in a final determination by the RPD, found to have been withdrawn or abandoned.

117 *IRPA*, *supra* note 105, s 109(2)(b). To date, 37 countries have been designated: see *Order Designating Countries of Origin*, (2012) C Gaz I 3378, *Order Amending the Order Designating Countries of Origin*, (2013) C Gaz I 317, *Order Amending the Order Designating Countries of Origin*, (2013) C Gaz I 1433 and *Order Amending the Order Designating Countries of Origin*, (2013) C Gaz I 1434. These include Hungary and Mexico, two of Canada's top source countries for refugee protection claimants: see www.cdp-hrc.uottawa.ca/projects/ refugee_forum/projects/documents/ REFUGEESTATSCOMPREHENSIVE1999-2011.pdf.

118 *IRP Regulations*, *supra* note 112, s 159.9(1)(a)(ii).

119 *Ibid*, s 159.9(1)(a)(i).

120 *Ibid*, s 159.9(3).

121 *RPD Rules*, *supra* note 111, ss 54(2) and (4).

122 E-mail from Janet Dench, Director – Canadian Council of Refugees, re: Summary of IRB consultative committee meeting (12 May 2011) (on file with author) [Dench e-mail]. Subject to operational limitations, the RPD must allow a claimant to change the hearing date on account of his or her counsel's unavailability only if the claimant retained counsel no later than five working days after the day on which the hearing date was initially fixed and the application to change the date is made within that time period. The new date must remain within the timelines prescribed for RPD hearings: *RPD Rules*, *ibid*, s 54(5).

123 *RPD Rules*, *ibid*, s 11.

support of their claim at least 10 days before the date fixed for the hearing.[124] Similarly, claimants wishing to call witnesses must provide witness information at least 10 days before the hearing date.[125] The IRB indicated in pre-reform consultations that its decisions would be based on the claimant's testimony and documentation that could reasonably be produced within the time available.[126]

Claimants are entitled to legal representation at their own expense.[127] Some provinces provide legal aid to cover some of the costs of hiring a lawyer, subject to strict financial eligibility requirements and, for some provinces, merit-based screening. Claimants unable to afford counsel can sometimes afford to be represented by immigration consultants. In contrast to RRT proceedings, where half the claimants appointed a representative to assist or represent them, pre-reform statistics show that over 90% of claimants benefited from representation before the IRB.[128]

The *IRPA* instructs the RPD to "deal with all proceedings before it as informally and quickly as the circumstances and the considerations of fairness and natural

---

124 *RPD Rules*, *supra* note 111, s 34(3)(a). The RPD may, in its discretion, allow the use of documents not disclosed in a timely way, taking into account their relevance and probative value, new evidence they bring to the hearing and whether the claimant could have with reasonable effort provided the document in a timely manner. Similarly, the RPD may allow the submission of documents after the hearing but before a decision takes effect: *ibid*, s 32.

125 *Ibid*, s 44. The RPD may, in its discretion, allow witness testimony where witness information has not been provided in a timely manner.

126 Dench e-mail, *supra* note 122.

127 *IRPA*, *supra* note 105, s 167(1). Only members in good standing (lawyers, notaries or paralegals) of a provincial law society or the Chambre des Notaires du Québec or of the Immigration Consultants of Canada Regulatory Council may represent refugee claimants for a fee: IRPA, s 91. See also *Regulations Designating a Body for the Purposes of Paragraph 91(2)(c) of the Immigration and Refugee Protection Act*, SOR/2011-142, s 2. The RPD must designate a representative for persons under the age of 18 or who, in the opinion of the RPD, is unable to appreciate the nature of the proceedings. The role of a representative includes deciding whether to retain counsel, instructing counsel and generally making decisions regarding the processing of the claim.

128 See Sean Rehaag, "2012 Refugee Claim Data and IRB Member Recognition Rates" (13 May 2013), online: http://ccrweb.ca/en/2012-refugee claim-data. Professor Rehaag's data indicate that, of 15,266 protection claims finally decided on the merits by the IRB in 2012, only 1,221 involved claims for which no counsel of record (which might include lawyers, notaries or immigration consultants) was reported by the IRB, resulting in a rate of representation of 92%. It is to be noted that these figures do not speak to the extent to which counsel assisted or represented a claimant throughout the refugee protection process. Rather, they confirm that, in 92% of cases decided, counsel was involved at some point and to some extent. The IRB has reported that rates of representation in 2009, 2010 and 2011 were 94%, 94% and 92% respectively (full data is not yet available for 2012): e-mail from Ken Sandhu, Deputy Chairperson, Refugee Appeal Division, Immigration and Refugee Board (12 June 2013) (on file with author).

justice permit."[129] It may inquire into any matter that it considers relevant to establishing whether a claim is well-founded,[130] is not bound by legal or technical rules of evidence[131] and may take official notice of generally recognized facts and information or opinion within its specialized knowledge.[132] It has broad powers and authority over the conduct of hearings and may issue summons, administer oaths, examine persons on oath, issue commissions and may do "any other thing" considered necessary to provide a "full and proper hearing".[133] At the hearing, the claimant is usually questioned first by the RPD member and then by his counsel,[134] an order which can be varied only in exceptional circumstances, including to accommodate a vulnerable person. The RPD is expressly authorized to limit the questioning of witnesses or claimants, taking into account the nature and complexity of the issues and the relevance of the questions.[135] Any representations must be made orally at the end of the hearing and RPD members must render oral decisions and reasons therefor at the hearing unless it is not practicable to do so.[136]

Before the recent legislative reforms, single-member panels of the RPD were assisted by an IRB Refugee Protection Officer ("RPO") who reviewed files to identify issues, conducted research, held interviews, presented evidence, called and questioned witnesses, made representations and generally insured a full and proper examination of the claim.[137] RPOs tested the credibility of applicants and posited legal reasons to reject their claims.[138] RPOs and RPD members would cross-examine the claimant to "flush out any weaknesses in the claimant's case that might lead to a determination that the claimant 'is not' a person in need of protection",[139] making the RPD hearing a relatively inquisitorial process.[140] This inquisitorial role is now assumed solely by RPD members.

---

129 *IRPA*, *supra* note 105, s 162(2).

130 *Ibid*, s 170(a).

131 *Ibid*, s 170(g).

132 *Ibid*, s 170(i).

133 *Ibid*, s 165.

134 *RPD Rules*, *supra* note 111, s 10(1). Where the Minister of Citizenship and Immigration intervenes in a proceeding to exclude the claimant or in other circumstances, the Minister will question the claimant before the claimant's lawyer.

135 *Ibid*, s 10(6).

136 *Ibid*, ss 10(7), (8). In 2011 consultations on the impending legislative reforms, the IRB stated that its target would be for 80% of decisions to be delivered orally: Dench e-mail, *supra* note 122.

137 *Ibid*, s 16.

138 Lorne Waldman, *Canadian Immigration & Refugee Law Practice* (Toronto: LexisNexis Butterworths, 2004) at 338.

139 *Thamotharem v Canada (Minister of Citizenship and Immigration)*, 2006 FC 16 (TD) at paras 70–1 [*Thamotharem FCTD*], reversed on other grounds, 2007 FCA 198 [*Thamotharem FCA*].

140 *Ibid* at para 44.

Claimants may appeal the RPD's decision to dismiss their protection claim to the newly launched Refugee Appeal Division ("RAD").[141] However, appeals are not available in several circumstances, including:[142]

- where the claimant is from a Designated Country of Origin;
- where the claimant is a "designated foreign national" defined as a foreign national who is part of a group whose arrival is designated by the Minister of Citizenship and Immigration as an "irregular arrival". The Minister may make such a designation if he or she is of the opinion that examinations (to determine identity) or investigations of persons in the group cannot be conducted in a timely manner or if he or she has reasonable grounds to suspect that human smuggling or trafficking has occurred;[143]
- where the RPD, in dismissing the protection claim, determined that it had no credible basis[144] or was manifestly unfounded;[145] and
- where the claimant made his or her claim at the Canada-US border and was found to qualify for an exception to the Safe Third Country Agreement, which normally renders ineligible for determination claims brought by claimants coming from the United States.[146]

Staffed by Governor in Council appointees,[147] the RAD may sit in panels of three or in single-member panels.[148] Its appellate jurisdiction extends to questions of law, fact and mixed law and fact.[149] It may decide to confirm the RPD decision, set it aside and substitute its own determination or, if it can do neither without hearing evidence that was presented to the RPD, it can refer the matter back to the RPD for re-determination.[150] It must proceed without a hearing on the basis of the record of the RPD proceedings, but may accept documentary evidence limited (for claimants) to evidence that arose after the rejection of their claim or that was not reasonably available or that the claimants could not reasonably have been expected

141 The RAD was launched on December 15, 2012: Canada, Immigration and Refugee Board, "Refugee Appeal Division", online: www.irb-cisr.gc.ca/Eng/tribunal/radsar/pages/index.aspx.

142 *IRPA*, *supra* note 105, s 110(2).

143 *Ibid*, ss 20.1(1), (2).

144 Where, in the opinion of the RPD, no credible or trustworthy evidence supported the claim: *ibid*, s 107(2).

145 Where the RPD is of the opinion that the claim is clearly fraudulent: *ibid*, s 107.1.

146 *Ibid*, s 101(1)(e).

147 *Ibid*, s 153(1).

148 Decisions of three-member panels have, for the RPD and single-member RAD panel, the same precedential value as the decision of an appeal court for trial courts: *ibid*, s 171(c).

149 *Ibid*, s 110(1).

150 *Ibid*, s 111.

to have presented to the RPD at the time of the rejection.[151] The RAD can only hold an in-person hearing where documentary evidence is submitted to the RAD by the Minister or claimant that raises a serious issue regarding the claimant's credibility that is central to the refugee protection decision and, if accepted, would justify allowing or rejecting the claim.[152] Absent such documentary evidence, the RAD will not be in a position to make its own in-person assessment of the claimant's credibility even if the RPD's findings in this respect are challenged on appeal.

Appeals to the RAD are also subject to short timelines. The claimant must file a notice of appeal within 15 days of the RPD decision, and must perfect the appeal by filing, within 30 days of the RPD decision,[153] an appellant's record which includes the RPD decision, transcripts of the RPD hearing relied upon, relevant documents that the RPD refused to accept as evidence, documentary evidence, case law and a legal memorandum of argument.[154] The RAD may extend each of these time limits for reasons of fairness or natural justice.[155] In deciding an application for an extension of time, the RAD will consider the justification for the delay, whether there is an arguable case, prejudice to the Minister and the nature and complexity of the appeal.[156] Unless it holds an in-person hearing, the RAD is required to render a decision on an appeal within 90 days after the date the appeal is perfected or, if that is not possible, as soon as feasible thereafter.[157]

The inquisitorial nature of refugee protection in Canada and the impact of reforms

Before the 2012 legislative reforms, the inquisitorial nature of RPD hearings and its impact on hearing fairness received judicial consideration. In *Thamotharem*, the Federal Court of Appeal found that the IRB's Guideline 7, which provided that the RPO or RPD member, not the claimant's counsel, would ordinarily question the claimant first,[158] did not breach the duty of procedural fairness. It held that, although the adjudicative nature of the RPD's functions, the finality of its decisions and the importance of the rights at stake demanded a high level of procedures, the content of the duty varied with the context, and in particular, Parliament's choice of an inquisitorial procedural model. In other words, "not all the elements of the adversarial procedural model followed in the courts are necessarily required for a

151 *IRPA*, *supra* note 105, ss 110(3), (4).

152 *Ibid*, s 110(6).

153 *IRP Regulations*, *supra* note 112, s 159.91(1).

154 *Refugee Appeal Division Rules*, SOR 2012-257, s 3(3) [*RAD Rules*].

155 *IRP Regulations*, *supra* note 112, s 159.91(2).

156 *RAD Rules*, *supra* note 152, s 6(7).

157 *IRP Regulations*, *supra* note 112, s 159.92.

158 This requirement has since been incorporated into the *RPD Rules*, *supra* note 111, s 10(2).

fair hearing of a refugee claim."[159] In fact, the fair adjudication of individual rights was "perfectly compatible" with the inquisitorial process.[160] The oral hearing held by the RPD "must ... be tailored to fit the inquisitorial and relatively informal nature of the hearing established by Parliament, as well as the RPD's high volume case load, considerations which reduce the power of the claim to aspects of the adversarial model used in courts, including the order of questioning."[161] The Court also rejected Thamotharem's claim that Guideline 7 interfered with his right to the assistance of counsel:

> Guideline 7 does not curtail counsel's participation in the hearing; counsel is present throughout and may conduct an examination of the client to ensure that the claimant's testimony is before the decision-maker. The right to be represented by counsel does not include the right of counsel to determine the order of questioning or, for that matter, any other aspect of the procedure to be followed at the hearing.[162]

With the 2012 legislative reforms, RPD hearings have conserved their inquisitorial nature and the powers of RPD members to conduct hearings are substantially unchanged. However, with the elimination of RPOs, RPD members now bear the full burden of this inquisitorial function.

At the time of writing, it is still too early into the implementation of the new refugee protection regime to obtain and analyze empirical data regarding its operation. However, it is likely that the most significant impact of these reforms may be to restrict refugee protection claimants' ability to secure representation for the refugee protection proceedings.[163] Most refugee claimants, having arrived in Canada at the most a few months before, will likely not have received a work permit and will require legal aid.[164] Refugee advocates have expressed concern that provincial authorities may take several weeks to approve legal aid, depleting the limited time available to retain counsel and for counsel to prepare for the hearing.[165] In his pre-reform assessment of legal aid for refugee claimants, Sean

159 *Thamotharem FCA*, *supra* note 113 at para 35.

160 *Ibid* at para 44.

161 *Ibid* at para 41.

162 *Ibid* at para 49.

163 For an overview of refugee claimants' primary legal services needs under the new legislation and the challenges facing provincial legal aid regimes to appropriately meet these needs, see Refugee Forum, "Legal Aid for Refugee Claimants in Canada" (June 2012), online: http://www.cdp-hrc.uottawa.ca/projects/refugee-forum/documents/ReportonLegalAidforRefugeeClaimantsRefugeeForumfinal.pdf.

164 Canadian Council for Refugees, "Proposed refugee appeal timelines are completely unworkable!" (on file with author).

165 Canadian Council for Refugees, "Protecting rights in a fair and efficient refugee determination system – Submission on Bill C-11" (5 May 2010), online: www.ccrweb.ca (accessed October 4, 2010) [CCR Submission on C-11] at 6.

Rehaag observed that, in Ontario, where close to 60% of refugee claimants reside, legal aid coverage is contingent on claimants meeting strict financial eligibility requirements and satisfying additional criteria.[166] Impecunious claimants from listed countries and/or who fear specific types of persecution there generally received legal aid certificates. Others received "opinion certificates" to pay private bar lawyers to prepare opinions on the merits of their claim which were reviewed by Legal Aid Ontario. Legal Aid Ontario has been working to expedite its process for funding applications from refugee claimants in order to accommodate the new legislation's shortened timelines by, among other things, defining claimant streams based on country of origin and the nature of the claim. Those claimants falling within "stream 1" receive a five-hour legal aid certificate to assist with the preparation of a Basis of Claim form. Others go on to a fuller merits assessment of their claim.[167] It is still too early to assess whether these measures are adequately addressing refugee claimants' needs for timely legal representation. At the time of writing, Legal Aid Ontario had just established a Review Committee to provide advice on implementation of its changes to refugee services over a one-year period.[168] There is urgency in making the system work. The more time the legal aid application processes take, the more likely refugee claimants risk attending the RPD hearing or RAD appeal (if they qualify and are able to navigate the strict time limits and procedural requirements) without counsel. In recent years, a growing number of refugee claimants were failing to qualify for legal aid certificates altogether, with increases in demand outpacing the increase in supply (22.8% versus 2.5% between 2006 and 2009).[169] While representation by immigration consultants is an option for some, claimants represented by lawyers have a much higher likelihood of success than claimants represented by consultants.[170]

The bottom line is that there may be more unrepresented (and less effectively represented) claimants due to the combination of expedited timelines and insufficient legal aid coverage, an outcome anticipated by the IRB in pre-reform

166 See generally Rehaag, *supra* note 19 at 94 et seq.

167 Legal Aid Ontario, News Release, "LAO accelerates application process for refugees" (8 February 2013), online: http:/www.legalaid.on.ca/en/news/newsarchive/1302-07_countrylist.asp.

168 Legal Aid Ontario, News Release, "LAO review committee to advise on implementation of refugee services transformation initiative" (8 May 2013), online: http:/www.legalaid.on.ca/en/news/newsarchive/1305-07_Refugee ServicesImplementation.asp. [LAO review committee].

169 *Ibid* at 95–6. Rehaag expressed similar concerns about legal aid in Québec, British Columbia and Alberta: *ibid* at 97–103.

170 Rehaag, *supra* note 18 at 92. Rehaag notes that this is seen most strongly for claimants from countries with low to average grant rates. This means that claimants from DCOs, which are characterized by low grant rates, would benefit from representation by counsel. Unfortunately, they are hampered in their ability to retain counsel in a timely manner by the expedited timelines.

consultations.[171] Tight timelines may prevent claimants from obtaining and presenting documentary evidence in support of their claim, including expert evidence (medical, psychiatric and psychological reports often required by vulnerable claimants) and documentation on the individual case and country conditions.[172] Though time may be extended as required by procedural fairness, the logic of the legislation will result in the RPD making determinations based on the claimant's testimony and documentation that can be reasonably produced within the time limits.[173] Many refugees, including victims of torture or sexual assault or LGBT persons, need to build trust in order to testify freely.[174] They may provide incomplete or inaccurate statements on their Basis of Claim form which must be filed within stringent timelines, potentially raising inconsistencies that will provide the foundation for adverse credibility determinations, as illustrated in *Applicant S154*.

Concluding Observations

Both the Australian and Canadian refugee protection systems are characterized as "non-adversarial" and "inquisitorial." Both the RRT and RPD have broad discretionary powers to obtain information they consider relevant to determining the merits of the refugee claim. Both have a large measure of control over the conduct of their proceedings. To date, a significant difference between the two systems had been the scope of the role played by counsel at the refugee protection hearings. In Canada, legal counsel, who before recent reforms were present at over 90% of hearings, can lead evidence and question the claimant to complete the evidence or address apparent inconsistencies or contradictions raised by the RPD member. In Australia, representatives, who are present at only half of the hearings, do not enjoy such participatory rights. The "inquisitorial" RRT was intended to allow a fair and accurate determination of protection claims in the absence of active representation of claimants. However, Australian courts have determined that, in all but exceptional circumstances, the RRT is under no statutory obligation to inquire, placing upon the Tribunal little external incentive to ensure, as the UNHCR Handbook and international law require, that each claimant present her case as fully as possible and with all available evidence. With the recent reforms to Canada's refugee system and the growing inadequacy of legal aid coverage in Canada, the IRB may soon find itself operating in a context similar to Australia's: an inquisitorial system functioning in a greater proportion of cases without the moderating influence of legal counsel effectively representing the claimant at the hearing. Moreover, the removal of RPOs at the hearing may place on the RPD

171 Dench e-mail, *supra* note 122.

172 CCR Submission on C-11, *supra* note 165 at 6–7.

173 Dench e-mail, *supra* note 122.

174 CCR Submission on C-11, *supra* note 165 at 6.

members, like their counterparts at the RRT, a greater burden to prepare for and conduct hearings and may produce pressures to "cut corners." As observed with regard to asylum appeals in the United Kingdom, tight time limits for the submission and determination of appeals put the asylum appeal process under pressure "to meet the demands of efficiency and cost-effectiveness" which, combined with restrictions to the availability of legal aid, challenged its ability to achieve fair and accurate decision-making.[175]

In such circumstances, would Canadian courts, like their Australian counterparts, refrain from subjecting the RPD to a robust duty to inquire? The Federal Court of Appeal indicated in *Thamotharem* that fairness requires that claimants "be given an adequate opportunity to tell their story in full, to adduce evidence in support of their claim, and to make submissions relevant to it."[176] A properly conducted inquisitorial hearing may in theory achieve this standard, but as illustrated by the Australian experience, much will depend on the members' experience and training in inquisitorial procedures and likely on the resources and time available to members to perform their function adequately.[177] One would expect a well-functioning inquisitorial refugee protection process to be lawyer or representative-neutral. Empirical research demonstrated that the pre-reform Canadian system was not. Representation matters: "access to competent and qualified counsel – and especially to experienced lawyers – is a key determinant of outcomes in life-and-death refugee determinations across the full range of countries of origin."[178]

There are few reasons to believe that the reforms to Canada's refugee protection system will improve fairness and accuracy in decision making. In fact, the contrary may be true. The new RPD will, at least in the short term, be staffed by individuals with less accumulated expertise in refugee determination than before. They will be facing tighter timelines than before. If anything, to face the challenges outlined above, the adjudicators at the new RPD will need more resources and more training than before to conduct inquisitorial hearings.[179] But, where some of them fail in their task, there is reason to believe that Canadian courts will

175 *Thomas*, *supra* note 56 at 477.

176 *Thamotharem FCA*, *supra* note 139 at para 39.

177 For a discussion of active or enabling adjudication of immigration and refugee appeals in the UK, see Robert Thomas, "From 'Adversarial v Inquisitorial' to 'Active, Enabling, and Investigative': Developments in UK Administrative Tribunals", at Chapter 3 of this volume.

178 Rehaag, *supra* note 18 at 93.

179 The availability of an appeal on the merits for some claimants (there is a long list of claimants, including those from DCOs and designated foreign nationals, for whom the appeal is not available) will not cure all deficiencies in first instance determination. The RAD's ability to properly review credibility determinations on a paper hearing is uncertain at best. The tight timelines to perfect a RAD appeal will make it difficult for counsel to secure the evidence required to trigger an in-person hearing allowing an adequate review of credibility determinations.

step in. In Australia, the courts' interpretation of the RRT's inquisitorial powers, which has privileged efficient and cost-effective adjudication over the delivery of accurate and independent decisions through fair procedures, is supported by the broad, discretionary language of the *Migration Act*, which trumps common law procedural fairness. In Canada, refugee claimants, whose security of the person is engaged by the refugee protection process, have a constitutional right to a hearing comporting with fundamental justice.[180] Accordingly, irrespective of the terms of the statute, they are owed an adequate opportunity to tell their story in full, adduce evidence in support of their claim and make submissions, and courts are bound to ensure that the RPD affords them this opportunity. Demands of efficiency and the high-volume, inquisitorial decision-making model adopted by Parliament will no doubt inform courts' analysis of whether the refugee determination process meets these basic requirements of procedural justice; however, these considerations cannot excuse procedures that are fundamentally unfair.[181]

A non-adversarial system of adjudication with inquisitorial features should be well-suited to refugee protection decision-making. In practice, however, there are problems. Until these are resolved, Canada's federal and provincial governments should ensure that legal aid for refugee claimants is well-funded. Failing this, Canadian courts should step in to prevent injustice in individual cases and subject the RPD to a robust constitutional duty to inquire.

180 *Singh v Canada (Minister of Employment and Immigration)*, [1985] 1 SCR 177.

181 *Charkaoui v Canada (Citizenship and Immigration)*, [2007] 1 SCR 350 at paras 23 et seq.

PART 2
EU Administrative Law and Polyjural Decision-making

Chapter 8

Inquisitorial Procedures and General Principles of Law: The Duty of Care in the Case Law of the European Court of Justice

Herwig C.H. Hofmann[1]

Introduction

The question of who is in charge of providing (and possibly proving) the relevant information for decision-making appears to be one of the key questions resulting in the classification of a procedure as "adversarial" or "inquisitorial."[2] Within the scope of application of European Union (EU) law, administrative decision-making generally relies on the generation and sharing of information, by highly integrated administrative networks consisting of EU and Member State institutions and bodies plus private actors.[3] EU administrative law provides rules and principles governing "who" has to generate information, by "what means", of "what quality", from "which source", and "how", finally, such information is to be used for the implementation of EU policies. The applicable rules and principles

1 This chapter is in parts taken from chapter 12 of Herwig CH Hofmann, Gerard C Rowe & Alexander H Türk, *Administrative Law and Policy of the European Union* (Oxford: Oxford University Press, 2011). By permission of Oxford University Press. www.oup.com.

2 The notion of "inquisitorial" procedures is used here in the sense of a juxtaposition with the notion of "adversarial" to describe certain archetypical types of administrative procedures. It is not used in the context of describing certain criminal procedures in pre-enlightenment times.

3 In EU administrative law, generally, the composition of a file is a joint, composite effort of Member State and EU administrations. Decision-making is then undertaken on the basis of that file by either an EU or a Member State body. An adversarial element comes into play in so far as that any decision affecting the rights of an individual is subject to judicial review in an independent Court. This right is guaranteed in Article 47 of the EU's Charter of Fundamental Rights (CFR). The first paragraph of Article 47 CFR states that "Everyone whose rights and freedoms guaranteed by the law of the Union are violated has the right to an effective remedy before a tribunal in compliance with the conditions laid down in this Article." The formulation of this article is slightly misleading, since it is the Court which will establish whether procedural or substantive rights of an individual have been violated. The claim of such violation opens the access to Court.

relate to all aspects of administrative activity, be it subordinate legislation and administrative rule-making, or single case decision-making (adjudication). They apply irrespective of whether a decision is to be based upon objective criteria, or whether the administration enjoys a certain level of discretion.[4]

Such rules and principles, as is usual in EU administrative law, have not been established by general legislation on administrative procedure. Instead, they have been established mainly with respect to individual policy areas. Nevertheless, certain standard structures and frameworks for handling information gathering and exchange have also emerged. Such general rules on information and its role in EU public administration arise from the protection of certain basic rights, from general principles of law and from certain important rules related specifically to the EU institutional structure. The key concepts of this general administrative law of the EU has largely been developed in the case law of the Court of Justice of the European Union (CJEU) and will be the main focus of this chapter. The approach of governing EU public law by the development and refinement of general principles of European Union (EU) law is a common approach of the CJEU. It is necessary to establish the legal backbone of a complex system of procedurally highly integrated administrations which implement EU policies jointly.

The purpose-driven generation of information prior to decision-making can involve the collecting or assembling of other pre-existing information. Within Europe's administrative network, as in national systems, decision-making by an authority (whether by an EU institution or a Member State) may rely not only on information gathered by that authority itself, but may also be generated by other public or private actors, for example, by an agency of (another) Member State, by (another) EU body, or by a private party. Correspondingly, such actors have both rights to request and obligations to maintain and to provide information.[5] In some cases, rules relating to the sourcing of information require an EU or Member State institution or body to generate and maintain all relevant information itself. This

4 This chapter is limited in that it exclusively deals with the administrative law of the EU. It does not give a comparative overview over the EU and its Member States' legal systems. The EU legal order often differs significantly from the structures in the Member States, as the legal systems of the Member States differ considerably amongst each other. Thereby, it is often less relevant whether a legal system belongs to a certain family of law. Important for the distinction are, in my comparative experience, factors such as, *inter alia*, whether a system has a written constitution, a constitutional court, a written Administrative Procedure Act, a specific system of administrative courts, a written catalogue of fundamental rights and many other more.

5 The topic of the law of information has been so far not been treated with great attention in legal writing on EU administrative law. A notable exception to this is the work by J Sommer, *Verwaltungskooperation am Beispiel administrativer Informationsverfahren im Europäischen Umweltrecht* (Berlin: Springer, 2003) and the summary thereof in J Sommer, "Informationskooperation am Beispiel des Europäischen Umweltrechts" in Eberhard Schmidt-Assmann & Bettina Schöndorf-Haubold, eds, *Der Europäische Verwaltungsverbund* (Tübingen: Mohr Siebeck, 2005) 57.

is so, for example, in competition law, where the EU Commission is the central enforcement authority together with Member States agencies. In other policy areas, the principle that individuals must supply pertinent information is common, for example, where they request authorizations to market a product, to register an intellectual property right, or a chemical compound. Finally, some policy areas' mix of inquisitive and adjudicatory roles in which, at different steps in a procedure (often under the influence of varying rules on the burden of proof), information is either directly collected by administrative actors or submitted by individuals, for example, in the area of state aid enforcement. Various instruments to obtain information exist but each requires for their application a legal basis in specific legislation regarding a policy area.

These instruments include investigations, controls, inspections, information injunctions and auditing procedures. Investigative powers are given to the "enquiring" administration such as the Commission or other EU authorities as well as Member States, including the right of one Member State to undertake an investigation in another EU Member State.[6] Inspections are specifically intensive forms of control serving the purpose of administrative information gathering. Through inspections, fact-finding takes place either physically, on the premises of the person or organization being inspected, or through the control of books and accounts or other documentation provided to the administrative bodies.[7] Information injunctions are decisions which can be issued on the basis of a specific legal basis to "specify what information is required and prescribe an appropriate period within which it is to be supplied."[8] Auditing is an important part of investigations into either private activity or that of other administrations. For example, in relations between the EU administration and the Member States, auditing plays an important role, for example in tracing Member States' distribution of EU moneys.

Information sourcing is a further part of often complex administrative procedures such as requests for authorizations, planning procedures or complaints procedures. In that respect, mostly private parties will request an administrative decision, or networks of administrative actors will enter into joint planning procedures. The

---

6 This is an exceptional arrangement; for example, in the area of supervision of banking and financial institutions, see Art 43(1) of *Directive 2006/48/EC of the European Parliament and of the Council of 14 June 2006 relating to the taking up and pursuit of the business of credit institutions (recast) Text with EEA relevance*, [2006] OJ, L 177/1 (which replaced EC, *Directive 2000/12/EC of the European Parliament and of the Council of 20 March 2000 relating to the taking up and pursuit of the business of credit institutions*, [2000] OJ, L 126/1).

7 For more detail consult especially Giacinto della Cananea's contribution in this volume.

8 An example is offered by Article 10(3) of the procedural regulation on state aids: EC, *Council Regulation 659/1999 of 22 March 1999 laying down detailed rules for the application of Art. 93 of the EC Treaty*, [1999] OJ, L 83/1 [Regulation 659/1999].

result is the requirement of providing the responsible administrative actors with relevant information such as to enable it to make an informed decision.

Despite the fact that the provisions governing inspections are spread across legislative acts relating to diverse single policy areas, limitations on the powers of inspection emerge from several general legal principles.[9] First, all administrative activity, whether undertaken by an EU body or a Member State authority acting within the sphere of European law, must be proportionate.[10] When undertaking inspections, especially *vis-à-vis* individuals, fundamental rights must be observed and protected.[11] Further discussion of these points is undertaken by the contribution of Giacinto della Cananea in this volume.

The "Duty of Care" as General Principle of EU Administrative Law

The principle of the duty of care arises from the administrative obligation to fully and impartially assess all the relevant factors leading to a decision prior to decision-making. Judicial review of administrative decision-making will review compliance of the administration of rules and principles of European administrative law relating to the use of information. This includes, for example, the issue of the level of information which must be established and quality demands which must be met by the information collected prior to decision-making. Courts establish and police these standards as to which information needs to be collected, and how – especially according to what standards – in order to serve as the basis of administrative decision-making under European administrative law. Judicial review regarding this point can thus become very strict, including full review of law and facts and, in certain cases having the effect of the reviewing Court replacing the administrative decision entirely. Although on its face based on procedural elements of decision-making, essentially it focuses on the questions directly related to its substance.

The level of information which needs to be brought together in order to allow an authority to take a decision within European administrative law is generally either explicitly or implicitly laid down in specific legal acts. Thus it will differ according to the policy field in question. As a general principle of EU administrative

9 See Jean-Bernard Auby, "Les pouvoirs d'inspection de l'Union européenne" (2006) 42 RTDE 131 at 136; Antje David, *Inspektionen im Europäischen Verwaltungsrecht* (Berlin: Duncker & Humblot, 2003) 277; Alberto Gil Ibañez, *The Administrative Supervision and Enforcement of EC Law* (Oxford: Hart, 1999) 71.

10 For example, Case 68/88 *Commission of the European Communities v Greece* [1989] ECR 2965. See with details Paul Craig, *EU Administrative Law* (Oxford: Oxford University Press, 2006) at 703 [Paul Craig]; Antje David, *Inspektionen im Europäischen Verwaltungsrecht* (Berlin: Duncker & Humblot, 2003) at 216–23 and 269.

11 Case 136/79 *National Panasonic v Commission of the European Communities* [1980] ECR at paras 17–22.

law, however, prior to an administrative decision, all relevant information must be assembled and assessed as to its potential influence on the final determination of the matter. This is the content of the general principle of the "duty of care", or sometimes also referred to as the "duty of diligent and impartial examination" by administrative actors. In EU case law, the duty of care is closely linked with the right to a fair hearing (the *audi alteram partem* rule)[12] and is now regarded as one of the general principles protected under the umbrella notion of "good administration."[13]

The duty of care was first explicitly mentioned in the case law of the CJEU (before entry into force of the Treaty of Lisbon, it was known as the ECJ) by van Gerven AG.[14] It has since been applied in reviewing the exercise of Commission discretion, especially in the context of economic regulation,[15] but also in cases of risk regulation.[16] The duty of care, or of diligent and impartial examination, is thus an important element of judicial review of inquisitorial-type administrative procedures. In particular, it sets the standard for the amount and detail of information to be established prior to taking a decision, and the way in which this information is then processed. The CJEU defined the duty of care to mean that the Commission was obliged to scrutinize the "information contained in the documents in the case ... with all the due care required."[17] It developed this obligation with respect to

12 HP Nehl, *Principles of Administrative Procedure in EC Law* (Oxford: Hart, 1999) at 103–5.

13 Also protected by Art. 41(1) CFR (Charter of Fundamental Rights of the European Union).

14 Opinion of Advocate General van Gerven in Case C-16/90 *Nölle v Hauptzollamt Bremen-Freihafen* [1991] ECR I-5163.

15 See, in particular, Cases T-211/02 *Tieland Signal Ltd v Commission* [2002] ECR II-3781 at para 37; Case T-54/99 *max.mobil v Commission* [2002] ECR II-313 at paras 48–51; Case C-449/98 *P IECC v Commission* [2001] ECR I-3875 at para 45; Case T-24/90 *Automec v Commission* [1992] ECR II-2223, para 79; Case T-95/96 *Gestevisión Telecinco v Commission* [1998] ECR II-3407 at para 53; Joined cases 142/84 and 156/84 *BAT and Reynolds v Commission* [1987] ECR 4487 at para 20. See also, with further detail, Paul Craig, *supra* note 10 at 374–5.

16 See, for example, Case T-13/99 *Pfizer Animal Health SA v Council* [2002] ECR II-3305, paras 170–2. The notions of risk and risk regulation have been element of several specific studies. See, for instance, with further references, J Neyer, "Risikoregulierung im Binnenmarkt: Zur Problemlösungsfähigkeit der europäischen politischen Verwaltung" in Christian Jörges & Joseph Falke, eds, *Das Ausschusswesen der Europäischen Union* (Baden-Baden: Nomos, 2000) 257; S Perez, "L'administration communautaire et la gestion du risque" (2001) 24 Annuaire Européen d'Administration Publique 323; E Fischer, "Risk and Challenges for Administrative Law" (2003) 15 ERPL/REDP 707.

17 The Court found this lacking in Nölle I, an anti-dumping case, and one of the first cases to explicitly refer to the duty of care. See Case C-16/90 *Nölle v Hauptzollamt Bremen-Freihafen* (Nölle I) [1991] ECR I-5163 at para 29.

anti-dumping matters in the *Nölle* cases,[18] and with respect to customs duties in *TU München*. In the latter, the Court found that the Commission was under the obligation to examine carefully and impartially all relevant facts and aspects of the particular case.[19] That case is important as the Court specifically based the annulment of the Commission decision *inter alia* on the violation of the duty of care by the Commission. The fault of the Commission was that, in its assessments of the facts, it had relied on "experts" who lacked the technical expertise needed for assessing the merits of the individual case.[20]

The principle of the duty of care applies to all steps of an administrative procedure. This has been established, for example, by the case law on multi-step competition procedures in which an initial investigation may be followed by a second phase in-depth investigation.[21] The duty of care is, therefore, applicable in the decision of the administrative body as to whether to follow up triggering information such as a complaint, whether to pursue a preliminary investigation in initial phase and finally, where a second in-depth phase is conducted, to what extent and depth the investigation needs to be taken in the path toward a final decision.[22] The application of the duty of care in competition law (antitrust) cases has for example led to the limiting of the Commission's discretion to react to an individual complaint about anti-competitive behaviors of a competitor. The

18 Nölle I was followed a few years later by Case T-167/94 *Nölle v Council and Commission* (Nölle II) [1995] ECR II-2589 at para 129 in which the GC (the former Court of First Instance, CFI) established the duty of care as a "rule protecting individuals."

19 Case C-269/90 *Technische Universität München v Hauptzollamt München- Mitte* [1991] ECR I-5469 at para 14. In that case, the technical university of Munich sought to benefit from an exemption from import duties in the EU customs code for imports of scientific instruments for which there was no equivalent produced in the EU. The university claimed that a microscope imported from Japan fell under this rule. The German customs officials and, upon review, the European Commission held that a microscope produced by a Dutch company was an equivalent to the imported Japanese product. Upon judicial review, the CJEU (then the ECJ) established that the Commission was obliged to base its decision on sufficiently qualified experts or else risking to violate the duty of care obliging the administration to fully and impartially investigate the case prior to taking a decision.

20 See Francis Jacobs AG in Case C-296/90 *Technische Universität München v Hauptzollamt München-Mitte* [1991] ECR I-5469 at paras 21, 30.

21 See, for example, Case T-7/92 *Asia Motor France and others v Commission* [1993] ECR II-669 at para 34: an antitrust case in which an initial *prima facie* investigation will require a subsequent full-scale investigation, should the Commission as administrative authority wish to prohibit certain activity for its anti-competitive effects or issue a fine for violation of EU competition law.

22 In German administrative law, the term "maturity" (*Entscheidungsreife*) is used indicating that an administrative decision may only be taken if the case file has sufficiently advanced in information gathering.

Commission is under an obligation "to examine carefully the factual and legal aspects of which it is notified by the complainant."[23]

The outcome of this examination must be communicated to the complainant in a reasoned decision, which is subject to judicial review.[24] In *Sytraval*, involving a complaint to the Commission from a competitor against an allegedly illegal state aid, the Court highlighted the importance of this understanding of the obligation.[25] The applicant had challenged the Commission's decision rejecting the complaint. The General Court (GC, prior to the entry into force of the Treaty of Lisbon known as the Court of First Instance, CFI) favored an expansive reading of the obligations upon the Commission arising from the duty of care. In deciding in state aid proceedings whether to embark upon a second phase, in which the complainant would have been procedurally entitled to present its arguments, the Commission had the "automatic obligation to examine the objections which the complainant would certainly have raised if it had been given the opportunity of taking cognizance of that information."[26] On appeal, the CJ (Court of Justice, formerly known as ECJ, now the highest-level Court within the CJEU) rejected this far-reaching view, but found that the Commission could be required "to conduct a diligent and impartial examination of the complaint, which may make it necessary for it to examine matters not expressly raised by the complainant."[27]

Where the Commission has entered into a formal investigation, the duty of care obliges the administration, in refining the matter to enable a final decision to be made, to conduct its investigation with "the requisite care, seriousness and diligence so as to be able to assess with full knowledge of the case the factual and legal particulars submitted for its appraisal."[28] The GC has in the past repeatedly sought to establish the duty of care as a general principle of law applicable in all policy fields within, where given, the framework of procedural rules laid out in secondary law. This raises the link between the duty of care and the general principle of good or sound administration. This approach was pursued in *max.mobil*,[29] a leading case in which an Austrian telecom company requested the annulment of those parts of a Commission decision rejecting *max.mobil*'s complaint against the abuse of a dominant position by a competitor, then under Article 82 EC (now Article 102 TFEU). The Court found that "it must be emphasized at the outset that the diligent and impartial treatment of a complaint is associated with the right to sound administration which is one of the general principles that are observed in a

23 Case T-24/90 *Automec v Commission* [1992] ECR II-2223 at para 79.

24 Case T-77/95 *Ufex and others v Commission* [2000] ECR II-2167 at para 42.

25 Case T-95/94 *Sytraval and Brink's France v Commission* [1995] ECR II-2651.

26 *Ibid* at para 66.

27 Case C-367/95 P *Commission v Sytraval and Brinks France* [1998] ECR I-1719 at paras 60, 62, linking this duty to the principle of sound or good administration.

28 Case T-206/99 *Métropole Télévision v Commission* [2001] ECR II-2707 at para 59.

29 Case T-54/99 *max.mobil v Commission* [2002] ECR II-313.

State governed by the rule of law and are common to the constitutional traditions of the Member States."[30]

The CJ has, however, been cautious in following the GC's lead in taking an expansive view of the duty of care. Instead it has traditionally focused more on the procedural obligations in each individual policy area. Although not contesting the link between the duty of care and the general principle of good or sound administration, in the appeal to *max.mobil* the Court linked it with particular obligations burdening the Commission in handling competition complaints under Article 82 EC (now Article 102 TFEU).[31] This more restricted view of the scope of the duty of care has not, however, prevented the Court from invoking the duty as a general specification of the criteria of investigatory diligence also in its case law in other policy areas and questions, especially risk regulation, as discussed in the following section concerning scientific evidence.

The duty to investigate fully and impartially all aspects of a case prior to taking a decision can also encompass the analysis of its potential impact on other collateral aspects.[32] Sharpston AG, in a matter concerning a Spanish support scheme for cotton producers, referred to the obligation of the institutions to explore the element of a decision fully, prior to taking a decision, as the obligation to undertake an "impact study."[33] This obligation is linked to the principle of proportionality insofar as it imposes "an obligation on Community institutions at least to satisfy themselves that the proposed measures are prima facie adequate to attain the legitimate aims pursued."[34] These questions are linked to the control over the exercise of discretion in judicial review. In that case, the CJ did not, however, explicitly refer to these significant issues raised by the Advocate General, nor to the conclusions which she drew. In two more recent cases, however this has been changed. The CJ now has established case law reviewing the legality of a measure under the principle of proportionality by establishing whether there is proof of the respect of the duty of care. The proof is supplied in both cases by means of an in-depth analysis of the

30 Case T-54/99 *max.mobil v Commission, supra* note 29 at para 48, with reference to Art 41(1) of the Charter of Fundamental Rights of the European Union proclaimed at Nice on 7 December 2000 (OJ 2000 C 364/1) confirming that "[e]very person has the right to have his or her affairs handled impartially, fairly and within a reasonable time by the institutions and bodies of the Union."

31 See especially the CJ's appeal decision in the *max.mobil* case, in which it overturned the GC: Case C-141/02 P, *Commission v max.mobil* [2005] ECR I-1283 at paras 68–75.

32 See, for example, the situation in Case C-310/04 *Spain v Council* [2006] ECR I-7285 at paras 123, 130: "[a] proper study of the effects of that reform on the profitability of cotton production requires an examination of the consequences the reform is liable to produce for ginning undertaking situated in the production regions."

33 This formulation of the Council's obligation should not be confused with the formal impact assessment procedure addressed below in this chapter.

34 Opinion of Sharpston AG in Case C-310/04 *Spain v Council* [2006] ECR I-7285 at para 80. The violation of the duty to care by the institutions was so severe that they were criticized as appearing arbitrary: "In the absence of any impact study, certain choices made by the Commission and the Council appear arbitrary" (para 94).

European Commission's impact assessment report drafted prior to the entry into force of the measure.[35] In both cases, however, the measures overturned by the CJ were of legislative nature. It remains to be seen whether this line of argument will also be developed with respect to the review of single-case measures in view of the duty of care. So far, the review of single case decisions has taken place in the context of the control of the duty of diligent and impartial examination of all aspects of the case. This is closely linked to the obligation to give reasons. Only a sufficiently reasoned decision will indicate compliance with the duty of care and the standards of investigation.[36] Especially in highly fact-based and context-determined competition law cases, the GC has limited the obligation of providing reasons for the final decision from the perspective of the satisfaction of the duty of care or diligence. In stating the reasons for decisions, the Commission is not obliged to adopt a position on all the arguments put forward by the parties, but may concentrate its presentation of facts and legal considerations on those having decisive importance for the decision.[37]

In a range of situations it will not be sufficient for administrative decision-makers to rely on pre-existing knowledge within the authority or on information provided by the parties. Instead, they must have recourse to scientific expertise.[38] The latter differs from general administrative information in that its generation complies with specific standards inherent in scientific method. It is based on gathering observable, empirical, measurable evidence, subject to specific principles of reasoning or analysis. That means that the information assembled has to be non-partisan, and those who generate the information have to answer to the standards of their scientific community. By referring to scientific expertise, an external and independently reviewable standard of information as basis for administrative decision-making is necessarily implied.[39] Decisions relying upon

---

35 Case C-176/09 *Luxembourg v EP and Council* [2011] ECR I-3727 at para 65; Case C-58/08 *Vodafone and Others* [2010] ECR I-4999 at para 55.

36 Joined Cases T-371 and 394/94 *British Airways and others and British Midlands Airways v Commission* [1998] ECR II-2405 at para 95.

37 See, for the development of the case law in cases other than Sytraval and Métropole, Cases T-7/92 *Asia Motor France and others v Commission* [1993] ECR II-669 at paras 31, 34; Case T-459/93 *Siemens v Commission* [1995] ECR II-1675 at para 31; Case T-387/94 *Asia Motor France and others v Commission* [1996] ECR II-961 at para 104; Case T-5/97 *Industrie des Poudres Sphériques v Commission* [2000] ECR II-3755 at para 199; Case T-187/99 *Agrana Zucker und Stärke v Commission* [2001] ECR II-1587 at para 84; Case T-206/99 *Métropole Télévision v Commission* [2001] ECR II-2707 at para 44; Case T-228 and 233/99 *Westdeutsche Landesbank Girozentrale v Commission* [2003] ECR II-435 at para 280. See Paul Craig, *supra* note 10 at 376 with further explanation.

38 For a background to the discussion see the contributions in Christian Joerges, Karl-Heinz Ladeur & Ellen Vos, eds, *Integrating Scientific Expertise into Regulatory Decision-Making* (Baden-Baden: Nomos, 1997) [Joerges, Ladeur & Vos].

39 The resulting judicial review of scientific expertise itself is then limited. It is restricted to a review of reasoning and its review takes place in the context of composite

scientific advice are "founded on the principles of excellence, transparency and independence" which the Court has held to be "an important procedural guarantee whose purpose is to ensure the scientific objectivity of the measures and preclude any arbitrary measures."[40] Generally, the reference to scientific expertise introduces the requirement for specifically structured, rational deliberation in administrative and regulatory decision-making. Even absent an obligation in secondary law to employ scientific expertise, it may still be necessary due to the principle of the administrative duty of care.[41] This holds true especially in matters where EU law requires a "high level" of protection to "be ensured in the definition and implementation in all Union policies and activities."[42] According to the CJ, the requirement of such a level of protection "implies that the Community institutions must ensure that their decisions are taken in the light of the best scientific information available and that they are based on the most recent results of international research."[43] EU authorities, when required to ensure that the best

---

procedures in a multiple-step procedure. See, for example, Joined cases T-74/00, T-76/00, T-83–85/00, T-132/00, T-137/00 and T-141/00 *Artegodan and Others v Commission* [2002] ECR II-4945 at paras 199, 200; Case T-27/98 *Nardone v Commission* [1999] ECR II-1293 at paras 30 and 88.

40 Case T-70/99 *Alpharma v Council* [2002] ECR II-3495 at para 183.

41 Reference to independent scientific expertise may, in certain cases, be protected in the framework of fundamental rights, especially the right to a fair hearing. This is illustrated by the case of Steffensen where the CJ gave a preliminary ruling to a question concerning the interpretation of an EU directive on quality controls of foodstuffs. That directive allowed Member States' authorities to take samples of foodstuffs for quality control whilst also obliging Member States to "ensure that those subject to inspection may apply for a second opinion." Depriving a party of the possibility to obtain a second opinion in the form of an independent scientific evaluation of the quality of the product, the Court held, was a violation of EU fundamental rights, notably the right to a fair hearing as protected in Art 6(1) ECHR if the evidence collected in the control of the foodstuffs will later be used as evidence in court against an alleged offender of food quality standards. See Case C-276/01 *Steffensen* [2003] ECR I-3735 at paras 73, 80.

42 Such a level is required under the Treaty in areas of regulation subject to the so-called "cross-section" clauses, that is, in matters concerning health (Article 114(3) and Article 168 TFEU), safety and consumer protection (Articles 12 and 114(3) TFEU) as well as environmental protection (Articles 11 and 114(3) TFEU). See Joined cases T-74/00, T-76/00, T-83–85/00, T-132/00, T-137/00 and T-141/00 *Artegodan and Others v Commission* [2002] ECR II-4945 at para 198; Case T-199/96 *Bergaderm and Jean-Jacques Goupil v Commission* [1998] ECR II-2805 at paras 64, 65; Case C-212/91 *Angelopharm v Freie und Hansestadt Hamburg* [1994] ECR I-171 at paras 31, 32 and 38.

43 Case T-326/99 *Fern Olivieri v Commission* [2003] ECR II-6053 at para 68; Case T-13/99 *Pfizer Animal Health v Council* [2002] ECR II-3305 at para 158; T-70/99 *Alpharma v Council* [2002] ECR II-3495 at para 171. This approach is in compliance with Art 114 TFEU (Art 95(3) EC), which obliges the Commission in the case of legislative proposals in these matters, to take into "account in particular any new development based on scientific facts."

scientific information forms the basis of a decision, are under the duty to check, wherever possible, "that all the information relating to the scientific evaluation of the product in question, whether it be favorable or unfavorable to the product, has indeed been made available to it." The fact that the applicable procedural rules do not provide how this is to be done "cannot prevent the Commission from obtaining information from a third party where such a course of action is indispensable in order to safeguard public health."[44]

Despite the benefits of requiring a more politically neutral, objectively rational approach to administrative decision-making through the requirement of referring to scientific evidence, there is a risk attached to the approach. Namely, that administrations may cloak essentially political decisions in scientific language and thereby disguise the real issues addressed, in order to be able to claim rational objectivity for the decision taken.[45] In this regard, the role of the courts in reviewing administrative decision-making must be to distinguish between, on the one hand, the requirement of gathering information as complete as possible and, on the other hand, the exercise of the discretion itself on the basis of the information collection. In this way the courts can acknowledge that uncertainty is inherent in scientific information, either due to incomplete data or differing opinions within the scientific community, and thus submit the decision-making to the measured review of discretion.[46] Addressing the needs of risk regulation in the face of scientific uncertainties has, however, led to the development of additional tools or precepts, most importantly the precautionary principle.

The necessity in some cases of basing a decision on the findings emerging from scientific expertise shows that there will often be a need for the administration, before making a determination, to engage in detailed information gathering concerning the nature and potential impact of a decision. Such information is, however, not always available either because it is simply lacking or because the science is inconclusive. In these cases the European courts, have accepted that "where there is uncertainty as to the existence or extent of risks to the health of consumers, the institutions may take protective measures without having to wait until the reality and the seriousness of those risks become fully apparent."[47]

---

44 Case T-326/99 *Fern Olivieri v Commission* [2003] ECR II-6053 at para 73.

45 M Shapiro, "The Frontiers of Science Doctrine: American Experiences with the Judicial Control of Science-Based Decision-Making" in Joerges, Ladeur & Vos, *supra* note 38 at 325–42.

46 This approach has been increasingly followed in the area of merger control, where the economic/scientific market analysis has been subject to closer control, see HCH Hofmann, "Good Governance in EU Merger Control: Due Process and Checks and Balances under Review" (2003) 24 ECLR 114.

47 Case T-13/99 *Pfizer Animal Health v Council* [2002] ECR II-3305 at para 139; Case C-157/96 *National Farmers' Union and Others* (BSE I-case) [1998] ECR I-2211 at para 63; Case C-180/96 *United Kingdom v Commission* (BSE II-case) [1998] ECR I-2265 at para 99; Case T-199/96 *Bergaderm SA and Jean-Jacques Goupil v Commission* [1998] ECR II-2805 at para 66.

This approach is generally referred to as the precautionary principle, which may be invoked in order to justify of a preventive measures in risk management.[48] The adoption of such measures requires, in principle, a scientifically based risk assessment identifying the "potentially dangerous effects deriving from a phenomenon, product or process."[49] The courts have confirmed that the existence or extent of risks cannot be based "on a purely hypothetical approach to the risk, founded on mere conjecture which has not been scientifically verified."[50] Prior to the application of the precautionary principle a risk assessment needed, therefore, to consider "the degree of probability of a certain product or procedure having adverse effects on human health and the seriousness of any such adverse effects."[51] Generally, risk assessment needs to be "as complete as possible"[52] and must be undertaken "on the basis of the most reliable scientific evidence available and the most recent results of international research."[53] Where, as often, such completeness and reliability does not obtain in fact, the precautionary principle provides some alternative. As a general principle of law, it is now being used by Member States and EU institutions in all fields of risk regulation and is the basis of many legislative approaches.[54] The precautionary principle thus establishes criteria for the amount of scientific information necessary to allow for preliminary measures taken in lieu of full information necessary for a final decision. From this perspective, the application of the precautionary principle is as much a question of the amount and use of discretion by an administration as a question relating to the management of information.[55]

---

48 See, for the more recent case law citing the precautionary principle in EU law, Case C-425/08 *EnviroTec v Etat Belge* [2009] ECR I-10035 at para 75; T-334/07 *Denka v Commission* [2009] ECR I-4205 at para 95.

49 European Commission, "Communication: On the precautionary principle", 2 February 2002, COM/2000/1 final.

50 Case C-236/01 *Monsanto Agricoltura Italy and others* [2003] ECR I-8105 at para 106; Case T-13/99 *Pfizer Animal Health v Council* [2002] ECR II-3305 at para 143; Case T-70/99 *Alpharma v Council* [2002] ECR II-3495 at paras 152–61.

51 Case T-13/99 *Pfizer Animal Health v Council* [2002] ECR II-3305 at para 148; Case T-70/99 *Alpharma v Council* [2002] ECR II-3495 at paras 152–61.

52 Case C-236/01 *Monsanto Agricoltura Italy and others* [2003] ECR I-8105 at para 107.

53 *Ibid* at para 113.

54 See, for example, the so-called REACH legislation on the control of chemical substances: Regulation 1907/2006 (EC) of the European Parliament and of the Council concerning the Registration, Evaluation, Authorisation and Restriction of Chemicals (REACH), establishing a European Chemicals Agency and amending Directive 1999/45/ EC, OJ [2006] L 396/1. See, for the first case law on the precautionary principle in the context of REACH, C-558/07 *SPCM and Others v REACH* [2009] ECR I-5783.

55 On the distinction between scientific advice, on the one hand, and that discretionary assessment of the competent authority, on the other, see, for example, the judgment in Case

The lack of information sufficient to decide a case may result from insufficient cooperation by the parties involved, especially where they are obliged to cooperate under secondary law. In that case, certain provisions in secondary legislation allow the EU institutions to act on the information available, even where not complete. Such provisions are essentially intended as sanctions for non-compliance with obligations for provision of information and are used as such.[56] Such rules, as an exception to the general duty of care and of diligent and impartial assessment of all relevant facts, are to be interpreted narrowly.[57]

Conclusion

This chapter offered a view of the distinction between inquisitorial and adversarial systems being chiefly a question of who gathers information to which extent and in which quality prior to decision-making. This information-centered view may not be a common perspective, neither amongst people classified as common lawyers nor amongst those labeled as members of the civil law families. The information-perspective on administrative procedure law, however, appears to be a parameter capable of explaining many aspects and specificities of a system of public law including the system of judicial review of administrative decision-making.

From this perspective, in this chapter, I have attempted to outline how in EU administrative law, the principle of the "duty to care" has become a central element of this administrative law of information. EU law has the specificities of a system allowing for a basically inquisitorial procedure linked with a system of judicial review, which is informed by a tradition of administrative courts with strong

---

C-405/92 *Mondiet v Armement Islais* [1993] ECR I-6133 at para 31, and the Opinion of Gulmann AG in that case at para 28.

56 See, for example, Art 18(1) of *Council Regulation (EC) 384/96 of 22 December 1995 on protection against dumped imports from countries not members of the European Community*, [1996] OJ, L 56/1 (as last amended by Regulation 2117/2005, [2005] OJ, L 340/17): "In cases in which any interested party refuses access to, or otherwise does not provide, necessary information within the time limits provided in this Regulation, or significantly impedes the investigation, provisional or final findings, affirmative or negative, may be made on the basis of the facts available. Where it is found that any interested party has supplied false or misleading information, the information shall be disregarded and use may be made of facts available." See also Art 12 of *Council Regulation (EC) 659/1999 of 22 March 1999 laying down detailed rules for the application of Art. 93 of the EC Treaty*, [1999] OJ, L 83/1: "If the Member State fails to comply with a suspension injunction or a recovery injunction, the Commission shall be entitled, while carrying out the examination on the substance of the matter on the basis of the information available, to refer the matter to the Court of Justice of the European Communities direct and apply for a declaration that the failure to comply constitutes an infringement of the Treaty."

57 The issue will often be combined in litigation with the question of the burden of proof of a party.

powers to control and overrule administrative decision-making. The availability of detailed judicial review generally introduces a strong adversarial component into the principally inquisitorial system. Adding such an adversarial element allows distinguishing unproblematic situations, in which inquisitorial decision-making is sufficient to allow for a fast and structured decision-making process, from the more controversial cases, in which a case will be brought before an independent judge deciding in the adversarial mode.

Chapter 9
The European Union and the "Legitimate Use of Force": Administrative Inspections and Legal Safeguards

Giacinto della Cananea*

Introduction

While less recent theories of public law insisted that the essence of government rested on authority,[1] contemporary narratives of public law tend to emphasize the importance of welfare concerns. A clear distinction, if not an opposition, is thus individuated between *imperium* and *dominium*,[2] which includes the State's direct and indirect intervention in the economic and social sphere, through the exercise of authority and delivery of a variety of goods and services (including money), respectively. As a matter of fact, thousands of public administrators make decisions that impinge on us not only from the cradle to the grave, but, as the American public lawyer Jerry Mashaw has argued, affect us from *before* the cradle to *beyond* the grave.[3] This provides the States with a legitimacy distinct from that deriving from representative processes,[4] and, according to some observers, characterizes contemporary states as providers of goods and services.[5]

---

* E-mail: della.cananea@economia.uniroma2.it. This chapter is based on a paper presented at the conference on "Inquisitorial Processes in Administrative Regimes: Global Perspectives" organized by the University of Windsor (Ontario, Canada), May 26–27, 2011.

1 For this theory, see Maurice Hauriou, *La puissance publique et le service public*, preface to the 11th ed of the *Précis de droit administratif et de droit public* (1926) and Otto Mayer, *Deutsches Verwaltungsrecht* (1895), vol I at 67. See also Martin Loughlin, *Public Law and Political Theory* (New York: Oxford University Press, 1992) at 11 [Loughlin].

2 This terminology is borrowed from Terence Daintith, "The Techniques of Government" in J Jowell & Dawn Oliver, eds, *The Changing Constitution*, 3rd ed (Oxford: Oxford University Press, 1994) 209.

3 Jerry Mashaw, *Due Process in the Administrative State* (New Haven: Yale University Press, 1985) at 12.

4 Jerry Mashaw, *Bureaucratic Justice* (New Haven: Yale University Press, 1983). See also Paul Verkuil, "*The Self-Legitimating Bureaucracy*", Book review of *Bureaucratic Justice* by Jerry L Mashaw (1984) 93 Yale LJ 780.

5 See Massimo Severo Giannini, *Il pubblico potere* (Bologna: Il Mulino, 1986) at 25.

The growing importance of the "benevolent" and friendly face of the State, however, should not obscure the fact that the principle of authority persists. Without the principle of authority, which lies at the heart of taxation, financial resources could not be gathered in order to cover the huge public spending for public services and subsidies to business. Without the authority exercised by spending ministries and departments, the use of public money by beneficiaries could not be checked through investigations and inspections. Nor has the use of force disappeared. In *fin-de-siècle* liberal democracies, disputes concerning the exercise of authority, particularly with regard to administrative investigations of business and citizens, continue to emerge. The US Supreme Court ruling in *Arizona v Johnson*, regarding the police's power to inspect a passenger in a vehicle,[6] is but the most recent example of this. Anti-terrorist legislation, almost everywhere, produces an increase of administrative activities, such as orders and inspections, often governed by *ad hoc* or derogatory rules. The persisting importance of the principle of authority explains why the study of the ways through which the use of force is limited, structured and checked is not simply of interest for historians, but is a crucial concern for modern public law.[7]

At the same time, the new dynamics of power beyond the State must not be neglected. More specifically, in Western Europe such dynamics have increasingly been influenced by European integration, in a twofold respect. First, European Union (EU) law requests national authorities to carry out investigations in a variety of fields, for example to ensure the proper and sound management of EU structural funds. Second, in the field of competition, the administration of the EU has the power to carry out investigations and inspections within the Member States' territory.

This chapter seeks to provide not only an overview of the emerging phenomena of EU law, but also to avoid a risk which is frequent in EU studies, that is to say to look at them only from a "*sui generis*" perspective. An attempt is thus made, drawing on a range of legal and political doctrines, to analyze such changes and to explore their broader theoretical implications, for the EU and its Member States. More precisely, the chapter examines briefly the traditional monopoly of the use of the force, as exposed by Max Weber, and the "realist" paradigm, according to which, in spite of growing integration, the Member States of the EU still retain such monopoly. As a following step, the chapter focuses on the twofold influence played by the EU: the gradual development of principles and rules governing the inspections which national authorities must carry out in order to ensure the respect of EU law, particularly in the field of agricultural and structural funds, and the

6 555 U.S. 2009. The Court held that, during a traffic stop, the police may order occupants to exit the vehicle pending completion of the stop. A police officer may pat down a driver once he exits a vehicle if the officer reasonably believes that the driver is armed and dangerous.

7 For this conceptualization of discretion, see Kenneth C Davis, *Discretionary Justice: A Preliminary Inquiry* (Baton Rouge: Louisiana State University Press, 1969).

more recent emergence of an autonomous power of inspection, attributed to the European Commission in the field of competition. To my knowledge, this is at the same time an unprecedented innovation and one for which there are no similar developments in Europe or elsewhere, which justifies the choice to focus on it. This is not the only reason, however. Precisely because the chapter argues that the European administration must now be regarded as an authority that may legitimately use force against undertakings, the question arises whether there are appropriate safeguards against the abuse, or improper exercise, of administrative power. Two such safeguards, are examined – a substantive one, namely, the inviolability of home, and a procedural one, more precisely the procedural requirements imposed on government. From both points of view, it will be argued that the law of the EC has been enriched by the European Court of Justice by referring to the European Convention on Human Rights (ECHR), although the Community was not a contracting party. This is arguably further proof of the interconnection between legal orders which characterizes the European legal space.[8]

The Realist Paradigm of Sovereignty and Force

The Normative Foundations of the Realist Paradigm

When scholars of different fields discuss EU law, one major difficulty derives from the different ideas about a fundamental concept of modern public law and political science – that of sovereignty.

The specialists of competition, agriculture or other fields of European integration emphasize the realities of public law, more specifically, the growing influence of the EU on the activities of its Member States, and even on their internal organization (for example, in the fields of monetary policy and telecommunications). But an important school of thought, without neglecting such realities, underlines the distinction, so central to more traditional theories of public law, between sovereign and non-sovereign entities, such as the Member States and the EU, respectively.[9] For all the binding effects of EU law, the argument goes, at the end of the day it is the States, and exclusively the States, that still retain the monopoly of the use of the force. Consequently, if the European administration wants to carry out an inspection on the use of EU funds, it must request in due form the cooperation of national authorities. Even the respect of the judgments of European courts, so central for the EU, is ensured by national authorities.

8 For this concept, see MP Chiti, *Lo spazio giuridico europeo*, in *Mutazioni del diritto pubblico nello spazio giuridico europeo* (Bologna: Clueb, 2003) 321; A von Bogdandy, *National legal scholarship in the European legal area – A manifesto*, 10 I-CON 614 at 618 (2012).

9 See Trevor C Hartley, *The Foundations of European Community Law: An Introduction to the Constitutional and Administrative Law of the European Community* (Oxford: Oxford University Press, 2007) at 109 (for a discussion from the point of view of subsidiarity).

In this picture, there is a fact whose importance may not be overlooked, that is to say the EU does not replace the States, nor does it aim to become a state of a new kind.[10] However, although this "realist" view of European integration tends to be presented as adherent to the "order of the things", it is influenced, like more or less all other theories, by some elements. From a normative point of view, this realist analysis does not draw only on Grotius and other international lawyers as far as sovereignty is concerned. It also draws on both Bodin and Hobbes. From Bodin, it derived the change from the analytical conception of sovereignty, based on a variety of supreme powers of the State (*summae potestates*, *compétences régaliennes*), to the synthetical conception, that is to say to sovereignty seen as whole and exercised in a given territory and a social body (nation).[11] From Hobbes, the traditional theory draws not only the replacement of reason with will as the foundation of political authority,[12] but also a normative argument in favor of a centralized exercise of force, seen as the only way an orderly society could be achieved and maintained.[13]

Weber and the State's Monopoly of the Legitimate Use of Force

A second fundamental element of the realist paradigm is the connection between internal sovereignty (as distinct from the relationships between sovereigns) and force. Perhaps no one more emphasized such connection than the German sociologist of law Max Weber.

In the early twentieth century, German public lawyers, in particular Georg Jellinek, had already pointed out that sovereignty and territory were, together with people, the essential features of a State, and of each State.[14] What Weber added, or specified, are the following three elements. First, he affirmed that States, unlike the political organizations of the past, were characterized by a professional bureaucracy. It is the latter which gathers the financial resources for delivering military and police activities, thus ensuring the functional legitimacy of the State.

Second, and more relevant for our purposes, Weber drew a distinction between force (*Macht, Gewalt*) and power (*Herrschaft*), and observed that the States have gradually assumed the monopoly of the use of force (*Gewaltmonopol des Staates*), at the expenses of other sites of authority, both universal (the empire) and local (municipalities and feuds). The State may confer legitimacy to other actors, either

---

10 This point is discussed in recent German scholarship: see Armin von Bogdandy & Jürgen Bast, eds, *Principles of European Constitutional Law*, 2nd ed (München: CH Beck, 2010).

11 Jean Bodin, *Les six livres de la Republique* (1576).

12 For further remarks, see Loughlin, *supra* note 1 at 79.

13 Thomas Hobbes, *The Leviathan* (1660), ch. XVIII. Jean-Jacques Rousseau, among other, pointed out the importance of force in his critical analysis of the Polish constitutional framework: see his *Considérations sur le gouvernement de Pologne* (1772), § VII and IX.

14 Georg Jellinek, *Allgemeines Staatslehre* (1900), vol I.

public (territorial militias) or private (for example, private security). But this does not undermine its exclusivity. In the Weberian perspective, the power to use force over individuals and things is granted by the State, and exclusively by the State.

Third, Weber defined the State's monopoly of force as a legitimate one.[15] By pointing out this aspect, the Weberian theory of the State went well beyond describing the evident fact that contemporary states have powerful military and police forces. To the extent that Weber emphasized the importance of legitimacy, the force exercised by the State was not simply force, let alone arbitrary force. It was qualified by legitimacy, or conformity with rules previously established.[16] The conformity with the rules previously established is typical of the legal–rational model of authority, as opposed to the traditional and charismatic ones, elaborated by Weber. As a further consequence, the exercise of force must not be disproportionate, but needs to be foreseeable and limited.

For our purposes, there is no need to discuss whether this theory had any moral basis[17] or was simply intended as an observation or reality. Suffice it to observe that this concept of internal sovereignty confirms the connection between unity and exclusivity, but adds a further important dimension, that of legitimacy.

The Frailty of the Realist Paradigm

The insightful theoretical framework which lays at the basis of the realist paradigm of the monopoly of the force is, nevertheless, not without its difficulties.

First, it is clear that an evident feature of modern states is that they can exercise force, internally and externally, by way of their police units and armed forces, respectively. However, after centuries of subtle debates, placing so much emphasis on force is questionable. The least that can be said is that such force increasingly needs to be characterized by legitimacy, as Weber convincingly pointed out. Otherwise, the monopoly of force or violence would not be a distinctive feature of the State, but, rather, a common feature with every private organization exercising physical control of a given territory. Indeed, rebels occupying a part of the State's territory and even criminal organizations (for example, those producing drugs in, say, a portion of a Latin American country) exercise a monopoly of force or violence.[18] This explains the importance attached by modern constitutions to the principles governing State interference with individual freedoms. In this

15 See Max Weber, *Wirtschaft und Gesellschaft* (1922) (VII.2, observing the connection between the monopoly of legislation and that of enforcement, and IX.7.3, arguing that State only has "*das Monopol legitimen physischen Zwanges*").

16 Alessandro Passerin d'Entreves, *Dottrina dello Stato* (Torino: Giappichelli, 1967) at 3.

17 According to Weber, any moral judgement must be suspended when describing the world as it stands: see his *Science as a Vocation* (*Wissentschaft als Beruf*, 1919).

18 For this remark, see Massimo Severo Giannini, "*Sovranità (diritto vigente)*" in *Enciclopedia del diritto* (Milano: Giuffrè, 1991) at 227.

respect, the Fourth Amendment to the US Constitution, recognizing "The right of the people to be secure in their persons, houses, papers, and effects, against unreasonable searches and seizures",[19] has a paradigmatic value.

Second, placing too much emphasis on armed forces and police corps is an excessive simplification of a complex legal reality. The judicial function, too, is a manifestation of sovereignty. When a judge or a court issues a judgment, this is undoubtedly an exercise of the supreme authority of the State. As a matter of fact, such judgment is binding on the parts and may not be reversed by another branch of government. Also, externally, that judgment is seen as a manifestation of sovereignty. Consequently, it produces its effects only within the territory of that state. Any further effect, within the territory of another state, must be justified and preceded by either a specific decision of such state or a general rule.

Third, although the traditional concept of sovereignty solved a variety of practical problems, and in particular cut the disputes concerning the possibility of including this or that power between the *summae potestates*, it is a cultural and historical product. It might have been useful to describe the reality of the great powers of the nineteenth century, such as United Kingdom and France. But it hardly applies as such to the post-1945 period, where even superpowers need external sources of legitimacy, such as UN clauses. Describing the exercise of sovereignty as consisting of unilateral measures by a single State is all the more puzzling, since in the last 25 or 30 years the States increasingly exercise their sovereign powers by acceding to a number of multilateral regimes.[20] As a result of this, even if the normative underpinnings of the realist conception of sovereignty are left unchallenged, a reductionist view of cooperation (that is to say one that emphasizes the autonomy and sufficiency of the State, of each State) is no longer justified. Nor is the reluctance to recognize the growing importance of regional and global regulatory regimes agreed to by the States justified. Indeed, such regulatory regimes impose binding limits on the founding States, though using a variety of incentives, disincentives, and sanctions in case of non-compliance.

EU Law and the Use of Force by Public Administrations

Administrative Investigations in EU Law

The binding effects of regulatory regimes are particularly relevant in the case of the European Community, and now of the Union. In this respect, a basic distinction ought to be made at the outset, between the centralized and decentralized

19 See US Const amend IV.

20 See Abraham Chayes & Antonia Chayes, *The New Sovereignty: Compliance with International Regulatory Agreements* (Cambridge: Harvard University Press, 1995) and Anne-Marie Slaughter, *A New World Order* (Princeton: Princeton University Press, 2004).

administration of EU policies,[21] although its importance has been attenuated by later developments.[22] When Jean Monnet elaborated the institutional structure of the European Coal and Steel Community (ECSC) in the early 1950s, his idea was that the High Authority, the Commission's forerunner, should have a strong political role, but a limited administration.[23] The salient political role of the High Authority emerges clearly when considering its tasks and powers. It was a truly supranational body with the power of decision-making. It took decisions binding on the Member States and within them. However, a general rule obliged the ECSC as a whole to carry out its mission with "limited interventions."[24] When the goals and the tasks of common institutions were enlarged by the Treaty of Rome (1957), the latter did not confer the power to execute EC policies on the European administration. Except in certain cases such as competition, execution was remitted to the national public authorities. In line with this choice, judicial review on the Member States was within the jurisdiction of national judges, although a connection between the latter and the European Court of Justice was established, by way of the preliminary reference procedure.[25] With the launch of the common agricultural policies in 1965, and the need to manage the new structural funds two decades later, the role of national departments and agencies has become even more important for the daily administration of EC policies.[26]

It is within the framework of such policies that several issues concerning administrative inspections has gradually emerged. Consider, for example, the financing of professional education by way of the European Social Fund (ESF).[27]

---

21 See, for example, Guy Isaac, *Droit communautaire général,* 3rd ed (Paris: Masson, 1990) at 193.

22 For further remarks, see Giacinto della Cananea, "The European Union's Mixed Administrative Proceedings" (2004) 68 Law and Contemporary Problems 197 (observing that often both national authorities and the Commission take part in multi-phase or "composite" decision-making processes) and Herwig CH Hofmann, Gerald C Rowe & Alexander Turk, *Administrative Law and Policy of the European Union* (Oxford: Oxford University Press, 2011) at 262 (observing that "the model of executive federalism no longer captures the reality of EU administrative law").

23 See Jean Monnet, *Mémoirs* (1976) at 546 (arguing that "*le pouvoir s'exerçait mieux avec des instruments légers*", "*il suffirait de quelques centaines de fonctionnaires européens pour mettre au travail des milliers d'experts nationaux et faire servir les puisssantes machineries ... des Etats*").

24 Article 3, ECSC Treaty, provided that "*la Communauté accomplit sa mission ... avec des interventions limitées.*"

25 For an analogy with the British "indirect rule", see Terence Daintith, ed, *Implementing EC Law in the United Kingdom: Structures for Indirect Rule* (Chichester: John Wiley & Son, 1995).

26 For a more detailed analysis, see Paul Craig, *EU Administrative Law* (Oxford: Oxford University Press, 2006).

27 See EC, *Council Decision 83/516 of 17 October 1983 on the tasks of the European Social Fund,* [1983] OJ, L 289; EC, *Council Regulation (EEC) No 2950/83 of 17 October*

Since what matters, for present purposes, is the legal framework for inspections, this sector's specific financial rules and procedures will be very briefly described. The funds are available under the budget of the EU, but are distributed by national authorities. The latter receive the applications, give money to producers, and request reimbursement from the Commission. In sum, although the Commission is responsible for implementing the budget of the EU, national agencies act as spending bodies. They are likewise responsible for carrying out the checks aimed at ensuring that the duties and conditions attached to funding under EU law are being observed. This solution is coherent with the underlying institutional policy of the Member States not to increase too much the administrative machinery of the EU, especially that of the Commission. But it has at least two drawbacks. The first is the lack of incentives for severe checks. The other is the risk of disparities between national enforcement performances. For these reasons, the Commission is responsible for checking that national authorities carry out their duty to monitor subsidy recipients by way of inspections performed with national administrations.

In order to understand how such inspections work concretely, we may consider an important ruling of the ECJ, *Lisrestal*.[28] An investigation, carried out in 1990 at the premises of the undertakings concerned revealed various irregularities in the management of financial assistance by some of such undertakings, in that they did not possess the necessary infrastructure and the staff necessary for carrying out the scheme. Moreover, some invoices were irregular. The inspectors thus suggested that a demand should be made for repayment of the Community funds paid to the respondents. After a long exchange of documents between *Directora-Geral do Departamento para os Assuntos do Fundo Social Europeu* (DAFSE) and the Commission, the latter decided that, on the basis of the inspectors' findings, the assistance granted to the beneficiaries should be reduced and part of the amounts paid had to be refunded the ESF. The beneficiaries then brought an action for annulment of the Fund's decision, ordering the repayment. The complaint was partly upheld by the Court of First Instance (CFI) and confirmed by the ECJ on procedural grounds. Two aspects of this dispute must be underlined, for present purposes. First, the Commission's decision specifies that "Where the management of an operation for which assistance has been granted is the subject of an investigation because of suspected irregularities, the Member State shall notify the Commission thereof without delay."[29] Therefore, although national administrative machinery retains the monopoly of the exercise of force, its legitimacy is determined by EU

1983 on the implementation of Decision 83/516/EEC on the tasks of the European Social Fund, [1983] OJ, L 289.

28 ECJ, Case C-32/95 P *Commission of the European Communities v Lisrestal* (24 October 1996) [*Commission v Lisrestal*]. For a fuller account of the facts, see the Court's ruling and the Opinion of Advocate General La Pergola in the same case, delivered on 6 June 1996 [La Pergola].

29 EC, *Commission decision 83/673 of 22 December 1983 on the management of the European Social Fund*, [1983] OJ, L 377/1.

law. Secondly, at least apparently there is a double legal relationship. The first is between the EU and each Member State, while the second is between each Member State and the undertakings receiving subsidies. The Member States bear responsibility for the "right outcome" of such interventions,[30] and, according to a consistent line of case-law, for recovering sums of money wrongly paid out.[31] However, since it is the Commission that decides that the subsidies allocated must be reduced or eliminated because of illegal behavior, according to the ECJ, a "direct relationship [arises] between the Commission and the contribution's beneficiary."[32] This finding implies that not only does EU law determine the legal conditions which must be respected by the conduct of national administrations, but the latter must obey the Commission. It is the national authorities, therefore, that specify the conditions for the legitimate use of force. The question thus arose whether the rights of the undertakings affected by the Commission's decision were safeguarded by EC and both Advocate General La Pergola and the ECJ answered positively. Another, more theoretical, question was whether the traditional realist paradigm, that (over)emphasizes the States' monopoly of the legitimate use of force, still catches current reality or whether new theories must be elaborated,[33] as it will be suggested in the following pages.

Commission's Inspections in Competition Cases: the Minoan Case

The question just raised becomes more evident when considering the role of the EU administration. Given its relatively limited centralized functions, the prominence of competition not only in early cases, but also in the more recent ones, is hardly surprising. Indeed, agriculture and competition cases accounted for the majority of cases reaching the ECJ and in particular for those concerning abuse of administrative powers.

---

30 ECJ, *Directora-Geral do Departamento para os Assuntos do Fundo Social Europeu (DAFSE) v Frota Azul*, Case C-413/98 (2001). See also Carol Harlow, *Accountability in the European Union* (Oxford: Oxford University Press, 2002) for further remarks on the anti-fraud initiatives [Harlow].

31 See ECJ, Case C-55/91, *Italy v Commission* (1993); Joined Cases C-89 & 91/86, *Etoile commerciale et CNTA v Commission* (1987). But see also La Pergola, *supra* note 28, § 21, pointing out that "this case differs from others in which the Court has ruled in this connection in recent years."

32 *Commission v Lisrestal*, *supra* note 28. See again La Pergola, *supra* note 28 at para 26 (observing that "the State is the interlocutor of the Commission, but it is the latter which takes the final decision"). For further remarks, see Sabino Cassese, "European Administrative Proceedings" (2004) 68 Law & Contemp Problems 31 (also examining other cases).

33 See also, for further remarks, Jean-Bernard Auby, "Les pouvoirs d'inspection de l'Union européenne" (2006) 42 Revue trimestrielle de droit européen 131.

The *Minoan* case provides an excellent basis for examining such powers and their conditions and limits.[34] *Minoan* is both a competition case and a paradigmatic example of the EU courts' predisposition to pursue the elaboration of the powers of the European administration in a way that anticipates and influences legislative change. The case involved an investigation on alleged anti-competitive practices concerning sea transport between Italy and Greece. Nine ferry operators provided passenger and vehicle transport services on the route between Patras (Greece) and three harbors on the eastern coast of Italy (Ancona, Bari and Brindisi). In 1992, a customer brought a complaint before the European Commission, alleging that the prices of the different ferries on these routes were all very similar. Hence the suspicion of illicit agreements or practices, prohibited by EC law.[35] After a *prima facie* analysis of the complaint, an inspection was carried out by Commission officials in Athens, in the buildings of the company deemed responsible for the anti-competitive practices, under the terms of the 1962 regulation. Commission officials carried out inspections on the premises of the ferry operators located in Athens and obtained copies of a large number of documents. The documents were treated by the Commission as evidence in deciding to fine several undertakings for having infringed Art. 81 of the Treaty. Minoan, however, argued that the inspection had been effected without the intervention of the national authority and had violated its procedural rights. In particular, the lack of cooperation with the Greek competition authority was asserted to violate both the existing regulation and the underlying constitutional reserve of the monopoly of force in favor of national institutions. The Commission replied that it had not sought a warrant or the assistance of the Greek police in order to carry out the inspection because its investigation was effected with the cooperation of the interested party.

The CFI upheld this line of reasoning,[36] dismissing the complaint that the Commission had exceeded its powers by inspecting the premises belonging to an undertaking different from the addressee of the latter's decision to carry out an investigation.[37] It began by reaffirming the traditional rights of defense and judicial review of the parties concerned must be fully respected in the administrative

34 CFI, Case T-66/99, *Minoan v Commission* (2003). An appeal was brought by Minoan before the ECJ, which dismissed it (see the order adopted on 17 November 2005, in Case C-121/04) [*Minoan*].

35 Art. 81. 1 of the EC Treaty provided that: "the following shall be prohibited as incompatible with the common market: all agreements between undertakings, decisions by associations of undertakings and concerted practices which may affect trade between Member States and which have as their object or effect the prevention, restriction or distortion of competition within the common market, and in particular those which: (a) directly or indirectly fix purchase or selling prices or any other trading conditions." Para (2) added that "Any agreements or decisions prohibited pursuant to this Article shall be automatically void." The basic regulation, n. 171962, was followed by regulation n. 4056/86, and later replaced by regulation n.1/2003, applicable from 1 May 2004.

36 *Minoan, supra* note 34 at para 93.

37 *Ibid* at paras 84–85.

procedures.[38] But this, the Court argued, did not diminish the Commission's wide powers of investigation, which included the power to seek documents. However, the conditions for the exercise of such powers were less clear. The CFI proposed a two-tier test for determining whether the Commission's behavior was consistent with EC regulations, thus confirming its opinion that the latter provided an adequate legal basis. The first part of the test was a consideration of whether the Commission's inspectors had exercised force anyhow, thus obliging the undertaking's officials to disclose documents which eventually proved the anti-competitive practices. In the Court's reasoning, only if this part of the test had a positive outcome, was the second part necessary. The second part of the test was whether the Commission's officials had failed to seek the assistance of the local (Greek) police, seen as the only legitimate site of authority and force. Since the Court accepted the Commission's view according to which its investigation had been completed with the cooperation of the interested party, it could dismiss the latter's complaint.

This did not call into question the persisting exclusive role of the State's authorities. However, their role must be exercised in accordance with the general principles of EC law. Such general principles require national courts to ignore or modify national procedures, when adjudicating under EU law. National procedural autonomy, the ECJ has repeatedly said, does apply as long as a rule of procedure does not render the exercise of rights stemming from the legal order of the EU virtually impossible or excessively difficult.[39]

Commission's Inspections in Competition Cases: Regulation n. 1/2003

A shift concerning the allocation of administrative powers to inspect derived from a new regulation,[40] enacted after *Minoan* by the Council of Ministers on a Commission's proposal.[41] The new Regulation confirms the Commission's power to request information from undertakings, competition authorities of Member

38 The discussion carried out in the text focuses primarily on the process rights of those undertakings alleged to have infringed the rules of free competition. But other parties may also take part in administrative procedures, in particular complainants: for further remarks, see Paul Craig, *EU Administrative Law* (2006) at 389 [Paul Craig].

39 ECJ, Case C-312/93, *Peterbroeck, Van Campenhout & Cie SCS v Belgian State*. See Diana-Urania Galetta, *Procedural Autonomy of the Member States: Paradise Lost?* (Berlin: Springer, 2010) (arguing that, though paying formal respect to procedural autonomy, the ECJ has substantially eroded it).

40 *Council Regulation n. 1/2003 of 16 December 2002 on the implementation of the rules on competition laid down in Articles 81 and 82 of the Treaty*, [2003] OJ, L 001 [Regulation n. 1/2003].

41 For an overview of Regulation n. 1/2003, see Claus-Dieter Ehlermann, "The Modernization of EC Antitrust Policy: A Legal and Cultural Revolution" (2000) 37 CML Rev 537. On the implementation of the new regime, see Philip Lowe, "Current Issues of E.U. Competition Law: The New Competition Enforcement Regime" (2003–2004) 24 Nw J Int'l L & Bus 567.

States, and national governments, which must afford the necessary assistance, including the exercise of police powers.[42] It provides penalties for non-compliance. Finally, it strengthens the Commission's power to inspect. Article 20 of the regulation entrusts the Commission with the power to inspect both undertakings and associations of undertakings. It specifies that its officials are:

> empowered: (a) to enter any premises, land and means of transport of undertakings and associations of undertakings; (b) to examine the books and other records related to the business, irrespective of the medium on which they are stored; (c) to take or obtain in any form copies of or extracts from such books or records ...[43]

A wide power to inspect is thus conferred upon the Commission. It may conduct all necessary inspections. It may enter all the premises and other properties of all undertakings, as well as of their associations (which would probably attenuate the problem of the exact identification of an undertaking, which emerged in *Minoan*). Last but not least, it has the power to gather any kind of document. Even a quick look at Article 21 of regulation, n. 1/2003 shows that such power of inspection is still wider, since this clause enables the Commission to carry out inspections in another kind of private property. Specifically, under Article 21, documents may be searched "in any other premises, land and means of transport, including the homes of directors, managers and other members of staff of the undertakings and associations of undertakings concerned."[44] If we read Article 20 in conjunction with Article 21, a twofold change emerges with regard to the Commission's power to inspect. First, the power to inspect lies in the hands of the Commission. Whether it decides to act only through its officials or to avail of other "accompanying persons", is a decision entirely left to its discretion, which is unbound from a substantive point of view, although subject to procedural limits, as we shall see later. Second, for the very first time, the Commission's inspecting powers go well beyond their traditional scope, which consisted of the undertakings' premises. Their scope now includes the homes of directors and managers, that it is to say private domiciles, in so far as it is suspected that business records are kept there.[45] The Regulation thus affects rights that are protected by national constitutions. An analysis focused on the competence of the European administration, in sum, leads to change the answer traditionally given to the main functional question concerning the locus of power. There is clearly a shift of administrative powers. Such powers regard the territory of the Member States and involve the adoption of coercive measures, that is to say the use of force.

---

42 See Annamaria Bonomo, *Administrative Enforcement of Community Competition Law* (Bruxelles: Bruylant, 2002).

43 See Council Regulation n. 1/2003, *supra* note 40.

44 *Ibid.*

45 This change has been pointed out by Paul Craig, *supra* note 38 at 391.

True, the Commission is obliged to consult the domestic competition authority, which shall provide active assistance. If the undertaking to which the Commission's decision to carry out an inspection opposes to it, the latter must ask the assistance of the national police authority and the authorization of the national judicial authority. However, the national police authority may not refuse its assistance, because its activity is bound by the principle of loyal cooperation, while the courts can carry out its review only on the authenticity and proportionality of the Commission's decisions.[46] They may not review its necessity and lawfulness. Indeed, as Article 21 (8) of the Regulation specifies, "the lawfulness of the Commission decision shall be subject to review only by the Court of Justice." Nor may the national judge demand that it be provided with information in the Commission's file, which is expressly ruled out. Whether the judicial review by EU courts of the choices made by the Commission is not merely formal, thus constituting a real barrier against the abuse of administrative powers, is another question and certainly not one of lesser importance. What is clear is that the State's administration is no longer the only site of authority which is empowered to use coercion against individuals (under Article 20 (4) the latter are "required to submit to inspections ordered by decision of the Commission"), albeit in a limited field, for which the EU has an exclusive competence. The Commission is empowered to exercise authoritative powers, or coercion, for achieving a fundamental goal of European integration, namely a workable competition. Its powers are established by EU law and fall basically, though not exclusively, under the judicial review of EU courts, with a limited space left for the intervention of national courts.

Legal Safeguards: the Inviolability of Home

A Constitutional Framework without a Bill of Rights

If not only national administrations, but also the administration of the EU may exercise coercion, the question arises whether the latter is subject to legal safeguards at least broadly comparable to those of the former. Two kinds of safeguards have

---

46 Under Article 21 (8), "Where authorisation as referred to in paragraph 7 is applied for the national judicial authority shall control that the Commission decision is authentic and that the coercive measures envisaged are neither arbitrary nor excessive having regard to the subject matter of the inspection. In its control of the proportionality of the coercive measures, the national judicial authority may ask the Commission, directly or through the Member State competition authority, for detailed explanations in particular on the grounds the Commission has for suspecting infringement of Articles 81 and 82 of the Treaty, as well as on the seriousness of the suspected infringement and on the nature of the involvement of the undertaking concerned. However, the national judicial authority may not call into question the necessity for the inspection nor demand that it be provided with the information in the Commission's file. The lawfulness of the Commission decision shall be subject to review only by the Court of Justice."

gradually emerged, both substantive (the inviolability of the home) and procedural (initially focused on the rights to the defense). Whether such safeguards constitute adequate barriers against abuses, however, it is to be seen.

Although much ink has been spilt by lawyers about the rule of law in the EC,[47] in the 1960s, when common institutions began to exercise administrative powers impinging on fundamental rights and liberties, there was not such a thing as a bill of rights. This was such an important gap that in that decade some public lawyers refused to recognize the existence of an administrative law of the EC.[48] Also three decades later, others hesitated to recognize that a European constitution existed.[49] This argument drew on an interpretation of Article 16 of the French Declaration of the rights of man and the citizen of 1789 ("Any society in which the guarantee of the rights is not secured, or the separation of powers not determined, has no constitution at all"), according to which the guarantee of the rights depends essentially on their inclusion in the bill of rights. Whatever the soundness of this interpretation, the ECJ found an original solution. Since its ruling in *Nold*,[50] the ECJ has held that fundamental rights are an integral part of the general principles of law, the observance of which the Court ensures, in accordance with constitutional traditions common to the Member States, and the international treaties on which the Member States have collaborated (and we shall see later the importance of this reference, with regard to the European Convention on Human Rights).

However, some problems remained. In particular, although most constitutions of the Member States recognized at least the essential content of some fundamental liberties, which represented boundaries to the powers of public authorities, such boundaries differed in several respects. Consider the freedom of home. Both the Greek and Italian Constitutions, those of the two Member States more directly affected by the anti-competitive practices emerged in the *Minoan* case, recognize such freedom solemnly (every person's home is a "sanctuary", according to the

47 For a recent reappraisal, see Armin von Bogdandy, "I principi fondamentali dell'Unione europea: Un contributo allo sviluppo del costituzionalismo europeo" (2011) Neapel 175.

48 See Massimo Severo Giannini, "Profili di un diritto amministrativo delle Comunità europee" (2003) Riv trim dir pubbl 979.

49 Luis-Maria Dièz-Picazo, "Una constituciòn sin declaraciòn de derechos? Reflexiones sobre los derechos fundamentales en la Unión Europea" (1991) 32 Revista espanola de derecho constitucional 135 (arguing that, though unified Europe had a constitution in the material sense, this was not coherent with constitutionalism).

50 ECJ, Case 4/73, *Nold v Commission* (1974). Few years later in *Hauer* (Case 44/79), the ECJ used the ECHR as an additional source of standards of legitimacy. The best narrative is still that of Joseph HH Weiler, "Fundamental Rights and Fundamental Boundaries on Standards and Values in the Protection of Human Rights" in JHH Weiler, ed, *The Constitution of Europe: "Do the New Clothes Have an Emperor?" and Other Essays* (Cambridge: Cambridge University Press, 1999) at 103 [Weiler].

former, the freedom of home is "inviolable" for the latter).[51] Both, moreover, establish the traditional nineteenth-century safeguards against the executive, consisting in allowing only parliamentary legislation to regulate this right (*réserve de la loi, riserva di legge, Vorrang des Gesetzes*) and in requesting the prior authorization of a court in individual cases. Other constitutions have higher standards. For example, Article 13 of the Basic Law (*Grundgesetz*) of Germany not only proclaims the inviolability of the home and required searches to be authorized by a judge, but it also specifies that any interferences and restrictions of such right could be allowed only to preserve another fundamental interest, such as averting a danger to the public or to the life of an individual.[52] In all the three constitutions, therefore, freedom of the home is one of the few freedoms picked out for special protection. But what this protection means could vary according to the reasons that public authorities must affirm when seeking to restrict the exercise of such freedom, by way of inspections and searches.

Another controversial issue was the scope of the constitutional protection. In Greece, for example, the inviolability of the home is extended to undertakings' premises. The same applied to Germany, as Advocate General Mischo observed in *Hoechst*, one of the main cases concerning inspections in the field of competition.[53] Interestingly, as A.G. Mischo observed, both the case-law and the legal writers are unanimous in considering that the term "home" covered business premises.

---

51 Article 9 (1) of the Greek Constitution reads as follows: "Every person's home is a sanctuary. The private and family life of the individual is inviolable. No home search shall be made, except when and as specified by law and always in the presence of representatives of the judicial power." Article 14 of the Italian Constitution is the following: "(1) The home is inviolable. (2) Inspections, searches or seizures may not be carried out except in the cases and in the manner set out by law and in accordance with the guarantees prescribed for the safeguard of personal freedom. (3) Controls and inspections for reasons of public health and safety or for economic and taxation purposes are regulated by special laws."

52 Article 13 (2) and (7) GG read as follows: "(2) Searches may be authorized only by a judge or, when time is of the essence, by other authorities designated by the laws, and may be carried out only in the manner therein prescribed. (7) Interferences and restrictions shall otherwise only be permissible to avert a danger to the public or to the life of an individual, or, pursuant to a law, to confront an acute danger to public safety and order, in particular to relieve a housing shortage, to combat the danger of an epidemic, or to protect young persons at risk."

53 AG Mischo, Opinion delivered in Joined Cases 46/87 and 227/88, *Hoechst AG v Commission* (1988) at para 57 [*Hoechst AG v Commission*]. Interestingly, the AG also pointed out that, although also in Italy the constitutional guarantee applied also to business premises, a fundamental distinction existed between, on the one hand, "*ispezioni o perquisizioni o sequestri*", which may be carried out only in the cases and in accordance with the methods provided for by law, in accordance with the guarantees laid down for the protection of personal liberty, and, on the other hand, "*accertamenti e ispezioni*" carried out on grounds of public health and hygiene or for economic and tax purposes, which are governed by special laws. Prior authorization by a court is in principle necessary only for searches (*perquisizioni*).

However, he added, this was not the case elsewhere. For example, in Belgium the application of the principle according to which "the home is inviolable" to legal persons and business premises was disputed and legislation granted very broad powers of investigation to inspectors without the need to obtain a court order in advance, in regard to taxation and social affairs and in regard to price control and commercial practices. In Denmark, although the Constitution was interpreted in the sense that a court order was necessary to enter a home or to seize or to examine letters and other papers, not only in the context of criminal proceedings, but also with regard to measures of administrative coercion, the legislature could provide for derogations.

A Common Boundary: the European Convention on Human Rights

The problems just mentioned explain the efforts made by the ECJ in order to find common standards, not only in common constitutional traditions, but also in the European Convention on Human Rights, to which all the Member States of the EC and which could, therefore, be regarded as a common boundary between public powers and individual liberties.[54] In particular, Article 8 ECHR, recognizing the right to respect for private and family life, expressly includes everyone's home and his correspondence, though enabling interference by public authorities only in accordance with the principles of legality and proportionality.[55] This meant, according to the European Court of Human Rights, that the protection accorded to the residence may, under certain circumstances, extend to business premises.[56]

Referring to the ECHR, however, did not solve all problems. First, according to ECJ itself, the EC could not become a member of the ECHR, because it lacked the necessary competence.[57] Moreover, the status of the ECHR in the Member States of the EU was not the same. In the UK it was not incorporated in national law until the Human Rights Act of 2000.[58] Elsewhere, the ECHR was incorporated, but it had the status of ordinary legislation. Consequently, it was subject, among others, to the principle *lex posterior derogat legi priori*, although this was manifestly in contrast with its nature of (multilateral) agreement aiming at recognizing and strengthening rights (at least potentially) enshrined into the national constitution.

54 See Weiler, *supra* note 50 at 105.

55 Article 8 (2) ECHR provides that: "There shall be no interference by a public authority with the exercise of this right except such as is in accordance with the law and is necessary in a democratic society in the interests of national security, public safety or the economic well-being of the country, for the prevention of disorder or crime, for the protection of health or morals, or for the protection of the rights and freedoms of others."

56 *Niemietz v Germany*, No 13710/88, [1992] ECHR.

57 ECJ, Opinion 2/94 (1996). Only in 2007, with the Treaty of Lisbon, has this issue been settled, in the sense that Under Article 6 TEU, the EU has now the competence to join the ECHR.

58 See Paul Craig, "The Courts, the HRA and Judicial Review" (2001) 117 Law Quart Rev 589 at 590.

Only recently, has the principle of the *lex posterior* been abandoned by higher courts.[59]

Second, and more relevant, neither the ECHR nor national legal orders provided uniform standards of conduct. Consider again the ruling of the ECJ in *Hoechst*. What was at stake was a Commission's decision imposing a penalty on some producers. Under regulation n.17/1962, the Commission found that there were grounds to suspect the existence of agreements or concerted practices for the fixing of prices. It then decided to carry out an investigation. But the applicant refused to submit to the investigation on the ground that it constituted an unlawful search. The German competition authority obtained from the *Amtsgericht Frankfurt am Main* a search warrant issued directly in the name of the Commission. The latter carried out the investigation and, after giving the applicant an opportunity to express its views, fixed the definitive amount of the periodic penalty payment. *Hoechst* brought an action to annul this decision arguing, *inter alia*, that the Commission's officials access to the documents held in its premises would infringe its fundamental right to the inviolability of home. But the Court dismissed this argument, on the grounds that, while such fundamental right was recognized in the Community legal order as a principle common to the laws of the Member States in regard to the private dwellings of natural persons, the same did not apply to business premises.[60] Nor did the Court found any limit to the intervention of public authorities, in this respect, in Article 8 ECHR.

Thirdly, in *Hoechst* the ECJ added that, if an undertaking opposes the Commission's investigation, the latter's officials may, without the cooperation of the undertakings, search for any information necessary for the investigation with the assistance of the national authorities. In this circumstance, the latter are required to afford them the assistance necessary for the performance of their duties. This had a twofold consequence. On the one hand, it was for each Member State to determine the conditions under which the national authorities would afford assistance to the Commission's officials while respecting the general principles of law. It followed that the appropriate procedural rules designed to ensure respect for undertakings' rights are those laid down by national law, although within the limits set by the general principles of law common to the legal orders of the Member States. On the other hand, national courts were responsible for checking whether the measures of constraint envisaged were arbitrary or excessive and to ensure that the rules of national law were complied with in the application of those measures. What was outside their judicial review was, instead, the need for the investigations ordered by the Commission and the lawfulness of its assessments of fact and law, which was subject only to review by the Court of Justice.[61]

59 See Helen Keller & Alec Stone-Sweet, eds, *A Europe of Rights – The Impact of the ECHR on National Legal Systems* (Oxford: Oxford University Press, 2008).

60 ECJ, Joined Cases 46/87 and 227/88, *Hoechst AG v Commission of the European Communities* (1988) at para 17.

61 *Ibid* at paras 34–37.

A functional rationale, therefore, emerged for providing EU officials and judges with better standards. However, this did not imply, not necessarily at least, that the Union should adopt a bill of rights, as it was decided in Nice in 2000. Indeed, another rationale existed, one that had a growing importance during the following decade, namely the widespread opinion that the legitimacy of the EU had to be strengthened, *inter alia*, by adopting a bill of rights.[62]

The EU Charter and the Reinterpretation of Fundamental Rights

Although the approach followed by the ECJ had always been more than a simple search for the appropriate legal basis and the adequacy of decision-making processes, its slow adaptation of general principles of law was not enough for European political leaders. They did not contest the importance of achieving legitimacy and accountability through law, one of the pillars of European integration.[63] However, the European Council of Nice in 2000 expressed the opinion that, especially in view of the widening of the Union which was to take place in the following years, EU courts would have needed to consult more directly the basic values that are enshrined in European constitutionalism. Hence the choice to adopt a bill of rights, as part of the strategy aiming at strengthening the ties between European institutions and the citizens of the Union.

Whatever the soundness of this political choice,[64] what matters for the purposes of this chapter is, more specifically, the content of the Charter concerning the freedom of home, its meaning and its legal effects. From the first point of view, Article 7 of the Charter aims at ensuring respect for private and family life. It establishes that "Everyone has the right to respect for his or her private and family life, home and communications."[65] In spite of the similarities with Article 8 ECHR, the word "correspondence" has been replaced with "communications", which covers a broader variety of technologies, and the respect of personal data falls within a separate clause, Article 8 of the Charter. With specific regard to

62 This view was endorsed by academic circles and political leaders, in spite of the doubts expressed by some scholars, including Joseph HH Weiler, "In Defence of the *Status Quo*: Europe's Constitutional *Sonderweg*" in Joseph HH Weiler & Marlene Wind, eds, *European Constitutionalism beyond the State* (Cambridge: Cambridge University Press, 2003) at 7 (arguing that the idea of a *pouvoir constituant* was but a "chimera") and Paul Craig, "Constitutions, Constitutionalism, and the European Union" (2001) 7 Eur LJ 125 (observing the difficulties that a constitutional process would have met, as it eventually happened, after France and the Netherlands did not ratify the Constitutional Treaty).

63 See Harlow, *supra* note 30 (in particular, chapter 6 "accountability through law").

64 See the critical remarks expressed by Joseph Weiler, "A Christian Europe? Europe and Christianity: Rules of Commitment" (2007) 6 European View 143 (arguing that European citizens do not need more rights, but a real empowerment).

65 In general terms, the Charter protects not only the right of EU citizens, but also those of other individuals: see Luis-Maria Diez-Picazo, *Constitucionalismo de la Uniòn europea* (Madrid: Civitas, 2002) at 34.

the respect for the "home", this expression has been interpreted broadly, so as to cover both the individual's residence and business premises.[66] This interpretation is founded on a general clause of the Charter, Article 52 (3). It lays down a general criterion for hermeneutics, by affirming that:

> Insofar as this Charter contains rights which correspond to rights guaranteed by the Convention for the Protection of Human Rights and Fundamental Freedoms, the meaning and scope of those rights shall be the same as those laid down by the said Convention. This provision shall not prevent Union law providing more extensive protection.[67]

Rather than preventing more extensive protection, as specified in the last indent of Article 52 (3), this provision requires an adjustment of the soft look traditionally followed by the ECJ. Consider again its ruling in *Hoechst*, where the ECJ took the view that the protection accorded by Article 8 ECHR to the "home" did not cover business premises.[68] This view was questionable, and was criticized, because it did not ensure to EC law a standard coherent with the constitutions of most Member States of the epoch. Moreover, it excluded completely the perspective of interest balancing as well as of the test of proportionality which was opened by the second paragraph of Article 8 ECHR. In a later ruling, *Roquette*, the ECJ partially coped with these weaknesses. It held that business premises are covered by the protection of the home, although in such a case the interference by public authorities may be more far-reaching, on the assumption that the interest at stake (that of a business) has a less intense protection than an individual's residence.[69] This standard looks more coherent with the case-law of the European Court of Human Rights mentioned earlier.[70] It should, therefore, be preferred to the less recent one. But Article 52 (3) of the Charter goes beyond this, to the extent to that it requires a dynamic adjustment of EU standards to those of the ECHR. As a result of this,

---

66 EU network of independent experts on fundamental rights, *Commentary of the Charter of Fundamental Rights of the European Union* (2006) at 83–84, online: http://158.109.131.198/catedra/images/experts/COMMENTARY%20OF%20THE%20CHARTER.pdf. I am indebted to Prof. Bruno Nascimbene for this reference.

67 Another provision, paragraph 4, adds that "Insofar as this Charter recognises fundamental rights as they result from the constitutional traditions common to the Member States, those rights shall be interpreted in harmony with those traditions." Limits of space preclude consideration of another aspect, notably the importance of the "explanations" given to the Charter: see Jacques Ziller, "Le fabuleux destin des explications relatives à la Charte des droits fondamentaux de l'Union européenne" in Jean-Claude Piris et al, eds, *Chemins d'Europe: Mélanges en l'honneur de Jean Paul Jacqué* (Dalloz-Sirey, 2010) at 765.

68 *Hoechst AG v Commission*, *supra* note 53.

69 ECJ, Case C-94/00, *Roquette Frères SA v Directeur général de la concurrence, de la consommation et de la répression des fraudes, and Commission of the European Communities* (2002) [*Roquette Frères SA v Commission*].

70 See also *Stés Colas and others v France*, No 37971/97), [2002] III ECHR.

although the ECJ has recognized some fundamental freedoms since its early cases, its standards of review must be adjusted to the new constitutional settlement, which accords priority to the higher standards elaborated by the Strasbourg Court.

Legal Safeguards: from the Right to the Defense to Due Process of Law

The Traditional Doctrine of the Right to the Defense

The approach of the ECJ, in its early cases, was quite similar to that of the French administrative judge. This is hardly surprising, since the influence of French administrative law especially on the EC system of judicial review is too well-known to require more than a hint. It was natural, therefore, to look first at French law, as Advocate General Warner did in *Transocean Marine Paint Association.*[71] But the French doctrine of *droit de la défense*, that had been developed in the 1940s, was based on the idea that, although general principles of administrative law could be identified without a textual basis, such principles could not prevail over statutory legislation.[72] The *audi alteram partem* was instead regarded as an unwritten constitutional principle in the other founding members of the EC, particularly in Germany and in Italy. Moreover, the doctrine of *droit de la défense* only applied where an administrative measure adversely affected an individual interest.[73]

Few years later, in *Hoechst*, as it was observed in section IV, the ECJ gave considerable weight to the differences between national legal orders in two respects. First, it accepted the Advocate General's finding that the fundamental right to the inviolability of the home was a principle common to the laws of the Member States. But, it specified, this applied only to the private dwellings of natural persons, not to he undertakings' premises. The reason was, according to the Court, that there were "not inconsiderable divergences between the legal systems of the Member States in regard to the nature and degree of protection afforded to business premises against intervention by the public authorities."[74]

---

71 ECJ, Case 17/74 *Transocean Marine Paint Association v Commission* (1974).

72 For further remarks concerning French case-law, see Benoît Jeanneau, *Les principes généraux du droit dans la jurisprudence administrative* (1954) and, for a comparative analysis, Giacinto della Cananea, "Minimum Standards of Procedural Justice in Administrative Adjudication" in Stephen W Schill, ed, *International Investment Law and Comparative Public Law* (Toronto: Oxford University Press, 2010) at 42 (arguing that, unlike rule-making, adjudication is subject to common standards in the liberal democracies that are members of OECD).

73 For this remark, see John Usher, *The General Principles of EC Law* (New York: Longman, 1998) at 73.

74 *Hoechst AG v Commission, supra* note 53 at para 17.

The second point is more complex and, therefore, requires a more detailed analysis. When considering the interests at stake, the ECJ gave considerable weight to the general interest of the Community. Such interest did not only justify the Commission's investigations, in order to "obtain evidence of infringements of the competition rules in the places in which such evidence is normally to be found, that is to say, on the business premises of undertakings." It implied also that its officials were not bound to have access only to documents or files which they could identify precisely in advance. On the contrary, the Court held, the Commission has the "power to search for various items of information which are not already known or fully identified." The justification was, not surprisingly, once again of functional nature. Without such a power, the ECJ affirmed, "it would be impossible for the Commission to obtain the information necessary to carry out the investigation if the undertakings concerned refused to cooperate or adopted an obstructive attitude."[75] Advocate General Mischo had gone even further, by affirming that:

> if the Commission's inspectors were entitled only to demand to be shown the classic files to be found in any undertaking, such as files of correspondence or other official Minutes of the governing bodies of the undertaking, they would probably never be able to find indications of an unlawful agreement. Such indications are more likely to be found on "loose pieces of paper", often hand-written, such as notes containing cryptic or coded references made at secret meetings held outside the undertaking, sometimes in a hotel situated in a country outside the Community.[76]

The Court's recognition of such wide discretionary powers did not imply, however, a sort of *carte blanche*. Quite the contrary, the ECJ held, in all the legal systems of the Member States, any intervention by the public authorities in the sphere of private activities of any person, whether natural or legal, must have a legal basis and be justified on the grounds laid down by law. This implied that an adequate protection against arbitrary or disproportionate intervention had to be provided. And the Court intended to ensure that such protection was provided at EC level, although it made no attempt to balance the interest of the Community, against the interests of the undertakings affected by the Commission's inspections.

The ECJ dealt only with the question of whether, also in summary procedures, certain rights of the defense had to be respected. In this respect, the ECJ confirmed

---

75 *Hoechst AG v Commission, supra* note 53 at para 19. The Commission's decision required the undertaking "to permit officials authorized by the Commission to enter its premises during normal office hours, to produce for inspection and to permit copies to be made of business documents related to the subject-matter of the enquiry which are requested by the said officials and to provide immediately any explanations which those officials may seek."

76 AG Mischo, Opinion delivered in *Hoechst AG v Commission, supra* note 53 at para 22.

its earlier case-law, according to which, although certain rights of the defense relate only to the contentious proceedings which follow the delivery of the statement of objections, other rights, such as the right to legal representation and the privileged nature of correspondence between lawyer and client must be respected as from the preliminary-inquiry stage and during inspections.[77]

Where the Court's reductive approach emerges more clearly is with regard to the duty to state reasons. It ought to be observed that, unlike in French or English administrative law, in the EC such duty is not a judge-made creation based on broad principles of fairness or natural justice, but a general rule laid down by the Treaty of Rome, and reiterated by Regulation n. 17/62. For its part, the ECJ had constantly, and convincingly, held that the Commission's obligation to specify the subject-matter and purpose of the investigation constituted a basic guarantee of the rights of the defense of the undertakings concerned. Consequently, as the Court said in *Hoechst*, the scope of the obligation to state the reasons on which decisions ordering investigations are based cannot be limited to general, if not generic, consideration concerning the need to ensure the effectiveness of Commission's investigations. At least, the Court added, the Commission must indicate the facts which it intends to investigate. Strangely, given the emphasis placed on the appropriateness of the procedure, at this point the Court expressed an unusually strong criticism of the Commission's conduct, but refrained from drawing the conclusions which could appear inevitable. It found, without any hesitation, that the statement of the reasons on which the contested decision was based "was drawn up in very general terms which might well have been made more precise."[78] It recognized that, under this perspective, the decision was therefore open to criticism. But, the Court added, such a decision none the less contained the essential indications prescribed by Regulation No 17/1962. However, when considering such indications, notably the "information" suggesting the existence and application of agreements or concerted practices and the need to contrast such deviations from the principle of free competition, it is difficult to dismiss the idea that they fall below the standard of "essentiality" (that is to say, the minimum standards concerning the essential information that must be provided to business). Interestingly, although in the same years the Court had constantly emphasized the connection between the statement of reasons and its judicial review, in this case it made no attempt to place the rights to the defense in a broader perspective. Otherwise, the least that can be said is that the Court resisted altering its methodology, but through that, each question

77 AG Mischo, Opinion delivered in *Hoechst AG v Commission*, *supra* note 53 at para 16, where the Court refers to its previous judgment in Case 155/79, *AM & S v Commission* (1982). A related issue is the Commission's duty of care, which is examined by Herwig CH Hofmann, "Inquisitorial Procedures and General Principles of Law: The Duty of Care in the Case Law of the European Court of Justice" in this volume (affirming that this is "amongst the most central general principles of law").

78 *Hoechst AG v Commission*, *supra* note 53 at para 42.

concerning the appropriateness of the administrative procedure followed by the Commission would be evaluated in context.

Towards Procedural Due Process of Law

A gradual change in the Court's approach to procedural constraints on administrative powers occurred more than ten years later, in *Roquette.*[79] While in *Hoechst* an undertaking had brought an action directly against a Commission's decision, in *Roquette* a French company brought to the *Cour de Cassation* an appeal against an order of the President of the *Tribunal de grande instance de Lille,* authorizing entry upon and seizures at the premises of that company with a view to gathering evidence of its possible participation in agreements and/or concerted practices. The French court then sent a preliminary reference to the ECJ. Why it had done so, is worth pointing out. In the distilled words of the ECJ's, the *Cour de Cassation* was "uncertain as to the possible effect on the principles established by the Court in *Hoechst.*" What was at stake, however, was a much more serious issue, that is to say whether the rather restrictive approach followed by the ECJ was coherent with the constitutional protection accorded to business premises.

In the previous two decades, the ECJ had faced similar issues arising from German and Italian judges. In both these countries, the constitutional courts had more or less grudgingly accepted the primacy of EC law over national law. But they had set limits to primacy, affirming that it did not affect the fundamental rights protected by the national constitution, of which they had the task to ensure the respect.[80] A similar position had not been taken by the French *Conseil constitutionnel*, but the step taken by the *Cour de Cassation* could open a new contrast. In fact, few years earlier, in 1983, the *Conseil constitutionnel* had ruled that investigations on private premises may only be carried out in conformity with Article 66 of the French Constitution, which entrusts to the judiciary the protection of individual liberty and, in particular, of the inviolability of the home.

As might be expected, the ECJ did not spend a single word on the French constitutional setting. On the other hand, it always refrains from making any comment to the description made by the referring court. It did, rather, mention what it euphemistically called "certain developments which have taken place in the field of the protection of human rights since delivery of the judgment in *Hoechst.*"[81] This meant, more concretely, that the ECJ took into due account case-law of the European Court of Human Rights subsequent to its own judgment in *Hoechst.* According to the rulings of the European Court of Human Rights in *Colas Est* and *Niemietz*, the protection of the home provided for in Article 8 of the ECHR could in certain circumstances be extended to cover such premises,

79 *Roquette Frères SA v Commission, supra* note 69.

80 See Alec Stone Sweet, *The Judicial Construction of Europe* (Oxford: Oxford University Press, 2004).

81 *Roquette Frères SA v Commission, supra* note 69 at para 22.

although the right of interference by public authorities might well be more far-reaching where professional or business activities or premises were involved than in cases concerning individuals, and the ECJ fully adhered to such standards. In other words, it very quickly adopted the citation of the precedents of the other Court as a substitute for a thorough revision of *Hoechst*. Whether the partial *revirement* was thus determined by some opportunistic view, is therefore, not an abstract question.

That said, there is much more in *Roquette* than a simple adjustment to new, and higher, substantive standards of protection of the home. The ECJ reiterated its emphasis on the need to prevent competition from being distorted to the detriment of the public interest.[82] But soon after that, although it was requested to clarify the purpose and the scope of the review to be carried out by the competent national court, it took the unprecedented attempt to draw a list of the procedural safeguards (or guarantees, to borrow its words) provided by Community law. Such safeguards, the Court noted, were of four kinds. First, the coercive measures for which application may be made to national authorities in the implementation of Regulation No 17/1962 are intended solely to enable EC officials to exercise the investigatory powers vested in the Commission, which are "clearly circumscribed." This echoes the continental conception of the principle of legality as a barrier against undue interference with the private sphere, or the rule of law ideal of a system of limited government. It produces an important consequence, underlined by the Court, that is to say that the Commission's power do not extend to documents of a non-business nature.[83] Let us suppose, for example, that under Regulation n. 1/2003 the Commission believes that an inspection must be carried in the home of a manager of the undertaking that is subject to an investigation. If documents of a non-business nature are excluded, then the correspondence of, say, the daughter of the manager may not be seized by Commission officials.

As a second safeguard, any undertaking has the traditional rights to the defense, including, in particular, the right to legal representation and the privileged nature of correspondence between lawyer and client. Third, the Commission must state the reasons for the decisions ordering an investigation, and, while in *Hoechst* the Court had certainly not insisted on this point, in *Roquette* it says that the Commission must state in that decision "as precisely as possible, what it is looking for."[84] According to the ECJ, this serves for protecting the rights of defense of the undertaking, which would be compromised if the Commission could rely on evidence against undertakings which was obtained during an investigation but that was not related to the subject-matter or purpose. There is not, in other words, an unlimited power to investigate and inspect.

Fourth, the conduct of the Commission is subject to judicial review. At least one implication of this ought to be specified. The Commission will be prevented

82 *Roquette Frères SA v Commission, supra* note 69 at para 42.

83 *Ibid* at para 45.

84 *Ibid* at para 48.

from using, for the purposes of its procedures, any document or evidence which it might have obtained in the course of its inspection, if the decision which orders it is annulled by the EU courts.[85]

It is probably fair to say that this ruling did not extend procedural rights. However, at least two innovative elements should not be neglected. *Roquette* is significant, first of all, because in earlier case law the ECJ had minimized the extent to which the protection of EC law could be granted in the face of the exercise of broad administrative discretion, particularly with regard to the duty to give reasons. The opposite of this approach was taken here, coherently with the growing emphasis placed by the ECJ on procedural constraints on power, which will later find its clearest manifestation in *Kadi*,[86] an important ruling concerning anti-terrorism measures.

As a second important element, unlike *Hoechst*, *Roquette* was a case in which the Court dealt with the orders enacted by national authorities, aiming at allowing the Commission to carry out its investigation and inspections. This case is significant, therefore, because coercive measures were not taken by the EC administration alone, but also by national authorities. Insisting on procedural protections in this context has, therefore, a different meaning. It is coherent, moreover, with the gradual extension of procedural safeguards, such as the right to be heard, in other areas of EC law, such as customs law.[87] In other words, it is part of a judicial trend towards procedural dialogue and hard-look process review.[88]

Conclusion: the Realist Paradigm Revised

In the light of the decades-long experience of EU law with inspections, certain specificities of national administrations are still unchanged. Two are especially significant. First, they dispose of military forces and police corps, while there is

85 ECJ, Case 85/87, *Dow Chemical Nederland v Commission* (1987) at para 34.

86 See ECJ, Case C-402/05 P, *Kadi v Council and Commission*. For further remarks, see G della Cananea, "Global Security and Procedural Due Process of Law Between the United Nations and the European Union" (2009) 15 Colum J Eur L 511 (arguing that the ECJ has restored procedural due process of law). But see also G de Burça, "The EU, the European Court of Justice and the International Legal Order after Kadi" (2010) 51:1 Harvard International Law Journal 1 (arguing that this judgment carries the risk of undermining the image of the ECJ as an actor committed to the respect of international law).

87 See ECJ, Case C-269/90, *Technische Universität München v Hauptzollamt München* (1991). For this reading of the Court's ruling, see Harlow, *supra* note 30 at 162 and Herwig CH Hofmann, "Inquisitorial Procedures and General Principles of Law: The Duty of Care in the Case Law of the European Court of Justice" in this volume.

88 Further developments of judicial review thus become possible, especially from the point of view of the principle of proportionality. For a theoretical perspective, see Alec Stone Sweet & Jud Mathews, "Proportionality Balancing and Global Constitutionalism" (2008) 47 Col J Transn L 72.

not yet a European equivalent to the US Federal Bureau of Investigation. Second, several units of national administrative systems are entitled to use force in order to fulfill certain public goals, including local authorities in some circumstances.[89] However, a twofold change has emerged, from a Weberian perspective, to the extent that not only is the legitimate exercise of force influenced by EU law, but also that, in the field of competition, the European administration, too, has both a benevolent face and that of the authority. It may not only issue orders affecting national physical and legal persons, but also decide to carry out inspections. The first point is to say that the State has lost the monopoly of legislation, and calls for no significant new departure in public law doctrines. Observing that national authorities have a prominent role in the legitimate exercise of force, but that they have no longer the monopoly of its exercise, raises instead a twofold question. Firstly, we should consider whether the traditional realist paradigm according to which the legitimate monopoly of force is an exclusive feature of the State (of each State), exists, and the appropriate answer is that this is no longer the case for the States that are members of the EU.[90] Secondly, and consequently, we should consider whether the exercise of force is subject to safeguards and, if so, whether they are adequate. With regard to this, the two kinds of inquiry carried out in the foregoing pages suggest that some safeguards have been introduced by the Court of Justice. Although initially the Court has been reluctant to limit the action of the Commission, it has gradually taken on the role of a constitutional court, by including the inviolability of home within the rights of which it has to ensure the respect. More recently, it has increasingly ensured that procedural requirements are respected in the EU administrations' activities powers upon business, in particular in the context of inspections. That this objective has been attained through judicial review, of course, does not diminish the importance of the formal constitutional restraints introduced by the Charter of fundamental rights and the Treaty of Lisbon, especially for its clause concerning the accession of the EU to the ECHR. But judicial review is likely to keep its importance to resolve the issues that always arise in the dialectic relationship between authority and freedom, especially if the institutional limitations of judicial review can, in part at least, be overcome through the development of better standards by courts of the EU and the European Court of Human Rights.

89 See Sabino Cassese, *Lo Stato introvabile* (Donzelli, 1998) at 35 (arguing that there is no such thing as a general power of this kind).

90 See Luis Dìez-Picazo, "Hacia una teoria de la coacciòn en el Derecho de la Uniòn Europea" in L Ortega Alvarez, ed, *La seguridad integral europea* (Lex Nova, 2005) at 115. See also D Curtin, *Post National Democracy: The European Union in Search of a Political Philosophy* (London: Kluwer Law International, 1997) (calling for a broader change of theoretical paradigms).

PART 3
Truth Commissions and Public Inquiries I – Views of Commissioners

Chapter 10
Reflections on the Public Inquiry into Pediatric Forensic Pathology in Ontario

Justice Stephen T. Goudge

Introduction

The Inquiry into Pediatric Forensic Pathology in Ontario was established on April 25, 2007. It reported to the government of Ontario on October 1, 2008.[1] In this chapter I will reflect on what happened in those 17 months to see what lessons there may be for the administrative tribunal community, particularly in balancing the objectives of efficiency and fairness. I will focus particularly on what we did that was more inquisitorial than the processes I am used to in my day job, in the sense that the Inquiry itself undertook initiatives to determine how matters would unfold.

It may be useful to begin with a brief description of what a public inquiry is, in the Canadian context. It is established by the executive branch of government through an order in council, passed pursuant to authorizing legislation. Its mandate is provided by that order in council. Its budget is set by the executive, and it reports to the executive. In a real sense, a public inquiry is a subordinate part of the executive branch of government. All provinces and the federal government have such legislation. Indeed, Ontario is in the process of bringing into effect new legislation which will enhance government's power to exercise control over public inquiries.

Much use has been made of public inquiries over our history. Since Confederation, there have been more than 400 such inquiries at the federal level alone. Some have engaged solely in the formation of policy for government. For example, we owe our public broadcasting system, our health care system, and our free trade arrangement with the United States in large measure to public inquiries.

Typically however, governments establish public inquiries in response to significant public controversies about the propriety of government activity, or significant public concern about particular tragic events. In such circumstances, the inquiry will typically be asked to find facts and make policy recommendations

---

1 Volume 4 of the Inquiry report is devoted to a detailed description of the processes used, in the hope that this may be of some use in future, online: http://www.attorneygeneral.jus.gov.on.ca/inquiries/goudge/index.html.

to government in order that the public interest may be better served in future similar circumstances. In this sense, mine was a typical inquiry.

How did the Inquiry come about? It hardly need be said that the tragedy of a child who dies unexpectedly in criminally suspicious circumstances is a devastating event for parents, for family, and for the entire community. It is vital for society to deal with the tragedy in a way that is right and just, and that allows all those affected to come to terms with it. The criminal justice system is central to this task. It must seek to determine whether there is truth to the suspicion that the child was killed, and if so by whom.

The consequences of failure are extraordinarily high: wrongful conviction; perhaps years unnecessarily suffered in penitentiary; shattered families; stigmatizing labels like child killer; exhausted financial resources; and potentially, unidentified killers going unpunished, all at huge cost to public faith in the criminal justice system.

Forensic pathology is often vital in determining the success or failure of the system in dealing with these difficult cases. The suspected parent or caregiver will often have been the only person in contact with the infant in the hours before death. Apart from this exclusive opportunity, there is often only the pathologist's opinion of the cause of death. That opinion can be decisive. If it is unsound, the risk of injustice is palpable.

In the 1990s, Dr. Charles Smith was the preeminent pediatric forensic pathologist working in the criminal justice system in Canada. Few others had his interest in the work. Like many in the field in that era, he was not formally trained in forensic pathology but was a clinical pathologist. However, he had the *imprimatur* of a world class institution, the Hospital for Sick Children, and a commanding court room presence. He got the most difficult cases and his opinion was often critical in determining the outcome.

Through the 1990s, however, there were warning signals in several of his cases. The last of these was one where a young man was convicted of first degree murder for sexually assaulting and strangling his four year old niece. The conviction was largely based on Dr. Smith's evidence. Some years later, after the young man had served over 12 years in penitentiary as a child killer, it became clear that Dr. Smith's opinion was completely wrong. There was no pathology evidence of either sexual assault or strangulation. It was the last straw. A courageous Chief Coroner for Ontario immediately called for a review by an internationally renowned panel of forensic pathologists of all of Dr. Smith's criminal cases from 1991 to 2001.

The results of the Review were announced on April 19, 2007. They were devastating. In 20 of the 45 cases the panel could find no reasonable support for Dr. Smith's opinions. In 12 of those 20 there were convictions or findings of guilt, many on very serious charges. As a consequence, public confidence in forensic pathology and its use in the criminal justice system was deeply shaken. Six days later, the Ontario government called the Inquiry and I was appointed Commissioner.

Seventeen months after my appointment, I tabled my report. Not surprisingly, I found significant failings by all the actors in the criminal justice system. This was far from a simple story of one rogue pathologist. There were too few forensic pathologists. They were poorly trained and routinely fell short of best practices in carrying out their work. They were poorly supervised by the institutions in which they worked. Counsel for the Crown and defence were inadequate in spotlighting flawed scientific evidence. And courts were inadequately vigilant in ensuring that the expert opinions they received carried a basic reliability sufficient to be acted upon. With hindsight, unjust results were no surprise. For each of these failings my Report offered recommendations to attempt, so far as possible, to prevent a recurrence of the tragedies that had been caused. Hopefully public confidence could thereby be restored.

The book ends of my Inquiry were its creation on April 25, 2007, and its report on October 1, 2008. I propose to examine what happened between these dates under four headings: establishing the mandate; the preparatory work; the hearing process; and the development of policy recommendations. My hope is to shed light on how these aspects of the methods we used may have assisted the achievement of both efficiency and fairness.

Establishing the Mandate

The results of the Chief Coroner's Review were released to the public on Thursday April 19, 2007. By the following Saturday, the media was filled with expressions of public alarm. At dinnertime that day, my phone rang and the Attorney General asked if I would take on this Inquiry. He had cleared my appointment with my Chief Justice. I agreed, and he invited me to meet with his deputy minister the next day to discuss the order in council that would be taken to Cabinet two days later.

I came to the meeting knowing no more than what I had read in the papers. Yet it was an opportunity not afforded to many tribunals to shape its own mandate, perhaps in quite specific ways that could enhance efficiency or fairness. A risk this presents, however, is that the Inquiry's jurisdiction is defined by the subordinate legislation by which it is set up, and if a subsequent challenge is raised that the Inquiry has exceeded that jurisdiction, the Commissioner may be in the awkward position of being asked to interpret the document that he or she had a hand in drafting. Fortunately, that did not happen in this instance.

The government had decided that the Inquiry would conduct a systemic review of the practice of pediatric forensic pathology in the criminal justice system in Ontario from 1981 to 2001. It would not be permitted to find criminal or civil liability, but would be called upon to make recommendations to restore and enhance public confidence in pediatric forensic pathology and its future use. And it would have a deadline. My contribution to the mandate's formation related to the latter and to matters of procedure.

Several of these ultimately proved invaluable. In particular, the order in council specified that the Inquiry was to rely "wherever possible on overview reports" submitted to it. The Inquiry was authorized to consider these reports in lieu of calling witnesses. The meaning of "overview reports" was not defined. The Inquiry was also instructed to rely wherever possible on representative witnesses on behalf of institutions. In addition, it was entitled within its approved budget to retain counsel, staff and expertise as it considered necessary to perform its mandate. It was authorized to make recommendations for funding for parties granted standing if they would otherwise not be able to participate. Finally, the Inquiry was empowered to ensure the provision of counseling services for "victims or families" of the events it was to examine. All of these are described below in more detail. They all contributed, some significantly, to the Inquiry being able to proceed as efficiently as possible and to attempt to fully discharge its mandate while preserving the fairness necessary for any adjudicative process. Whether such explicit and binding prior authorization of procedures is something that can be emulated by administrative tribunals generally may be a matter of debate. Where, as here, the tribunal is definitively authorized by subordinate legislation there can be no doubt about the efficiency that can thereby be achieved.

The Preparatory Work

Unlike most administrative tribunals, in its first day in business, the Inquiry was a pure "green fields" operation, with one staff member, the Commissioner. The hearing of witnesses did not commence until November 2007. The intervening six months were ones of intense activity. Early on, there were matters of pure logistics such as securing space, hiring staff, constructing a hearing room, discussing the budget with government and so on. Beyond that however a number of the steps taken in that time frame were absolutely critical to the way the Inquiry was able to proceed.

Most important was the obtaining of Commission counsel. I was tremendously fortunate to be able to retain Linda Rothstein. I had previously worked closely with her and knew how able a litigator she is. I knew, as well, how well she would be able to interact with other counsel. I was also confident she could act as Commission counsel must, pursuing the truth wherever it leads in an objective and non-partisan way. The Inquiry's ability to employ inquisitorial methods while retaining the perception of fairness among the participants was due in large part to her skills.

The second important step was to take the time necessary to understand the issues that would be faced as well as possible before any hearings commenced. This required Commission counsel to obtain, review, and organize documentation from a variety of sources. Importantly, the criterion used was not possible relevance, but a narrower more focused search only for documents that would be helpful to the systemic nature of the mandate. 36,000 documents were collected, scanned, and put in a searchable database. Commission counsel and her staff also spent much of their investigative time conducting interviews of persons with knowledge of information relevant to the work of the Inquiry. Interview summaries were prepared of each of these. All this was made available to the parties. Finally, because few of us began with any detailed understanding of the death investigation process, arrangements were made for seminars to be conducted for the participants on the subject of forensic pathology generally. All counsel and staff were invited to attend.

This preparatory work was absolutely essential in allowing us to proceed efficiently when the hearings themselves commenced. It permitted preparation of an early, although obviously tentative, list of the issues to be addressed. It allowed the critical task of time allocation for witnesses to be undertaken in an informed way. And it allowed the Inquiry to begin its own targeted research program.

That program was headed by Prof. Kent Roach of the University of Toronto Law School with the able collaboration of Dean Sossin of Osgoode Hall Law School, then a colleague of Prof. Roach. Over the summer of 2007, they retained experts from Australia, Canada, the United Kingdom and the United States to prepare 11 different studies on various aspects of forensic pathology and its interaction with the justice system. Importantly, the research and fact finding phases of the Inquiry's work were not kept separate. The studies were made available to all when they were ready and most of the authors participated as panelists in our policy roundtables. In the end, this work provided many insights that were of great assistance in identifying issues of importance, comparing alternative approaches, articulating questions for witnesses, and considering final submissions.

All this allowed us, well before the public hearings began, to compile and circulate to the parties a list of the systemic issues that should be addressed if we were to do our job. Those issues were identified as the things that went wrong with the role played by forensic pathology in the criminal justice system, as exemplified by the cases we reviewed, and that must be addressed if similar mistakes were to be prevented in the future. We made it clear that the list was not intended to be exhaustive, nor did it represent anyone's final view of which were the key issues. But it vastly assisted in many ways, including in the ongoing discussions with the parties concerning the limits of the Inquiry, as guidance for the preparation of and cross-examination of witnesses and in the development of recommendations.

The questions of standing and funding also had to be resolved as part of the preparation work. After hearing oral submissions on August 17, 2007, I granted standing to 11 parties including the Office of the Chief Coroner of Ontario, Dr. Smith, the Hospital for Sick Children where he was on staff, two groups of affected individuals and families, and five organizations involved in the criminal justice system. I determined that seven of those required funding in order to participate. In the end, all were ably represented by counsel. It is impossible to overemphasize how essential the contribution of good counsel is to the effective conducting of any hearing, including this one.

As is apparent, many of the parties had interests that were starkly in conflict. To assist in the management of this, Commission counsel met regularly with counsel throughout the process to discuss and address their various concerns and interests. I was available to resolve any concerns that could not be otherwise dealt with, but was never called upon. Those discussions not only provided essential lubrication for our procedures, but allowed the Inquiry to anticipate and address in advance problems that could arise at the hearing.

To take advantage of the mandate to use overview reports in lieu of calling witnesses Commission counsel prepared an overview report of each of the 18 cases reviewed by the Chief Coroner's panel of experts that we intended to examine. Each summarized the facts of the case in a neutral non-argumentative way, and the steps taken in the death investigation, the criminal proceedings, and the child protection proceedings that took place. Counsel for all parties were asked to comment on these reports before they were finalized. Because of the care taken in their preparation, there were few suggested revisions. Had any irreconcilable differences emerged, the parties could have addressed these with evidence at the hearing but that proved unnecessary. In the end, given that they were not tested for their truth, the parties were free to argue the weight I should attach to these reports and the information in them.

The same was true of the institution reports that were sought from the Chief Coroner for Ontario and the Hospital for Sick Children (SickKids). Like the overview reports, these reports dramatically reduced the number of witnesses needed from those institutions and the length of the testimony from those who were called.

Finally, an important part of our preparation consisted of meetings with individuals and families whose lives had been profoundly changed by what we were examining. I wanted to hear from them because the events that so affected them had precipitated the Inquiry. It was useful context for my work. As well, I wanted to give them the opportunity to be heard in some way, and to offer to them the provision of counseling if they wished. None were obliged to meet with me. I made it clear to them and to the parties that I would use nothing I heard in these meetings as evidence. The meetings were private and confidential. I was accompanied only by one staff lawyer. No transcripts were kept. The families were told that this was not a fact finding part of the process but one that was to provide context for the work of the Inquiry.

I found these meetings a sad but deeply moving experience. However, I was heartened by the response of those I met with, who made it clear that even though I would not be acting on what they told me, it helped their healing process to be able to tell their stories to someone who was charged by government with recommending improvements to the system. They wanted to offer whatever limited assistance they could. In return, we were able to offer the provision of counseling paid for by the government. A number accepted. In a small way, I came to understand the immense benefits that a truth and reconciliation process can provide.

The Hearing Process

Nowhere was the balance of efficiency and fairness more important to strike than in the fact finding process which was conducted through formal hearings. Efficiency was important not only because public funds were being used but because of the need for timely recommendations to help restore public confidence in forensic pathology as soon as possible, given its vital role in criminal justice. Fairness was equally important. Many facts were contested and public reputations were very much at stake, particularly given the intense media scrutiny under which the Inquiry was carried on.

The preparatory work I have described was very important in achieving this balance. By the time the hearings began, we had a preliminary list of issues to be addressed that was understood by all. This provided much focus for examination and cross-examination. Interview summaries served as will say statements, and in several cases as evidence-in-chief. The use of overview and institutional reports to lay out uncontested facts without the need for witnesses allowed us to start the hearing by tabling them as 2,055 pages of evidence. Continual meetings between Commission counsel and counsel for the parties, with the Commissioner available as backstop if necessary smoothed the process significantly.

All this allowed us to commence the fact finding hearings in November 2007 with a 60 day hearing schedule mapped out in advance that was acceptable to all. The hearings ran continuously, with the exception of holiday breaks. It was an intense process, five days a week from 9 to 4:30 with an hour for lunch. Because counsel knew well before we actually began what witnesses would be called, when, and generally what they would say, preparation was greatly facilitated.

Perhaps most important was the imposition of time limits on all counsel, including Commission counsel, for examination and cross-examination and the process that was used for doing so. The total time for each witness was proposed in the first instance by Commission counsel who was in a position to do this because of all the preparatory work. If other counsel contested the allocation I was available to decide. However, I was never called on to do so. I then divided the time allocated to each witness among counsel. With one exception, Dr. Smith, Commission counsel led all the witnesses-in-chief in fulfillment of her truth seeking role. Commission counsel was allotted half the time for each witness. After taking requests for cross-examination time I subdivided the other half of the time among requesting counsel according to the interests of their clients. Parties understood my basis for doing so. It was done well before and in a transparent and reasoned way. That contributed significantly to the acceptability of the allocations made. In addition, I encouraged cross-examining counsel to consult in advance and avoid duplication. Importantly, I tried to ensure that these various limitations on counsel, having been set in advance, were carefully observed. The result, perhaps in large measure facilitated by the skill of counsel, was pointed and effective cross-examination that was informed by the principle of proportionality, that is giving witnesses only the time their relative importance deserves. Because of the various steps taken by the Inquiry no sense of unfairness was ever voiced by counsel. In the end, I came away firmly persuaded that examination and cross-examination is made much more effective by time limits, just as I have learned from 15 years' experience on my court that the same is true for argument.

Finally, in some cases we were able to call fact witnesses in panels. For example, the Chief Coroner's Review Panel gave their evidence about Dr. Smith's work in this way. Since much of this was opinion evidence I found it very useful to have panelists comment in real time on the opinions offered by their colleagues. This too allowed us to proceed more effectively. This procedure is one that is already in widespread use in the administrative tribunal world.

The Development of Policy Recommendations

There were two aspects to this stage of the work of the Inquiry, policy roundtables and final submissions. The Inquiry held a series of 18 roundtables in February 2008 at the conclusion of the fact finding process. Each was designed around a particular theme and many comprised both domestic and international experts. The purpose of the roundtables was to ensure that the most difficult policy questions could be addressed by leading academics and practitioners.

Commission counsel carefully selected the participants. Some roundtables had as many as six panelists, others as few as two. Input was sought from those who could speak to both the theoretical and practical aspects of the various systemic issues. Participants included academics, pathologists, and lawyers from around the world together with a number of professionals from Ontario's legal, medical, and child care protection communities. Some had previously testified at the formal hearings. Others had prepared research studies while still others had played no previous role in the work of the Inquiry.

For each roundtable, Commission counsel prepared a series of questions to be discussed and debated by the participants. They and the parties were advised that these were not exhaustive nor would they all necessarily be addressed in the final report. The themes and the proposed questions were circulated in advance to all counsel who were invited both to comment on them and add their own questions. The Inquiry also provided participants and counsel with a compendium of relevant articles and documents for each roundtable.

Commission counsel led the roundtables using a question and answer format. There were no opening statements nor were the participants sworn. Dialogue amongst them was encouraged. All counsel were afforded their own opportunity to ask questions. I was also very much involved in these discussions. This proved to be a process that was open, engaging, dynamic, full of important insights, and was consistent with both efficiency and fairness.

The final step consisted of the submissions by the parties. Written submissions were exchanged in advance, and were filed by March 20, 2008. There was no page limitation. Oral submissions were time limited and were made on March 31 and

April 1. Parties were expressly asked to set out any specific findings of fact or systemic recommendations they wished the Inquiry to make.

The following four and a half months involved the relentlessly intense task of writing the report following by six weeks of editing, translation, printing and binding. On October 1, 2008, I delivered my report. It consisted of four volumes: an executive summary; the systemic review of the practice of pediatric forensic pathology in the criminal justice system; policy recommendations; and a description of the processes used.

The recommendations were directed at the government, at the practice and organization of forensic pathology in Ontario, at the Office of the Chief Coroner of Ontario and at the roles of coroners, Crown, defense, and the courts.

Having delivered my report it would be inappropriate for me to comment on the response of government and its institutions since it is important that the judiciary stay out of politics. I would only say that I have been gratified.

I do not think the same constraint applies to my recommendations for counsel or the courts. That context provided the last example of how a public inquiry can be activist, in a way that an inquisitorial tribunal might be but a court could not be. My recommendations concerned the participation of both counsel and the judiciary in the criminal justice system and attempted to suggest ways that both might better keep flawed scientific opinion evidence from affecting outcomes. Following my report, I have spoken to many groups of lawyers and judges on this topic. I have viewed this as part of my mandate. And while it is due I am sure to far more than my Inquiry I think it accurate to say that there is now a very lively and widespread conversation going on in both communities on the subject of expert evidence and how better to deal with it. It reflects the reality that our criminal justice system is very fortunate to have participants who are constantly seeking for ways to make the system better.

I hope the criminal justice system has benefitted from the work of the Inquiry. If the administrative law system can also benefit in any way from the Inquiry and the processes we used, particularly with the difficult task of balancing efficiency and fairness, it will simply enhance the privilege it was to serve as the Commissioner of the Inquiry into Pediatric Forensic Pathology in Ontario.

Chapter 11
Reflections on the Braidwood Inquiry

Hon. Thomas R. Braidwood, Q.C.

Introduction

In October 2007, at the Vancouver International Airport, an officer of the Royal Canadian Mounted Police (RCMP), in the company of three other RCMP policemen, deployed a conducted energy weapon (CEW) against Mr. Robert Dziekanski, who died within seconds. The total time that elapsed between the first encounter with the police and his death was less than two minutes. The public reaction to this conduct, which was caught on a video camera, was immediate and intense. At a more general level, concern was expressed regarding the deployment and use of conducted energy weapons by policing bodies in British Columbia. Accordingly, I was appointed to conduct two separate inquiries under the British Columbia *Public Inquiry Act*: (1) a study commission "... to inquire into and report on the use of conducted energy weapons by constables, sheriffs, and authorized persons in British Columbia;" and (2) a hearing and study commission "... to inquire into and report on the death of Mr. Dziekanski."[1]

The Study Commission

I conducted the study commission first. The Terms of Reference[2] designated to me by the Attorney General were exceptionally broad. They invited me to:

- review the current rules, policies, and procedures applicable to constables, sheriffs, and correctional officers respecting their use of conducted energy weapons, including their training and re-training;
- review research, studies, reports, and evaluations respecting the safety and effectiveness of conducted energy weapons when used in policing and law enforcement; and
- make recommendations respecting the appropriate use of conducted energy weapons, including appropriate training and re-training.

---

1 "Purpose and Terms of Reference: Braidwood Inquiry" (30 June 2009), online: http://www.braidwoodinquiry.ca/terms_of_reference.php [Purpose and Terms of Reference].

2 *Ibid.*

It was obvious to me at the outset that my primary concern, arising from the unfortunate events at the Vancouver International Airport and other conducted energy weapon incidents, was an erosion of public confidence in our law enforcement agencies. This led me ultimately to call my report "Restoring Public Confidence."

To address this mandate, I developed a two-pronged approach. In order to further my own understanding of the complexities of these issues, and to assist in educating the public so that they would have confidence in my recommendations, Commission Counsel and Associate Commission Counsel organized a series of informal public forums. A wide range of people with varying interests and perspectives were invited to make presentations. We advertised in numerous newspapers and established a website to invite participants. We invited to the hearings almost everyone who applied, but obviously Taser International had many experts who testified in the open hearings and presented many briefs and studies. Our counsel called experts to cover all aspects of the issue as did the RCMP, the mental health organizations and other such organizations.

In order to pursue the many technical and policy issues in more depth, our research Counsel brought together a team of legal, medical, empirical, and policy researchers who analyzed an enormous volume of Canadian and international materials and prepared research papers, which I relied upon in preparing my report.

Under the heading "Study Commissions" in the *Public Inquiry Act*,[3] section 20 sets out that a study commission may engage in any activity necessary to effectively and efficiently perform the duties of the commission, "including (a) conducting research, including interviews and surveys; (b) consulting with participants, privately or in a matter that is open to the public …; (c) consulting with the public generally …"

Furthermore, the commission was empowered to make certain directives, which included:

> (a) the notification of participants and the public regarding a consultation under this section;
> (b) the holding of public meetings …
> (c) …
> (d) the receipt of oral and written submissions.[4]

Additionally, s. 20(3) provides that "a study commission must not exercise the power of a hearing commission."

Accordingly, in order to carry out my objectives as stated above, I decided, and my counsel arranged for participants to attend the forums. I set out the rules ahead of time and they were simply that only my counsel could lead the witnesses, while the others simply be present and listen. There would be no questions from anyone

3 *Public Inquiry Act*, SBC 2007, c 9 [*Public Inquiry Act*].

4 *Ibid*, s 20(2).

except my counsel. At the end of the witness giving his or her testimony, which I took under Oath, there would be a five-minute adjournment. This would enable that any questions people present may have had could be given to my counsel, who in their sole discretion based on public concern, could put further questions.

To address fairness I did not believe that there was a need to allow cross examination. The exercise was a study session on the future of the use of the CEW. If a witness gave evidence that did not please a particular group or individual, including counsel, then of course they were invited to present their own brief or evidence. The few questions that were allowed as described above were really to clarify issues, not to challenge.

As one can see, this study commission was not an adversarial process.

Fairness was accomplished by the ability of interested parties to suggest witnesses to be called. We also invited "studies" to be presented. In my report, I stated that "I found every presentation to be well prepared, thoughtful, and respectful ... I learned a great deal and gained an appreciation of the complexity of the important issues."[5]

The medical reports and the evidence from various medical specialists that were called was quite conflicting, ranging from the fact that the CEW could not possibly have any effect on a person's health as opposed to its immediate effect, to the likelihood that in certain circumstances, the discharge of a CEW could result in death.[6] The policing authorities and manufacturers of CEWs frequently observe that autopsies find no physical evidence suggesting that the weapon's electrical current triggered a heart attack or other cardiac or respiratory malfunction causing or contributing to the death. Rather, it is suggested that death is attributable not to the deployment of a CEW, but to the so called "excited delirium."

---

5 Braidwood Commission on the Death of Robert Dziekanski, W*hy? The Robert Dziekanski Tragedy* (May 2010) at 36, online: http://www.braidwoodinquiry.ca/report/P2_pdf/00-TitlePage.pdf [Why? The Robert Dziekanski Tragedy].

6 I will not list everyone who was called, but those that had a commercial interest would of course include Mr. Thomas Smith, Chairman of the Board of TASER International, Inc. Four doctors were called with specialities in electrical and biometrical engineering. Doctors with specialties in emergency medicine were called; namely four in all. Four specialists in cardiology were called; one epidemiologist; one pathologist; a psychologist; three psychiatrists; and three persons in the area of mental health, including the executive director of the Canadian Mental Health Association.

Under the heading of law enforcement, I heard ten various witnesses. I heard a Staff Superintendent from the Toronto Police Department, and from the Vancouver Police Department I heard from six officers; two more from the Victoria Police Department, and also officers from the Corrections and Sheriffs branches, policing policy witnesses, and civilian oversight, including Mr. Dirk Ryneveld, QC, the Police Complaint Commissioner from Victoria, BC.

Mr. Ujjal Dosanjh, PC, QC, Member of Parliament, gave evidence. He was the former Attorney General and Premier of British Columbia. He allowed the use of CEWs within the province.

However, I was able to find that in those circumstances there was nearly always the use of cocaine or heroin, or some other illegal drugs, usually coupled with alcohol, and often with a psychosis. As a result, I was able to conclude that in certain extreme circumstances the use of the CEW can result in death.

With reference to the syndrome called "excited delirium" the underlying causes are not particularly well known but as mentioned above the individual is nearly always under the influence of cocaine or heroin or often coupled with alcohol and often with an underlying psychosis. When he or she is in this state, to put it in simple terms, his or her adrenalin reaches a very high state and that means that on rare occasions if he or she is shocked with a CEW, this shot continues to even further heighten the degree of his or her underlying adrenaline level which can result in death. The evidence also led me to believe that when the prongs that are shot from the CEW weapon penetrate the skin near the heart, then what is called a capturing of the heart can occur. This means that there is an electronic capture that can result in an interference with the functioning of the heart and cause death.

Some of the evidence was duplicated in the second hearing when the actual cause of death of Mr. Dziekanski was explored and in the circumstances of Mr. Dziekanski which will be explained in more detail later, he was in a high state of frustration so he was not in a state called excited delirium for there was no alcohol or cocaine or underlying psychosis, but his adrenaline level was exceptionally high by reason of a prolonged state of frustration and the multi-tasering of him resulted in a very high level of adrenaline rush which eventually caused his death.

As a result of this process, I was able to make a number of recommendations to the Provincial Government, which included a threshold test of when the CEWs should be used, discussions of the use on emotionally disturbed people, the effect of multiple deployments, the necessity of prior medical assistance, use of automated external defibrillators, various provincial regulations, training and re-training, and so forth.

I am happy to express that my Report[7] was met with great favor and the threshold for the use of the CEW was adopted in the manner I set forth.

The contract between the Province of British Columbia and the Royal Canadian Mounted Police came up for renewal in 2012 and I have been informed that, in the course of negotiations with reference to that contract, both sides have accepted the standard I had set forth with reference to when it was appropriate to discharge a CEW.

The study commission is to be contrasted with the second inquiry, which was a hearing commission discussed below.

---

7 Braidwood Commission on Conducted Energy Weapon Use, *Restoring Public Confidence: Restricting the Use of Conducted Energy Weapons in British Columbia* (June 2009), online: http://www.braidwoodinquiry.ca/report/P1Report.php.

Litigation in Relation to the Study Commission Report

TASER International, Inc., manufacturer of CEWs, was less than pleased with the result of my Study Commission report and brought a petition to the Supreme Court of British Columbia that the Honourable Mr. Justice Sewell quash all of my findings and recommendations as they related to the use of the CEW.

TASER argued that my report should be subject to judicial review, because it fundamentally affected their interests.[8] They also submitted that they had a legitimate expectation of fairness based on statements made by myself and Commission counsel about the Study Commission's process.[9] This duty of fairness was allegedly unfulfilled since they did not receive prior notice of the Study Commission report, and were not given an opportunity to respond.[10]

The judge, in my opinion, correctly noted that what I was giving was an opinion to the government, and not a decision. Therefore, it did not fall under section 2 of the *Judicial Review Procedure Act* (JRPA).[11] The relevant sections are as follows:

> Application for judicial review
> 2 (1) An application for judicial review is an originating application and must be brought by way of a petition proceeding.
> (2) On an application for judicial review, the court may grant any relief that the applicant would be entitled to in any one or more of the proceedings for:
> (a) relief in the nature of mandamus, prohibition or certiorari;
> (b) a declaration or injunction, or both, in relation to the exercise, refusal to exercise, or proposed or purported exercise, of a statutory power.
> [13] "Statutory power of decision" and "statutory power" are defined in s. 1 of the JRPA as follows:
> "statutory power of decision" means a power or right conferred by an enactment to make a decision deciding or prescribing
> (a) the legal rights, powers, privileges, immunities, duties or liabilities of a person, or
> (b) the eligibility of a person to receive, or to continue to receive, a benefit or licence, whether or not the person is legally entitled to it,
> and includes the powers of the Provincial Court;
> "statutory power" means a power or right conferred by an enactment
> (a) to make a regulation, rule, bylaw or order,
> (b) to exercise a statutory power of decision,
> (c) to require a person to do or to refrain from doing an act or thing that, but for that requirement, the person would not be required by law to do or to refrain from doing,

8 *Taser International Inc v British Columbia,* 2010 BCSC 1120 at para 20 [*Taser*].
9 *Ibid* at para 45.
10 *Ibid* at para 49.
11 RSBC 1996, c 241 [*JRPA*].

> (d) to do an act or thing that would, but for that power or right, be a breach of a legal right of any person, or
>
> (e) to make an investigation or inquiry into a person's legal right, power, privilege, immunity, duty or liability.[12]

Justice Sewell found that s. 2(2)(b) of the JRPA was not applicable to the Study Commission Report as none of the Commission's terms of reference constituted the exercise of a statutory power of decision.[13]

The learned Judge, however, went on to consider whether or not there is jurisdiction pursuant to the prerogative writ of certiorari and found that in cases with certain special circumstances, such jurisdiction does exist. Justice Sewell concluded that in the special circumstances of this case, the Study Commission owed a duty of fairness to the petitioner.[14]

In considering the nature and extent of that duty, his Lordship referred to the non-exhaustive factors set out in *Baker*:[15] the nature of the decision being made; the nature of the statutory scheme; the importance of the decision to the individual affected; the legitimate expectations of the persons challenging the decision; and the choices of procedure made by the agency itself. The main issue was whether the procedures followed the duty of fairness in terms of the petitioner presenting his or her case fully, and in terms of the decisions being made using a fair, impartial and open process.[16]

His Lordship then went on to discuss the nature of the proceedings under review, and found that due to the advisory nature of the decision and the Study Commission's mandate to review research material, it seemed inappropriate to burden the Study Commission with an obligation to act in a judicial or quasi-judicial manner.[17]

He further found that the *Public Inquiry Act* placed significant limits on the proceedings of the Study Commission, consistent with the legislative intent that Study Commissions should not be expected to act with a high degree of formal procedural fairness.[18]

His Lordship then considered the distinction between the importance of the decision to the petitioner's commercial interests and the importance of the decision to its reputation and status. His Lordship concluded that there was nothing in the Study Commission report which a fair-minded person would construe as an attack or criticism of the petitioner's reputation as a corporate citizen, or its right to carry on business and market its products. He mentioned that the Commissioner did

---

12 *JRPA*, *supra* note 11, s 2.

13 *Taser*, *supra* note 8 at paras 28–29.

14 *Ibid* at paras 32 and 34.

15 *Baker v Canada (Minister of Citizenship and Immigration)*, [1999] 2 SCR 817.

16 *Taser*, *supra* note 8 at paras 36–37.

17 *Ibid* at para 39.

18 *Ibid* at para 40.

recommend the continued use of the conducted energy weapon and commented favorably on the advantages of using such a weapon in certain circumstances. His Lordship then mentioned the great caution that should be exercised by a reviewing Judge in assessing the complaints that were before him. He mentioned that the essential mandate of the Study Commission was to conduct a risk-benefit analysis with respect to a particular product. He wrote that it "is a mandate which inherently invokes an exercise of judgment as opposed to a determination of rights or status."[19]

In conclusion, his Lordship found that the proceedings were fair. He wrote that there was nothing to show that the Commissioner had handled the inquiry in any way that was inconsistent with his express intentions. He found that the Commissioner gave the petitioner ample opportunities to come forward with information and evidence. Justice Sewell concluded that the Study Commission had discharged any duty of fairness owed to the petitioner in terms of how the mandate was carried out, and the decision-making process.[20]

Lastly, Justice Sewell considered whether or not the decision of the Commissioner was patently unreasonable. He considered the submission that the report's conclusion that conducted energy weapons have the capacity to cause death was patently unreasonable and unsupported by any credible evidence. Justice Sewell found no merit in that submission. His Lordship expressed doubt as to whether the court should even embark upon such a review.

Accordingly, the method by which the inquiry was conducted was held to be fair. The concept of fairness depended on the provisions of the statute and also the manner in which the proceedings were conducted. In particular, everybody who had an interest in the matter, especially TASER International, had an opportunity to submit whatever evidence they wished. Many doctors and professionals suggested by them were called forward as witnesses and various studies that they conducted were received by the commission.

The Hearing Commission

I was also appointed after I finished the Study Commission, to commence a Hearing and Study Commission. The hearings were entirely adversarial. Here, it was obvious that the role of various persons as they encountered Mr. Dziekanski at the airport would be under close scrutiny, particularly the four RCMP officers, along with various airport and other staff members.

Before the hearings, I distributed a set of Rules as to the conduct of the hearings. These included the right to apply for status as a Participant. Once status was granted, these participants were allowed to attend, call witnesses, cross-examine, make submissions, and receive any of the necessary documents that would be

19 *Taser*, *supra* note 8 at para 42.

20 *Ibid* at paras 47–48.

available. I had the power to issue summons, which I did, and the hearings were generally conducted as a full trial. There is power in the *Act* to apply to a court if need be. Examples would be the need for a direction for a person to comply with a summons; authorization to inspect a private place, including the copying of records; citing a person for contempt, and so forth.

Under the *Public Inquiry Act*, Lieutenant Governor in Council must define the purposes of the commission. The purposes of the study and hearing commission, established under section 2(2), were set forth as follows:

- to provide Mr. Dziekanski's family and the public with a complete record of the circumstances of and relating to Mr. Dziekanski's death;
- to make recommendations referred to in section 4(2)(c).

Terms of Reference

4 (2) the terms of reference of the inquiries to be conducted by the hearing and study commission established under section 2(2) are as follows:

- to conduct hearings, in or near the City of Vancouver, into the circumstances of and relating to Mr. Dziekanski's death;
- to make a complete report of the events and circumstances of an relating to Mr. Dziekanski's death, not limited to the actual cause of death;
- to make recommendations the commissioner considers necessary and appropriate; and
- to submit a report to the Attorney General on or before a date to be determined by the Attorney General in consultation with the Commissioner.[21]

It should be noted the requirements of the *Public Inquiry Act* state at section 21 that subject to the *Act* and the terms of reference, a hearing commission can do what is necessary to complete its duties, including:

(a) issuing directives respecting any of the matters set out in subsection (2);
(b) holding written, oral and electronic hearings;
(c) receiving submissions and evidence under oath or affirmation;
(d) making a finding of misconduct against a person, or making a report that alleges misconduct by a person.

I granted Participant status for counsel who represented interested persons. They included counsel for the Government of Canada; various RCMP officers, including the four officers who took Mr. Dziekanski down; the mother of the deceased; the Attorney General of British Columbia; the City of Richmond Fire Department; the Government of Poland; TASER International; Vancouver Airport Authority; Public Service Alliance of Canada; the BC Civil Liberties Association; and so forth. These evidentiary hearings were conducted over a period of some 61

21 Purpose and Terms of Reference, *supra* note 1.

days, during which 91 witnesses testified under Oath or affirmation, and I granted official participation status to sixteen individuals and organizations.

Once again, the medical evidence was in conflict. Various cross examiners were able to bring out the weaknesses and strengths of the various witnesses. The issue of excited delirium was in the forefront of TASER International's position, but I was able to conclude that while the use of the CEW in the particular circumstances did not interfere with the functions of the heart of the individual, they did add to his overall stress and significantly contributed to his ultimate demise.

I was able to find as follows: (1) Mr. Dziekanski did not likely have alcohol cardiomyopathy, nor was he experiencing alcohol withdrawal when he arrived in Vancouver; (2) all the stresses and pre-existing medical conditions alone did not lead to a fatal arrhythmia in Mr. Dziekanski (3) descriptions such as "sudden death during restraint" or "excited delirium" are not applicable to Mr Dziekanski's case as he was aware of his surroundings, followed directions, was not intoxicated, and did not have a history of serious mental illness.[22]

The evidence did not let me decide precisely how much the weapon and physical altercation with the RCMP contributed to the hyperadrenergic state that led to Mr Dziekanski's death, but I was able to reasonably infer from the evidence that the multiple deployment of CEW played a more substantial role.[23] In conclusion, I was able to determine – I hope with a great degree of exactitude – the events that occurred at the airport, and was also able to make recommendations as to appropriate civil oversight of police activities.

Litigation in Relation to the Notices of Misconduct

As noted prior, a hearing commission can make a finding of misconduct against a person, or make a report that alleges misconduct by a person.[24]

Section 11 establishes procedural safeguards, before a finding of misconduct can be made:

> (2) If a hearing commission intends to make a finding of misconduct against a person, or intends to make a report that alleges misconduct by a person, the hearing commission must first provide the person with
> (a) Reasonable notice of the allegations against that person, and
> (b) Notice of how that person may respond to the allegations.[25]

Near the conclusion of the evidentiary hearings, Commission Counsel delivered several Confidential Notices, which advised recipients that "the Commissioner may make the following findings that may amount to misconduct", and then

22 Why? The Robert Dziekanski Tragedy, *supra* note 5 at 327–8.
23 *Ibid.*
24 *Public Inquiry Act*, *supra* note 3, s 21(2).
25 *Ibid*, s 11.

itemized those possible findings. Counsel for the recipients of those Notices had the opportunity to address the allegations during their closing written and/or oral submissions.

On May 12, 2009, counsel for the four RCMP officers who had dealt with Mr. Dziekanski at the Airport applied to me confidentially, under our Practice and Procedure Directive for Evidentiary Hearings, for an Order that the Notices did not sufficiently particularize the misconduct alleged against them. In a confidential written Ruling dated May 22, 2009, I ordered further particulars in relation to one paragraph of the Notices, but otherwise dismissed the applications. Commission Counsel subsequently delivered revised Notices of Misconduct.

On June 2, 2009, counsel for the same four officers applied to me confidentially for an Order that the Notices of Misconduct be quashed as being beyond the authority of a provincial inquiry and outside the Terms of Reference of this particular Commission. On June 9, 2009, I issued a confidential Ruling dismissing these jurisdictional arguments.

The four officers applied to the BC Supreme Court for judicial review of both these Rulings and, in the course of doing so, disclosed the identity of their clients and the allegations of misconduct made against them. On June 15, 2009, Mr. Justice Silverman issued oral Reasons for Judgment dismissing the officers' claims.

Three of the four officers appealed that decision to the BC Court of Appeal. On December 29, 2009, the Court issued written Reasons for Judgment unanimously dismissing the appeal.

Reasons were written by the Honourable Madam Justice Saunders and agreed to by the Honourable Mr. Justices Chiasson and Groberman. In the Reasons, the Court described notices of misconduct in paragraph 7 as follows:

> The Notices of Misconduct as amended contain four allegations common to all appellants …:
> 1. failing to properly assess and respond to the circumstances faced in relation to Mr. Dziekanski;
> 2. deploying the taser in circumstances that did not justify such deployment;
> 3. after deploying it, failing to adequately reassess the situation before further deploying it;
> 4. making further deployments of the instrument when they were not justified in the circumstances;
> 5. misrepresenting facts in notes and statements which had been made;
> 6. misrepresenting facts in evidence given before the Commission;
> 7. providing misleading information of the witness' notes and statements in the evidence before the Commission.[26]

The appellants raised essentially three points:

26 *Bentley v Braidwood*, 2009 BCCA 604 at paras 7–8 [*Bentley*].

1. the notices of misconduct reflect an exercise in criminal law beyond the jurisdiction of a provincially appointed commission;
2. the notices reflect an exercise of jurisdiction that interferes with the management or administration of a federally created agency, namely the Royal Canadian Mounted Police; and
3. the particulars were not sufficient.

Her Lordship said that the standard of review was correctness.

Madam Justice Saunders found that a description of the possible findings in common, non-technical language as done in the Notices of Misconduct did not make the public inquiry a criminal investigation.[27] She rejected the appellant's argument that the findings of the Commissioner in the terms set out in the allegations would be tantamount to findings of criminal conduct.[28]

With reference to the second argument, namely infringing federal powers over the Royal Canadian Mounted Police, the Court noted that policing in general is a matter of provincial jurisdiction by 92 (14) of the *Constitution Act, 1867*. However, to the extent that the provincial function of policing is performed by the federally established RCMP, the province is "limited from interfering in or direct[ing] its management or administration."[29]

After reviewing many cases, Madam Justice Saunders agreed with Justice Silverman that the allegations of misconduct did not intrude on the federal jurisdiction of the RCMP's management and supervision.[30] She stated that it was important to consider that the administration of justice allows a commission to reflect on matters that relate to the public confidence in the administration of justice, such as the response of police officers to Mr. Dziekanski's situation.[31] She thus did not see a reason related to the federal nature of the RCMP to interfere with Justice Silverman's order.[32]

The Court also dismissed the issue of particulars. Particulars go to the issue of procedural fairness and an appropriate notice. The Court also commented that since the appellants had testified at length, they would not be unclear as to the parts of their evidence that might be relevant to the issues identified in the Notices of Misconduct.[33]

As I mentioned above, the procedure that I followed was very close to that of a trial. My counsel kept all participants fully informed of all relevant matters, including the disclosure of documents, and would call witnesses, lead them in chief, and the witness would then be open to cross-examination by any one of the

---

27 *Bentley, supra* note 26 at para 38.
28 *Ibid* at para 39.
29 *Ibid* at para 45.
30 *Ibid* at para 50.
31 *Ibid* at para 51.
32 *Ibid* at paras 49–52.
33 *Ibid* at para 73.

various lawyers who were granted Participant status. Also, counsel was able to suggest witnesses to be called, and could call witnesses on their own behalf. The four policemen were called by their various counsel and led in chief, then cross-examined by Commission Counsel.

In my report under the headings "Findings of Misconduct" I emphasized that the Supreme Court had ruled that a commission of inquiry could make findings of misconduct.[34] Since the Court also acknowledged that findings of misconduct could damage someone's reputation, these findings should only be made when they are required to fulfill the inquiry's mandate.[35] The commissioner should avoid making findings that would use the same terms as courts finding civil or criminal liability, but the commissioner could not completely avoid language that could be read as a legal finding.[36]

34 Why? The Robert Dziekanski Tragedy, *supra* note 5 at 37.

35 *Ibid.*

36 *Ibid* at 38.

PART 4
Truth Commissions and Public Inquiries II – Observers’ Reflections

Chapter 12
Public Inquiries: Independence is the Key

Gus Van Harten*

Introduction

The accountability of a public inquiry depends on its independence and, ultimately, on the independence of its commissioner. Among all statutory decision-makers, a public inquiry calls for the most rigorous protection of its institutional independence because the inquiry must review official conduct at any place or level of decision-making, including at the highest levels of government; it must investigate thoroughly and fairly matters of grave concern and potential embarrassment to the powerful; and it must report fully on what is uncovered. If Cabinet is a buckle between the legislature and the administration,[1] then an inquiry, in rare cases of profound scandal or tragedy, offers suspenders to hold up government in the eyes of the public.[2]

An inquiry may be divided in three periods. The first period, which begins with the announcement of the inquiry, usually occurs in a context of great controversy about apparent failures of government. This is a time at which the delays following the announcement of the inquiry may help the government to avoid a public reckoning in the short term.[3] The second period, after the inquiry's hearings are underway, often heightens attention and generates revelations about matters that many governments would prefer to keep under wraps. Over time, however, many inquiries then reach a third period in which public attention has waned prior to the completion of the inquiry's investigation. It is at this time that a government, having reaped the political benefit of the inquiry in earlier periods, may be tempted to take steps to reduce the political cost.

By understanding an inquiry as an unfolding process of investigation, it is possible to identify possible threats to independence over the months of document

* gvanharten@osgoodeyorku.ca; former assistant to the commissioner of the Walkerton Inquiry and the Arar Inquiry in Canada. The views and opinions expressed in this chapter are those of the author alone.

1 Walter Bagehot, *The English Constitution* (1867), no. II (The Cabinet).

2 *Phillips v Nova Scotia (Commission of Inquiry into the Westray Mine Tragedy)*, [1995] 2 SCR 97 at 138; Rt Hon Sir Cyril Salmon, *Tribunals of Inquiry* (London: Oxford University Press, 1967) at 5.

3 Robert Centa & Patrick Macklem, "Securing Accountability Through Commissions of Inquiry: A Role for the Law Commission of Canada" (2001) 39 Osgoode Hall LJ 117.

review, interviews, hearings, deliberations, drafting, and reporting. In this chapter, a series of potential threats are examined in order to highlight institutional aspects of inquiries that counteract these threats and support public confidence in the inquiry. In particular, the discussion focuses on the stages of an inquiry where:

- the commissioner is appointed;
- the commissioner appoints counsel, staff, or expert advisors;
- the commissioner and commission counsel design the investigation according to the inquiry's mandate;
- the commissioner and commission counsel review documents, conduct interviews, and decide what to put in evidence in public hearings;
- the commissioner decides what conclusions to draw from the evidence;
- the commissioner's report of findings and conclusions is submitted and released; and
- the inquiry is concluded.

The discussion is supplemented by examples from past inquiries, drawn mainly from Canada, the United Kingdom, and the United States, in which concerns about independence arose. However, no suggestion is intended that any particular inquiry or investigation lacked impartiality or fairness. In addition, the discussion turns to some examples of past and current dangers – in the form of statutory reform, especially in the United Kingdom[4] – to the independence of inquiries.

As an aside, proposals to reform the statutory framework for inquiries are often justified in the name of accountability, presumably meaning something beyond an inquiry's accountability to the public for its truth-seeking mission. In light of this, the discussion in this chapter turns occasionally to the question of accountability. That said, accountability is a far-reaching notion that begs further questions: to whom, for what, and with what implications? These are not examined in any depth in this chapter. The key point elaborated here is that, in a public inquiry, accountability depends entirely on independence. There is no such thing as accountability to the truth-seeking mission of a thorough, open, and fair investigation if a public inquiry is not protected institutionally from the suspicion of inappropriate interference in its decision-making process. For this reason, concerns about, for example, the speed or cost of an inquiry – clearly important issues in any inquiry – become most pressing when they affect public confidence in the inquiry and, by extension, its ability to remain independent.

4 *Inquiries Act 2005* (UK), c 12, s 19 [*Inquiries Act*]. Marny Requa, "Truth, Transition, and the Inquiries Act 2005" (2007) European Human Rights LR 404.

Appointment of the Commissioner

An inquiry investigates matters that are embarrassing to persons or organizations of power. For the inquiry to be independent, its commissioner must above all be independent of powerful actors. This requires that the commissioner be free of pre-set notions or inappropriate influences on what she or he is prepared to investigate and conclude within the inquiry's mandate. Independence must exist in the mind of the commissioner but must also be apparent to the reasonable and concerned member of the public. In all respects, the perceived independence of an inquiry is traceable to the perceived independence of its commissioner.

Thus, a critical stage for the independence of an inquiry is the appointment (usually, in Canada, by Cabinet) of the commissioner. To appoint a commissioner who is or who appears predisposed toward the government's position would undermine the promise of independent truth-seeking. On the other hand, the issue of appointment bedevils any decision-making process for the reason that no decision-maker who relies on another for her or his office can be fully and originally independent. In the context of public inquiries, this conundrum is resolved often by the appointment as commissioner of someone who was appointed previously to an independent office: a judge.[5] Thus, the commissioner (who is an administrative officer) carries the institutional safeguards of independence of the judge, presumably supported by a record of respected decision-making as a judge.[6] Or, where the commissioner is a retired judge, she or he is protected by a secure pension and by the apparent liberation, via the passage of time, from a need to win clients or contracts in the marketplace or to pursue advancement in a government or corporate bureaucracy.

Yet there may be criticisms of this approach to appointment. For example, a judge may be said to lack expertise in the subject matter of the inquiry. Underlying this criticism is an assumption that expertise is as or more important than independence in an inquiry. This assumption is misplaced because, while it is possible for one who is independent (and adequately funded) to call on the expertise of others, it is not possible for one who is dependent on others to avoid that dependency by invoking her or his expertise. Likewise, the more an area of expertise is relevant to an inquiry, the more it will enmesh the expert – based on a career of specialized research, training, and professional activity – to interests affected by the inquiry. Thus, for the rare but vital role of a public inquiry, the commissioner's independence must trump any case for substantive expertise. For this reason, generalist judges are often well-suited to the role of commissioner.

Another concern about the reliance on judges to run public inquiries is external to the independence of the inquiry itself. It is the concern that the controversy

5 Ed Ratushny, *The Conduct of Public Inquiries* (Toronto: Irwin Law, 2009) at 144–5 [Ratushny].

6 Jack Beatson, "Should Judges Conduct Public Inquiries" (2005) 121 LQR 221 at 234–5.

swirling around a public inquiry may follow the commissioner to the bench after the inquiry is finished. In time, this could erode public belief in the political detachment of the judiciary. Beatson cites Lord Simon of Glaisdale for the observation that: "every time that a judge is called to conduct [a difficult and controversial] inquiry, he is embroiled in a controversial issue and his detachment may be compromised. Indeed the reputation of the judiciary as a whole may be compromised."[7]

This concern about political blowback to the bench is important; a government should not attend to discrete crises, however urgent, in a way that saps public faith in the judiciary. Where inquiries are used with caution, though, there is probably room to expend some of that capital to address a crisis of public confidence in government that cries out for independent investigation. The question of when to make that investment might not best be left entirely to Cabinet, as at present, but this is not the critical issue for the present discussion. Also, the problem of blowback goes beyond the independence of any single inquiry; suffice it to say that it emphasizes the need for inquiries to be used sparingly and for judges, when acting as commissioners, to maximize their insulation from the heat of the moment in order to minimize the wider risk to the judiciary.

Other aspects of the appointments process go directly to the independence of the inquiry itself. Above all, one may ask, which judge has a government appointed? Any observer will know that a government may be tempted to find a judge who is predisposed to its perspective. An acute concern arises where there is something in the judge's background that gives reasonable cause for concern about possible bias in light of the subject of the inquiry.[8] However widely respected the individual, it would not be appropriate to appoint a judge whose main client base in private practice was the food industry in order to inquire into a tainted meat scandal. Awkward facts about a judge's background are bound to surface, whether at the time of appointment or at a later stage, and to be used to connect the commissioner to an interest affected by the inquiry. In turn, this could reasonably undermine confidence in the inquiry.

Those who decide who to appoint as commissioner must therefore examine the implications for perceived independence. Beyond this check, however, are there other ways to constrain Cabinet's power to appoint? The options are limited because of the root problem: whoever else in the administration might make the decision will also be open to a concern about possible influence by powerful interests in government. One might alternatively envision other judges certifying the decision to appoint, but only so long as this did not transfer to the judiciary a role to supervise the administration generally. Perhaps best is a practice by which Cabinet, when dealing with a matter of grave scandal, is expected to go first to the highest court in the jurisdiction and seek the consent of its chief judge before

7 Beatson, *supra* note 6 at 234–5, citing Lord Simon of Glaisdale, [572] HL Deb Col 1282 (5 June 1996).

8 Ratushny, *supra* note 5 at 145–6.

appointing a judge from that court.[9] Also, perhaps a summary of this process could be reported publicly when news of the appointment is announced. Even then, this check would serve primarily as a way to channel and inform public concern on the inquiry's independence. As with other institutional safeguards that protect inquiries, the aim is to make it possible for the public to identify possible threats to independence and, in turn, to enable a judge better to resist any threat.

Appointment of Commission Counsel and Staff

Commission counsel is the alter ego of the commissioner and subject always to the commissioner's direction.[10] However, commission counsel makes all sorts of decisions in the course of an inquiry's investigation that affect its thoroughness, fairness, and independence.[11] So it is important that the selection and ongoing employment of commission counsel rests with the commissioner. Likewise, other staff – financial officers, press relations staff, expert advisors – must be subject to the ultimate authority of the commissioner. Only under these conditions can an inquiry draw on staff who represent a range of backgrounds, perspectives, expertise, and interests without compromising its perceived independence. Thus, when the U.S. 9/11 Commission was criticized for the close association between its executive director and the Bush White House,[12] the only clear response is to resort to the responsibility and authority of the commissioner (in this case the congressional members of the commission). Similarly, criticisms of the Sponsorship Inquiry[13] in Canada that the commission's chief counsel was a former chief of staff to the former Prime Minister (of a competing political party to that under investigation) is answerable only by the perceived independence of the commissioner.[14]

It may seem straightforward that these staffing issues would be in the hands of the commissioner. Yet it is not an idle concern that a government, whether at the outset or in the course of an inquiry, would try to influence the commissioner's choice of counsel, staff, or experts. Government officials will be aware of the role

---

9 *Inquiries Act*, *supra* note 4, s 10(1). Canadian Judicial Council (CJC), *Position on the Appointment of Federally Appointed Judges to Commissions of Inquiry* (March 1998).

10 John Sopinka, "The Role of Commission Counsel" in Allan Manson & David Mullan, eds, *Commissions of Inquiry: Praise or Reappraise?* (Toronto: Irwin Law, 2003) 75 at 77–8 [Sopinka].

11 Ratushny, *supra* note 5 at 176–7, 195, 219–20, 240–3, and 248.

12 David Ray Griffin, *The 9/11 Commission Report – Omissions and Distortions* (Olive Branch Press, 2005) at 7–14.

13 Commission of Inquiry into the Sponsorship Program and Advertising Activities, *Who is Responsible? Fact-Finding Report* (2005–06), online: http://epe.lac-bac.gc.ca/100/206/301/pco-bcp/commissions/sponsorship-ef/06-03-06/www.gomery.ca/en/phase1report/index.asp.

14 Online: http://en.wikipedia.org/wiki/Gomery_Commission (last accessed 1 May 2011).

that those actors play in ensuring that a range of perspectives are taken seriously at the inquiry. It is vital, then, that a government not succeed in any efforts to pressure the commissioner on such matters. For the public, there are few ways to protect against this possibility – barring the unlikely prospect of whistle-blowing by the person who is refused or removed from a senior position – than to depend on the integrity and fortitude of the commissioner. In this respect, the perceived independence of staff is an extension of the commissioner's perceived independence.

Design of the Investigation

Subject to judicial review, it is up to the commissioner, as advised by commissioner counsel, to determine the scope of her or his mandate. Although the commissioner's understanding of the mandate may evolve, the determination of this issue can be formative in early stages because it sets in motion the investigation. That is, it guides the requests for document production, the selection of persons to interview, the questions pursued, and the issues addressed. The interpretation of the mandate is also largely a process that takes place internal to the inquiry. Although it is possible to adjust the orientation of an investigation once it is in motion, this becomes more difficult as the inquiry proceeds.

The shaping of the mandate is critical, less for what is deemed to fall within the mandate and more for what is excluded. At the U.K. Hutton inquiry, which was tasked to investigate the death of a government scientist who acted as a confidential source for a BBC journalist's reporting on the government's case for invading Iraq, the commissioner was criticized for his interpretation of his mandate.[15] The inquiry's terms of reference required the commissioner "urgently to conduct an investigation into the circumstances surrounding the death of Dr Kelly", which the commissioner characterized as a mandate to consider the circumstances "preceding and leading up to" the death of Dr. Kelly.[16] However, the commissioner rejected the argument that his mandate allowed him to consider the controversy about whether the government's intelligence on weapons of mass destruction was sufficiently reliable to justify the invasion, even though this was clearly a major factor in Dr. Kelly's engagement with the BBC journalist. The commissioner reached this conclusion based mainly on the amount of evidence that the issue would involve.[17]

---

15 For example, Conor Gearty, "A Misreading of the Law", *London Review of Books* (19 February 2004) 3.

16 UK, *Report of the Inquiry into the Circumstances Surrounding the Death of Dr. David Kelly C.M.G.* by Lord Hutton (UK: House of Commons Library, 2004) at para 9 [Hutton Inquiry].

17 *Ibid.*

A related question on the interpretation of the mandate is the issue of when that interpretation is conveyed to the parties and the public. Where a decision to narrow the mandate is made in the late stages of an inquiry, then it reinforces the degree to which the internal decision-making of an inquiry shapes the process in ways that are difficult to reverse. On the other hand, a commissioner must be able to focus the mandate in order to balance the principles of thoroughness and expeditiousness. Although speed and efficiency are only a means to the ultimate end of truth-seeking, they are important because they can affect public confidence in the inquiry and, in turn, undermine the commissioner's ability to resist inappropriate pressure. Also, there are diminishing returns in the pursuit of final answers to every aspect of the mandate. Thus, a degree of compromise on the mandate is in many respects unavoidable[18] so long as the inquiry remains relentless in investigating the role of key actors in the relevant events. In these respects, the independence of an inquiry is not compromised so long as the commissioner is not predisposed or influenced inappropriately in the balancing of thoroughness and expeditiousness. Where an inquiry is criticized for sidestepping an important question or for taking too long, the key concern is whether the commissioner can be trusted to form an independent view about the appropriate balance.

In some cases, governments will attach time limits to an inquiry by setting, for example, a date for delivery of the inquiry's report. A requirement for time limits may be found in the statute under which a public inquiry is called or alternatively in its terms of reference. This may have the benefit of creating a general expectation about the timeline and of focusing the minds of those involved on the end point.[19] Even so, ironically it is also critical to allow for the extension of time limits. In particular, a time limit may be seen to affect the independent judgment of the commissioner about how to balance thoroughness and expeditiousness, especially if it frustrates the investigation of matters that, in the commissioner's judgment, need to be investigated.

To elaborate, in mature stages of an inquiry (say, after one to two years) time limits make it more difficult to extend the investigation (or to obtain Cabinet approval for an extension) into questions that come to light only in the course of the unfolding investigation. For example, document production by the government in matters of institutional decision-making may be approaching completion only at this mature stage. Further, a key lever for an inquiry in the face of apparent delays or inadequacy of document production is to communicate that its hearings will be renewed or that a supplementary report will be issued, however late in the process, if further information of importance comes to light. One example, outlined in the Walkerton Inquiry report, illustrates the point.[20] After reviewing

18 Ratushny, *supra* note 5 at 185 and 202–3.

19 Simon Ruel, *The Law of Public Inquiries in Canada* (Toronto: Carswell, 2010) at 17 [Ruel].

20 *Report of the Walkerton Inquiry – the Events of May 2000 and Related Issues*, Part I (Queen's Printer for Ontario, 2002) at 488–9.

documents produced by central agencies of the government, the commission found that few documents had been produced by the Premier's Office and that no documents had been produced from files of the Premier's chief of staff. In light of this, the commission made further requests for documents from the Premier's Office. Government counsel responded that documents relevant to the Inquiry might have been deleted by the Premier's chief of staff in the normal course. On the advice of RCMP personnel, the commission then requested that the government take a mirror image of various computers to obtain any relevant deleted files that were stored on the hard drives. The analysis of documents obtained in this mirror imaging was ongoing at the time of the Inquiry's report. The commissioner stated in his report that, if anything was disclosed by the search that warranted comment by him, he would issue a supplementary report.

In this case, then, the commissioner retained the option to report further where the document review process required additional time.[21] There was no strict deadline for the submission of the final report of the Inquiry other than those set by the commissioner. It was thus possible for the commissioner to issue a supplementary report even after the main activities of the Inquiry had been wound down. On the other hand, the imposition of a strict time limit for an inquiry's final report could provide an opportunity for government officials to use delay as a tactic to avoid scrutiny, with knowledge that it will be difficult to force an in-depth investigation in later stages of the inquiry. This is especially problematic where the matters under review involve high-level decision-makers. In such circumstances, Cabinet may have an interest to refuse to extend a pre-set deadline.

More practically, it is difficult to predict at the outset of an inquiry the complexity of an investigation into government and the challenges of uncovering relevant information. If the purpose of including a deadline in an inquiry's terms of reference is to highlight the trite point that the inquiry should be expeditious, then the costs and risks appear to outweigh the benefit. When time limits are dealt with in legislation on public inquiries, Cabinet should at most have a discretionary power to stipulate and vary a deadline for an inquiry. Even in this respect, rote provision by Cabinet of one- or two- or three-year time limits for inquiries is either of limited value – where it carries the implicit option to allow extensions – or a potential threat to independence. Especially, a requirement to deliver a report by a set deadline may require the commissioner to curtail the thoroughness of the investigation or refuse to submit a report and then resign. After a substantial investment of public funds, the latter option will be unattractive, putting pressure on the commissioner to compromise with Cabinet on the scope of the inquiry. This runs contrary to the promise of an investigation that is independently thorough. It can be avoided by leaving to the commissioner – who was presumably chosen judiciously by the government in part because of an ability to run a major investigation – the announcement of target dates and of periodic updates on the inquiry's progress.

---

21 Ratushny, *supra* note 5 at 244.

Review of Documents, Conduct of Interviews, and Calling of Evidence in Public Hearings

The step-by-step process of investigation is central to an inquiry. The process involves document production and review, interviews with potential witnesses, and the calling of evidence at hearings.[22] It would of course be shocking for an inquiry's independence if any party attempted to pressure an inquiry overtly in these activities. Yet there are more subtle ways to influence or frustrate the investigative process.

Most obviously, a party could withhold information or refuse to make available a witness. Facing such resistance, the commissioner typically has the statutory power to compel document production or witness testimony, backed by the threat of criminal sanction.[23] Yet, in some cases, investigations into matters of grave public concern (including even so-called public inquiries[24]) may take place without coercive powers. In such cases, an outside observer has good reason to ask whether the investigation was thorough and whether it answered the questions that prompted public outrage.

To illustrate, after a tainted meat scandal in Canada caused a major Listeriosis outbreak and the deaths of 22 people, the federal government declined to establish a public inquiry and instead appointed a distinguished health services administrator and chief executive, Sheila Weatherill, to conduct an "independent investigative review" into the affair. The review was not supported by coercive powers, raising the question of whether it got to the bottom of the tragedy. On at least one set of issues – the adequacy of the federal meat inspection program – it apparently did not. Ms. Weatherill reported that she was unable to reach conclusions about the adequacy of a new approach to federal meat inspections (introduced months before the outbreak) because, "[d]ue to the lack of detailed information and differing views heard", her investigation "was not able to determine the current level of resources as well as the resources needed to conduct the CVS [Compliance Verification System] activities effectively."[25]

It is fortunate that this review of the Listeriosis tragedy was at least not presented by the government as a public inquiry. Indeed, it perhaps should not have been described as an independent investigation if there was no assurance that the investigator would be provided the information required, in her judgment,

---

22 Sopinka, *supra* note 10 at 79–81.

23 Ruel, *supra* note 19 at 42–6; Thomas J Lockwood, "A History of Royal Commissions" (1967) 5 Osgoode Hall LJ 172 at 176–7; George W Keeton, *Trial by Tribunal* (London: Museum Press Ltd, 1960) at 12.

24 For example, the Hutton Inquiry, *supra* note 16, was conducted without coercive powers.

25 *Report of the Independent Investigator into the 2008 Listeriosis Outbreak* (20 July 2009), online: http://www.cmc-cvc.com/sites/default/files/files/ListeriaIndependentInvestigatorReport_July212009.pdf.

to answer the questions put to her. For present purposes, the key point is that an investigation that is branded as a public inquiry and that carries the promise of a thorough and independent investigation should have the power to compel document production and witness testimony.[26] Many important investigations occur without such powers and this is appropriate in many circumstances. But it is a deceit on the public to claim that such investigations are independent public inquiries.[27]

Even where a party to an inquiry is subject to coercive powers, the party may refuse to cooperate in document production or the answering of questions. To an extent, a degree of tactical behavior on such matters is inevitable in any lawyered-up process. That is, some parties may succumb at times to temptations to be unable to find documents or to recall conversations. In the face of coercive powers, however, these ways to frustrate an investigation are limited, especially when dealing with questions of government policy that have been discussed and recorded widely in government. In that context, other means may be used to frustrate the investigation, such as delays in the process of document production.

Delay tactics may frustrate independence particularly when one party can influence or control what evidence is heard in the inquiry's hearings. This issue arose in the Arar Inquiry in Canada due to the sensitivities of the national security context of the investigation.[28] Where an investigation is subject to confidentiality requirements, this may create a back-and-forth dynamic between the inquiry and the government over whether and how to admit information in public hearings. An interest of the inquiry will be to maximize openness, albeit with a degree of manageability in the planning of hearings. In the Arar Inquiry, this back-and-forth dynamic was primarily under the control of the commissioner because he was authorized to decide what information should be made public. Secondarily, the commissioner's decisions on the disclosure of information were subject to judicial review under the *Canada Evidence Act*.[29] Thus, it was not up to the Attorney General of Canada (on behalf of the Canadian Security Intelligence Service, the RCMP, or the Canada Border Services Agency, for example) to authorize in

---

26 Gus Van Harten, "Truth Before Punishment: A Defence of Public Inquiries" (2003) 29 Queen's LJ 242 at 252–7 [Van Harten].

27 Recently, the Quebec government announced a public inquiry into allegations of corruption in the construction industry. The inquiry was at first not given powers to compel document production or testimony. However, in response to a request from the commissioner, the government granted these powers to the commission. Rhéal Séguin, "In About-face, Charest Gives Construction Probe Full Powers", *The Globe and Mail* (9 November 2011).

28 *Report of the Events Relating to Maher Arar, Factual Background*, vol I, II, and Analysis and Recommendations, Addendum (Analysis and Recommendations) (released 9 August 2007), online: http://publications.gc.ca/site/eng/298241/publication.html [Arar Inquiry Report].

29 RSC 1985, c C-5, s 38 to 38.15 [*Canada Evidence Act*].

advance the disclosure of any and all information heard in the inquiry's public hearings.

In other contexts, the executive has the direct authority to control public disclosure of information uncovered by an inquiry's investigation. Following reforms to the U.K.'s statutory framework for inquiries in 2005, the government was given the power to restrict public access to the inquiry.[30] According to the *Inquiries Act 2005*, a Minister under whose authority an Inquiry is called may impose restrictions on "attendance at an inquiry, or at any particular part of an inquiry" and on "disclosure or publication of any evidence or documents given, produced or provided to an inquiry."[31] In imposing such restrictions, the Minister has a broad discretion to do whatever she or he "considers to be conducive to the inquiry fulfilling its terms of reference or to be necessary in the public interest" with regard to a broad list of matters.[32] The listed matters include:[33]

- the extent to which any restriction on attendance, disclosure or publication might inhibit the allaying of public concern;
- any risk of harm or damage[34] that could be avoided or reduced by any such restriction;
- any conditions as to confidentiality subject to which a person acquired information that he is to give, or has given, to the inquiry; and
- the extent to which not imposing any particular restriction would be likely to cause delay or to impair the efficiency or effectiveness of the inquiry, or otherwise to result in additional cost (whether to public funds or to witnesses or others).

These provisions give the government a broad power to decide what information can be introduced in an inquiry's public hearings or otherwise released, including in the inquiry's report. The issue of what to disclose to the public is central to any public inquiry and goes to the core of the inquiry's independence for at least two reasons.[35]

First, to have a process in which a government official approves the content of an inquiry's hearings, there must be a process by which the commission notifies the government on what the commission intends to put into evidence and then

30 *Inquiries Act*, *supra* note 4, s 19.

31 *Ibid*, s 19(1).

32 *Ibid*, s 19(3).

33 *Ibid*, s 19(4).

34 The terms "harm or damage" are defined further, in *ibid*, s 19(5), to include death or injury; damage to national security or international relations; damage to the economic interests of the United Kingdom or of any part of the United Kingdom; or damage caused by disclosure of commercially sensitive information.

35 UK, Parliament, Joint Committee on Human Rights, *Fourth Report* (25 November 2004) at para 2.19 [Joint Committee].

allows the government (but not other parties to the inquiry) an opportunity to influence the inquiry on what information should be disclosed and what should be suppressed. Where there was disagreement, the government has the further power to ban disclosure. This presents a major threat to the independence of an inquiry and, by extension, its thoroughness and fairness because it gives the government a running veto over the conduct of the investigation and over public access to the fruits of the truth-seeking process. In effect, it appears to replace a public inquiry with an internal investigation that is co-managed by the commissioner and the government and that may take place in private.

Second, there is good reason to anticipate that a government would use these powers to limit public disclosure of information that is damaging or embarrassing to the government. An indication of how a government could use such powers to stifle an inquiry is provided by the Arar Inquiry. In that case, disagreements arose between the Inquiry and the government over what information – already disclosed by the government to the Inquiry – should be released to the public. These disagreements continued until after the inquiry's report was released, at which point they were referred to the Federal Court of Canada for resolution under the *Canada Evidence Act*.[36] The court authorized release of a series of additional information[37] over which the government had maintained objections to disclosure.[38] One item released in the authorized disclosure was the information that the RCMP (via a task force, Project A-O Canada, that was established in the aftermath of the events of 11 September 2001) supported a search warrant application to a Canadian court by relying on foreign-sourced information that might have been the product of torture. Further, the RCMP did so without drawing the court's attention to that risk and to its implications for the reliability of the information.

It seems reasonable to conclude that one reason for the government's assertion of a national security confidentiality claim over this information was a concern that its release would be embarrassing. The information did not disclose the identity of any informant, country, investigative technique, or ongoing investigation and had been found by the commissioner of the Arar Inquiry to be relevant to the terms of his mandate and to warrant disclosure on the basis that disclosure would not threaten Canada's national security. Importantly, the government was able to avoid scrutiny of this information by various parties to the Inquiry because the confidential claim extended beyond the conclusion of the Inquiry's hearings and beyond the release of its main report.

This example from the Arar Inquiry provides a basis for reflection on the power of a Minister to issue restriction notices under the U.K. *Inquiries Act 2005*. While ministerial restrictions on access may be warranted in many government

36 *Canada Evidence Act*, *supra* note 29.

37 *Canada (Attorney General) v Canada (Commission of Inquiry into the Actions of Canadian Officials in Relation to Maher Arar)*, [2008] 3 FCR 248.

38 Arar Inquiry Report, *supra* note 28 at 99.

investigations, the *Inquiries Act 2005* replaced longstanding legislation in the U.K.[39] that allowed for independent inquiries into matters of a national significance arising from a major scandal or tragedy. As such, the Act must be evaluated according to whether it continues to allow the establishment of an inquiry that carries the utmost assurances of independence and thoroughness. Based on the Arar Inquiry example, it is reasonable to expect that a statutory power to block content of an inquiry's hearings may be used by government to filter the investigation to shield the government from embarrassment. Including this provision in the governing legislation of an inquiry thus undermines on its face the inquiry's truth-seeking mission.

As an aside, objections to the provision for restriction notices in the *Inquiries Act 2005* were expressed before the adoption of the Act. Lord Saville of Newdigate, a former inquiry commissioner, stated that the Act "makes a very serious inroad into the independence of any inquiry; and is likely to damage or destroy public confidence in the inquiry and its findings."[40] Former Supreme Court of Canada Justice Peter Cory, who was in 2002 appointed to investigate several killings in Northern Ireland in which official collusion was alleged, stated that "the proposed new Act would make a meaningful inquiry impossible" and that "the Minister, the actions of whose ministry was to be reviewed by the public inquiry would have the authority to thwart the efforts of the inquiry at every step" and in turn advised Canadian judges "to decline appointment [under the Act] in light of the impossible situation they would be facing."[41] Nonetheless, these objections did not prompt the government to revise the Act's provisions on restriction notices and, as a result, there is now a strong basis in the U.K. to doubt the institution of the public inquiry as classically employed to respond to matters of grave public concern about the role of government.

Drawing of Conclusions from the Evidence

Similar to the discussion above, it is important that a commissioner be able to draw from the evidence heard at an inquiry the findings and conclusions that he or she considers appropriate. In this respect, it is possible – perhaps surprisingly, it does happen – that a government or other party may attempt overtly to pressure

---

39 *Tribunals of Inquiry (Evidence) Act, 1921*, which provided a statutory basis for establishing (on a resolution of both Houses of Parliament) an inquiry into matters of urgent public importance but was repealed by the *Inquiries Act*, *supra* note 4.

40 As reported in Amnesty International, "UK: Amnesty urges judges not to be part of Finucane inquiry" (20 April 2005), online: www.amnesty.org.uk/news_details.asp?NewsID=16053.

41 Ruel, *supra* note 19 at 179. See also Letter from the Honourable Peter Cory to Chairman Chris Smith (15 March 2005), reported online: http://www.patfinucanecentre.org/cory/pr050315.html.

a commissioner in this regard. Where this occurs, an independent commissioner must be relied on to resist strongly such pressure. However, just as concerning is the possibility that the institutional framework of an inquiry could allow the government to influence an inquiry's decision-making (short of terminating the inquiry and assuming the political consequences[42]) by replacing the commissioner or altering the terms of reference. This presents a major threat to independence. While there may be reasons to doubt the performance of some inquiries on criteria such as cost and delay,[43] it should not be the government – a subject of the investigation – that decides how to implement its views about performance by replacing the commissioner or otherwise intervening directly in the investigation.

Facing such encroachments on his or her independence, the ultimate remedy for the commissioner is to resign. However, it may be difficult to take this step, especially in late stages of an inquiry or in the face of certain forms of intervention. Further, the option of resignation may be constrained significantly where the statutory framework for the inquiry provides expressly, from the inquiry's outset, that the government has the relevant powers of intervention. To illustrate, the *Inquiries Act 2005*, s 12,[44] provides clearly that the Minister may at any time terminate the appointment of a member of an inquiry panel on various grounds, including that, in the Minister's view, the member "has failed to comply with any duty imposed on him by this Act."[45] In Ontario, provisions included in the *Public Inquiries Act, 2009* in its original form (although not as enacted)[46] would have given Cabinet the power to revise an inquiry's terms of reference and to terminate the appointment of a commissioner, to appoint a substitute commissioner or to appoint additional commissioners.[47] In both respects, these provisions present concerns for independence because they sanction in the statute itself the possibility of serious encroachments on the inquiry's decision-making and appear to permit the government to control an inquiry without shutting it down outright. The provisions may reflect powers that are otherwise available to the government for an inquiry that it has established. However, their inclusion in the statute gives a powerful justification for their exercise at any time and for any purpose, which is out of place in the modern history of public inquiries.

---

42 Ratushny, *supra* note 5 at 280–1.

43 Michael J Trebilcock & Lisa Austin, "The Limits of the Full Court Press: of Blood and Mergers" (1998) 48 UTLJ 1 at 48; Bryan Schwartz, "Public Inquiries" in Allan Manson & David Mullan, eds, *Commissions of Inquiry: Praise or Reappraise?* (Toronto: Irwin Law, 2003) 443 at 444–50 and 453–6.

44 *Inquiries Act*, *supra* note 4, s 12(3).

45 *Ibid*, s 12(3)(b).

46 Bill 212, *Good Government Act, 2009*, 1st Sess, 39th Parl (Sched 6: *Public Inquiries Act, 2009*), s 3(5). These provisions are not found in the final version of the Bill.

47 *Ibid*, s 3.

Submission and Release of the Report

It was suggested earlier that inquiries are accountable ultimately to the public for their truth-seeking mission. This framing of an inquiry's purpose may appear rhetorical. Formally, in the Canadian context, inquiries are established by Cabinet to deliver a report to Cabinet and so it is Cabinet alone that decides whether and how to publish the inquiry's report.[48] The commissioner lacks the authority to publish the report directly and, where Cabinet does not release it, it is up to the public to hold the government accountable for the apparent suppression of the truth. On the other hand, non-release of a report by the Cabinet may put a commissioner into a dilemma. The furor that led to the inquiry will have subsided and those who were vindicated by, or most interested in, the commissioner's findings and conclusions may lack the political power to ensure public release. In these circumstances, the commissioner may be inclined to release the report to the public in the face of a deliberate cover-up by the government of embarrassing information. It may be that a commissioner sees it as part of his or her independence, and commitments at the time of appointment, to release the report once the government has had a reasonable time to review it. While such a decision would not be straightforward or without controversy, it seems that it should remain an option for the commissioner to consider in some cases.[49]

Yet, even if a commissioner did not release a report directly to the public after a government refused to do so, in principle there remains an accountability relationship between the inquiry and the public. The relationship is not altered by the formal dynamic of reporting by the inquiry to the government because, by the submission of the report, the commissioner will have completed the investigation and recorded her findings and conclusions. Once the report is delivered to the government and the public is informed of this fact by the commissioner, the commissioner has presumably satisfied the truth-seeking role and accounted publicly. To maintain this line of accountability, however, the commissioner must retain the ability to determine exactly what to include in the report for public release. Otherwise, the report, although under the signature of the commissioner, becomes a report from the government to the public.

For this reason, it is quite remarkable that statutory reforms have given, or proposed to give, government a power to affect the very content of inquiry reports. In the U.K. *Inquiries Act 2005*, s 25,[50] the responsible Minister is authorized to withhold portions of an inquiry's report from publication "to such extent ... as [the Minister] considers to be necessary in the public interest."[51] Thus, the Minister

48 Ratushny, *supra* note 5 at 400.

49 *Ibid* at 402–4.

50 *Inquiries Act*, *supra* note 4, s 25.

51 *Ibid*, s 25(4)(b).

has broad discretion to determine content, limited only by a requirement to have regard to various matters, including:[52]

- the extent to which withholding material might inhibit the allaying of public concern;
- any risk of harm or damage[53] that could be avoided or reduced by withholding any material;
- any conditions as to confidentiality subject to which a person acquired information that he has given to the inquiry.

Based on these provisions, a Minister can override a commissioner's judgment about whether it is necessary to include findings or conclusions in the report in order to allay public concern. By overriding the commissioner's authority to decide independently what to publish, these provisions encroach very seriously on the principle of an inquiry's accountability to the public for truth-seeking.[54]

A similar encroachment on the investigative function of inquiries was proposed in Ontario's *Public Inquiries Act, 2009*, which in its original form (although not as enacted) would have given a Minister the authority to "publish any unfinished work of a commission if the commission does not for any reason deliver its report, and that work shall be considered to be the official report of the commission for all purposes."[55] This authority could be exercised by the Minister where a commission was shut down by the government or where the commissioner resigned, for example. In any case, it is difficult to see how this provision could be implemented without encroaching on independence. All reports go through various drafts and the process is never complete until deemed so by the commissioner. The drafting process involves editorial choices that may change significantly the meaning of findings and conclusions going to the core of the commissioner's mandate. Giving a Minister the authority to decide whether and to what extent unfinished work should be published as an official report of the commission substitutes the government for the commissioner as author of the report.

Conclusion of the Inquiry

Once an inquiry is concluded and its report released, one may think that its independence has been secured. This may be true in the great majority of cases. The report will be a matter of public record, the hearings recorded for posterity, and the findings and recommendations passed into the public forum. The outcome of the inquiry will have become a historical fact.

52 *Inquiries Act*, *supra* note 4, s 25(4)–(5).

53 The terms "harm or damage" are defined further in the Act; see *supra* note 34.

54 Joint Committee, *supra* note 35 at para 2.20.

55 *Inquiries Act*, *supra* note 4, s 20(4).

Yet there remain potential threats to independence even after the inquiry has concluded. One involves subsequent activities of those who worked on the inquiry as counsel, staff, or experts. For those who appear to have played an important role, especially in the inquiry's factual investigation or policy research, it could undermine the inquiry's perceived independence for such persons subsequently to take up positions with organizations whose interests were engaged at the inquiry. For example, it would obviously be problematic if an inquiry into the public health system led to a policy recommendation in favor of two-tier health care and the inquiry's research director then took up a position with a private health care provider. This points to a need for caution in the commissioner's contracting of staff and in limiting what staff may do in the aftermath of the inquiry.

More acutely, persons involved in an inquiry may publish their own report on the inquiry, perhaps as a book, that elaborates on or may even contradict the commissioner's report. In some respects, it may be appropriate for information to be published in this way. In the case of the Somalia Inquiry in Canada,[56] the publication of a book by one of three commissioners to the inquiry, after the inquiry was shut down by the government, could be said to have enhanced the inquiry's public accountability.[57] Even so, the publication alongside the commissioner's report of an account by someone who worked on an inquiry is fraught with risk, as illustrated in the case of *Chrétien v Gomery*.[58] In that case, it was alleged that the commissioner of the Sponsorship Inquiry in Canada, John Gomery, made public statements that established a reasonable apprehension of bias against some of the parties to the inquiry, including the former Prime Minister Jean Chrétien. Teitelbaum D.J. of the Federal Court of Canada concluded, after reviewing a series of statements by the commissioner, that there was a sufficient basis for this apprehension and struck down portions of the commissioner's report. Teitelbaum D.J. did so based partly on statements in a book authored by a staff member of the inquiry that was described by the commissioner, in the foreword of the book, as "accurate."[59] Teitelbaum D.J. concluded, based among other things on the book's inaccurate reports of communications between the inquiry and members of the public, that there was evidence to lead a reasonable observer to conclude that the commissioner had prejudged the outcome of the investigation.[60]

---

56 *Dishonoured Legacy – The Lessons of Somalia Affair – Report of the Commission of Inquiry into the Deployment of Canadian Forces to Somalia*, vol 1 (Ottawa: Minister of Public Works and Government Services Canada, 1992).

57 Peter Desbarats, *Somalia Cover-Up – A Commissioner's Journal* (McClelland & Stewart, 1997). Tamar Witelson, "Interview with Mr. Justice Gilles Létourneau, Somalia Commission Chair" in Allan Manson & David Mullan, eds, *Commissions of Inquiry: Praise or Reappraise?* (Toronto: Irwin Law, 2003) at 361–78.

58 *Chrétien v Canada (Ex-Commissioner, Commission of Inquiry into the Sponsorship Program and Advertising Activities)*, 2008 FC 802, [2009] 2 FCR 417 at paras 86 and 89–92 [*Chrétien v Canada*].

59 François Perreault, *Inside Gomery* (Douglas & Mcintyre, 2006).

60 *Chrétien v Canada, supra* note 58.

This example demonstrates the hazards of a staff member publishing information about an inquiry, let alone in a book endorsed by the commissioner, alongside the commissioner's report and the surrounding official record. Such publications may convey information about the parties to the inquiry that is unfair or inaccurate. More broadly, the integrity of the inquiry could be compromised in unanticipated ways by the (potentially) more salacious details in the book, which will unavoidably prompt questions about whether the commissioner was aware of and agreed to the content. To address this issue, a commissioner may consider requiring a confidentiality undertaking in the contracts of inquiry staff in order to limit the possibility of a staff person disclosing information that was learned in the inquiry, and is not otherwise public, without the commissioner's consent.

This brings us to the most serious post-inquiry risk to independence: that the commissioner will opine further on his or her findings and conclusions after the official report has been issued. In circumstances where this may be interpreted as a revision of the report, it raises serious concerns. An example arose in the context of the 2009 report by a UN fact-finding mission on the Gaza conflict, headed by South African former judge Richard Goldstone.[61] In April 2011, Goldstone published an opinion article in the *Washington Post* that stated in part:

> We know a lot more today about what happened in the Gaza war of 2008–09 than we did when I chaired the fact-finding mission appointed by the UN Human Rights Council that produced what has come to be known as the Goldstone Report. If I had known then what I know now, the Goldstone Report would have been a different document.[62]

This was interpreted by some commentators as a retraction of the report and has led to speculation that former judge Goldstone succumbed to outside pressure in his decision to publish the statement.[63] It also prompted a reply by the three other members of the mission, who lamented that press articles and comments had "misrepresented facts in an attempt to delegitimize the findings of [the UN mission's] report and to cast doubts on its credibility" and emphasized that "the mission ended when it presented its report" and that the report "is now an official

---

61 *Report of the United Nations Fact-Finding Mission on the Gaza Conflict*, submitted to the Human Rights Council, 12th Sess., UN Doc. A/HRC/12/48 (25 September 2009).

62 Richard Goldstone, "Revisiting Gaza", *Washington Post*; re-printed in *The Hamilton Spectator* (7 April 2011) A11.

63 "Lieberman Hints that Israel Exerted Pressure on Goldstone to Recant his UN Report's Findings", *Middle East Monitor* (5 April 2011), online: http://www.middleeastmonitor.org.uk/news/middle-east/2201-lieberman-hints-that-israel-exerted-pressure-on-goldstone-to-recant-his-un-reports-findings (last visited: 2 May 2011); Oudeh Basharat, "Goldstone's 'Regret' Is a Result of Emotional Pressure", *Haaretz* (8 April 2011), online: http://www.haaretz.com/print-edition/opinion/goldstone-s-regret-is-a-result-of-emotional-pressure-1.354841 (last visited: 2 May 2011).

UN document …".[64] The example demonstrates that the post-inquiry activities of a commission member may affect an inquiry's perceived independence and, in turn, highlights the need to protect from inappropriate influence those who authored the report.

Conclusion

Public inquiries are an important institution in the democratic governance tradition of Canada, the United Kingdom, and elsewhere. In rare cases of tragedy or scandal that threaten public confidence in government, they are a vehicle for government to make credible commitments to an independent, thorough, open, and fair investigation. It is true that the vehicle may be used too often or may not in all cases deliver on expectations. For example, an inquiry may take too long or cost too much or, worse, may not live up to the promise of independence that makes it a unique administrative instrument. Even where individual inquiries fall short of expectations, however, the failures may be attributable as much to other actors in the inquiry, including the government, as to the commissioner.[65] In any event, where governments lament the cost or apparent irrelevance of a particular inquiry, the obvious answer is to take this into account when considering the establishment of future inquiries.[66] On the other hand, where a government – in the name of speed, efficiency, or accountability – encroaches directly on a commissioner's autonomy or on the institutional independence of inquiries in general, this should be understood as an attempt to evade government accountability to the public, often precisely at the moment when there is a powerful case for independent truth-seeking.

64 Hina Jilani, Christine Chinkin & Desmond Travers, "Goldstone Report: Statement Issued by Members of UN Mission on Gaza War", *The Guardian* (14 April 2011).

65 Ratushny, *supra* note 5 at 199 and 201–2.

66 Van Harten, *supra* note 26 at 280–1.

Chapter 13
Australian Royal Commissions and Public Inquiries: Their Use and Abuse and Proposals for Reform

Scott Prasser

Introduction

This chapter focuses on the use and abuse of public inquiries in Australia with particular reference to inquisitorial inquiries. "Public inquiry" in this chapter refers to temporary *ad hoc* bodies appointed by executive government to provide advice or to investigate some issue; whose members are drawn from outside government; have public processes; seek community input and release their reports. This excludes: parliamentary committees; permanent government advisory bodies; internal government reports; and inquiries initiated by government bodies such as ombudsmen, anti-corruption bodies and departments.

As suggested by the Australian Law Reform Commission's (ALRC) recent review of the *Royal Commission Act 1902*[1] and research by the Victorian Parliamentary Research Library[2] and academics,[3] Australian public inquiries are classified as being inquisitorial/investigatory or policy advisory bodies.

Inquisitorial/investigatory inquiries are those appointed to investigate allegations of impropriety and maladministration or some catastrophic event (for example, flood, bushfire or accident). Inquisitorial inquiries focus on finding the "truth" about an allegation or incident and are therefore inquisitorial by nature and process. Their recommendations are prescriptive. The ALRC saw the functions of these inquiries as, "establishing accountability and responsibility; allowing stakeholders to learn what happened; providing catharsis or reconciliation; and providing and rebuilding public confidence."[4] Although the prime focus of inquisitorial inquiries is to clarify the facts about an issue, to check an allegation

1 Australian Law Reform Commission (ALRC), *Making Inquiries: A New Statutory Framework*, Report 111 (Sydney: Australian Government, 2009) at 57 [ALRC].

2 Adam Delacorn, *Royal Commissions in Victoria: 1854–2009* (Research Service, Parliament of Victoria, 2011).

3 Scott Prasser, *Royal Commissions and Public Inquiries in Australia* (Sydney: Lexis/Nexis, 2006) [Prasser, *Royal Commissions*].

4 ALRC, *supra* note 1 at 57.

and often to allocate responsibility, such inquiries also provide recommendations on broader policy issues pertaining to their particular topic.[5] Appendices 2 and 3 outline State and Commonwealth inquisitorial inquiries into corruption, improprieties and maladministration appointed since 1960. Appendix 4 lists Commonwealth and State public inquiries in Australia since 1960 into major catastrophic events.

Most inquisitorial inquiries appointed in Australia by Commonwealth, State and more recently Territory governments[6] take the form of royal commissions that are appointed under specific legislation (see Appendix 1 for legislation details across Australian jurisdictions) as occurs in other Commonwealth countries. Such legislation confers wide ranging coercive powers of investigation on these inquiries (for example, abilities to call and cross-examine witnesses, obtain evidence, rights of entry, phone-tapping) while also providing protection to witnesses and inquiry members from legal action such as defamation.

There are also forms of inquisitorial inquiries other than royal commissions. In New South Wales inquiries with similar powers and processes of appointment (that is, by the State Governor issuing *Letters Patent*) to royal commissions have been established under the more recent *Special Commissions of Inquiry Act (1983)*.[7] In Victoria boards of inquiry with similar powers to royal commissions have also been established.[8] Some State inquisitorial inquiries have been appointed under their own specific legislation with powers similar to royal commissions.[9] A few Commonwealth inquisitorial public inquiries have been appointed under the umbrella of other legislation to provide them with necessary powers of investigation.[10] In a limited number of cases the Commonwealth government has appointed inquisitorial inquiries without a statutory base and therefore without

5 For instance the 1991 Commonwealth *Royal Commission into Aboriginal Deaths in Custody* made recommendations across a range of social, health and economic issues as well as concerning deaths in custody; The 2001 Commonwealth *Royal Commission of Inquiry into HIH Insurance* proposed changes to the financial system that went beyond the immediate issues of the HIH insurance company collapse.

6 Australia has two main territories, the Australian Capital Territory (where the national capital, Canberra, is located) and the Northern Territory. Since both have gained self-government status in the 1980s they have enacted their own legislation in relation to public inquiries.

7 J Ransley, "The Powers of Royal Commissions and Controls over Them" in Patrick Weller, ed, *Royal Commissions and the Making of Public Policy* (Melbourne: Macmillan, 1994) at 22–31 [Ransley, 1994].

8 Leonard Arthur Hallett, *Royal Commissions and Boards of Inquiry: Some Legal and Procedural Aspects* (Sydney: Law Book Company, 1982).

9 The 2004 South Australian inquiry into child abuse was established under the *Commission of Inquiry (Children in State Care and Children on APY Lands) Act 2004*.

10 The 1996 *Inquiry into the Manner in which DFAT has Dealt with Allegations of Pedophile Activities* was appointed under the *Public Service Act 1922*.

investigative powers.[11] The Howard Coalition Commonwealth Government (1996–2007) established one inquisitorial inquiry without legislative backing[12] and two other inquiries under different legislation than the *Royal Commissions Act 1902*.[13] The Rudd Labor Commonwealth Government's (2007–10) 2008 *Inquiry into Dr M. Haneef* was an inquisitorial inquiry that had no formal statutory backing.

Policy/advisory inquiries provide advice, information, research and options to governments about a particular policy problem. Most policy inquiries take the form of reviews, taskforces, panels, working parties, committees of inquiry, independent inquiries and royal commissions. With the exception of royal commissions most policy inquiries, have no legislative backing to provide them with investigatory powers or to protect witnesses or inquiry members. There have been some exceptions. A small number of policy inquiries, other than royal commissions, have been established under either general[14] or occasionally their own specific legislation.[15] Policy inquiries are established by ministerial or sometimes cabinet decision, not *Letters Patent* issued by the Crown. Non-statutory policy inquiries constitute the bulk of public inquiries in Australia. They rely on their appointment by executive government, membership profile and topicality of their subject to attract submissions and public interest.

This lack of any statutory base for most policy inquiries has caused some concern. The ALRC assessed whether the Commonwealth *Royal Commissions Act 1902* should be changed in relation to the nomenclature of royal commissions, their coercive powers and processes of accountability. It also considered whether policy public inquiries required a legislative base as in Canada and more recently in the United Kingdom and New Zealand to provide them with powers of investigation and legal protection of witnesses and inquiry members.

---

11 The Hawke–Keating Commonwealth governments (1983–96) appointed ten non-royal commission inquisitorial inquiries to investigate allegations of impropriety. Most had no legislative base (see Prasser, *Royal Commissions*, *supra* note 3 at 25).

12 *Inquiry into the Circumstances of the Immigration Detention of Cornelia Rau* appointed in 2005.

13 *Independent Inquiry into Allegations of Corruption in the Australian Federal Police* and the *Inquiry into Allegations of Pedophile Activities in the Department of Foreign Affairs* were established under the *Public Service Act 1922* (Cth); The 2007 *Equine Influenza Inquiry* was established under the *Quarantine Amendment (Commission of Inquiry) Act 2007* (Cth).

14 The 1975 *Commission of Inquiry into Ranger Uranium Development in the Northern Territory* and the later *Inquiry into the Shoalwater Bay Training Area* were established under the *Environmental Protection Act* (Cth).

15 The 1987 Commonwealth *Inquiry into the Lemonthyme and Southern Forests* was established under the *Lemonthyme and Southern Forest* [*Commission of Inquiry*] *Act 1987*.

Brief History of Trends in Australian Public Inquiries

Public inquiries have a long history in Australia. Numerous public inquiries, mostly in the form of royal commissions, were appointed by Australia's six States prior to federation in 1901. Since then, the States have continued to appoint public inquiries, usually, but not only royal commissions. Altogether the States have established over 1,000 public inquiries since federation.[16]

Nationally, the newly formed Commonwealth government was quick to appoint a public inquiry in the form of an inquisitorial royal commission soon after federation in early August 1902: *Royal Commission on Transport of Troops from Service in South Africa in the SS Drayton Grange and the circumstances under which Trooper H. Burkitt was not landed at Adelaide from the SS Norfolk.* Two weeks later the Commonwealth hastily passed the *Royal Commissions Act 1902*, one of the Commonwealth's earliest pieces of legislation. This was deemed necessary, as the then Attorney-General and later Prime Minister, Alfred Deakin explained, because although the government could appoint a royal commission through *Letters-Patent* issued by the Governor-General, the Commission had "no means by which witnesses could be compelled to attend or ordinary penalties could be imposed for perjury."[17] The *Royal Commissions Act 1902* provided this and other powers. The legislation had only eight clauses and was similar to existing State legislation.

This early Commonwealth legislation and comparable State legislation concerning royal commissions highlights an important difference with their then United Kingdom counterparts. From the outset Australian royal commissions were established under specific legislation that provided for extensive coercive powers of investigation. By contrast, royal commissions in the United Kingdom were not established under any legislation. Since the 1920s only inquiries established under *Tribunals of Inquiry Act 1921* (UK) have similar powers to Australian royal commissions and only rarely have these been called royal commissions.[18] These arrangements in the United Kingdom only changed recently with the new *Inquiries Act 2005* (UK) that replaced 30 separate laws and the *Tribunals of Inquiry Act 1921* and provided for the establishment of inquiries with specific powers of investigation.

At the Commonwealth level in Australia royal commissions were once the dominant form of public inquiry. They reached their peak during 1910–29 when

---

16 DH Borchardt, *Commissions of Inquiry in Australia* (Bundoora: La Trobe University Press, 1991); DH Borchardt, *Checklist of Royal Commissions, Select Committees of Parliament and Boards of Inquiry, Vol III: Victoria, 1856–1960* (Sydney: Wentworth Books, 1970); J Ransley, *Inquisitorial Royal Commissions and Investigations into Political Wrongdoing* (PhD Thesis, Faculty of Arts, Griffith University, 2001).

17 Austl, Commonwealth, House of Representatives, *Parliamentary Debates* (21 August 1902) at 15355 (Mr A Deakin, Attorney-General).

18 For example, the 1924 *Royal Commission into Lunacy and Mental Disorder*.

54 were established. Subsequently, royal commission numbers declined. Twelve royal commissions were appointed from 1929–40 and only seven from 1950–72. From the 1940s non-statutory public inquiries became the preferred inquiry form. Though used relatively sparingly compared to recent times (see Table 13.1), such inquiries provided advice on important topics: tertiary education, taxation, economic policy, poverty, environment and population.[19] Of seven royal commissions appointed during this period two provided policy advice, while the remainder were of the inquisitorial type.

The election of the Whitlam Labor Commonwealth Government (1972–75) saw public inquiry numbers increase greatly. Some 70 non-statutory mostly policy public inquiries were appointed along with 13 royal commissions.[20] Only one of these royal commissions could be classified as an inquisitorial inquiry.[21] Despite criticism from the then conservative Coalition (Liberal–National Party) Opposition about this proliferation of inquiries[22] the public inquiry genie was out of the bottle and subsequent Commonwealth governments have continued to appoint public inquiries more often compared to earlier times. The Fraser Coalition Government (1975–83) appointed just over 80 general public inquiries and eight royal commissions. The Hawke–Keating Labor governments (1983–96) appointed 189 public inquiries and 12 royal commissions. The Howard Coalition Commonwealth Government (1996–2007) established over 80 general public inquiries (mostly policy) and four inquisitorial royal commissions. The Rudd and Gillard Labor Commonwealth governments (2007–) initiated nearly 40 public inquiries, but notably have eschewed establishing any royal commissions despite calls for their appointment into several major administrative scandals until very recently (see page 249).[23]

This increase in inquisitorial inquiries, especially royal commissions, at the Commonwealth level during the 1980s and 1990s (see Appendix 3) was partly a response by successive governments to a range of scandals involving elected officials and public servants, key government agencies and serious maladministration across a number of key programs. Similar problems, especially

---

19 EV Spiegel, *Study of Ad Hoc Committees of Inquiry Appointed by the Commonwealth Government between 1957 and 1969* (PhD Thesis, Department of Government, Faculty of Economics, University of Sydney, 1973) for assessment of Commonwealth inquiries during the 1950s and early 1960s.

20 CJ Lloyd & GS Reid, *Out of the Wilderness: The Return of Labor* (Melbourne: Cassell, 1974).

21 This was the 1974 *Royal Commission into Alleged Payments to Australian Maritime Union.*

22 M Fraser, MP, Press Release, "Review of Bodies Conducting Inquiries" (2 February 1976).

23 The Opposition has called for a "judicial" inquiry into the home insulation batts scandal (see C Lewis, "The Home Insulation Program Policy Debacle: Haste Makes Waste" (2011) 5:2 Public Policy 83).

in relation to police corruption erupted across most States resulting in numerous inquisitorial inquiries being established (see Appendix 2).[24]

In summary, since the 1970s the number of policy and inquisitorial public inquiries increased in comparison with previous times. Non-statutory policy advisory public inquiries particularly proliferated and were the dominant inquiry form. Most of the royal commissions appointed at both national and State levels have been inquisitorial. Since 1979 only three of the 23 Commonwealth royal commissions could be classified as policy inquiries. A more recent trend evident during the last decade has been that all Australian governments have become reluctant to appoint inquisitorial inquiries like royal commissions unless there was no other viable alternative or it was into a more neutral topic that was less directly related to government performance.[25] This reflects growing concerns not only about the costs of such inquiries[26] and their exercise of powers, but also the adverse impacts that previous inquisitorial inquiries had on governments during the 1990s when a number of State and Commonwealth governments lost office as a consequence of inquisitorial inquiry findings (see Appendix 3).[27] Hence, until November 2012 the last Commonwealth royal commission was the 2005 *Commission of Inquiry into Possible Breaches of Australian Law in relation to the UN Oil-for-Food Programme* only appointed by the Howard Coalition Government after considerable political pressure.[28] Some regard the 2007 *Equine Influenza Inquiry* established by the Howard Government under the *Quarantine Amendment (Commission of Inquiry) Act 2007* (Cth) as a royal commission as it has most of the powers of a royal commission, but has been treated differently in this analysis as it was neither appointed under the *Royal Commission Act 1902* nor were *Letters Patent* issued by the Governor-General (see footnote 13). Other explanations for the decline in inquisitorial public inquiry numbers include new Commonwealth and State integrity mechanisms such as anti-corruption bodies and integrity commissioners and expanded roles for existing integrity agencies like ombudsmen. Some of these which were themselves outcomes of royal commission recommendations have provided governments with alternative mechanisms for dealing with allegations of impropriety and maladministration.

Nevertheless, public inquiries of the inquisitorial royal commission type still remain the "institution of last resort" for governments when all other bodies are deemed unsuitable for handling issues of high political salience and sensitivity.

24 Rodney Tiffen, *Scandals: Media, Politics and Corruption in Contemporary Australia* (Sydney: University of New South Wales Press, 1999) [Tiffen].

25 Scott Prasser, "Royal Commissions in Australia: When Should Governments Appoint Them?" (2006) 65:3 Australian Journal of Public Administration 28.

26 The 2001 *Royal Commission of Inquiry into the Building and Construction Industry* cost $60m.

27 Tiffen, *supra* note 24.

28 L Botterill, "Doing it for Growers in Iraq?: The AWB Oil-for-Food Scandal and the Cole Inquiry" (2007) 66:1 Australian Journal of Public Administration 4.

In 2005 the Queensland Beattie State Labor Government appointed not one, but two royal commissions into the overseas doctors' scandal after exhausting every alternative.[29] State governments following major fire and flood disasters in Victoria and Queensland in 2009 and 2011 quickly appointed the inquisitorial commissions of inquiry to investigate the causes of disasters[30] and to advise on post-disaster management.

A major development nationally was the announcement by Prime Minister Julia Gillard in November 2012 of a Commonwealth Royal Commission into "institutional responses to instances and allegations of child sexual abuse in Australia"[31] (*Royal Commission into Institutional Responses to Child Sexual Abuse*). This announcement came as a surprise. The current Labor Commonwealth government that has held office since the end of 2007 (though with a change in prime minister from Kevin Rudd to Julia Gillard in June 2010) has resisted many calls for other royal commissions across a range of areas. Moreover, this issue is primarily a State responsibility where a number of public and parliamentary inquiries have been completed or were under way. Indeed, the suddenness of the decision was reflected by the fact that the exact terms of reference and members of this royal commission were not announced till January 2013 – some time after the November 2012 announcement. Further underlining this was the unusual step of issuing of a consultation paper seeking views as to the royal commission's terms of reference and possible membership.[32] Although opinion polls indicate strong public support for this royal commission, there have been criticisms. Some warned that it must not evolve into a "witch-hunt" against individuals and institutions like the Catholic Church.[33] Others suggested it could be too wide ranging, impinge on State inquiries and responsibilities, go on for too long and cost too much (estimated costs in the May 2013 Commonwealth budget were over $400m) and was too politically motivated.[34] Regardless of these concerns the issue is that the

29 This concerned issues of overseas doctors working in public hospitals. The first royal commission had to be disbanded because of the perceived bias of its chair and was replaced by a new commission (see Scott Prasser, "The Queensland Health Royal Commissions" (2010) 69:1 Australian Journal of Public Administration 79) [Prasser, Queensland].

30 These were: *Royal Commission into Victorian Bushfires* and Queensland appointed the *Commission of Inquiry into the 2010/11 Floods.*

31 PM Gillard, *Media Statement* (12 November 2012).

32 Austl, Commonwealth, Department of Prime Minister and Cabinet, *Consultation Paper – Royal Commission into Institutional Responses to Child Sexual Abuse* (November 2012).

33 Scott Prasser, "Royal Commission Must not Be Turned into a Witch-hunt", *The Australian* (13 November 2012).

34 P Kelly, "Commission on Child Sex Abuse: A Depressing Example of Populist Politics", *The Week-End Australian* (17 November 2012); G Johns, "Commission Impossible: Sex Probe Will Over-promise and Under-deliver", *The Australian* (20 November 2012).

Table 13.1 Number of Public Inquiries established by Australian Commonwealth Governments 1900–2005 by Decade[(a)]

Decades	Royal Commissions	Other inquiries	Total
1900–09	15	2	17
1910–19	27	2	29
1920–29	27	6	33
1930–39	10	10	20
1940–49	5	14[(b)]	19
1950–59	3	20	23
1960–69	3	19	22
1970–79	18	151	169
1980–89	13	151	164
1990–99	3	96	99
2000–05	4	44	48
Total	**128**	**515**	**643**

Notes: [a] Sources: Based on: Borchardt 1991; Prasser 2006 and surveys of Commonwealth Parliamentary Papers series 1901–2005. [b] Includes 11 inquiries appointed under *National Security (Inquiries) Regulations* which allowed the Attorney-General to appoint an inquiry on "any matter in relation to public safety or defence of the Commonwealth" (Section 1A). Such inquiries have sometimes been counted as royal commissions (Fraser 1986 – see footnote 69), but are excluded as such in this table as they did not exercise full royal commission powers nor were all their reports released publicly.

royal commission instrument, though less used than previously, still remains a viable option for government.

Issues of Use and Abuse of Public Inquiries

Public inquiries, including those of the inquisitorial type serve a wide range of legitimate purposes in a democracy. At the same time, they are also vulnerable to possible abuse. Key to understanding public inquiries is to appreciate that they are first and foremost executive government inquiries, appointed by executive government to serve executive government purposes. Executive government motivations in their establishment impact on their potential use and abuse.

Appointing public inquiries for legitimate and politically expedient reasons

Understanding why public inquiries are appointed is fundamental to appreciating their potential use and abuse by executive government. As Cartwright, writing of public inquiries in the United Kingdom observed, "one of the perennially fascinating questions about royal commissions and departmental committees" is why governments appoint public inquiries.[35] Similarly in Canada, Walls observed some time ago:

> Many citizens today are speculating as to why royal commissions are necessary – why they last so long and why they appear to be so costly to the taxpayer. On all sides one hears such remarks as: "Why should government have to appoint a commission when they themselves are elected to solve such problems."[36]

Stated reasons for appointing any inquiry only reflect the explanations a government wants to present publicly. Such explanations are usually framed in terms of rational decision making, seeking expert advice, promoting consultation or, in relation to inquisitorial inquiries, of seeking the "facts" to identify the causes of some calamitous event, to allocate responsibility or to provide independent assessment about an allegation of impropriety. These may be deemed as a legitimate use of public inquiries. Walls summed up this rational policy making and legitimate role of public inquiries:

> The principal function … is to place before government … a cold blooded impartial survey followed by an equitable solution to the problem submitted to it, a solution without concern as to its implication or on whose toes it may figuratively step.[37]

In Australia[38] and overseas[39] public inquiries, especially of the policy variety, were seen as a means for governments to access the latest social science knowledge to tackle emerging public policy problems, employ outside experts, develop options and promote public debate on emerging policy issues. Certainly, in Australia, many public inquiries through their research, consultation and analysis have paved the way for policy change. While there is a necessary "political" element to this process, the legitimacy of such inquiries is not diminished if these aims are explicit and underpinned by a rigorous inquiry process and appropriate membership. Similarly, it is also legitimate for executive government to appoint an inquisitorial inquiry to identify the causes for some disaster or to probe an

---

35 TJ Cartwright, *Royal Commissions and Departmental Committees in Britain* (London: Hodder and Stoughton, 1975) at 84.

36 CS Walls, "Royal Commissions – Their Influence on Public Policy" (1969) 12 Canadian Public Administration 365.

37 *Ibid* at 365.

38 Geoffrey Hawker, "The Use of Social Scientists and Social Science in the Inquiries of the Labor Government 1972–75" (Paper delivered at the 48th ANZAAS Congress, Sociology Section, Melbourne, 1977).

39 Martin Bulmer, *The Uses of Social Research: Social Investigation in Public Policy Making* (London: Allen and Unwin, 1982) [Bulmer, 1982].

allegation of corruption and even, as one royal commissioner observed, to assuage a community experiencing trauma.[40]

However, the problem is that assessing executive government's motivations is not always easy. Public explanations for appointing an inquiry "cannot necessarily be taken at their face value"[41] and may involve "highly cynical and self-serving motives."[42] These include: decision postponement, issue smothering, interest group pacification and co-option, providing symbolic action, blame avoidance and as "a device to enable governments to do what they want to do anyway … clothing it in the legitimacy provided by research … mobilising support … providing an aura of objectivity and … prestige."[43] Inquiries, according to this perspective, are "not so much for digging up the truth but for digging it in."[44]

Tests concerning whether executive government's motivations in establishing a public inquiry are primarily for politically expedient purposes that abuse the inquiry process or serve more legitimate reasons of research, independent analysis and fact finding include:

- Terms of reference (how wide or narrow)
- Powers (how extensive and/or statutorily backed)
- Reporting timeframes (how rushed or inflexible the deadlines)
- Resourcing (how adequate and responsive to inquiry requests)
- Membership (how expert, unbiased and independent)
- Inquiry processes (how consultative and transparent)
- Post inquiry reactions by government (implementation of recommendations, formal responses within given timeframes).

Policy advisory inquiries are generally more prone to be established for politically expedient purposes. Such inquiries cover not only a broad range of policy areas, but their proposals are more contestable, open to interest group debate and criticism. Also, their membership is often large, drawn from a wide pool: experts, academics and representatives from particular interests and hence more easily manipulated by governments to obtain the outcome desired. In public choice parlance analysis shows that the composition of Commonwealth policy inquiries during the 1980s was heavily dominated by representatives from producer groups (that is, key interest groups who may benefit from inquiry outcomes) compared to consumers or independent and expert members.[45]

---

40 Susan Pascoe, "The 2009 Victorian Bushfires Royal Commission: Lessons for the Conduct of Inquiries" (2010) 69:4 Australian Journal of Public Administration 392.

41 Gerald Rhodes, *Committees of Inquiry* (London: Allen and Unwin, 1975) at 67.

42 Bulmer, 1982 *supra* note 39 at 97.

43 *Ibid* at 99.

44 AP Herbert, "Anything but Action: A Study of the Uses and Abuses of Committees of Inquiry" in R Harris, ed, *Radical Reactions* (London: Hutchison, 1961) 251.

45 Prasser, *Royal Commissions*, *supra* note 3 at 127–8.

There is no lack of examples of policy advisory inquiries being perceived to serve politically expedient roles and at the mercy of executive government whims. The 1983 *Committee of Inquiry into Industrial Relations Law* was seen by the business community as being composed of members from the "industrial relations club"[46] and therefore biased. The Chair of the 1980 *Independent Public Inquiry into Domestic Air Fares* complained that the inquiry was so rushed by the government that it prevented "further desirable examination of the submissions."[47] Harding highlighted how the Fraser Coalition Commonwealth Government (1975–83) used several public inquiries to highjack the political agenda,[48] delay decision making and to divert attention from other policy failures.[49] The *Committee of Inquiry into Australian Institute of Multicultural Affairs* was condemned on the basis that its report "could not sustain its conclusion that the Institute was inefficient and ineffective", and "lacked objectivity from beginning to end."[50] The now highly regarded 1981 Campbell *Committee of Inquiry into the Australian Financial System*[51] established by the Fraser Coalition Government was attacked by the Labor Opposition as being too ideologically based in its terms of reference, membership and recommendations.[52]

Government responses to inquiry reports is another indicator of their motivation. The Fraser Government's quick dismissal of the inquiry into unemployment benefits and the Howard Government's immediate rejection of the *Committee of Inquiry into Fuel Taxation* questions the motives of these governments in appointing such inquiries. Indeed, implementation or rather non-implementation of inquiry recommendations has long been the "greatest degree of dissatisfaction with royal commissions"[53] and public inquiries in Australia and overseas. Non-implementation of inquiry recommendations reinforces the perception that governments only appointed an inquiry to be seen to be "doing something" with no real intention to act on the issue. That all public inquiries in

46 Editorial, *Australian Financial Review*, 24 May 1984.

47 Austl, Commonwealth, Independent Public Inquiry into Domestic Air Fares, *Report of the Independent Public Inquiry into Domestic Air Fares* by WJ Holcroft (chair) (Canberra; Australian Government Publishing Service, 1981) at x.

48 *Committee of Review of the Commonwealth Employment Service* (1976); *Committee of Inquiry into Education and Training* (1976); *Committee of Inquiry into Unemployment Benefit Policy* (1977); *Committee of Inquiry into Technological Change* (1978).

49 A Harding, "Unemployment Policy: A Case Study of Agenda Management" (1985) 44:3 Australian Journal of Public Administration 224.

50 F Galbally, QC, *Sydney Morning Herald* (12 December 1983).

51 The Campbell Report heralded the deregulation of the Australian financial system in the 1980s, largely achieved by the Hawke–Keating Labor Commonwealth Government.

52 Austl, Commonwealth, House of Representatives, *Parliamentary Debates* (17 November 1981) at 2850–2 (Mr R Willis).

53 Martin Bulmer, "Increasing the Effectiveness of Royal Commissions: A Comment" (1983) 61 Public Administration 440.

Australia, including inquisitorial royal commissions, are only temporary bodies that disband after they report and have no powers of oversight or to enforce the implementation of their proposals means it is easy for executive government to ignore inquiry recommendations.

However, inquisitorial inquiries in general and royal commissions and their equivalent in particular, are regarded as being less able to be manipulated by executive government. They are appointed to investigate the causes of some major disaster or allegations of impropriety and are expected to provide definable answers based on much clearer evidence than policy inquiries. Much of this evidence is gained from the exercise of extensive coercive powers[54] that policy inquiries do not have. The high political salience of the issues inquisitorial inquiries investigate (for example, corruption, major disasters) make governments less willing to interfere too openly in their activities. Further, royal commissions and like bodies are appointed by the Crown rather than ministers and their formal reporting to the Crown underpins their independence compared to other public inquiries. Indeed, their formal nomenclature of such inquiries as "royal commission" or "special commission" gives these bodies greater prestige compared to other *ad hoc* non-statutory inquiries. The ALRC noted that "the title 'royal commission' is helpful in that it indicates how the highest form of public inquiry is established"[55] and concluded that the term "royal commission" is "well-known" and therefore "can communicate to the public the extraordinary nature of such an inquiry" and should be retained for such high order investigations.[56] Also, inquisitorial inquiries are overwhelmingly constituted by current or former senior members of the judiciary or legal profession who tend to be less tolerant of government interference, delays and non-implementation of recommendations. Indeed, since 1960 chairs of the 31 Commonwealth inquisitorial public inquiries have been largely drawn from the senior ranks of the legal profession or current and former members of the judiciary, with a few exceptions.[57] Although employing current members of the judiciary is not without criticism, it nevertheless has given those bodies so chaired considerable prestige and a perceived independence other public inquiries can rarely match.

Nevertheless, inquisitorial inquiries are not immune from being seen to be used for politically expedient reasons by executive government. The 1954 *Royal Commission on Espionage* (*Petrov Royal Commission*) appointed by the Menzies Coalition Commonwealth Government (1949–66) in the wake of the defection of

54 See s 7 of the *Royal Commission Act* (Cth).

55 ALRC, *supra* note 1 at 107.

56 *Ibid* at 107.

57 Mike Codd, former Secretary of the Department of the Prime Minister and Cabinet conducted the 1994 *Inquiry into the Conduct of the Hon Alan Griffiths MP*; Former Coalition MP, Ian McPhee in 1992 reviewed the Civil Aviation Authority's tender process; retired Australia Federal Police Commissioner, Mick Palmer headed the 2005 inquiry into Cornelia Rau.

two Soviet embassy staff (the Petrovs) and concerns about Communist infiltration was seen by some as "one of the most blatant abuses of royal commissions"[58] designed to inflict maximum damage on the Labor Party prior to the 1955 federal election. This view has now been seriously challenged.[59] The 1980 *Royal Commission into the Activities of the Federated Ship Painters' and Dockers' Union* (*Costigan Royal Commission*) appointed by the Fraser Coalition Commonwealth Government, was initially seen to be established to embarrass the then Labor Opposition.[60] The Hawke Labor Commonwealth Government's 1984 *Royal Commission into British Nuclear Tests in Australia* chaired by former Whitlam Labor minister Jim McClelland, was condemned by the Coalition parties as being a flawed, biased and politically motivated.[61] For some, the Howard Government's 2001 *Royal Commission into the Building and Construction Industry* was a vehicle to attack the trade unions, to justify anti-union legislation already decided upon and to take attention off other political problems.[62]

One particular inquisitorial inquiry widely attacked for its perceived politically expedient role was the 1995 Western Australian *Royal Commission into Use of Executive Powers* (*Marks Royal Commission*). This was appointed by the Court Coalition State Government to investigate issues relating to the former Labor government and its then Premier, Dr Carmen Lawrence. By the time the royal commission had started Dr Lawrence had left State politics and was Health Minister in the Keating Labor Commonwealth Government (1992–96). The *Marks Royal Commission's* findings forced Lawrence to stand down as Health Minister and to face trial for alleged perjury. Many commentators saw the inquiry as being deliberately designed to besmirch Lawrence.[63] As Prime Minister Keating (1995) in one of the strongest attacks on a royal commission said the *Marks Commission* was:

> … conceived as an act of political malevolence by the Court Government … the basic principles of natural justice were ignored … the terms of reference were

58 EG Whitlam quoted in *Sydney Morning Herald* (26 September 1984); N Whitlam & J Stubbs, *Nest of Traitors: The Petrov Affair* (Brisbane: Jacaranda Press, 1974); see R Manne, *The Petrov Affair: Politics and Espionage* (Sydney: Pergamon, 1987) for an overview.

59 JR Nethercote, "The Timing of the 1954 Election", *Quadrant* (June 1995) 50; JR Nethercote & D Martin, "New Light on the Petrov Affair", *Quadrant* (June 1995) 46; G Henderson, "Cold War Secrets and the Spies Who Came out of Canberra", *Sydney Morning Herald* (12 April 2011).

60 M Grattan, "Libs Caught in Crime Fight", *The Age* (28 August 1982).

61 Austl, Commonwealth, Senate, *Parliamentary Debates* (13 March 1986) at 1001–2 (Mr J Carrick).

62 J Marr, *First the Verdict: The Real Story of the Building Royal Commission* (Sydney: Pluto Press, 2003).

63 "Time to End Marks Commission", Editorial, *The Australian* (11 September 1995).

> deliberately narrow … drawn up to put Dr Carmen Lawrence and the Labor Party on trial … the establishment of the Royal Commission was unique and uniquely disreputable …[64]

Also, inquisitorial inquiries including royal commissions, can despite their prestige, membership and profile suffer from non-implementation, sabotage and even attack[65] from executive government, be denied extensions of time[66] and resources.[67] Numerous members of such inquiries have expressed frustrations on these matters.[68]

Appointment of Judges and Legal Professionals to Chair Inquiries

Another possible abuse in relation to inquisitorial public inquiries concerns their heavy reliance on members and former members of the judiciary as chairs. It is argued that the deployment of judges is an intrusion by executive government into judicial independence, a breakdown in the separation of powers and a possible depletion of limited judicial resources. Such concerns are not new.[69] In the 1930s the Chief Justice of the Victorian Supreme Court, Sir William Irvine, resolved not to allow members of the Victorian judiciary to serve on executive-appointed inquiries such as royal commissions. For Irvine, the proper role of judges was:

> … to hear and determine issues of fact and of law … There begins and ends the function of the judiciary. It is mainly due to the fact that, judges in all British communities have, except in rare cases, confined themselves to this function, that they have attained … the confidence of the people.[70]

While the Irvine Doctrine has been adhered to in Victoria, it has not been followed in the other States or at the Commonwealth level. However, this concern was

---

64 P Keating, MP, Press Release, "Marks Royal Commission" (14 November 1995).

65 Prime Minister Fraser attacked the 1982 *Royal Commission into the Australian Meat Industry*: Austl, Commonwealth, House of Representatives, *Parliamentary Debates* (21 September 1982) at 1621–57 (Mr M Fraser).

66 The *Costigan Royal Commission* was arguably closed down prematurely by the Hawke Labor Government.

67 The Hawke Government refused to provide additional major resources and to extend timelines for the 1984 *Royal Commission into the Use and Effect of Chemical Agents on Australian Personnel in Vietnam*.

68 A Moffitt, *Quarter to Midnight: The Australian Crisis – Organised Crime and the Decline in the Institutions of State* (Sydney: Angus and Robertson, 1985) at 19; P Woodward, "Too Hot to Handle", *The Australian* (18 March 1989); Tony Fitzgerald, "What Went Wrong with Queensland", *The Courier-Mail* (29 July 2009).

69 G Fraser, *Judges as Royal Commissioners* (Melbourne: Victorian Law Foundation, 1986) [Fraser].

70 W Irvine quoted in Fraser, *supra* note 69 at 11.

renewed in recent times with the growth in royal commission numbers since the 1970s. The controversial nature of some of their topics and the attacks several royal commissioners received from some governments were added factors. In addition, some have questioned the skills of such legal representatives in "sifting the evidence" on matters about which they may have little real expertise.[71]

Nevertheless, the continued reliance on judges, former judges or senior legal professionals to chair inquisitorial inquiries continues. The 2009 *Victorian Bushfire Royal Commission* was chaired by a former judge. The Queensland Government's 2011 *Flood Commission of Inquiry* is chaired by a sitting member of the State Supreme Court. Though this latest appointment was criticized[72] it has been generally welcomed as an indication of the Commission's status and independence. Importantly, Queensland's *Commissions of Inquiry Act* confers additional powers of investigation if a royal commission is led by a member of the State Supreme Court.[73]

Mr Justice Athol Moffitt, who chaired several royal commissions in New South Wales, believed sitting judges should conduct royal commissions as they promoted public confidence in the inquiry and brought needed skills to the investigation. He was aware how executive governments could manipulate such appointments to give efficacy to a royal commission with covert political goals. Moffitt suggested as a safeguard against abuse a statement of practice concerning what cases a judge may preside over after the inquiry they have chaired has been completed.[74] Neither the ALRC nor the Law Council of Australia, believe there should be any limits on the role of members of the judiciary serving on public inquiries. However, the ALRC did support a statement of independence being included in the new legislation to reinforce this important principle.[75]

Powers of Investigation: Too Intrusive?

The coercive powers of statutory based inquisitorial inquiries have raised concerns about their potential to undermine civil liberties. Royal commissions and other inquisitorial inquiries established under similar legislation, have coercive powers to probe, force documents to be presented, make witnesses not only appear before them, but also give testimony even if it is self-incriminating and in some cases to

71 D Solomon, "The Lawyers, the Politicians and the Commissions", *Australian Financial Review* (4 November 1983).

72 N Brown, "Politics Has No Place in Courtroom", *The Spectator* (Australian edition) (29 January 2011).

73 E Campbell, *Contempt of Royal Commission* (Melbourne: Faculty of Law, Monash University, 1984) at 13 concerning powers of inquiries so chaired to issue warrants.

74 A Moffitt, "Judges, Royal Commissioners and the Separation of Powers", *Quadrant* (May 2000) 36.

75 ALRC, *supra* note 1 at 144.

conduct phone-tapping and other related activities. Fines and imprisonment can result if individuals do not cooperate with such inquiries.

There is some variation of the nature and extent of these coercive powers across Australian jurisdictions. For instance, Commonwealth royal commissions have power to search, enter and seize documents without needing a warrant, while in some States a warrant must be issued through an independent officer of the courts. In New South Wales, royal commissions cannot apply for a search warrant, but may use seconded police officers to do so. In the Northern Territory no warrant is needed. In Queensland, a royal commissioner can issue a search warrant without recourse to the courts.

What has increased concern about this aspect of inquisitorial inquiries has been that in response to requests from several Commonwealth and State major inquiries during the 1980s, governments have provided for additional powers for these bodies. For instance, the 1980–84 *Costigan Royal Commission* sought and received increased powers to issue search warrants and fine witnesses who were uncooperative. The 2004 *Royal Commission into the NSW Police Service* gained additional powers of investigation.[76] In Queensland, the 1987–89 *Commission of Inquiry into Police Misconduct* (Fitzgerald Commission) gained extra powers on five separate occasions. Executive government has generally been loath to reject demands from such high profile inquisitorial inquiries for extra powers, time or resources, lest it be seen as interfering with inquiry outcomes.

Supporters of inquisitorial type inquiries believe such coercive powers "enable commissions to unearth hidden evidence"[77] not normally available to other agencies. It is these very powers, it is argued, that have made such inquiries so effective compared to other agencies. Others are less positive. Justice Ronald Sackville, who himself chaired a royal commission, believed that increased powers of royal commissions "undercut protections against the intrusions of the state" and that "investigative royal commissions constitute a serious and continuing threat to civil liberties in Australia."[78]

The ALRC review heard from the Law Council of Australia, Liberty Australia, Department of Immigration and Citizenship and Australian Government Solicitor concerning the need for inquiries to exercise such powers.[79] Overall, the ALRC concluded:

> The availability of information gathering powers is a fundamental and characteristic feature of royal commissions. It is necessary for them to possess the power to obtain information relevant to their terms of reference, by requiring

---

76 Royal Commission into New South Wales Police Service, *Final Report*, Vol 1 at 17.

77 Ransley, 1994, *supra* note 7 at 22.

78 R Sackville, "Royal Commissions in Australia: What Price Truth?" *Current Affairs Bulletin* 60:12 (May 1984) 10.

79 ALRC, *supra* note 1 at 253–5.

> the production of documents and other things or by requiring a person to attend oral examination or hearing to answer questions.[80]

The need for coercive powers has also been acknowledged in recent reviews of royal commission powers in New Zealand.[81]

However, not all requests for increased inquiry powers have been supported. In Tasmania, the 2000 *Royal Commission into the Death of Joseph Gilewicz* requested more powers including access to listening devices. The Tasmanian government accepted the advice by the Tasmanian Law Reform Institute (TLRI)[82] not to provide these additional powers. The ALRC concurred that Commonwealth inquisitorial inquiries should not be empowered to initiate interception of telecommunications, but believed royal commissions should be able to receive intercepted information legally gained.[83] Also the Tasmanian government agreed with recommendations from the TLRI that warrants sought by royal commission had to be formally sought through the courts and decided against giving commissions greater powers in this area.[84]

The other issue of possible abuse has not been excessive powers, but rather the lack of them for non-statutory inquiries. This particularly affects policy inquiries that lack any legislative basis to call witnesses, obtain information, to protect witnesses giving evidence or to ensure inquiry members do not suffer legal action. The recent Commonwealth inquisitorial inquiries into the Cornelia Rau and Dr Haneef affairs were seen as being unable to conduct their inquiries effectively because of this deficiency.[85] The ALRC's solution is to create a new *Inquiries Act* that would allow for a two-tier system of inquiries: royal commissions as the highest-ranking inquiry and with basically the same powers and processes of appointment as now; and a second tier of inquiries designated as "official inquiries" to be appointed by a minister. These "official inquiries" would have less coercive powers than royal commissions concerning accepting intercepted information, issuing of warrants for imprisonment of uncooperative witnesses or in relation to entry, search and seizure.[86] However, legal protection to witnesses and inquiry members would be afforded.[87] Such "official inquiries" could be made into royal commissions should circumstances prove that they have inadequate

80 ALRC, *supra* note 1 at 259.

81 New Zealand Law Commission, *A New Inquiries Act*, Report No 102 (2008) at para 5.4.

82 Tasmanian Law Reform Institute (TLRI), *Report on Commissions of Inquiry Act 1995*, Final Report No 2 (August 2000) at 10–14 [TLRI].

83 ALRC, *supra* note 1 at 285–6.

84 TLRI, *supra* note 82 at 10–14.

85 Scott Prasser, "Informal and 'Judicial' Haneef Inquiry a Paper Tiger", *Courier-Mail* (2 May 2008).

86 ALRC, *supra* note 1 at 256.

87 *Ibid* at 96.

powers to complete their investigations successfully. This is a worthwhile reform and one that makes the inquiry instrument more flexible than in the past.

Procedural Fairness

Another possible abuse of citizens' rights includes the lack of procedural fairness by inquisitorial inquiries and the potential loss of reputation for individuals who are mentioned during proceedings. Australian courts have strongly applied procedural fairness principles in relation to inquiries.[88] Parties should be heard, given reasonable notice to respond to allegations and the reputation of a person or organization should be relevant in assessing such cases.

One of the issues in relation to royal commissions and similar inquiries is that the six principles of procedural fairness laid down by Lord Justice Salmon in the United Kingdom[89] have not been formally adopted in the legislation governing these bodies in Australia. The Commonwealth *Royal Commissions Act 1902* does not refer to any of these principles of procedural fairness. Nor, until recently did any other State or Territory inquiry require legislation. However, the Salmon principles are not without their critics overseas[90] or in Australia.[91] The ALRC concluded: "The Salmon Principles provide a useful guidance on the kinds of procedural measures that may improve the fairness of inquiry procedures ... however, the applications of these principles may not be appropriate or practicable in every inquiry."[92]

Consequently, the ALRC did not recommend their inclusion in its proposed new legislation governing public inquiries federally in Australia, suggesting that these matters could be covered in guidelines for any new inquiry. The ALRC did suggest that under its proposed new *Inquiries Act* the inquiries in their reports "should not make any finding that is adverse ... unless the inquiry has taken all reasonable steps to give notice of the proposed adverse findings" to those concerned.[93] Only recently has Tasmania incorporated these principles into its legislation governing royal commissions so there is now statutory guarantee of procedural fairness that reflects the Salmon Principles.[94] This approach reflects the Canadian model under s 13 of the *Inquiries Act*, RSC 1985.

88 *Kioa v West*, (1985) 159 CLR 550, Mason J at 584.

89 Rt Hon Lord Salmon, *Royal Commission on Tribunals of Inquiry* (London: HMSO, 1966) at 17–18.

90 R Scott, Procedures at Inquiries – The Duty to be Fair" (1995) 111 Law Quarterly Review 596.

91 G Lindel, *Tribunals of Inquiry and Royal Commissions* (Sydney: Federation Press, 2003) at 40-55 for discussion.

92 ALRC, *supra* note 1 at 387.

93 *Ibid* at 383.

94 TLRI, *supra* note 82 at 14–15.

Judicial Review: Accountable to Whom and for What?

According to the Australian Administrative Review Council, judicial review is "the function or capacity of courts to provide remedies to people adversely affected by unlawful government action."[95] An emerging issue about public inquiries in general, and inquisitorial royal commissions in particular, is how much judicial review should they be subject to in the future. Previously, royal commissions faced limited external review. They have tended to operate outside the system of responsible government as they are not required to be established by parliament. Nor are they part of the legal system with the normal checks and balances despite their impact on future legal proceedings, prosecutions and court cases.[96] To do so and to expose royal commissions to increased judicial review, would and already is, as several former royal commissioners have argued, to undermine the very reasons why the royal commission instrument was employed in the first place. It would slow down investigations and potentially impose the same restrictions in relation to evidence and processes as the legal system and crime enforcement agencies, which had been unable to deal with the very issue now assigned to a royal commission.[97]

While courts and more especially governments have been reluctant to intervene in inquiry processes that may be seen to curb their powers or hinder their operations[98] such inquiries have gradually been brought under partial judicial review. The *Administrative Decisions (Judicial Review) Act 1977* (ADJR Act) now applies to the administrative decisions of Commonwealth royal commissions on a number of areas, for instance, whether a commission has issued a summons appropriately. A royal commission can also be challenged if it is seen to be acting beyond its terms of reference, breaches the principles of procedural fairness and if a commissioner is perceived to be biased against certain witnesses.[99] This issue of perceived bias was spectacularly seen in Queensland in the first of the royal commissions into the overseas doctors' scandal,[100] the 2005 *Royal Commission into Bundaberg Hospital* chaired by Tony Morris QC. Two senior staff of Bundaberg Hospital lodged an action in the Supreme Court against the Morris Commission on the basis of an "apprehended bias" in their treatment by Morris.[101] As Justice

95 Administrative Review Council, *The Scope of Judicial Review*, Report No 47 (Canberra: Australian Government, 2006) at 1.

96 Ransley, 1994, *supra* note 7 at 22–23.

97 See Royal Commissioner, the Hon Terence Cole (*Royal Commission into the Building and Construction Industry*), comments in ALRC, *supra* note 1 at 358.

98 See *Ross v Costigan (No 2)*, (1982) 64 FLR 55 at 69.

99 ALRC, *supra* note 1 at 356.

100 Several overseas doctors in Queensland public hospitals did not have proper qualifications.

101 *Keating v Morris & Ors,* [2005] QSC 243 [*Keating*]; *Leck v Morris & Ors,* [2005] QSC 243.

Moynihan said, the issue was "not whether the decision maker is in fact biased, but whether a fair minded observer might reasonably apprehend that the decision maker might not bring an impartial or unprejudiced mind to bear on the task."[102] Justice Moynihan was "satisfied that each of the applicants has made out a case of ostensible bias"[103] and that the actions of the Morris Commission "would give rise … to a reasonable apprehension of lack of impartiality on the Commissioner's part in dealing with issues relating to each of the applicants." This judgment highlighted that a royal commission "cannot lose sight of the legal framework" within which they have to operate and that "the process … should be fair and not some kind of kangaroo court."[104] As a consequence the Morris Commission was disbanded and replaced by another royal commission chaired by a former judge and successfully completed its investigations.[105]

In response to these concerns, the ALRC did not believe that future inquiries including royal commissions should have to be formally established by parliament. This would improve accountability at one level, but also introduce a level of rigidity that again would undermine the very purpose of such bodies. However, ALRC concluded that as inquisitorial inquiries "are not subject to the supervision of a government department or a body with oversight powers",[106] suggestions to "fast-track" existing review processes should be rejected.

The other related issue is whether there should be any requirement for reports to be tabled in parliament. At the Commonwealth level no such requirement exists and arrangements vary across the States. Improved reporting to parliament would enhance the accountability of inquiries, if only marginally. The ALRC recommended that reports be tabled by the government within 15 days of receiving the inquiry report.[107]

Review of Court Decisions

Another possible abuse by inquisitorial inquiries has been their appointment by executive government to review court decisions and processes. The most recent example was the 2005 South Australian *Kapunda Road Royal Commission*. Although about a particular road accident it was in effect, a review about police procedures, court arrangements and the operations of the Director of Public Prosecutions. As one commentator said, as a result of this royal commission

102 *Keating v Morris & Ors*, *supra* note 101 at para 37.

103 *Ibid* at para 158.

104 J Ransley, "Fair Play Must Rule", *The Courier-Mail* (5 September 2005); D Hamer, "*Keating vs Morris; Lack vs Morris*: Politics and Procedure in the Dr Death Inquiry" (2006) 24:1 University of Queensland Law Journal 131.

105 Prasser, Queensland, *supra* note 29 at 79–97.

106 ALRC, *supra* note 1 at 360–1.

107 *Ibid* at 162.

the "potential remains for a lasting public perception of the politicisation of the judiciary."[108]

Other inquisitorial inquiries into court decision include the 1959 South Australian *Royal Commission in Regard to Rupert Max Stuart* that reviewed the evidence concerning a convicted murderer.[109] At the Commonwealth level there was the 1986 *Royal Commission into the Chamberlain Convictions.*[110] The 1987 *Royal Commission into Aboriginal Deaths in Custody* was a case-by-case reassessment of 99 Aboriginal deaths in prisons which involved reviewing State Coroners' decisions.

Whether executive appointed inquiries are an appropriate mechanism to review another arm of government is an issue needing further consideration.

Enforcing Inquiry Recommendations

As discussed, an area of great dissatisfaction with public inquiries is non-implementation of their recommendations. Governments are not required by law to respond formally to inquiry reports, although in several jurisdictions there are requirements for government responses to parliamentary committee reports. The ALRC saw no need to change current arrangements.[111]

On implementation of inquiry recommendations the issue is whether governments should be forced by legislation or some other administrative oversight mechanism to implement recommendations. The ALRC was not in favor of any oversight mechanism and concluded that decisions to implement inquiry recommendations "should be a matter for the Australian Government."[112] However, it did suggest that its proposed new legislation should, for reasons of transparency and accountability, ensure government publishes an update on implementation progress of an inquiry's recommendations within 12 months of a report's release.[113] This reform could have implications about a long-term problem, if not an abuse, that has long plagued public inquiries.

---

108 G McCarthy, "Public Outrage, Media Spectacle and the Kapunda Road Royal Commission" (2008) 67:1 Australian Journal of Public Administration 39.

109 R Chamberlain, *The Stuart Affair* (Adelaide: Rigby, 1973).

110 This reviewed the case of Lindy Chamberlain who was convicted of murdering her daughter, but who was later released following the royal commission that found the conviction "unsafe."

111 ALRC, *supra* note 1 at 164.

112 *Ibid* at 169.

113 *Ibid* at 171.

Conclusions

Public inquiries continue to serve many useful functions in Australian democracy. Policy inquiries can bring fresh ideas and outside views to bear on key issues and promote consultation. Inquisitorial inquiries, especially royal commissions, are seen to be more independent and effective than existing institutions in investigating particular events, allegations and complaints. Their open processes, external membership, expertise and, in the case of royal commission and similar type inquiries, real powers of investigation, have successfully exposed major issues of corruption and reviewed underlying problems concerning catastrophic events. Overall, the benefits of public inquiries, especially inquisitorial ones, far outweigh any abuses. Of course, there are problems. The lack of legislation covering a large number of inquiries has limited their effectiveness. The growing powers of inquisitorial inquiries raise legitimate concerns about civil liberties. These issues have been recognized by the ALRC, but its assessment is that these coercive powers need to be retained if the usefulness of the inquiry instrument is to be preserved, albeit with some safeguards. Overall, the ALRC's proposals have sought to retain the virtues of existing laws covering public inquiries, while proposing a new flexible system of legislation that responds to current inadequacies, affords protections and creates certainties. However, four years on, the Commonwealth Government has yet to make a formal response to the ALRC's recommendations.

Appendix 1

LEGISLATION IN AUSTRALIA GOVERNING ROYAL COMMISSIONS AND RELATED INQUIRIES

Commonwealth
Royal Commissions Act 1902

Queensland
Commissions of Inquiry Act 1950

New South Wales
Royal Commissions Act 1923

South Australia
Royal Commissions Act 1917

Tasmania
Commissions of Inquiry Act 1995

Victoria

Royal commissions are appointed under ss 88B and 88C of the *Constitution Act 1975* and ss 14–21C of the *Evidence Act 1958*

Western Australia

Royal Commissions Act 1968

ACT

Royal Commissions Act 1991
Inquiries Act 1991 (ACT)

Northern Territory

Inquiries Act 1945

Other legislation pertaining to public inquiries in Australia

Special Commissions of Inquiry Act 1983 (NSW)
Commission of Inquiry (Children and State Care and Children on APY Lands) Act 2004 (SA)
Public Sector Management Act 1994 (WA)
Commission of Inquiry (Deaths in Custody) Act 1987 (NT)

Appendix 2

STATE PUBLIC INQUIRIES INTO CORRUPTION, IMPROPRIETIES AND MALADMINISTRATION 1960–2011

(Inquiries are listed by State in chronological order with family name of chair and year of appointment in brackets)

NEW SOUTH WALES

Royal Commission into Organised Crime in Clubs in New South Wales (Moffitt: 1973)
Royal Commission into Drug Trafficking (Woodward: 1977)
Royal Commission into New South Wales Prisons (Nagle: 1978)
Royal Commission into New South Wales Police Administration (Lusher: 1979)
Royal Commission into Allegations Against Mr Kevin Humphreys, SM (Street: 1983)
Special Commission of Inquiry into Certain Allegations by the Right Honourable Ian McCahon Sinclair (Cross: 1984)
Special Commission of Inquiry into Certain Allegations by R. Bottom (Cross: 1984)
Special Commission of Inquiry into the New South Wales Early Release Scheme (Cross, then Slattery: 1984)

Special Commission of Inquiry into the Police Investigations of the Death of Donald Bruce Mackay (Nagle: 1986)
Royal Commission into Deep Sleep Therapy (Slattery: 1988)
Royal Commission into Productivity in the Building Industry in New South Wales (Gyles: 1990)
Royal Commission into NSW Police (Wood: 1994)
Special Commission of Inquiry into the Medical Research and Compensation Foundation Established by the James Hardie Group (Jackson: 2004)
Special Commission of Inquiry in Sydney Ferries Corporation (Walker: 2007)
Special Inquiry into Child Protection Services in NSW (Wood: 2008)
Special Commission of Inquiry into Acute Care Services in NSW Public Hospitals (Garling: 2008)
Special Commission of Inquiry in New South Wales Crime Commission (Patten: 2011)

QUEENSLAND

Royal Commission into the National Hotel Allegations (Gibbs: 1963)
Inquiry into the Southport Betting Case (O'Connell: 1975)
Committee of Inquiry into Sexual Offences involving Children and Related Matters (Sturgess: 1984)
Committee of Inquiry into the Enforcement of Criminal Law in Queensland (Lucas: 1976)
Commission of Inquiry into Possible Illegal Activities and Associated Police Misconduct (Fitzgerald: 1987)
Parliamentary Judges' Commission of Inquiry (Gibbs: 1989)
Commission of Inquiry into the Care and Treatment of Patients in the Psychiatric Unit of the Townsville General Hospital between 2 March 1975 and 20 February 1988 (Carter: 1990)
Royal Commission into Bundaberg Hospital (Morris: 2005)
Royal Commission into Queensland Health (Davies: 2005)

SOUTH AUSTRALIA

Special Inquiry into the Police Special Branch Security Records (White: 1977)
Royal Commission into the Dismissal of Commissioner of Police, Harold Hubert Salisbury (Mitchell: 1978)
Royal Commission into the State Bank of South Australia and the State Bank Group of Companies (Jacobs: 1991)
Inquiry Concerning the Minister of Tourism (Worthington: 1992)
Inquiry concerning Hon Dale Baker MP (Anderson: 1997)
Kapunda Road Royal Commission (James: 2004)

TASMANIA

Royal Commission into the Edmund Rouse Bribery Affair (Carter: 1991)
Commission of inquiry into the Death of Joseph Gilewicz (Mahoney: 2000)

VICTORIA

Board of Inquiry into Allegations of Corruption in the Police Force in connection with Alleged Abortion Practices in the State of Victoria (Kaye: 1970)

Board of Inquiry into the Purchase of Land in Victoria by Alan Humphrey Croxford (Harris: 1972)

Board of Inquiry into Allegations against Members of the Victorian Police Force (Beach: 1975)

Board of Inquiry into Certain Land Purchases by the Housing Commission and Questions Arising Therefrom (Gowans: 1977)

Royal Commission into Certain Housing Commission Land Purchases and Other Matters (Frost: 1979)

Board of Inquiry Relating to Certain Matters within the City of Richmond (Nicholson: 1981)

Inquiry into the Victorian Economic Development Corporation (Ryan: 1988)

Royal Commission into the Tricontinental Group (Woodward: 1990)

Royal Commission into the Metropolitan Ambulance Service (Lasry: 2000)

WESTERN AUSTRALIA

Report of Inspector on a Special Investigation into Rothwells Ltd (McCusker: 1989)

Royal Commission into Commercial Activities of Government and Other Matters, Western Australia (Kennedy: 1991)

Royal Commission into Use of Executive Power (Easton Petition issue) (Marks: 1995)

Royal Commission into the City of Wanneroo (Davis: 1996)

Royal Commission into whether there has been any corrupt or criminal conduct by Western Australian Police Officers (Kennedy: 2002)

Appendix 3

COMMONWEALTH PUBLIC INQUIRIES INTO CORRUPTION, IMPROPRIETIES AND MALADMINISTRATION 1960–2011

(Inquiries are listed in chronological order with family name of chair and year of appointment in brackets)

1960–1969

Royal Commission on Alleged Improper Practices and Improper Refusal to Cooperate with the Victoria Police Force on the part of Persons Employed in the Postmaster-General's Department in Victoria in relation to Illegal Gambling (Taylor: 1962)

1970–1979

Royal Commission into Alleged Payments to Australian Maritime Unions (Sweeney: 1974)

Royal Commission of Inquiry into Certain Matters relating to Electoral Redistribution of Queensland in 1977 (McGregor: 1978)

1980–1989

Royal Commission into the Activities of the Federated Ship Painters' and Dockers' Union (Costigan: 1980)*

Royal Commission of Inquiry into Drug Trafficking (Stewart: 1981)*

Royal Commission into the Activities of the Australian Building Construction Employees and Builders Labourers Federation (Winneke: 1981)

Royal Commission into the Australian Meat Industry (Woodward: 1981)

Royal Commission of Inquiry into the Activities of the Nugan Hand Group (Stewart: 1983)

Inquiry into Circumstances Surrounding the Customs Declaration by the Hon M.J. Young at Adelaide 5 July 1984 (Black: 1984)

Inquiry into Allegations of SP Gambling Against Telecom (Vincent: 1984)

Inquiry into the Financial and Administrative Arrangements of Grants made Under the Community Housing Expansion Program (O'Donovan: 1985)

Royal Commission of Inquiry into Alleged Telephone Interceptions (Stewart: 1985)

Special Parliamentary Commission of Inquiry into the Alleged Conduct of the Hon Mr Justice Murphy (Blackburn: 1986)

Review of Alleged Entry of Suspected War Criminals into Australia (Menzies: 1986)

Review of Tender Procedures for Coastwatch Contracts (Menzies: 1987)

Royal Commission into Aboriginal Deaths in Custody (Muirhead and then Johnson: 1987)*

Inquiry into Allegations as to the Administration of Aboriginal Affairs (Menzies: 1988)

*Supported by State governments

1990–1999

Independent Review of the Civil Aviation Authority's Tender Evaluation Process for the Australian Advanced Air Traffic System (McPhee: 1992)

Inquiry into Circumstances of Leo McLeay's Compensation (Street: 1993)

Independent Inquiry into the Circumstances surrounding the Non-Payment of a Deposit for Satellite Pay TV Licences and related matters (Pearce: 1993)

Commission of Inquiry into Relations between the CCA and Seaview Air (Staunton: 1994)

Royal Commission of Inquiry into the Leasing by the Commonwealth of Accommodation in Centenary House (Morling: 1994)

Inquiry into the Conduct of the Hon Alan Griffiths MP (Codd: 1995)

Independent Inquiry into Allegations of Corruption in the Australian Federal Police (Harrison: 1996)
Inquiry into the Manner in which DFAT (Department of Foreign Affairs and Trade) has Dealt with Allegations of Paedophile Activities (Hunt then O'Neill: 1996)

2000–2011
Royal Commission of Inquiry into the Building and Construction Industry (Cole 2001)
Royal Commission of Inquiry into HIH (Owen: 2001)
Inquiry into Centenary House Lease (Hunt: 2004)
Commission of Inquiry into Possible Breaches of Australian Law in relation to the UN Oil-for-Food Programme (Cole: 2005)
Inquiry into the Circumstances of the Immigration Detention of Cornelia Rau (Palmer: 2005)
Inquiry into Dr Mohamed Haneef (Clarke: 2008)

Appendix 4

COMMONWEALTH AND STATE PUBLIC INQUIRIES INTO CATASTROPHIC EVENTS 1960–2011

(Inquiries are listed by jurisdiction in chronological order with year of appointment in brackets)

COMMONWEALTH
Royal Commission on the Loss of HMAS *Voyager* (1964)
Royal Commission on the Statements made by Lieutenant-Commander Cabban and Matters Incidental to the HMAS Voyager Royal Commission (1967)

STATES
New South Wales
Special Commission of Inquiry into the Glenbrook Rail Disaster (2000)
Special Commission into the Waterfall Incident (2003)

Queensland
Commission of Inquiry into the 2010/11 Floods (2011)

Victoria
Royal Commission into the Failure at Kings Bridge (1962)
Royal Commission into the Failure of West Gate Bridge (1970)
Royal Commission into the Esso Longford Gas Plant Incident (1998)
Royal Commission into Victorian Bushfires (2009)

Chapter 14

Home Truths about Truth Commission Processes: How Victim-Centred Truth and Perpetrator-Focused Adversarial Processes Mutually Challenge Assumptions of Justice and Truth

Jula Hughes*

Introduction

Truth is back. The notion of a single, knowable and objective truth had taken a significant poststructuralist vacation in the second half of the twentieth century. During this time, speaking about the truth had become a quaint exercise in defying the *zeitgeist*.[1] Recently, truth is once again much debated, both in broader public discourse and, more narrowly, in legal *fora*. After three vignettes that illustrate the multi-faceted reemergence of a discourse about truth, this chapter explores how current court procedures are subject to three distinct but related challenges to discovering truth. In addressing at least some of these challenges, court reformers might wish to consider how the Canadian Truth and Reconciliation Commission on Indian Residential Schools has devised processes that are different from both adversarial and inquisitorial proceedings in Canadian and foreign courts and administrative tribunals.

---

* Thank you to the editors of this volume, Laverne Jacobs and Sasha Baglay, for their helpful editorial comments on earlier drafts of this chapter, discussant Ian Greene for his insightful comments on the original presentation, my research assistant James Strickland for able, thorough and timely research assistance and to my colleagues Myron Gochnauer and Vanessa MacDonnell for their spirited critique and generous suggestions for improvements. I am also grateful to the Endowment of the Law Foundation of New Brunswick for enabling my attendance at the conference "The Nature of Inquisitorial Processes in Administrative Regimes: Global Perspectives" in Windsor, Ontario in 2011.

1 For a very useful discussion of the implications of the poststructuralist challenge to the assumption of objective truth in legal epistemology, see Jill Anne Farmer, "A Poststructuralist Analysis of the Legal Research Process" (1993) 85 Law Libr J 391 at 392.

The chapter explores three themes. One, the critical and postmodern philosophical preoccupation with the constructed nature of truth as a response to the trauma of the Holocaust: here, I am interested in the historical context of the emergence of a critical discourse on truth. It appears to me not accidental that objective truth becomes problematic in European societies in the aftermath of World War II. The division of entire societies into perpetrators, bystanders and victims may have acted to sensitize us to the power dimensions of truth claims.

Two, the ways and means by which courts pursue truth: adversarial and, to a lesser extent, inquisitorial approaches to the truth-seeking function of the courts and the ways in which the truth emerging from adversarial proceedings may be suited for some purposes like allocating liability, but fall short where the truth sought is for broader societal purposes: under this theme, I am exploring two related ideas. The first is that our rules of evidence and trial procedures aim at a fact-finding process that constructs truth as the absence of things that are untrue rather than attempting to capture the richness of augmenting, mutually informing and mutually challenging narratives. The second idea is that our courts are unsafe for many witnesses which results in the loss of their truths from our fact-finding processes. This in turn negatively affects the ability of legal processes to produce truths that have external credibility, particularly for marginalized communities.

Three, I am exploring how the Canadian Truth and Reconciliation Commission (TRC) draws on a victim-centred paradigm to pursue a form of truth-seeking that is designed to facilitate participation in its process with a view to contributing to the broader goal of reconciliation between indigenous and settler society Canadians. I am querying whether courts can take inspiration from some of the process decisions made by the Commission despite the difference in purpose.

Ultimately, I conclude that the procedural innovations of the TRC can assist us in addressing some of the systemic difficulties facing both adversarial and inquisitorial proceedings. The TRC and courts share some fundamental challenges that makes cross-pollination of procedural ideas promising while recognizing that the differences in purpose will require adjustments. Both the TRC and the courts require witnesses to come forward and tell their stories; and while courts have considerable coercive powers at their disposal, voluntary participation is preferable and necessary for courts as well. Both the TRC and the courts frequently need to hear from witnesses who bring a background of marginalization to the hearing. These witnesses pose particular problems to the fact-finding enterprise as they may face barriers to participation. There are further communalities inherent in the reception of witness testimony. The testimony must not only be elicited, it must be heard, contextualized, evaluated and translated into factual findings. This is the case whether the purpose is to generate a historical (for the TRC) or a judicial record. Again, both court and TRC processes need to perform these functions for marginalized witnesses who often face greater barriers when mainstream credibility criteria are being applied without adjustment.[2] Beyond the immediate needs of the process, both the TRC and the courts need institutional legitimacy and credibility with participants and the broader community. All of these challenges relate to the truth-seeking function of the TRC and the courts. Considering how the TRC tackles its process can assist us in devising and revising court processes to be more inclusive, to remove participatory barriers and to come to more reliable, legitimate factual determinations.

Three Vignettes about the Renewed Interest in Truth

Vignette 1: Aboriginal author and Massey lecturer of "The Truth About Stories: A Native Narrative",[3] Thomas King, begins a guest lecture by proposing that it does not matter whether a story is true. The statement riffs off the title of his book, "The Truth About Stories." Applying a poststructuralist lens, one would accept this proposition without hesitation. Stories are powerful in themselves. Being false does not deprive them of their power. History is full of false but powerful stories. King's audience reacts strongly and negatively to the proposition, however: Surely, it matters whether the stories we tell or do not tell about aboriginal people in this country are true. Surely, it matters that lies abound. Surely, it matters that the truth is being silenced. We could understand the audience reaction as an expression of a renewed positivism, but it seems to me that we would be selling the audience short. It is precisely because we have become sensitized to the power relationships in the narrative construction of truth that the audience rejects the apparent moral relativism of King's statement. And yet, the audience is likely underestimating King. King's story "You're not the Indian I had in mind", which is part of the "The Truth about Stories" lecture cycle, is a counterpoint to the narrative stereotypes of indigeneity in North America. He notes:

> We see race. Never mind that race is a construction and an illusion. Never mind that it does not exist in either biology or theology, though both have, from time to time, been enlisted in the cause of racism. Never mind that we can't hear it or smell it or taste it or feel it. The important thing is that we believe we can see it.[4]

---

2 The difficulties inherent in the judicial reception of evidence by vulnerable and marginalized witnesses are well documented. See Janine Benedet & Isabel Grant, "Hearing the Sexual Assault Complaints of Women with Mental Disabilities: Evidentiary and Procedural Issues" (2007) 52 McGill LJ 515; John Borrows, "Listening for a Change: The Courts and Oral Tradition" (2001) 39 Osgoode Hall LJ 1; Nicholas Bala et al, "Judicial Assessment of the Credibility of Child Witnesses" (2005) 42 Alta L Rev 995.

3 Thomas King, "Quick and Slick: Why Narrative Will Not Save the World" (John McKendy Memorial Lecture in Narrative delivered at St. Thomas University, October 21, 2009) [unpublished]. See also Thomas King, *The Truth about Stories. A Native Narrative* (Toronto: House of Anansi Press, 2003) [King, 2003].

4 King, 2003, *ibid* at 44.

The truth about stories for King, then, is that they create realities as much as they reflect them. This is instructive for the work of the TRC and the courts. In the process of hearing evidence and finding facts, both are not only engaged in seeking the truth, they are also engaged in constructing new realities through the narratives of reports and decisions.

Vignette 2: The Canadian Association of University Teachers revises its policy statement on academic freedom. The policy under review stated that one of the purposes of universities was to serve the common good of society through the search for truth. The revision suggests deleting "seeking the truth" as one of the primary objects of academic work. This suggestion is hotly debated. Social scientists on the committee charged with the review scorn the idea that we still think about "the truth" as a monolith, particularly one that could be found. Others are not willing to give up on seeking the truth as an academic purpose and are more prepared to allow for a small "t" construction of truth that may or may not commit to monolithic, external or objective conceptualizations. Ultimately, the Council of CAUT accepts an amended version of the policy in which "knowledge" takes the place of "truth."

The advantage of characterizing the truth as a "knowledge" is that it reminds us of the complex and dialectic nature of truth-seeking. The object of the pursuit is neither completely divorced from external realities (there is such a thing as a lie or an untruth), nor is it independent of the fact-finder who shapes the truth as found through evaluation, contextualization and narration. Again, these are useful reminders for the TRC and for courts. Getting it wrong is a hazard any fact-finder will be exposed to. What is more troublesome is that there are many ways of getting the facts right that nevertheless fall short of the task of constructing a legitimate and credible narrative.

Vignette 3: Faced with a class action lawsuit, the federal government agrees to establish a Truth and Reconciliation Commission on Indian Residential Schools. The task of seeking the truth about the experience of aboriginal children, families and communities is taken out of the court system and transferred into a body specifically created for this purpose. There is undeniable symbolic value in creating a truth commission. Beyond the symbolism, though, there seems to be an acknowledgment implicit in the settlement that our courts may not be suited to finding a truth that would build a foundation for reconciliation between highly conflicted groups: colonial settlers and first peoples. This resonates with some of the literature promoting alternative dispute resolution. There is something about the way we seek truth in courts that does not promote or sustain ongoing relationships. Again, there are important lessons here for the TRC and the courts. Seeking truth is not an abstract process. We had already seen that truth is contextual. It appears that one important context is the purpose for which the truth is sought. It might be tempting to construct the courts' purposes for truth-seeking narrowly: to determine rights or to attribute liability, for example. However, courts also rely on broader purposes related to justice or the rule of law for their institutional legitimacy. We need to keep these broader purposes in mind when we think about court procedure.

Why Knowing the Truth is Difficult – and Necessary

The history of ideas of the twentieth century has a large chapter on truth. In the first half of the century, the ancient binaries of φύσις (physis, the nature of a being) and εἶδος (eidos, that which appears) and the queries about their respective ontological status,[5] the enlightenment's grand debate of empiricism and rationalism resonated as much in Heidegger's ontology as in Wittgenstein's Tractatus.[6] Fundamental epistemological questions of what we can know and how we know it were being pursued with rigour not only in philosophy, but also in physics. The emergence of both critical and post-modern schools in the second half of the 20th century challenged our assumptions about the promise of rational and enlightened systems of adjudication. Having looked into the abyss of the Holocaust and the horrors of World War II, it became difficult to believe in the perfectible universe of the enlightenment[7] and, even more discouragingly, in the possibility of adequate responses to mass murder and global warfare.[8] Adorno's famous dictum about the impossibility of writing poetry after Auschwitz was but the tip of the iceberg in a new reality of muteness in the face of mass human rights violations and genocide. Language, a potential mediator and possible vanishing point of the binary poles of physis and eidos, became the primary philosophical battleground of the 1980s, and it was language's hidden meanings, subtexts and undercurrents that came to preoccupy interpretive theory. By century's end, many had come to the conclusion that truth was unknowable and, in any event, unspeakable.

The last decade of the 20th century and the new millennium brought about the considerable mainstreaming of these ideas. We know that deconstruction has lost its radical edge because we can now order deconstructed Caesar salad and students write essays in which "deconstruct" has come to take the place of "analyze." The return of realism in literature and art similarly suggests that we have moved on from the epistemological crisis that dominated much of the philosophical and social science discourse in the second half of the 20th century. And yet, the questions that were raised about the limits of knowledge and expression of truth, significantly it seems to me, in Germany and France post-Holocaust, are resurfacing in the Canadian context post-residential schools.

5 Aristotle, *Metaphysics*, 1032a12–1032a27.

6 Martin Heidegger, *Being and Time*, translated by Joan Stambaugh (Albany: State University of New York Press, 1996); Ludwig Wittgenstein, *Tractatus Logico-Philosophicus*, translated by Pears & McGuinness (London and New York: Routledge, 2002).

7 Max Horkheimer & Theodor W Adorno, *Dialectics of the Enlightenment: Philosophical Fragments*, Gunzelin Schmid Noerr, ed, translated by Edmund Jephcott (Stanford: Standford University Press, 2002).

8 Martha Minow, *Breaking the Cycles of Hatred: Memory, Law, and Repair* (Princeton: Princeton University Press, 2002).

Let me revisit briefly, and with admitted oversimplification, the difficulties related to the knowability of the past.

There seem to be at least three possible obstacles to knowing the truth[9] about a historical event:

- One, there may be no objective reality to be known or, at the very least, there is no decision-maker who could decide when it has become known.
- Two, if we see objective reality as an agglutination or processing of subjective truths, too many perspectives are lost, silenced or otherwise inaccessible.
- And finally, at least some important aspects of a given truth are impossible to communicate – they may not be spoken or cannot be heard.

How do these various ways of unsettling a positivist understanding of truth play out in legal processes?

Challenges to the Truth as Object of Legal Process

The first, most fundamental objection – that there may be "no there there" – is in some sense no ultimate bar to adjudication because notwithstanding ontological uncertainties, practical reason must have her pound of flesh in law. Its corollary, however – that the truth requires an arbiter – is of abiding interest to the law. Legal processes have built-in arbiters of facts, and as long the decisions of judges and juries are acceptable to the relevant constituencies, the truth as found is secure. Judgments in this sense are true because the arbiter of truth has legitimacy and is trusted by the community. Positivists might argue that a determination that is accepted would still fall short of actual truth. However, while we might reserve some doubt about all *ex post facto* determinations of historical events on a principled basis, it is impossible to distinguish between the accepted truth and the real truth at any given time. As argued by Thomas King, it does not matter whether the story is true as long as it is believed.

We can therefore understand the critical stance as an expression of doubt about the legitimacy of the decision-maker who finds truth. Institutionally, a legal fact-finding is ultimately true because the judge determined it to be so. It should be noted that does not release the judge from his or her obligation to seek the truth. *Ex ante* legitimacy may not be sufficiently weighty. Rather, legitimacy accrues in part

9 This chapter is concerned with what some writers have described as the forensic or factual aspect of truth, i.e. the question of what happened and how we find out, not about interpretive or normative truth (inquiry into the meaning of events) in the broadest sense. For a useful discussion of different conceptions of truth, see Joanna Quinn, *The Politics of Acknowledgment: Truth commissions in Uganda and Haiti* (Vancouver: UBC Press, 2010) at 45–47.

because of a track record of reliable findings and is threatened by demonstrations of error. This relationship between sound fact-finding and legitimacy is important for truth commissions and courts alike.

It is noteworthy that many societies are now less willing to simply accept the say-so of their appointed decision-makers. Indeed, the legitimacy and reputation of justice institutions has long been declining along with the reputation of other governmental bodies.[10] Courts are aware of this decline and have arguably become more preoccupied with the reputation of the justice system and its outcomes in response to this ongoing deterioration. The empirical base for gauging how specific reforms affect legitimacy and reputation of justice institutions is only now slowly evolving. For example, the European Social Survey, in its fifth round, is collecting data on legitimacy and trust of police and the criminal justice system for various national populations based on a methodology developed by Jackson et al.[11]

Canadian courts are very alert to this problem. For example, the recent recasting by the Supreme Court of Canada of the test for admissibility of evidence under s. 24(2) of the *Charter* in *R v Grant* in terms of the long-term interest of the reputation of the administration of justice can be understood as a rhetorical answer to a threat of loss of legitimacy.[12]

The legitimacy of courts is negatively affected by many factors entirely outside of the control of the courts such as trust in governmental institutions and community support for police. That said, there are also concerns that arise directly from the fact-finding process itself.[13] Chief among these latter concerns is the

10 Jürgen Habermas, *Legitimation Crisis* (Boston: Beacon Press, 1975); David Beetham, *The Legitimation of Power* (London: Macmillan, 1991).

11 Jonathan Jackson et al, "Developing European Indicators of Trust in Justice" (2011) 8:4 European Journal of Criminology 267 [Jackson et al].

12 *Canadian Charter of Rights and Freedoms*, Part I of the *Constitution Act, 1982*, being Schedule B of the *Canada Act*, 1982 (UK) *R v Grant*, 2009 SCC 32, [2009] 2 SCR 353 [*Grant*]. It is likely significant that the decision is anchored in the constitutional text as opposed to the prior jurisprudence since the dominant academic threat to the legitimacy of constitutional judicial review comes from quarters associated with originalist leanings. Reliance on the constitutional text as an extra-judicial guarantor of legitimacy is not as common in the constitutional jurisprudence of the Canadian Supreme Court as in its American counterpart, but it surfaces particularly in places where some members of the Court appear to perceive the Court's legitimacy to be in issue. The most curious examples of this kind of recourse arise in the area of judicial independence where the textual basis is thin, but reliance is placed on the preambular text to support guarantors of independence. See *The Queen v Beauregard*, [1986] 2 SCR 56 at para 29.

13 Tom R Tyler, "Psychology and Institutional Design" (2008) 4:3 Review of Law and Economics 801 [Tyler]; Wojciech Sadurski, *Equality and Legitimacy* (Oxford: Oxford University Press 2008).

growing appreciation that courts are getting their fact-finding wrong by convicting the factually innocent.[14]

The Legitimacy Challenge arising from Wrongful Convictions

It is very arguable that the repute of the administration of justice has been very negatively affected by the slate of confirmed wrongful convictions in Canada, particularly in cases where the accused is found to have been wrongfully convicted after a fair trial and full appellate review.[15] For example, David Milgaard was wrongfully convicted for the murder of Gail Miller and served 22 years in prison before being released in 1992. His wrongful conviction was the subject of a reference to the Supreme Court of Canada[16] and, after his DNA exoneration, of a provincial judicial inquiry.[17] The Supreme Court in *Milgaard* opened its remarks by stating:

> It is appropriate to begin by stating that in our view David Milgaard had the benefit of a fair trial in January 1970 … Milgaard was represented by able and experienced counsel. No error in law or procedure has been established. At the conclusion of the trial, there was ample evidence upon which the jury, which had been properly instructed, could return a verdict of guilty.[18]

The word "truth" does not appear once in the reasons, nor is there a reference to "facts" or "findings" in relation to Mr. Milgaard. Tellingly, the only reference to a finding relates to a possible prosecution of the new suspect, Mr. Fisher.

As far as the accused is concerned, it appears, the truth is not a legally cognizable value. The accused has no right to the truth, merely a right to a fair trial. Conversely, the Crown seems to have a right to the truth at least to the extent

---

14 The obverse problem of acquitting the factually guilty is typically not blamed on faulty fact-finding, but is instead attributed to admissibility rules that result in incomplete factual records.

15 The threat to legitimacy seems more attenuated where the trial was procedurally flawed or where a subsequent inquiry can point to systemic or specific problems in the investigation or prosecution of the wrongfully convicted. It is easier to accept that systemic racism would have caused Donald Marshall and William Mullins-Johnson to be wrongfully convicted or that flawed expert evidence, tunnel vision, police and Crown misconduct would have contributed to the wrongful convictions of Guy Paul Morin Robert Baltovich, James Driskell, Gregory Parsons, Thomas Sophonow, Steven Truscott and Erin Walsh than to accept that fair trials can lead to wrongful convictions.

16 *Reference re Milgaard (Can),* [1992] 1 SCR 866 [*Reference re Milgaard*].

17 Canada, Government of Saskatchewan, Report of the Commission of Inquiry into the Wrongful Conviction of David Milgaard (September 2008) (The Honorable Mr Justice Edward P MacCallum, Commissioner).

18 *Reference re Milgaard, supra* note 16 at 870.

that the assertion of that right does not deprive the accused of her right to a fair trial. This balancing of truth and fairness interests is cold comfort to the person who is wrongfully convicted.

Courts have long been concerned with the relationship between procedural justice and truth. In adversarial systems, the relationship is often described as a trade-off between the interests of the accused in procedural justice and the interests of the Crown, the court and society at large in the discovery of the truth. For example, in *Levogiannis*, the Supreme Court of Canada describes the attainment of truth as the chief object of legal proceedings and identifies a trend in the rules of evidence "to remove barriers to the truth-seeking process."[19] At the same time, the Court acknowledges that there is an obligation to provide "the accused with the opportunity to make full defence."[20]

Conceptualizing the relationship between truth and fairness as a trade-off appears to be a necessary consequence of the adversarial nature of the criminal trial. Since the ability of the Crown to obtain a conviction is contingent on the court accepting the truth of the allegation, and the right to a fair trial is allocated to the defence, the criminal trial emerges as a contest between truth and fairness.

The highly problematic nature of this conceptualization is apparent in wrongful conviction cases. Despite the fair trial rhetoric, the defence has a direct interest in the truth, at least in those cases where the accused is factually innocent. This defence interest in the truth is obliterated, however, in the characterization of the accused's interest in having a fair trial only. The Supreme Court of Canada has on occasion diverged from this bifurcation of interests, albeit only in ways that further favour the prosecution. For example, Lebel J in dissent in *Graveline* declared:

> The accused has a right to a fair trial in accordance with the substantive and procedural rules of criminal law and the principles of the Constitution. The Crown, which represents the state and the public interest in the proper administration of the criminal law, has the same right.[21]

This is consistent with the view, expressed forcefully in *Grant*,[22] that the public has a constitutionally cognizable interest in the adjudication on the merits, as well as with the view that the role of the Crown is ultimately adversarial as explained in *Cook*:

> Nevertheless, while it is without question that the Crown performs a special function in ensuring that justice is served and cannot adopt a purely adversarial role towards the defence ... it is well recognized that the adversarial process

19 *R v Levogiannis*, [1993] 4 SCR 475 at para 23.

20 *Ibid* at para 20.

21 *R v Graveline*, 2006 SCC 16, [2006] 1 SCR 609 at para 31. There is no discussion as to the source of the Crown's right to a fair trial.

22 *Grant, supra* note 12.

> is an important part of our judicial system and an accepted tool in our search for the truth … Nor should it be assumed that the Crown cannot act as a strong advocate within this adversarial process. In that regard, it is both permissible and desirable that it vigorously pursue a legitimate result to the best of its ability. Indeed, this is a critical element of this country's criminal law mechanism … In this sense, within the boundaries outlined above, the Crown must be allowed to perform the function with which it has been entrusted; discretion in pursuing justice remains an important part of that function.[23]

It would be preferable in my view to rethink the relationship between truth and fairness (or procedural justice) not as a trade-off, but as mutually informing goals of the justice system, both intimately linked to the reputation of the administration of justice. An important condition for accomplishing this re-conceptualization appears to me to lie in reallocating the interests in truth and fairness.

As long as each party in the adversarial proceeding is associated with one of the two values, it is difficult to conceive of the relationship as anything other than a contest. Instead, we would do well to recognize that both the prosecution and the defence have an interest in the truth and similarly, that the trial must be fair to the parties to the proceeding. One might go further and argue that courts must also take account of the fairness and truth interests of non-parties (such as complainants) and that it likely must be seen to be fair to outsiders to sustain the normative legitimacy of the adjudication process. Legitimacy scholars building on the work of Hardin[24] and Hinsch[25] have argued for a subjective–objective analytical framework of trust and legitimacy. They have emphasized the need for both subjective moral alignment between individual values and the values expressed by the justice system, and objective or normative legitimacy in terms of efficiency, accountability or legality.[26]

We might wish to amplify the factors contributing to normative legitimacy to include independence and impartiality among others, but the basic notion that the truth as found by courts is as much a function of trust and legitimacy of the system as it is a matter of factual accuracy is noteworthy. Conversely, we must take account of the fact that erroneous factual determinations are not merely detrimental to immediate participants, but also undermine the legitimacy of the system.

---

23 *R v Cook*, [1997] 1 SCR 1113 at para 21.

24 Russell Hardin, *Trust and Trustworthiness* (New York: Russell Sage 2002).

25 Wilfried Hinsch, "Legitimacy and Justice" in Jörg Kühnelt, ed, *Political Legitimation without Morality?* (London: Springer 2008).

26 Jackson et al, *supra* note 11. This approach to a democratic legitimacy of justice institutions may be contrasted with what Douglas Hay so ably described in "Property, Authority and the Criminal Law" in Douglas Hay et al, eds, *Albion's Fatal Tree: Crime and Society in Eighteenth Century England* (London: A Lane, 1975) 17 at 26–31, where the legitimacy of the courts rides on the coattails of royal authority expressed in language, architecture and court room paraphernalia.

To address the first challenge to determining truth in legal processes then, courts have to find ways to improve their track record of avoiding erroneous factual determinations and at the same time ensure that their processes reflect societal values that support court legitimacy. Adversarial systems of adjudication may be particularly vulnerable to erroneous fact-findings that arise from a trade-off conceptualization of trial fairness and factually correct outcomes. Rethinking the relationship between trial fairness and truth in terms of systemic normative legitimacy may assist in making visible the shared interests of all participants in truth and fairness.

Missing Voices: Challenges arising from Exclusionary Processes

As noted, a second challenge to the discovery of truth lies in the necessary incompleteness of perspectives. This is the case whether the purpose of the truth-seeking process is legal or historical. No retrospective will ever capture all possible perspectives on a past event. Additionally, a process that loses voices in a biased or discriminatory way will be more vulnerable to distorted truth findings. There is a dual concern here: one, that we fail to capture a sufficient number of perspectives and two, that our processes are irreparably biased towards the perspectives of those privileged few who are able to show up and make themselves heard.

On the broader issue of failing to capture a sufficiency of voices, we need to consider the role of evidence law. In the adversarial system, rules of evidence are driven by concerns about lay adjudication. In order for our juries to produce acceptable outcomes, we streamline what evidence may be received. Almost without exception, evidentiary rules govern admissibility rather than weight. The rules are about how to keep out potentially relevant evidence because we are concerned about evidence that is more prejudicial than probative or too inherently unreliable. The net result of the application of these rules is that truth obtains through a process of subtraction. Of the possible universe of truths, only those parts that pass the filters of relevance, materiality and admissibility become potential components of the constructed truth.

At the fact-finding stage, this is further refined to silence all truths that fail to meet the applicable standard of proof. These may of course appropriately include statements that are found to be not credible, but very commonly also include statements where the court is left in doubt about contradictory evidence (in criminal cases) or where the court favours, however slightly, the alternate version.

The truth as constructed in adversarial justice is what is left over after we remove from the universe of possible truths all those things that the parties choose not to adduce, all things that are unavailable, all things that are rendered inadmissible at the objection of a party, all things that are found to be unpersuasive, all things that are found to be untrue and all things that, though potentially true, are fundamentally unfair. What remains may appropriately be described as "nothing but the truth", but not as "the whole truth."

By contrast, inquisitorial systems (not necessarily as imagined by the Supreme Court of Canada, but actual up-and-running inquisitorial systems like those of France and Germany) impose an obligation on the judge to ensure that the full case is before the court.[27] Despite this, a highly developed form of case management means that the full case is often no less contained than that of an adversarial trial.

The impact of putting the judge in charge of ensuring that the full case is before the court is acutely felt on appeal or judicial review as the failure in this regard constitutes a reviewable error.[28]

On the related second concern, we need to consider the potential exclusionary effects of court processes that do not meet the needs of vulnerable or marginalized witnesses. For many potential participants, our court processes are neither accessible nor safe. The threat of losing the evidence of complainants has driven the development of some procedural innovation in this regard. For instance, sexual assault complainants may be shielded from cross-examination by a self-represented accused[29] and child witnesses may testify from behind a screen.[30] These innovations may be subject to constitutional challenges on the basis that they interfere with the fairness rights of the accused. In upholding some of these innovations, the Supreme Court of Canada has focused on constructing these innovations as minimal changes to the routine adversarial trial.

For example, the Court in *Levogiannis* emphasizes the similarity of the proceedings in which a child is giving testimony behind a one-way screen with those of the usual adversarial trial:

> The screen does not obstruct the view of the complainant by the accused, his counsel, the Crown or the judge. All are present in court. The evidence is given and the trial is conducted in the usual manner, including cross-examination.[31]

---

27 See the discussion of inquisitorial processes by Laverne Jacobs in this volume.

28 Section 244 of the German procedural code in criminal matters (*Strafprozess-ordnung*) requires the court to gather all evidence necessary for ascertaining the truth.

29 *Criminal Code*, RSC 1985, c C-46, s 486.3.

30 *Ibid*, s 486.2. A further significant, but underutilized innovation is found in s 6 of the *Canada Evidence Act* which, since 1998 has enabled the court to admit evidence of witnesses with disabilities by alternate means as long as the evidence so elicited is intelligible. Subsection 1 provides: "If a witness has difficulty communicating by reason of a physical disability, the court may order that the witness be permitted to give evidence by any means that enables the evidence to be intelligible." Subsection 2 provides for analogous powers for witnesses with mental disabilities. In some ways, the exception more aptly describes the limits of our system than the general rules, most pertinently subs 16(4) which provides that "A person (...) who neither understands the nature of an oath or a solemn affirmation nor is able to communicate the evidence shall not testify." The locus of the disability is clearly identified as resting with the witness and the focus is on the evidence, not the person's right of participation.

31 *Levogiannis*, *supra* note 19 at para 18.

After a lengthy exposé on the difficulty children face when testifying, particularly about issues of sexual abuse, not a single line in the judgment asks whether the child is comfortable in this minimally altered setting. The child is not there to have an opportunity to be heard. Instead, the alteration is cast as contributing to the truth-seeking function of the court.[32] The alteration is thus focused on enhancing the court, not on improving the experience of the witness beyond what is minimally necessary to extract her evidence.

This rather stingy approach is driven by the litigation context in which defence counsel is challenging the constitutionality of the alteration as potentially interfering with his right to make full answer and defence. One could imagine a different approach in a context that looks at the issue of child participation through an equality lens, i.e. one that challenges the norms established for child testimony on behalf of the child. Changes of this kind are difficult to imagine in a system in which trial fairness is equated with adversarial process.

In inquisitorial systems, one of the interesting consequences of the judicial obligation to obtain the whole truth is that courts have had to put more effort into ensuring that vulnerable witnesses can be heard. While much of the North American literature on child victims of sexual abuse is preoccupied with keeping out false memory, unreliability and threshold admissibility,[33] the German courts and attendant academic literature is typically focused on enabling testimony and appropriate credibility evaluation.[34]

For example, in a criminal proceeding against the father of a perpetrator of a horrific school shooting for negligent homicide (failure to store weapon appropriately), a German court ordered the trial moved to juvenile court because the highly traumatized survivors required the supports and experience of a judicial process designed for youth.[35] Similarly, in compensation and social benefits

32 See also the chapter by Mary Liston in this volume which discusses the historical trajectory of children's representation and participation in the specific context of state institutions designed for child welfare.

33 For an excellent review of the history of the treatment of child witnesses and the continuing difficulties, see Nicholas Bala et al, "A Legal and Psychological Critique of the Present Approach to the Assessment of the Competence of Child Witnesses" (2000) 38 Osgoode Hall LJ 409. See also Dianne Cakoni, "Les défis diagnostiques posés par l'évaluation clinique des allégations de sévices sexuels concernant des enfants" (1996) 37:3 Canadian Psychology/Psychologie Canadienne 145.

34 See *supra* note 28.

35 "Winnenden Prozess" (24 January 2010), online: http://www.focus.de/panorama/welt/winnenden/winnenden-prozess-trauma-erschwert-aussage-der-zeugen_aid_473726.html. This transfer is authorized by § 26 of the *Gerichtsverfassungsgesetz* (GVG) which provides: "(1) *Für Straftaten Erwachsener, durch die ein Kind oder ein Jugendlicher verletzt oder unmittelbar gefährdet wird, ..., sind neben den für allgemeine Strafsachen zuständigen Gerichten auch die Jugendgerichte zuständig.*" ("For offences of adults that have injured or directly endangered a child or youth ... youth courts have jurisdiction additionally to the courts generally responsible for criminal offences." My translation.)

proceedings for Holocaust survivors, German courts have looked to psychological experts to adapt their procedures to make them more accessible and acceptable to these witnesses. The changes included offering hearings abroad, chiefly in Israel, reorganization of hearing spaces, training for judges on re-traumatization and, most importantly, psychological expert assistance to judges in making credibility findings.[36]

In order to address the related concerns of insufficiency of perspectives and discriminatory bias in adversarial proceedings, it appears therefore necessary to reconsider how our admissibility-focused rules of evidence may need to be tweaked to ensure that nothing-but-the-truth remains at least a reasonable facsimile of the whole truth. Beyond this, we need to continue to make progress on lowering participatory barriers and devising more inclusive court processes.

Hard Truths: Challenges arising from Testimony about Traumatic Events

The concerns discussed thus far apply broadly to legal proceedings. The remaining issues relate more narrowly to the reception of evidence about traumatic events. We had seen that in the philosophical debate about truth, there was a sense of collective muteness as a response to mass trauma. This has close analogues in court proceedings where witnesses testify to traumatic events.

Some of the difficulties that arise inhere in the witness who may experience dissociation or memory loss in response to trauma. Others occur at the interface between the witness and the fact-finder. The usual tools for credibility findings may not work. Finally, there may be psycho-social responses by the adjudicator to the evidence that make it difficult for the adjudicator to appropriately hear the testimony. Let me deal with each of these concerns in turn.

Memory and Communication

When witnesses testify to traumatic experiences, the memory of those experiences may itself be affected by the traumatic experience. In some of the literature, this is understood as a variant of memory function with specific characteristics.[37] Other theorists prefer to think of these trauma narratives as indicators of a

36 Ilka Quindeau, "Credibility Testing of Forced Labourer Claims in German Pension" (Paper delivered at the ILSA conference, Montreal, 29 May–1 June 2008); Ilka Quindeau, "Indemnification for Holocaust Survivors 60 Years Later: Juridical and Psychological Problems Concerning Memory and Trauma" (Presentation delivered at the International Conference "Beyond Reconciliation – Dealing with the Aftermath of Mass Trauma and Political Violence", 2–6 December 2009, University of Cape Town).

37 Gottfried Fischer & Peter Riedesser, *Lehrbuch der Psychotraumatologie* (Munich: Reinhardt, 1998).

trauma-induced psychological pathology.[38] Thus, the individual may present with memory dysfunction in the form of dissociative amnesia.[39] There are empirical limitations to taking a pathological view of trauma narratives. Pathological interpretations are frequently misleading since amnesia is often not manifest and the narrative does not appear unusual on its face.[40] Whether one prefers a pathological lens or thinks of trauma narratives as simply a variant, it is generally agreed that trauma affects memory in predictable ways. As will be elaborated below, this has important implications for the application of credibility indicators.

Further, trauma has significant effects on the ability of individuals to trust others. While the courtroom experience can be unsettling for many witnesses, it may take trauma victims longer to build a relationship with the examining lawyer or the judge and it may be more difficult to overcome a sense of being disconnected from the proceedings. This impacts the testimonial narrative, as the narrative act is invariably relational. We might anticipate that where the cause of the trauma has an institutional character as is the case for residential school survivors, trust in institutions, particularly related institutions, would be undermined. The likely result of this lack of trust is that aspects of the truth will be more difficult to access and may go missing altogether. These missing truths may result in a deformation: the truth as constructed in the legal discourse of a judgment may reflect these absences as distortions.

Trauma not only alters memory function and impacts relational capacity, it also affects the ability of individuals to capture traumatic experiences symbolically through language. Testimonial muteness of trauma victims has been well documented.[41] It was evident in hearings involving Holocaust survivors in the German courts and is likely going to affect the process of the Canadian Truth and Reconciliation Commission in its interaction with residential school survivors.

It is important not to treat testimonial muteness as a defect of the witness. As literary scholars in particular have pointed out, testimonial muteness or silence before the aporia of trauma simultaneously fails to communicate and succeeds in expressing the experience of trauma.[42] Instead, we will need to adjust our process to allow for the eloquence of silence and to give space and time building trust to enable the participation of traumatized witnesses.

---

38 Luise Greuel, Thomas Fabian & Michael Stadler, *Psychologie der Zeugenaussage: Ergebnisse der rechtspsychologischen Forschung* (Weinheim: Beltz, 2010).

39 Diagnostic and Statistical Manual of Mental Disorders, Fourth Edition (DSM-IV) (The American Psychological Institute, 1994).

40 Ilka Quindeau, "Zeugnis und Wahrheit: Fragen an das hermeneutische Geschichtsdenken Paul Ricoeurs aus psychoanalytischer Perspektive" in Burkhard Liebsch, ed, *Bezeugte Vergangenheit oder versöhnendes Vergessen* (Deutsche Zeitschrift für Philosophie, Sonderband, 2010).

41 Marianne Hirsch & Leo Spitzer, "The Witness in the Archive: Holocaust Studies/ Memory Studies" (2009) 2:2 Memory Studies 151.

42 Sara R Horowitz, *Voicing the Void: Muteness and Memory in Holocaust Fiction* (New York: SUNY Press, 1997) at 40.

Credibility Evaluations

Even where witness is able to give voice to the trauma experience, the usual credibility criteria may not be adequate as they are based on everyday experiences and regular memory function, or, more precisely, a common sense or lay approach to credibility evaluation. The common law generally takes a particularly committed lay approach. It tends to reject almost all attempts to bring scientific insights into the evaluation and appreciation of *viva voce* evidence to bear on the adversarial adjudication process.[43] There is reason to believe that these criteria may fail us even in the evaluation of testimony not impacted by trauma.[44] Additionally, narratives of traumatized people differ significantly and in predictable ways from narratives by individuals unaffected by trauma.[45] Psychology of memory and neurobiological research both demonstrate that trauma affects both the encoding and the recall of the traumatic memory.[46] This means that we should expect differences between trauma narratives and other *viva voce* testimony.

For example, important credibility indicators are commonly missing from trauma narratives.[47] These absences include precise indications of time and place or internal coherence of a statement. While these indicators of credibility are intuitive and frequently relied upon by adjudicators, they are not helpful in evaluating trauma narratives. This is because these absences are not only possible but instead are to be expected. The hallmark of a traumatic (as opposed to a merely painful) experience is that it disrupts the ability of the individual to integrate the experience meaningfully into their life story.

---

43 A rare exception to the general rule that judges and juries are fully competent to make credibility findings in even the most complex cases arose in *R v Lavallee*, [1990] 1 SCR 852 where the Supreme Court of Canada ultimately permitted the use of expert evidence to assist the jury in evaluating the evidence of a battered woman, albeit at the expense of exceptionalizing and pathologizing the witness.

44 This is apparent in the demeanor evidence debate, recently revived in the Canadian courts in the context of veiled witnesses. *R v N.S,* 2010 ONCA 670. Natasha Bakht, "Objection, Your Honour! Accommodating Niqab-Wearing Women in Courtrooms" in Ralph Grillo et al, eds, *Legal Practice And Cultural Diversity* (Surrey: Ashgate Publishing Ltd., 2009) 115.

45 Sabine von Hinckeldey & Gottfried Fischer, *Psychotraumatologie der Gedächtnisleistung* (Munich: Reinhardt 2002).

46 Bessel A van der Kolk, Alexander C McFarlane & Lars Weisaeth, eds, *Traumatic Stress: The Effects of Overwhelming Experience on Mind, Body, and Society* (New York: The Guilford Press, 1996); Natan P F Kellermann, "Die Kinder der child survivors" in Hartmut Radebold, Werner Bohleber & Jürgen Zinnecker, eds, *Transgenerationale Weitergabe kriegsbelasteter Kindheiten. Interdisziplinäre Studien zur Nachhaltigkeit historischer Erfahrungen über vier Generationen* (Weinheim: Juventa, 2008).

47 Friedrich Arntzen, *Psychologie der Zeugenaussage. System der Glaubhaftigkeitsmerkmale* (München: Beck, 2007).

A lack of precision in time and place and internal coherence are therefore not sufficient reasons to doubt the truth of the statement; in fact, the opposite may be the case. This is somewhat analogous to sexual assault law where judges and juries were prone to using prior sexual activity as a red flag for complainant credibility. This issue has now been addressed legislatively, one of the few instances where Parliament has given statutory guidance to credibility evaluation.[48] The experience demonstrates that these types of problems are susceptible to reform within our existing legal structures. There is more work to be done. As a result of the application of standard credibility criteria to trauma narratives, testimony by traumatized witnesses is still frequently and disproportionately disbelieved in court and other legal and quasi-legal proceedings.[49]

When a person may make a statement, but finds their evidence disbelieved or discounted even though sound reasons exist for the acceptance of their evidence, the individual (and possibly, their community) will feel disenfranchised. Credibility barriers include methods of credibility assessment relying on mainstreamed credibility factors, failure to provide appropriate supports, or physical arrangements limiting full participation.

Clearly, adjudicators will have to make credibility determinations for vulnerable and marginalized witnesses in some contexts. For this reason, it is important to develop credibility criteria that are informed by and connect with the particularities of trauma narratives. Ultimately, only if those who participate are appropriately evaluated, will the effort of attracting their participation lead to increased legitimacy and reputational gain.

Some Truths are Hard to Hear: Psycho-social Difficulties in Adjudication

A final reason why trauma narratives pose difficulties for judges and juries is that just as the experience of a traumatizing event is difficult to integrate into the life story of the individual, it is difficult for the listener to integrate what they are hearing into their existing frameworks of understanding. Put simply, there are certain things we would all prefer to believe were not true.[50] This adjudicative stance is further promoted by the stance of institutional distrust that is common

---

48 *Criminal Code*, *supra* note 29, s 276 (1)(b).

49 Kirsten Stang & Ulrich Sachsse, *Trauma und Justiz. Juristische Grundlagen für Psychotherapeuten: psychotherapeutische Grundlagen für Juristen* (Stuttgart: Schattauer, 2007).

50 The unwillingness or inability of mainstream adjudicators to adopt a victim perspective is well documented in sexual assault trials. Assumptions about violence against women and rape myth reasoning persist despite clear evidentiary foundations for their rejection. See Susan Ehrlich, *Resisting "Utmost Resistance": Using Rape Trauma Syndrome to Combat Underlying Rape Myths Influencing Acquaintance Rape Trials: Representing Rape: Language and Sexual Consent* (London and New York: Routledge, 2001).

in trauma survivors. We might understand these interactions as a self-protective attempt on the part of the fact-finder to not be personally unsettled by the evidence in a situation that strongly invites their empathy. This is compounded by the general legal preference for rational discourse and carefully controlled emotion.[51]

In sum then, court processes are vulnerable to all three threats to appropriate fact-finding suggested in the philosophical challenge to positivist notions of truth. As a result of broader challenges to the legitimacy of governmental institutions and a highly publicized track record of erroneous determinations, their legitimacy as authoritative arbiters of truth is somewhat weakened. Further, courts are insufficiently accessible and are subject to considerable participatory barriers. These barriers apply in biased and discriminatory ways to vulnerable and marginalized people. This renders the truth as found subject to discriminatory distortions. Finally, rules of process and evidence may conspire to lead fact-finders astray when they receive and evaluate trauma narratives.

Inspiration for Reform: the Canadian Truth and Reconciliation Commission

The Canadian Truth and Reconciliation Commission on Indian Residential Schools (TRC) was created as part of a settlement of a national class action of residential school survivors against the Canadian government and three large churches involved in the operation of Indian Residential Schools. It is hearing from survivors about their experiences in and impact from attending residential schools. The TRC is also seeking to hear from people who operated or worked in residential schools. It lacks any coercive powers, which makes attendance of perpetrator groups much less certain. The ultimate objects of the TRC are to provide survivors with a forum to share their stories and to create a historical record of residential schools for all Canadians. The TRC is headed up by three commissioners: the chief commissioner, Murray Sinclair, is a sitting judge of the Manitoba provincial court who is of aboriginal descent, co-commissioner Wilton Littlechild is an aboriginal lawyer and co-commissioner Marie Wilson is a journalist with long work experience in Canada's North.

The TRC faces many similar difficulties to those discussed above for court processes. It has to create a legitimate process, address participatory barriers and receive testimony from witnesses with complex and intersectional backgrounds.

There are, of course, significant differences between the TRC and courts. Some of these differences may ultimately operate to limit its usefulness as a model for reform, but some differences are helpful. Because it is not operating in a highly constitutionalized environment and because its purposes are clearly not

51 Jeremy A Blumenthal, "Law and the Emotions: The Problems of Affective Forecasting" (2005) 80 Ind LJ 155 at 160. The display of emotions also impacts credibility. See Geir Kaufmann et al, "The Importance of Being Earnest: Displayed Emotions and Witness Credibility" (2003) 17:1 Applied Cognitive Psychology 21.

oriented towards determining individual rights, it has more freedom to experiment with procedural innovation. Further analysis will clearly be needed to identify those innovations that might be transferable to the justice system, but it seems worthwhile to closely observe and document the procedural innovations of the TRC and their effects on the way survivors testify.

The TRC deals with witness issues of extraordinary complexity. Most witnesses are indigenous, have a history of abuse that frequently includes sexual abuse, many are elderly, many have or have had substance abuse problems, and many describe a fraught relationship with settler society justice institutions including experiences of criminalization.

The TRC is responding to these challenges with a broad range of highly innovative procedures, most of which appear to be designed to increase participation of witnesses.

The institutional design literature generally focuses on majoritarian legitimacy and trust.[52] What is missing, however, is a theory of legitimacy and legitimation based on substantive equality principles. Even if a justice system appears legitimate to a societal mainstream, it may lack legitimacy among marginalized groups. To the extent that these groups are significantly represented in the justice system, their perception of legitimacy becomes important.[53] Yet, there are few studies about how marginalized people experience the court system.[54] Stories gathered in the context of access to justice initiatives provide some evidence suggesting that the legitimacy gap is exaggerated for marginalized communities.[55] Assuming that these stories are representative, there are very significant barriers to participation in justice processes for marginalized people.

---

52 See *supra* notes 21–23.

53 The overrepresentation of marginalized groups in the criminal justice system is well documented. See, for example, *R v Gladue,* [1999] 1 SCR 688.

54 For a useful up-to-date review of the existing literature, see Margret E Bell et al, "Battered Women's Perceptions of Civil and Criminal Court Helpfulness: The Role of Court Outcome and Process" (2011) 17:1 Violence Against Women at 73. For the Canadian experience, see British Columbia (Attorney General), *Court Design Issues Affecting Children and Other Vulnerable Witnesses: A Background Study Based on a Key Informant Consultation and Literature Review* by Andy Wachtel (Burnaby, BC: United Way Research Services, Commissioned by the British Columbia Ministry of Attorney General, Community Justice Branch, Victim Services Division, Child Abuse Committee, 1997).

55 Leonard T Doust, Foundation for Change: *Report Of The Public Commission On Legal Aid In British Columbia* (Vancouver, 2011); Province of New Brunswick, *If there were Legal Aid in New Brunswick. A Review of Legal Aid Services in New Brunswick* by Jula Hughes & Ernest MacKinnon, (Fredericton: Province of NB, 2007); Attorney General of Ontario, *Report of the Legal Aid Review 2008* Report submitted to the Honourable Chris Bentley, Attorney General of Ontario by Michael Trebilcock (Toronto: AG Ontario, 2008).

Creating Legitimacy

A number of TRC innovations seek to address legitimacy concerns. Some relate to the preparatory stage of the statement-taking events. For example, prior to its first National Event, the TRC promulgated various brochures that were available on-line before the event and in print at the event that informed potential participants about the background of the TRC and advised them of the various options for making a statement. The TRC was also seeking to build individual trust through dissemination of biographical information of the Commissioners and other TRC participants.[56]

Other innovations sought to give participants a direct procedural stake. For example, all the sharing circles permitted statements of up to six minutes in length. A number of survivors spoke for longer and were permitted to do so. Rather than imposing the time limit externally, it was self-enforced and survivors were reminded at the beginning of the circle that taking more than the allotted time would make it more difficult for others to also make a statement. There was no time-keeping during the statement-taking.

The terms of the statement-taking events were described as somewhat negotiable; significantly the Chair assured participants that they would make sure everyone got an opportunity to speak and asked for patience before "you accuse us of not knowing how to run a proper circle."[57]

This suggested to me that the participants were implicitly permitted and even expected to critique the way the Commissioners managed the statement-taking event. Permitting participants some measure of control may operate to increase legitimacy.

Creating Inclusionary Processes

Offering procedural choice

Universal design literature suggests some principles underlying accessible and inclusionary systems. One key principle is flexibility in use. This principle is implemented chiefly through providing users with choice about how they want to access a facility or service.[58]

At the first national event in Winnipeg, there were at least three different modes offered to survivors who wanted to make a statement. They could register for a one-on-one meeting with a TRC volunteer at a hotel located adjacent to the event; they could participate in a survivor sharing circle held in an event tent with one

---

56 Tyler, *supra* note 13, states (at 815) that personal legitimacy can powerfully support institutional legitimacy and that this may partially explain the greater compliance with ADR resolutions compared to court orders.

57 Notes of the author, Winnipeg, June 18, 2010.

58 Molly Follette Story, "Maximizing Usability: The Principles of Universal Design" (1998) 10:1 Assistive Technology 4 at 8.

or more of the Commissioners present; or they could participate in a women-only circle in a theatre.[59] The choice was entirely that of the survivor, though space management proved difficult in a number of cases.

Modeling

Unfamiliarity with process acts as a participatory barrier. Since the TRC is developing its process *ad hoc*, this problem is particularly pressing. There are no ready-made resources explaining the process. One of the most interesting (and potentially problematic) innovations at the first National Event was the staging of a model sharing circle.

Early in the three-day meeting, there was a sharing circle offered where the participants had obviously been preselected and briefed extensively. This circle operated as a frame of reference for many attendees as to the format, length and style of presentations.[60] From a procedural fairness perspective, one might be concerned that modeling statements could lead to the tailoring of evidence much in the same way that we might be concerned about witness statements where there is no witness exclusion order. On the other hand, the ability to listen to the testimony of others appears to have assisted people in finding their voice.

Trauma Narratives: Culturally Appropriate Responses

As discussed above, traumatized witnesses face peculiar barriers to participation and appreciation. Since practically all witnesses before the TRC will fall into this category, finding culturally appropriate ways to facilitate participation is a pressing concern. The TRC has responded to this in a number of innovative and inspirational ways.

Throughout the statements, ceremonial supports through contact with sacred objects, emotional support through touching and encouraging words and empathetic gestures were provided. This is startlingly different from court processes which tend to isolate witnesses and where proceedings are typically interrupted when a witness breaks down in tears.

During the statement-taking, crying, even wailing, was the norm. Both speakers and listeners were frequently reduced to tears. Each Commissioner had a personal spiritual advisor to support them through the hearing. This clearly signaled to participants that the Commissioners expected to be and in fact were, profoundly affected by what they heard.

There was no legal or other representation though survivors were able to bring support persons with them to the statement-takings. Indeed, it would have

---

59 The women's circle was intended to be held in a tent also, but severe rainstorms caused the event to be relocated.

60 Modelling statements is an important mechanism for the TRC. It also provides this kind of information in videos online: http://www.youtube.com/TheTRCCanada#p/u/18/-BQgPrTbsqs.

been difficult to see what role lawyers could have played given that there were no questions other than introductory open-ended invitations to speak by the Commissioners. Consequently, there was also an absence of cross-examination and of oaths.

The supports for survivors did not end with the conclusion of the statement taking. Counselling was offered through Health Canada and members of the Indian Residential School Survivor Committee were on hand during the entire event to provide support. The TRC also offers a 24-hour/7-day telephone Indian Residential Schools Crisis Line.

Do the Procedural Innovations Encourage Participation?

Participation at the first National Event was smaller than the TRC had anticipated; at least, fewer people gave statements than had been expected. However, turnout was strong and the venues were crowded. Subsequent regional hearings have been very well attended and the TRC has found it necessary to even discourage some people from attending the subsequent national event in Inuvik because it was anticipated that the demand for statement-taking opportunities would outstrip the capacity of both the community and the commissioners.

One might therefore tentatively conclude that the TRC's procedural innovations have been successful in attracting participation of survivors, no small feat given the complexity of the task. It is much less clear whether a more recent initiative of the TRC to attract participation of workers at the residential schools will meet with success. It does appear from the publications of some of the churches that there will be participation by church officials.[61] Whatever the final outcome, the TRC presents a unique opportunity to observe a natural experiment in procedural justice.

---

61 All three respondent churches were represented at the first national event of the TRC, though not as individuals giving testimony. The Anglican and Catholic churches were represented at the second national event through a number of bishops offering apologies. The *Catholic Register*, the United Church paper *Observer* and the Anglican paper *Anglican Journal* all routinely reports on the TRC. In fact, denominational publications provide more press coverage of the TRC than any other media outlet.

PART 5
Hybrid Models of Oversight – Specialized Ombuds, Legislative Officers and Investigations

Chapter 15
Evaluating Ombuds Oversight in the Canadian Access to Information Context: A Theoretical and Empirical Inquiry

Laverne Jacobs*

Introduction

Outside of administrative law hearing processes, polyjural[1] approaches to dispute resolution are also found in broader, more policy-oriented administrative regimes. The complaint resolution processes of the legislative officers established to oversee the executive branch of government represent one such example. This chapter examines the models of dispute resolution used by the legislative officers that have been statutorily created to resolve "access to information"[2] (ATI) complaints in Canada. Since the enactment of Canada's first freedom of information legislation by the federal government in 1983, a debate has emerged as to whether an investigatory approach based on the ombuds[3] tradition or

* An earlier version of this chapter was presented at *The 1st Global Conference on Transparency Research* (Rutgers University, May 19–20, 2011), at the *Nature of Inquisitorial Processes in Administrative Regimes: Global Perspectives* (University of Windsor, May, 26–27, 2011) and at the *7th International Conference of Information Commissioners* (Ottawa, October 3–5, 2011). I am grateful to the participants of these conferences, as well as to the anonymous reviewer of this chapter, for their constructive feedback. Thanks also to the Law Foundation of Ontario for its generous support and to Melissa Kwok and Ki Lin Tay for their excellent research assistance.

1 In keeping with the rest of this volume, I use the term "polyjural" to describe administrative justice systems that foster the coexistence of elements from more than one legal tradition. In the case of legislative oversight for access to information, the legal traditions that are relevant are the inquisitorial, adversarial, and ombuds traditions. For discussions of the use of polyjural approaches in administrative hearing processes, please see the chapters by Robin Creyke, Robert Thomas, Michael Asimow, Jean-Bernard Auby, and Samantha Green and Lorne Sossin in Part 1 of this volume.

2 The expressions "access to information" and "freedom of information" will be used interchangeably throughout this chapter.

3 Throughout this book, the following terminology has been adopted, in order to promote gender neutrality while also respecting the names of ombuds institutions. The capitalized expression, "Ombudsman" has been used for specific names (e.g. the

an adversarial adjudicative approach is most suitable for achieving effective regulatory oversight. This debate resurfaces often, as it did, for example, in 2009, when major reforms to the *Access to Information Act*[4] were yet again suggested by the responsible standing committee of Parliament.[5] Indeed, the discussion about appropriate administrative process lays just beneath the surface of many policy issues relating to access to government information in Canada, such as avoiding delays and saving public funds. This chapter engages with the debate over choice of institutional design by considering both the theoretical nature of the different models that exist, and the concrete goals that an access to information complaint resolution regime should seek to further.

Part I defines three typologies for access to information dispute resolution processes. These three dispute resolution typologies are: investigatory, adjudicative, and mixed investigatory–adjudicative. Each typology shows some connection to the ombuds tradition. An examination of the access to information resolution processes established in each of the fourteen territorial jurisdictions in Canada reveals these three typologies in existence along a spectrum. Although Canada has been used as a case study, these typologies may be appropriate in other jurisdictions as well.

Part II begins the case study of Canada's federal Office of the Information Commissioner (OIC). The extent to which the OIC's investigatory dispute resolution process reflects the ombuds tradition is considered, keeping in mind that to ameliorate the effectiveness of an investigatory system based on the ombuds model, it may be possible to develop on the general policy goals and powers inherent to the ombuds tradition.

Part III then examines more closely the debate over the suitability of investigatory and adjudicative approaches to delivering effective regulatory oversight. It does so through a theoretical and empirical inquiry. In Part III, I first suggest that the debate over the appropriate dispute resolution model can be analyzed from the perspective of four, often competing and sometimes overlapping, theoretical values: i) institutional competence, ii) access to justice, iii) efficiency, and iv) effectiveness in promoting government transparency. I argue for a reconciliation of these theoretical values that would place greater emphasis on the fourth factor – that is, on the effectiveness of the dispute resolution regime in promoting government transparency. I next take an empirical look at how

Swedish Ombudsman, the Ombudsman of Ontario). The lowercase words "ombudsman", "ombudsperson" and "ombuds" have been used, as nouns and adjectives, to represent general institutions, with preference for the use of the gender-neutral forms of "ombudsperson" and "ombuds" wherever possible.

4 *Access to Information Act*, RSC 1985, c A-1 [ATIA].

5 See *Report of the Standing Committee on Access to Information, Privacy and Ethics "The Access to Information Act: First Steps Towards Renewal"* (June 2009), online: http://www.parl.gc.ca/content/hoc/Committee/402/ETHI/Reports/RP3999593/ethirp11/ethirp11-e.pdf [First Steps].

Canada's federal Office of the Information Commissioner is faring with respect to the four theoretical values. The empirical data for this part of the discussion is taken from the preliminary results of an online survey administered to access officials in the federal government. An analysis of the survey results suggests that the OIC's investigatory complaint resolution process can play a significant role in achieving the four values inherent in access policy; however, fundamental aspects of institutional design, which would enable the Information Commissioner's work to have a longer-term impact, first need to be addressed.

Defining Adjudicative, Investigatory, and Mixed Models of ATI Dispute Resolution: Three Typologies

"Adjudicative" (also termed "quasijudicial") and "investigatory" models of ATI dispute resolution are widely referenced in ATI literature and practice,[6] though defined with little precision. In common ATI parlance, the two concepts are used as synonyms for "order-making" and "ombudsman" models, respectively. Given the widespread use of this terminology and the current, prolific development of access to information regimes around the world,[7] it is useful and timely to seek deeper definitions of these terms. In this section, I define adjudicative, investigatory, and mixed investigatory–adjudicative models. These definitions find their source in the legal literature relating to dispute resolution and in a close analysis of the statutes across Canada used to resolve ATI disputes at the federal level, in the provinces, and in the territories.

---

6 For example, the Access to Information Task Force describes Information Commissioners around the world as capable of being classified as either "quasijudicial" or "investigative." See, in particular, chapter 6 "Ensuring Compliance: The Redress Process" of *Access to Information: Making it Work for Canadians – Report of the Access to Information Review Task Force* (Ottawa: Public Works and Government Services, 2002) at 92, online: http://publications.gc.ca/collections/Collection/BT22-83-2002E.pdf [*Access to Information: Making it Work for Canadians*]. One of Canada's federal Information Commissioners has used similar language in a report requesting changes to the Commissioner's enabling statute. Former Commissioner John Reid stated in 2009:

> "The debate surrounding the authorities allocated to Information Commissioners has generally involved the examination of two models: the ombudsman model and the quasi-judicial model. The ombudsman model is based on investigation and moral suasion while the quasi-judicial model provides for order-making powers."

A more global iteration of this idea is given by Laura Neuman in "Enforcement Models: Content and Context" (Washington: World Bank Institute, Access to Information Working Paper Series, 2009), online:

http://siteresources.worldbank.org/EXTGOVACC/Resources/LNEumanATI.pdf.

7 See John M Ackerman & Irma E Sandoval-Ballesteros, "The Global Explosion of Freedom of Information Laws" (2006) 58 Admin L Rev 85.

Adjudicative ATI Dispute Resolution

The terms *adjudication* and *investigation* refer to methods of settling disputes. As a dispute resolution method and a legal term of art, the more common of the two, *adjudication*, has been described as a court-like procedure in which evidence is brought before a decision-maker by the parties, the parties are given an opportunity to be heard, and a decision of some sort is issued to the parties, at minimum, if not also to the public. In "The Forms and Limits of Adjudication", Lon Fuller provided the following core definition of adjudication:

> the distinguishing characteristic of adjudication lies in the fact that it confers on the affected party a peculiar form of participation in the decision, that of presenting proofs and reasoned arguments for decision in his favor.[8]

A more detailed definition, which looks beyond Fuller's emphasis on individual participation in the hearing to the overall process itself may be found in this more recent definition by Bruce Archibald, who describes adjudication as:

> a process based on individual rights in which a neutral adjudicator will apply pre-existing and democratically established rules to facts as found by a neutral fact finder in order to achieve a fair or just outcome – one which will then be deemed authoritative and legitimate …[9]

---

8 Lon L Fuller, "The Forms and Limits of Adjudication" (1978) 92 Harv L Rev 353 at 364. I am also mindful of Fuller's observation that defining the "pure essence" of anything is often chimerical. However, it is useful to have essential models in order to examine their forms and limits.

9 Bruce P Archibald, "Progress in Models of Justice: from Adjudication/Arbitration through Mediation to Restorative Conferencing (and Back)" in Ronalda Murphy & Patrick A Molinari, eds, *Doing Justice: Dispute Resolution in the Courts and Beyond* (Montréal: Canadian Institute for the Administration of Justice, 2007) 129 at 134. Archibald's definition stems from ideas that have been debated by American procedural scholars, Owen Fiss and Judith Resnick (see for example, O Fiss & J Resnick, *Adjudication and its Alternatives: An Introduction to Procedure* (New York: Foundation Press, 2003)). Australian academic Peter Cane asserts, contrary to Fuller, that the adversarial presentation of arguments is not necessary for adjudication in the context of administrative law. Instead, an essential distinction in administrative law lies in the difference between decision-making over cases in which individual interests are pitted against those of the state (*adjudication*) and decision-making to implement broader social objectives (*implementation*). This distinction, found in Australia and the UK, is understood as the distinction between *adjudication* and *rulemaking* in the United States. See generally Peter Cane, *Administrative Tribunals and Adjudication* (Oxford: Hart Publishing, 2009) at 9–16. "Adjudication" has also been employed in some countries simply to refer to external review by courts and tribunals of administrative decision-making. In this sense, the use of the term relates to the structural apparatus of the administrative justice system.

This definition proposes five central elements to adjudication: 1) a dispute relating to individual rights; 2) a neutral adjudicator; 3) pre-existing and applicable legal principles; 4) facts determined by a neutral fact finder; and 5) a just and authoritative outcome. Each of these five elements is worthy of examining within the access to information context.

Some of these elements are relatively uncontested within the realm of access to information law. The dispute over whether one should have access is plainly one over a right. The right to see government records is statutorily (and/or sometimes constitutionally) granted to all individuals. Similarly, access legislation typically provides the applicable legal provisions, such as the mandatory and discretionary exemptions that dispense with an individual's right of access. These provisions and the body of case law that they generate as they are applied in particular circumstances provide the pre-existing applicable legal principles to which the third part of the definition of adjudication refers. Finally, while the justice of any outcome may fall within the eye of the beholder, any legislative ATI regime that specifies a binding order enables the outcome to be authoritative.

Where matters become murky is with respect to the existence of a neutral adjudicator and a neutral fact finder. When the Information Commissioner is both the fact finder and decision-maker in the same case, to what extent can he or she be conceived to be neutral? On one level, this question points to the co-existence of two dominant legal traditions that both fall within the contours of adjudication. Two of the most common systems of adjudication in the Western legal tradition are the adversarial and the inquisitorial systems. Across the fourteen statutory access to information dispute resolution regimes that have been set up territorially in Canada, elements of both the adversarial and inquisitorial tradition can be found along a spectrum. On another level, this question speaks to a misperception about bias that those trained in the adversarial tradition sometimes see in the inquisitorial tradition.

With respect to the two dominant legal traditions, adjudication may be performed in two ways. In both, order-making powers are present, and a binding order is the result that one obtains from the Commissioner before venturing on to judicial review or appeal. As discussed in the introductory chapter to this volume,[10] the first, adversarialism, espouses the idea that it is the parties who control what evidence should be brought forward to be considered by a neutral decision maker in reaching his or her decisions. The parties are responsible for initiating the process and are largely responsible for the way that the proceedings will unfold, although they are required to work within the limits of strict procedural rules designed, in part, to preserve ethical conduct.

Within the Canadian ATI context, adversarialism exists when the requester and the government institution with which the requester disagrees are each expected to proffer representations and evidence to the Information Commissioner. The Information Commissioner then acts as a neutral and passive adjudicator, deciding

10 Please see the Introduction to this volume.

the matter based on the information brought forward. The adversarial design of access to information adjudication presumes that the information required to determine the dispute will be made available by the parties.[11] However, in no Canadian jurisdiction does there exist an absolute version of the adversarial adjudicative process for ATI dispute resolution. While certain jurisdictions present a strong form of adversarial adjudicative design, these ATI decision-makers have generally also been granted powers to conduct investigations so that they may obtain whatever additional information they need from the government institutions before them. In other words, there is a reserve function that allows the Commissioner to conduct independent fact-finding.

The Québec *Commission d'accès à l'information* (CAI) is the strongest example among Canadian jurisdictions of an adjudicative system set up for ATI regulation that possesses distinct adversarial qualities. Québec's *Act respecting access to documents held by public bodies and the protection of personal information*[12] allows any person whose request for access to a record has been denied, to apply to the Commission for review. The *Rules of Proof and Procedure* provide for a public, oral hearing at which the Commission, an administrative tribunal presided by at least one member, may admit any form of evidence.[13] The adjudicative division of the Commission, which is the division that holds hearings to review access complaints, does not have the power to enter premises on its own initiative and inspect documents there. As seen through Tables 15.1 and 15.2 at the end of this chapter, this feature distinguishes the CAI from almost all other access dispute resolution regimes in the country.[14] The inability of members of the CAI's adjudicative division to enter premises also contrasts sharply with the powers of the Commission's inspectors, who are appointed to ensure the compliance of public bodies with the Act's requirements against inappropriate retention, disclosure, and collection of personal information.[15] Inspectors are not only permitted to

11 Please see the Introduction to this volume.

12 RSQ, c A.2.1 [Québec *Access to Public Information Act*].

13 See *Rules of Proof and Procedure before the* Commission d'accès à l'information c A-2.1, r. 2 [CAI *Rules of Proof and Procedure*], ss 13, 18 and 22. In order to protect the confidentiality of documents, the Commission may hold part of its hearing *in camera* to avoid releasing information that qualifies for protection under the statute. See CAI *Rules of Proof and Procedure*, ss 18, 20.

14 The only other exception is Nunavut. See Table 15.2.

15 In this respect, contrast the provisions dealing with the powers of inspectors appointed to help ensure that Québec public bodies are complying with statutory requirements regarding the retention, disclosure etc of information (ss 123.1–123.3 of the Québec *Access to Public Information Act*, *supra* note 12) with the provisions setting out the powers of the members of the adjudicative division when they are sitting to determine access complaints. Most of these provisions are found at ss 13–24 of the CAI *Rules of Proof and Procedure*, *supra* note 13. The powers of inspectors show them to be much more active in determining the evidence than the adjudicators. For instance, although the adjudicators may be able to call any witnesses to testify and admit any form of evidence, the provisions

enter premises but also to request a person on the site to present any information or document required.[16] Quite clearly, if the Québec legislature had wanted the resolution of complaints to accord more closely with a non-adversarial model, it could have used similar language to that used for the Commission's inspectors.

Yet, the Commission has powers that allow it flexibility in the way that it manages its hearings. For example, the Commission "may, of its own motion or on application, call any person to appear before it and compel him to testify under oath."[17] It may also, "where it deems it expedient, order witnesses to give evidence in the absence of any other witness."[18] These approaches show a deviation from a strict adversarial approach. Nevertheless, while these powers appear to be similar to fact finders under an inquisitorial process and to administrative actors designed on an ombuds tradition, the brevity in their description[19] and their location in the legislation as a supplementary feature of the CAI process, signal that they are not meant to replace the primarily adversarial adjudicative nature of the CAI. In summary, while not an absolute form of the adversarial adjudicative model, Québec's CAI illustrates what an adjudicative model of ATI dispute resolution that is strongly adversarial looks like.

The second adjudicative design found within Canadian access dispute resolution is an inquisitorial one. Both adversarial and inquisitorial approaches to adjudication lead to binding orders. Features of the inquisitorial adjudication process are a presumption that the decision-maker will play an active role in

---

relating these powers, appear only after the legislature has set out the default, baseline procedure of the CAI, which is to hold a preliminary meeting and then a hearing with the parties.

16 The provision relating to the powers of inspectors reads:

> 123.2. Persons acting as inspectors may
> (1) enter the establishment of a body or person subject to the oversight of the Commission at any reasonable time;
> (2) request a person on the site to present any information or document required to exercise the Commission's oversight function; and
> (3) examine and make copies of such documents.

17 *Ibid*, ss 23, 24.

18 *Ibid*.

19 Compare the brevity in legislative drafting used to describe the Quebec CAI's power to summons persons who may be relevant to the hearing, as quoted above, to the expansively drafted wording of the same function in PEI, which incorporates, by reference, s 3 of the PEI *Public Inquiries Act* (RSPEI 1988, c P-31), as reproduced below:

> **3.** The commissioner may summon before him any witnesses, and may for that purpose under his hand issue a subpoena requiring and commanding the person therein named to appear at the time and place mentioned therein to testify to all matters within his knowledge relative to the subject matter of the investigation, and to bring with him and produce any document, book or paper, which he has in his possession or under his control relative to any such matter as aforesaid; and any such person may be summoned from any part of this province by virtue of the subpoena.

gathering the evidence that will then be used to decide the matter.[20] In the ATI dispute resolution context, one sees manifestations of this approach in jurisdictions where the Commissioner or a delegate will conduct an independent investigation of the facts once a request for review has been brought by a requester. This independent investigation allows the Commissioner or delegate to compel production of the relevant records from the government department and examine them, in order to determine whether access should have been granted. From a reading of Canadian ATI legislation, and as illustrated in Table 15.1, this model has been adopted in provinces such as Alberta, British Columbia, Ontario, and Prince Edward Island where the default approach to procedure does not leave it primarily to the parties to present evidence, and the available powers to compel the production of evidence are quite coercive.[21] In practice, however, through administrative discretion, the forceful statutory tools of inquiry granted to these Commissioners are rarely used by them.[22]

Interestingly, doubts over the suitability of the adversarial process for access to information dispute resolution have been raised in the jurisprudence. It has been suggested that access to information disputes do not have opposing parties at all; rather, what is fundamentally at stake in every access dispute is simply a policy question about the types of information that should be revealed.[23] This opinion shows preference for the use of an inquisitorial approach to ATI adjudication. If one conceives of access to information as primarily an executive branch accountability mechanism, then an inquisitorial approach is also compelling for another reason. One can argue that, as the designated administrative body, the Information Commissioner should take the lead to determine if transparency standards are being met. Doing so may require more than passive adjudication over files brought forward by the government. Finally, lawyers trained in the adversarial tradition sometimes perceive bias in the fact-finding role of the inquisitorial adjudicator. These misperceptions of bias overlook, however, that the adjudicator's involvement is not driven by an aim to further the interests of any party but rather, by the goal of obtaining the fullest set of information possible in order to further the public interest.[24]

---

20 Please see the Introduction to this volume.

21 See, for example, s 52(4) of Ontario's *Freedom of Information and Protection of Privacy Act*, RSO 1990, c F.31 [*FIPPA*] which reads:

> **Powers of Commissioner**
>
> (4) In an inquiry, the Commissioner may require to be produced to the Commissioner and may examine any record that is in the custody or under the control of an institution, despite Parts II and III of this Act or any other Act or privilege, and may enter and inspect any premises occupied by an institution for the purposes of the investigation.

22 See *Access to Information: Making it Work for Canadians*, *supra* note 6.

23 See *Spooner v Commission scolaire des Sommets*, [2008] JQ No 10690 at para 36.

24 The inquisitorial tradition and misperceptions of bias by lawyers steeped in the adversarial tradition are discussed in greater detail in the chapters by Robin Creyke, and Samantha Green and Lorne Sossin, in this volume.

Investigatory ATI Dispute Resolution

Adjudication finds itself alongside other contemporary models of dispute resolution such as negotiation, conciliation and mediation.[25] However, although adjudication, negotiation, conciliation, mediation, and others are often discussed in the dispute resolution literature, *investigation* as a distinct form or phase of dispute resolution is largely absent. The concept of *investigation* is also largely absent from Canadian administrative law theory.[26] Given its significant role in access to information regulation around the world, however, it is useful to attempt a theoretical definition of *investigation*. Unlike adjudication, an investigation leads to a recommendation as opposed to a final authoritative outcome. Yet, as a dispute resolution model, investigation is not just about outcomes but about the tools used to gather information and to reach factual conclusions. In this section, I identify the distinguishing characteristics of ATI investigation. These distinguishing characteristics derive from the information-gathering processes and outcomes adopted by Information Commissioners in Canada in the resolution of access to information disputes.

Starting from a broad theoretical perspective, at least two types of investigation can be found in administrative law: a) investigatory models based on the ombuds tradition and b) investigatory models that further the goals of commissions of inquiry. The former are most germane to ATI dispute resolution regimes as Information Commissioners across the country all share some powers and family likenesses with the institution of the classical ombudsman.[27] In the Introduction to this volume, the history and nature of this institution is described. Several central tenets may be drawn from that description. First, an ombuds is normally established as an officer of the legislature that works to have officials in the executive branch of government correct and avoid instances of maladministration. To achieve this objective, the ombuds is endowed with forceful tools of investigation that enable its office to ascertain the factual information necessary for determining if an individual has been mistreated by government. These tools typically include the ability to issue subpoenas, compel testimony, produce documents, and so on. Information Commissioners across Canada share the family likeness of being

---

25 For a definition of these terms, please see Julie MacFarlane et al, eds, *Dispute Resolution: Readings and Case Studies* (Toronto: Emond Montgomery, 2011).

26 The major Canadian administrative law texts pay some attention to commissions of inquiry with emphasis on issues such as procedural fairness, however, they do not devote much time to the concept of investigation as a standalone institution. See for example, Gus Van Harten, Gerald Heckman & David J Mullan, eds, *Administrative Law: Cases, Text, and Materials*, 6th ed (Toronto: Emond Montgomery, 2010) and Colleen M Flood & Lorne Sossin, eds, *Administrative Law in Context* (Toronto: Emond Montgomery, 2008).

27 The latter, investigatory models designed for commissions of inquiry, is discussed in detail earlier in this volume. Please see the chapters by Van Harten, Prasser, Goudge and Braidwood.

legislative officers. In the particular case of access to information, the legislative officers oversee the executive branch of government's adherence to prescribed transparency principles. Information Commissioners generally also possess many of the same investigative tools as a classical ombuds.

Other defining elements of ATI investigation can be gleaned from a reading of the enabling statutes of Information Commissioners across the country, as seen in Tables 15.1 and 15.2. During the course of an investigation, an ATI Commissioner will be obliged to give the parties an opportunity to make representations,[28] though the issue of whether the parties may know each other's representations is generally either left to the Commissioner's discretion,[29] or resolved against shared representations, in the enabling legislation.[30] Some of the enabling statutes also indicate that any investigation undertaken is to be conducted in private.

Several post-investigation powers possessed by ombuds are also replicated in Information Commissioner legislation across Canada. After investigation, if an ombuds is of the opinion that correction is required, the ombuds will use negotiation, persuasion, education and publicity as the primary mechanisms for convincing the government to make the recommended changes. These tools of moral suasion are central to the ombuds tradition and available to Information Commissioners as well. In Canada, the power to educate and to publish reports is usually available to ombuds and Information Commissioners expressly through their enabling legislation.[31] By contrast, powers of negotiation and persuasion are usually implicit tools drawn from the reserve of administrative discretion for both types of legislative officer. The government is normally not bound by an ombuds' recommendations and an ombuds will generally not be endowed with order-making powers that lead to a legally binding result. So, too, with many Canadian Information Commissioners. As illustrated in Tables 15.1 and 15.2, more than half of the Information Commissioners in Canada do not have order-making powers.

In summary, in its ideal form, an investigatory model of ATI dispute resolution results in non-coercive recommendations to government as opposed to legally binding orders. The investigation is conducted by a legislative officer that is endowed with extensive and coercive tools of investigation as well as explicit powers of public reporting and education. In the investigatory model, Information Commissioners rely on powers of persuasion and negotiation to convince governments to adopt their recommendations, although these powers are generally exercised as implicit acts of administrative discretion, as opposed

28 All Information Commissioners in Canada have this obligation. See, for example, *Freedom of Information and Protection of Privacy Act*, RSA 2000, c F-25, s 69(3).

29 See e.g., *Freedom of Information and Protection of Privacy Act*, RSBC 1996, c 165, ss 56(4).

30 See e.g., *Freedom of Information and Protection of Privacy Act*, RSA 2000, c F-25, ss 69(3).

31 See e.g. *Access to Information and Protection of Privacy Act*, SNL 2002, c A-1.1.

to being generated by express statutory powers. Finally, if the Commissioner's recommendations are not adopted by government then the enabling legislation generally allows for an appeal or a review *de novo* before a court. Judicial review may alternatively be sought.

In conclusion, an investigation is a dispute resolution model that endows coercive tools on state actors to determine truth. An investigation may be conducted in private as opposed to in a public hearing. Investigations generally do not lead to a binding or authoritative outcome. In the ATI context, Information Commissioners are endowed with specific tools of education and generally employ negotiation in resolving disputes.

Mixed Investigatory–Adjudicative ATI Dispute Resolution: Building on the Ombuds or Independent Accountability Agencies?

Many of the tools of the investigatory model that derive from the ombuds institution, such as forceful investigatory powers, powers of education and a tendency to negotiate, have equally been granted[32] to adjudicative Information Commissioners endowed with the power to grant binding orders. A question therefore arises as to whether it is possible to identify adjudicative Information Commissioners as specialized ombuds with order-making powers. Put another way, is it equally legitimate to conceive of the *adjudicative* ATI dispute resolution model as also being built on the ombuds institution?

Arguments in favour of designating such bodies as specialized ombuds see this development as an innocuous, natural expansion of the ombuds institution.[33] By contrast, those who challenge the classification, do so with practical and constitutional arguments. A common practical argument is that order-making powers will reduce the flexibility that an investigatory commissioner may have in using its tools of negotiation and persuasion. The argument suggests that if endowed with order-making powers, commissioners will have to be more careful about being procedurally fair and will feel obliged to produce more precedents which will limit them in future decision-making.[34] Another is that acceptance of the notion of an ombuds with order-making powers changes the institution from being one that stands on the sidelines, out of the fray of the three branches of government and in a position from which it could validly critique government.

32 Such powers are legislatively granted to or derive from the discretion of the Commissioner.

33 Reif and Marshall, for example, accept access to information commissions as part of newer specialty ombudsman, without any protest. See Mary A Marshall & Linda C Reif, "The Ombudsman: Maladministration and Alternative Dispute Resolution" (1995) 34 Alta L Rev 215.

34 See Jennifer Stoddart, "Cherry Picking Among Apples and Oranges: Refocusing Current Debate About the Merits of the Ombuds-Model Under PIPEDA" (October 2005), online: http://www.priv.gc.ca/information/pub/omb_051021_e.cfm.

With order-making powers, an ombuds is said to be pulled into the world of administrative tribunals by being subjected to the oversight of the judiciary through judicial review. Finally, the idea of the adjudicative Information Commissioner as an ombuds has been rejected because the ombuds institution has, at its core, the tradition of being a citizen's defender. Concerns arise, therefore, that the adjudicative ATI Commissioner will not be seen as neutral decision-maker of fact and law but perceived as an advocate in favour of "the cause" of public requesters.

From an administrative law perspective, it is questionable whether these arguments are well-founded. For example, negotiation is always possible in administrative law contexts and may lead to a settlement. Many administrative tribunals offer alternative dispute resolution before entering into an inquiry that will lead to a binding order. In fact, alternative dispute resolution is already a common practice among those Canadian ATI commissions that produce binding orders and it is valued because it staves off the need, time and costs associated with binding adjudication. The argument that an ombuds will lose flexibility in the ability to use negotiation and persuasion is therefore not convincing. Moreover, the degree of procedural fairness required in any given instance will always be determined on a case-by-case basis. Although more procedural fairness is generally required in adjudicative, court-like, administrative hearings, this does not mean that no procedural fairness is required at all in more informal situations leading to recommendations.[35] As for the concern about binding precedents, one should note that there are no formal requirements of *stare decisis* in Canadian administrative law, although administrative bodies generally aim to be consistent in their decision-making for reasons of efficiency and to assist their users in predicting outcomes.

Finally, the concern about loss of neutrality by an order-making ombuds can be avoided. In the ATI context, concerns about the Commissioner favouring one party, usually the requester, are sometimes instigated by the image of an Information Commissioner as an ombudsperson for the citizen. I argue that the appropriate conception of Information Commissioners endowed with ombuds-like powers and also possessing order-making capacities is to understand them as independent accountability agencies. Independent accountability agencies are designed to promote and pursue transparency in government.[36] The notion of an independent accountability agency avoids the "citizen defender" image and instead promotes the idea that the agency, led by the Information Commissioner, has been put in place with the mandate of furthering of principle of transparency wherever legally possible. In so doing, the Commissioner will decide individual complaints fairly,

---

35 See *Baker v Canada (Minister of Citizenship and Immigration)*, [1999] 2 SCR 817.

36 See John M Ackerman, "Understanding Independent Accountability Agencies" in Susan Rose-Ackerman & Peter L Lindseth, eds, *Comparative Administrative Law* (Northampton, MA: Edward Elgar, 2010) 265.

interpreting the statute in a way that allows for transparency whenever possible but which also respects the limits on access provided in the statute itself. I argue that an Information Commissioner should be seen as an agent for the principle of transparency, following and enforcing the mandate of the access to information legislation. Moreover, concerns about partiality are misplaced in that they focus on the possibility of party favouritism as opposed to the information void that may exist if the parties alone were left to decide what evidence should be determinative in a public interest dispute.

In conclusion, ATI dispute resolution is an administrative law context in which polyjuralism abounds. In light of the foregoing analysis, it is possible to picture the range of ATI dispute resolution as a spectrum that incorporates regulatory processes and tools commonly found within Canadian administrative law. The three broad typologies, which apply in Canada and may also apply elsewhere, can be seen to fall along the spectrum. On the spectrum, the processes of the various Information Commissioners (adversarial–adjudicative, inquisitorial–adjudicative) are paired with the tools provided for resolving the dispute (enforceable orders, recommendations, and so on). At one end of the spectrum lies adjudication with enforceable orders. At the opposite end of the spectrum is investigation that results only in recommendations. In the middle lay less formal adjudicative processes supplemented by investigative powers, that result in enforceable orders. The three typologies may therefore be set out according to this depiction:

- adjudicative/enforceable
- investigatory–adjudicative/enforceable
- investigatory/non-enforceable

Canada's Federal Office of the Information Commissioner

How closely can the dispute resolution system designed for federal ATI complaints in Canada be aligned with the ombuds model of dispute resolution? The value of this question is that it provides insight into the ways in which the dispute resolution process might be naturally improved. For example, to ameliorate the effectiveness of a system based on the ombuds model, it may be possible to develop on the general policy goals and powers inherent to the ombuds tradition. At the same time, knowledge of the historical roots of traditional processes is not meant to serve as a limitation to creative policy development. Certainly, it may be that despite the traditional tenets of any dispute resolution process, the contemporary political and legal context requires the development of innovative approaches. Otherwise, access policy in Canada may not be effectively fulfilled.

In this second part of the chapter, the investigatory procedure used by the federal Office of the Information Commissioner is examined against the theoretical backdrop of the ombuds tradition. From this analysis, I suggest that the ombuds tradition does not adequately capture the complexity of the administrative processes currently used. However, the mixture of traditions that is present offers possibilities for developing on the existing dispute resolution mechanisms so that they more fully achieve the policy goal of fostering governmental transparency.

Canada's federal Office of the Information Commissioner (OIC) is most commonly described as a specialized ombuds.[37] From a reading of the literature produced by the OIC, one sees signs that the office considers itself an ombuds primarily because it does not have the ability to make binding orders. The current website of the office states, for example: "As an ombudsperson, the Commissioner may not order a complaint to be resolved in a particular way, though she may refer a case to the Federal Court for resolution."[38]

Linda Reif has usefully delineated three characteristics of classic parliamentary ombuds: i) they investigate complaints and allegations, ii) they secure redress in cases where a complaint is found to be justified, and iii) they help to bring about improvements in administrative systems and procedures generally.[39] Under its enabling statute, the federal Information Commissioner possesses powers that reflect traditional ombuds characteristics. First of all, with respect to complaints and allegations, the Commissioner is statutorily obliged to receive and investigate all written complaints that come into the office.[40] The issues for which complaints may be brought include denial of access to records requested,[41] concerns that unreasonable fees have been requested by an institution for providing access to records,[42] delays,[43] complaints that records were not provided in the official language requested or in an alternative format,[44] and essentially any other matter relating to requesting or obtaining access to records under the *Act*.[45] In addition to investigating complaints brought to the Commissioner, the Commissioner also has

37 The Access to Information Review Task Force described it as such without question in its report. See *Access to Information: Making it Work for Canadians*, *supra* note 6.

38 See Office of the Information Commissioner for Canada (OIC), "What we do", online: http://www.oic-ci.gc.ca/eng/abu-ans_what-we-do_ce-que-nous-faisons.aspx (last accessed on June 24, 2012). The OIC has also described itself as an ombudsman in various published reports and in its appearances before parliamentary committee. See, for example, OIC *Annual Report 2009–10 "Achieving Results, Building for Success"*, online: http://www.oic-ci.gc.ca/eng/rp-pr_ar-ra.aspx [OIC Annual Report, 2009–10]; see also the transcript of the appearance by Mr. Robert Marlow, Information Commissioner, before the Standing Committee on Access to Information, Privacy and Ethics (March 4, 2009) at 5.

39 See Linda C Reif, *The Ombudsman, Good Governance and the International Human Rights System* (Boston: Martinus Nijhoff Publishers, 2004) at 218. See also the discussion of traditional ombuds characteristics in the Introduction of this book.

40 See ATIA, *supra* note 4, ss 30(1) and 31.

41 *Ibid*, s 30(1)(a).

42 *Ibid*, s 30(1)(b).

43 *Ibid*, s 30(1)(c).

44 *Ibid*, s 30(1)(d), (d.1).

45 *Ibid*, s 30(1)(f).

the discretion to investigate any matter relating to requesting or obtaining access to records if he or she is convinced that there are reasonable grounds to do so.[46]

One concern that has been repeatedly raised by Information Commissioners regards the inability to choose which complaints to pursue.[47] Nevertheless, the obligation to investigate complaints and the power to initiate investigations into the executive branch of government's compliance with the *Access to Information Act* is very much in keeping with the ombuds tradition. In 2006, under the *Federal Accountability Act*, the Information Commissioner was granted the ability to examine Officers of Parliament as well.[48] While the *Access to Information Act* does not apply to judicial bodies, there has been debate over whether the Commissioner's powers should be so extended.

The resemblance between the classic parliamentary ombuds and the Information Commissioner is strong when it comes to investigating complaints and allegations. It is equally compelling with respect to the second of Reif's distinguishing features – namely, securing redress where the complaint is found to be justified. The tools used traditionally by an ombuds are recommendations to the executive branch of government and publicity. The Information Commissioner's Office fits within this model as it has the power to recommend to government institutions that they release records that the Commissioner has reviewed. The Commissioner's office reports on a selection of cases in its annual report to Parliament. Finally, the office can also report on the specific issues into which it has initiated investigations.[49]

The final aspect of securing redress within the ATIA framework enables a complainant to ask the Federal Court for "a review of the matter"[50] if a government institution has not provided access to records and the Information Commissioner has completed an investigation, regardless of whether the Information Commissioner found that the complaint was justified. Interestingly, the Information Commissioner has a variety of roles that it can play at this point, at its discretion. The Commissioner may bring the matter to the Federal Court with the consent of the requester, or may act on behalf of a requester who has applied for review of the government's nondisclosure. In the final alternative, the Commissioner may appear as a party to any review of nondisclosure brought by a complainant. In this final scenario, it seems that the Commissioner's interests would usually be united

46 See ATIA, *supra* note 4, s 30(3).

47 See Recommendation Number 4 in Information Commissioner of Canada, *Strengthening the Access to Information Act to Meet Today's Imperatives* (Appearance before the Standing Committee on Access to Information, Privacy and Ethics, March 4, 2009) [*Strengthening Access*].

48 SC 2006, c 9 [*Federal Accountability Act, 2006*]. These parliamentary officers include the Privacy Commissioner, the Auditor General and the Information Commissioner itself.

49 ATIA, *supra* note 4, ss 39–40.

50 *Ibid*, s 41.

with those of the complainant; it is possible, however, that the Commissioner may not support disclosure to the extent sought by the complainant. The various roles that the Commissioner may play in a review before the Federal Court are therefore applicant (with consent), advocate or interested party.[51]

There are at least two possible ways of conceiving of the federal Commissioner's functions in securing redress. The first option views the Commissioner as a recommendatory ombudsperson whose territory is circumscribed to investigating and making recommendations to government institutions. This idea is described well in a special research report on the Commissioner's investigative procedures written by Barbara McIsaac 2002. McIsaac writes:

> The federal Information Commissioner investigates complaints relating to the refusal to disclose information under the *Access to Information Act* and other matters relating to the *Act*, but, as an ombudsman, the Commissioner can only recommend a solution. He has no binding order power. Final determinations as to whether exemptions have been properly claimed or not are made by the Federal Court.[52]

The second way shows the Commissioner to have a distinct role to play in the Federal Court as well. Instead of their role being restricted to investigatory and recommendatory functions, the Commissioner is also a valuable player in assisting the court to determine the facts. In examining the complaint and establishing the facts, the Commissioner has an impartial investigatory role similar to the court appointed officer in the inquisitorial process; once the matter moves to review by the court, the Commissioner plays a variation on the role of inquisitorial examiner, becoming an applicant, advocate or interested party.[53] The first conception sees the Commissioner as a specialized ombuds. The second suggests a variation on traditional inquisitorial process.

With respect to the last of Reif's descriptive features of an ombuds – that is, helping to bring about improvements in administrative systems and procedures generally – the Information Commissioner's statutory mandate could be significantly strengthened. Outside of the investigatory powers and the ability to make special reports, there are no powers designed to allow the Information Commissioner to work with institutions to improve systemic issues. This contrasts

---

51 ATIA, *supra* note 4, s 42.

52 Access to Information Review Task Force, *Report 28- The Information Commissioner Investigative Powers and Procedures* by Barbara A McIsaac (Ottawa: The Task Force, 2002).

53 Indeed, the fact that the Federal Court may rely on the Commissioner's factual findings can be seen clearly in some cases such as *3430901 Canada Inc v Canada (Minister of Industry)* (1999), 177 FTR 161 (TD). The approach is not always consistent, however. The issue of records disclosure has also been examined as a pure question of statutory interpretation in which the factual record does not figure prominently.

to jurisdictions such as Ontario or Québec where compliance, education and policy functions are clearly outlined in the enabling statutes.[54]

In conclusion, although it is possible to see connections to the classical parliamentary ombuds, the federal Information Commissioner's functions go beyond this to incorporate aspects of the inquisitorial tradition as well. Nevertheless, what appears to be missing from the federal Information Commissioner's statutory functions is the ability to provide more guidance to governmental institutions on maintaining transparency on a day-to-day basis. This will be further discussed from an empirical perspective in the next part of the chapter.

Investigatory or Adjudicative Complaint Resolution? A Preliminary Empirical Inquiry

In this third and final part of the chapter, I take a closer look at the debate over whether the most appropriate complaint resolution model for access to information at the federal level should be an investigatory or an adjudicative one. This section outlines the debate, theorizing that four competing values can be seen within it and argues that ensuring governmental transparency should be more highly prioritized. It then sets out and analyzes the preliminary findings of an online empirical study designed to evaluate the effectiveness of the current federal investigatory approach with respect to these four values.

Revisiting the Investigatory–Adjudicative Debate over Federal Access Complaint Resolution

Canada's federal Information Commissioner has often offered recommendations for improving the effectiveness and functioning of the office. Additional ideas for improving the OIC have been generated by a Task Force set up to study the matter in 2002,[55] and through a collection of hearings and reports by the parliamentary committee responsible for Access to Information Privacy and Ethics (AIPE).[56] Despite these many calls for change, there has been only one legislative reform affecting the ATIA[57] and no major overhauls of the Act or its complaint resolution process. One debate that has resurfaced consistently since the inception of the

---

54 See, for example, the Ontario Information and Privacy Commissioner's powers at s 52 of *FIPPA*, *supra* note 21, and *An Act respecting Access to documents held by public bodies and the protection of personal information*, RSQ, c A-2.1, ss 122–134, especially ss 122.1 and 123.

55 See *Access to Information: Making it Work for Canadians*, *supra* note 6.

56 See, for example, First Steps, *supra* note 5.

57 The *Federal Accountability Act, 2006*, *supra* note 48, extended the reach of the ATIA to approximately 70 additional bodies including parliamentary officers and crown corporations.

federal access to information regime is the question of whether an adjudicative or an investigatory approach should be used for the resolution of access disputes.

This debate shows four underlying policy values at play and sometimes in competition: i) institutional competence, ii) access to justice, iii) efficiency, and iv) effectiveness in promoting governmental transparency. I will go through each of these values and suggest that the last one, effectiveness, merits more attention in discussions over the appropriate access complaint resolution mechanism.

Institutional competence

In 1977, a Green Paper was issued by the Secretary of State that examined policy options for creating Canada's federal legislation on access to information.[58] The Green Paper discussed, generally, the challenge of balancing the need for access to government records to enable citizens to participate effectively in public decision-making with circumstances in which government functioning requires confidentiality. With respect to the review of access complaints, the author of the Green Paper considered several options and, for each option, queried whether an appropriate balance could be struck between deterring ministers from being overly protective in their decisions regarding disclosure, and respecting their political expertise about the implications of releasing material. The Green Paper rejected the option of allowing direct appeals to the Federal Court as it gave members of the judiciary the political role of deciding the merits of questions that were constitutionally within the realm of the executive branch of government. The drafters of the Green Paper manifested concerns about institutional competence through a discussion of constitutionality and polycentricity:

> [a] judge cannot be asked, in our system of government, to assume the role of giving an opinion on the merits of the very question that has been decided by a Minister. There is no way that a judicial officer can be properly made aware of all the political, economic, social and security factors that may have led to the decision in issue. Nor should the courts be allowed to usurp the constitutional role that Parliament plays in making a Minister answerable to it for his actions.[59]

Such concerns about institutional competence have hardly dissipated since the time of the 1977 Green Paper. In fact, one may argue that we have seen the reverse: a surge in concern about the proper role of the courts in both constitutional law, due to the advent of the *Charter*, and in administrative law as a result of acute attention over the past three decades to standard of review analyses in judicial review. One of the recent proposals suggested by the Information Commissioner is to allow direct access to the Federal Court by requesters who have been denied

58 Canada, Secretary of State, *Legislation on Public Access to Government Documents* (Ottawa: Ministry of Supply and Services Canada, 1977) (Honourable John Roberts) [Green Paper].

59 *Ibid* at 18.

access to records.[60] If the proposed recourse to the Federal Court is designed as a *de novo* review, the same issues of institutional competence that lurked in 1977 will arise. If couched as judicial review, the current standard of review analysis to be conducted under *Dunsmuir v New Brunswick*[61] would likely invite a standard of reasonableness in order to give deference to the expertise of the department and in light of the nature of the question and the decision-maker, regardless of whether there is a strong privative clause. However, reasonableness review may not satisfy the general public that there has been sufficient scrutiny of executive decisions to withhold government records.[62] The Supreme Court has held that the question of disclosure is merely one of statutory interpretation, albeit with broad implications, and engaged in judicial review on a correctness standard.[63] But, if this standard is adopted consistently, the issue of institutional competence will once again arise as it would with *de novo* review at the Federal Court. Institutional competence is definitely one of the underlying factors to be considered in designing an appropriate review mechanism for access complaints.

Access to justice

The idea of direct access to the Federal Court is also animated by concerns for access to justice. The right to government information has attracted constitutional protection in some contexts by the Supreme Court of Canada.[64] The requirement that each complaint first be investigated by the Commissioner's office can be seen as an obstacle to obtaining a timely resolution and to receiving a remedy if the right has been improperly violated. This is especially so given that the Commissioner does not have discretion to choose the complaints that will be investigated. As a consequence, all complaints, including frivolous and vexatious ones must be dealt with. Not surprisingly, the OIC has been plagued by backlog for several years.[65]

---

60 See Recommendation Number 11 in *Strengthening Access*, *supra* note 47, which asserts: "That the *Access to Information* Act allow requesters the option of direct recourse to the Federal Court for access refusals." This recommendation was endorsed by AIPE in its report to Parliament of June, 2009.

61 [2008] 1 SCR 190 [*Dunsmuir*].

62 See *Canada (Information Commissioner) v Canada (Commissioner of the Royal Canadian Mounted Police)*, 2003 SCC 8.

63 Recently, the Supreme Court of Canada applied the correctness standard in *Canada (Information Commissioner) v Canada (Minister of National Defence)*, [2011] 2 SCR 306.

64 See *Ontario (Public Safety and Security) v Criminal Lawyers' Association*, [2010] 1 SCR 815 where it was held that access to information legislation may violate the constitutional right to freedom of expression if the denial of access effectively precludes meaningful public discussion on matters of public interest and there are no countervailing considerations inconsistent with production.

65 See OIC Annual Report, 2009–10, *supra* note 38, in which the Information Commissioner discusses strategies adopted over the year that assisted with reducing the backlog.

Will changing to a system of direct access to the Federal Court provide greater access to justice? On the one hand, a complainant who would nevertheless have ended up before the Federal Court may receive a quicker resolution by bypassing one step in the process. On the other hand, a significant challenge arises for this complainant in terms of securing the evidentiary record that he or she will need. The Information Commissioner plays a valuable role by being able to examine records, the confidentiality of which is in dispute. If the Commissioner is not involved in the process, complainants will be required to construct their cases without benefitting from a full investigation or from the strong investigatory powers of the Information Commissioner. If direct access to the Federal Court were adopted, it would be wise for ancillary statutory reforms to be made allowing for the Commissioner to be called upon to investigate and present facts to the Court in the public interest.

Concerns about access to justice must also ensure that there is a balance between the interests of the requester and the department, whatever the procedural design. Both the requester and the department should be able to contribute to the discussion and know that their points of view will be fully and fairly considered.

Efficiency

The Information Commissioner's efficiency and access to justice concerns are closely related. It has already been noted that there is a significant backlog of cases at the Commissioner's office. The delay caused by this backlog is another reason given in support of allowing complainants to bypass the Commissioner and ask the Federal Court for the first level of review. However, the court system is well known to suffer from backlog as well. There is no guarantee that direct access to the Federal Court will provide a quicker solution to the complainant. Moreover, unless the issues discussed above relating to the complainant's disadvantage in obtaining the factual record are addressed, direct Federal Court access may be quicker for the complainant but not as effective. It would be more advisable to provide resources to the Information Commissioner's office in order to ensure that it can do its work efficiently and effectively instead of pursuing first level review at the Federal Court as, regardless of the change, there may still be delay and the Information Commissioner may still need to be involved.

Effectiveness in promoting governmental transparency

Finally, one must address the greater issue of effectiveness that spans beyond the satisfaction of any one complainant. The purpose of the federal access to information legislation is not only to provide access to government-held records in individual cases but to promote a cultural shift in government that accepts transparency as a default position and secrecy as an exception. The stated purpose of the Act suggests this quite clearly:

> The purpose of this Act is to extend the present laws of Canada to provide a right of access to information in records under the control of a government institution

> *in accordance with the principles that government information should be available to the public, that necessary exceptions to the right of access should be limited and specific* and that decisions on the disclosure of government information should be reviewed independently of government.[66]

One way in which the access to information regime may achieve greater effectiveness in promoting governmental transparency is by investing a wider panoply of tools in the Information Commissioner. The complaint resolution process as it currently stands focuses on strong investigation and fact-finding. The Information Commissioner has little if any mandate to pursue broader educational goals with the government institutions with which it deals; yet, as an ombuds, the OIC is in a perfect position to persuade, negotiate and teach government institutions in order to bring about change with a longer-term impact. Such a mandate would fit very well with the traditional role of an ombuds, as an ombuds has the ability to make meaningful connections with the government institutions that it sees repeatedly. This type of longer-term educational impact may not necessarily be as easily derived from an adversarial system that results in orders. The OIC has asked for a public education mandate;[67] it would be useful if this legislative reform were realized.

The Impact of the OIC's Investigations: Empirical Methodology and Preliminary Findings

How is the federal access complaint resolution process faring on the ground? Should it be replaced with an adversarial model? In this section, I report on the methodology and early findings of an ongoing empirical study which aims to gather information and reasoned opinions as to whether the investigatory and adjudicative processes employed in different jurisdictions in Canada have an impact on changing the culture of government institutions. In particular, the research project seeks to understand how, if at all, the results of investigations or adjudicative decisions relating to freedom of information are translated into longer-term effects (policies, practices, and so on) that further a culture of transparency within government departments and ministries.

Empirical methodology

The research instrument used in this part of the study was an online web-based survey, sent to access to information coordinators in the federal government.[68]

---

66 ATIA, s 2(1) [emphasis added]. Subsection 2 (2) supports this idea further by stating that ATIA's enactment is in no way designed to limit open government practices that already exist.

67 See Recommendation Number 5 in *Strengthening Access*, *supra* note 47.

68 An access to information coordinator is the person or team of individuals responsible for determining whether access to records held by a government department (or

There are three parts to the overall research study, each with its own designed survey.[69] The first engages with access to information officials in the Canadian federal government where an investigatory approach is used to resolve access to information disputes. This write-up reports on the results of the first part only. The second part of the research study surveys access officials in Québec, a jurisdiction in which an adjudicative tribunal has been adopted for the same purpose. Finally, a survey has been designed for media associations and other members of the public who frequently make access to information requests. Each part of the study employs its own independent survey instrument.

Potential federal government respondents were asked to participate in a 20-minute online survey sent by e-mail link. The questions asked respondents to provide reasons why they believe that investigatory or adjudicative approaches to access complaint resolution have a greater impact on governmental transparency, timeliness and fairness within their institutions, and to indicate whether any practices or policies have developed to promote transparency, timeliness and/or fairness as a result of encounters with the federal ATI regulator, the OIC.

The survey was sent in two waves. Initially, it was sent to a select group of 33 federal government departments. These departments were chosen based on the federal Information Commissioner's *Report Cards* over the five-year period of 2005–2010. The *Report Cards* track institutions for which the OIC has received at least five complaints relating to timeliness of response.[70] The majority of the institutions chosen for the survey had been subject to the *Report Card* exercise at least once between 2005 and 2010; two institutions were included because they were institutions affiliated with those who had undergone the *Report Card* exercise. Ultimately, all institutions were chosen because the *Report Card* initiative indicated that they had had extensive experience dealing with the OIC. Because of a low response rate, the survey was sent out a second time to all of the publicly listed access to information coordinators across the federal government.[71]

---

institution) should be granted to requesters. Under the ATIA, the coordinator is by default the head of the government department (or institution), though this responsibility may be delegated to a designated public official or team of public officials. The survey is on file with the author.

69 A second and third instrument have also been created for Quebec ATI officials and for some of the most significant users ATI legislation (i.e. media associations and their representatives) respectively. With respect to Québec, the ministries total approximately 40 and all will receive the survey (REB# 10-237). federal government

70 This is the criterion as it was defined in 2008–09. It is unclear how the OIC chose the institutions examined for its *Report Cards* prior to 2008. Information about the OIC's Report Card exercise can be found on its website: http://www.oic-ci.gc.ca/eng/rp-pr_spe-rep_rap-spe_rep-car_fic-ren_3_yrs_plan.aspx.

71 There are approximately 75 publicly listed federal access coordinators although not all of the government departments or institutions with which they are affiliated have had experience before the federal Information Commissioner.

Part A of the survey asked whether the respondent considered the investigatory approach of the OIC to be effective in balancing interests of the requester and the department, in encouraging the department to maintain a workplace culture of government transparency, and in encouraging timely responses to future requests. Respondents were asked to explain the reasons for their responses. Part B then asked for their opinions on whether an adjudicative approach in which a tribunal or court had first review of the issues and responsibility for issuing binding orders, would be more effective in balancing the interests of the department and requesters with regard to fairness, furthering a workplace culture of transparency, and encouraging timely responses.

The access officials were subsequently asked to consider their responses in Parts A and B in light of two of the most common types of access to information request – requests for personal information and for information for which exemptions relating to national security and defense could be invoked – and to provide any additional comments. The survey then asked questions regarding the existence and genesis of any policies and/or practices that may have been established by the department regarding how documents should be handled on a day-to-day basis in case access to information requests are filed.[72]

The empirical methodology therefore sought to explore, through questioning, reasoned opinions about the qualitative effectiveness of the investigatory access complaint dispute resolution systems designed by Parliament. Taken together, the survey questions were designed to examine how the four theoretical values of institutional competence, access to justice, efficiency, and effectiveness are succeeding within the institutional design of investigatory oversight constructed for the federal access information regulatory context.

Empirical findings

The response rate to the survey was an interesting finding in of itself, and leads the empirical data gathered to be more suggestive than definitive. After an initial slow start,[73] a number of access coordinators replied to explain that their department/institution could not participate in the survey due to a lack of resources/personnel, because their departments received an insignificant number of access requests, had no exposure to the OIC, or because of lack of permission from their department or institution to take part in the survey. Twelve substantive responses surfaced altogether and form the basis of the discussion below. Although this is a small number of respondents, given that a number of departments could not participate and the reasons that prevented them from contributing, the respondent pool is still qualitatively significant.

72 Respondents were also asked if they could be contacted for a follow-up conversation/interview.

73 In the first wave, although 33 government departments were approached and all given at least two weeks to respond, with reminders, only one response surfaced. The second wave produced more respondents and a more robust set of information.

With respect to the first question which asked "whether the current investigatory approach was effective in balancing the interests of departments and requesters", 60% of respondents felt that the investigatory approach was effective. A repeated theme among these respondents was that the OIC attempts to consider all information provided by both the requester and the department, and that the process allows requesters a chance to review the department's application of exemptions so that they can ensure that their right of access has not been unduly restricted. Concern was expressed, however, that the OIC process still seems confrontational even though described as investigatory. Interestingly, one respondent expressed concern that there was no long-term impact of the investigations and that similar requests often led to a re-initiation of the entire process at the departmental level. Concern was also expressed that investigators are not as knowledgeable as they once seemed to be. These last two concerns seem to point to a need for greater resources, both educational (so that departments learn to be more efficient after their mistakes) and in terms of investigator training.

In response to the question of whether the current investigatory approach is effective in encouraging their departments to maintain a workplace culture of government transparency, only 40% of those who answered felt that it was. This contrasted to 60% who felt that it was not effective in doing so. The minority highlighted that negotiations with the investigators provide openness to the parties and that the threat of an investigation is a good motivation for employees who are reluctant to positively engage in the process. Those who felt that it was not effective indicated, for the most part, that their departments already had a workplace culture of openness that was independent of the complaint process. In response to a variety of questions, a significant group of officials responded that a culture of transparency begins with strong leadership at the department level. These officials felt that a workplace culture of transparency could not be inculcated by the "threat" of either investigatory or adjudicative oversight.

As for the impact of the investigatory oversight process on timeliness, 50% of those who responded felt that the current investigatory approach succeeded in encouraging departments to provide timely responses to future requests. They emphasized the "helpful guidance and recommendations" that the OIC investigation provides and that the OIC's *Report Cards* are effective in encouraging departments to respond in a timely fashion as institution heads do not like the negative publicity. By contrast, an interesting repeated concern arose from those who were of the view that departmental timeliness in responding to requests had not been enhanced by the investigatory process. They emphasized that investigations take up resources that could be used to address other current complaints in a timely fashion.

With respect to whether an adjudicative approach, in which a tribunal or court had first review of the issues and responsibility for issuing binding orders, would be more effective, the survey-takers were largely in favour of the investigatory approach already in place. With regard to balancing interests, almost 78% of those who responded chose the investigatory approach. They emphasized advantages in terms of costs, collaboration, and balanced outcomes. The investigative approach was perceived as less expensive and one that permitted the parties to place more emphasis on the interests related to access than on saving time and money. Moreover, the approach was seen as collaborative, and any outcome was therefore perceived as one that had assessed relevant competing interests. As regards furthering a workplace culture of transparency, again approximately 78% of respondents preferred investigation. They believed that an adjudicative approach could create a culture of fear rather than one of transparency, and that the will to be transparent had to come from within the organization. For similar reasons, approximately 73% of respondents were of the opinion that an adjudicative approach would not be effective in encouraging timely responses to access requests. These respondents also felt that tribunal or court decisions would not have the same "political impact" on government that investigations through an office such as the OIC would have. The minority who preferred an adjudicative approach emphasized that the time and costs of litigation, as well as being forced to adhere to a binding order, would likely encourage institutions to think twice before deciding access requests.

When asked to consider whether they believed that an investigatory or adjudicative approach would be more effective in resolving access complaints relating to personal information and national security, the preferences changed little. Fifty-six percent of those who responded to the question felt that an investigatory approach would be less expensive and more effective for resolving personal information complaints, an area where transparency was not too heavy a concern for government. With respect to national security, where government transparency was more of a concern, the collective response was simply to favour any approach that would least risk revealing confidential information. Approximately half of the respondents chose the investigatory approach out of concern that it would be awkward to discuss potential state secrets in open court, and because ombuds investigation offers a better opportunity to manage competing interests. The other half of the respondents suggested that their choice of approach would depend on the circumstances of the case but held that neither approach should have the power to overturn a legitimate concern for national security and defense.

Finally, when asked whether departments had developed policies to efficiently address access requests, a third of the respondents answered "yes", a third answered in the negative, and a third simply did not respond. Officials were asked what prompted the creation of any existing policies. Interestingly, none of the respondents indicated that the investigatory process had specifically prompted its policies, although one department indicated that the implementation of the Act had led to the creation of its policies. Most survey-takers chose not to respond to the question of whether policies in existence have been helpful in improving the willingness to be transparent on the part of department officials. However, those who said that it did indicated that it is easier for officials to adhere to a policy than to have to grapple with the intricacies of the legislation. Overall, it is difficult to draw a conclusion that regulatory oversight has led to a long-term development of departmental policies and procedures. Indeed, more information would be needed to draw any connection between the OIC's regulatory work and any policies that do exist within federal government departments. To be taken into account, as well, is that the Treasury Board also has a generative role to play in the development of policies across government relating to a variety of matters including access to information.

One respondent had particularly thoughtful opinions to convey on the value of the investigatory approach. This official perceived that a strong value of the investigatory approach is that it offers an opportunity for those under investigation to "buy into" the results. The respondent was of the opinion that an adjudicative process with binding results may not have the same potential. With respect to promoting government transparency, adjudication may, in the words of this respondent, "actually do the opposite and drive an already nervous workforce to create even less records than at present."[74]

In addition to the chance to buy into the results, the survey-taker also found that the investigatory approach took the emphasis away from court and lawyers' fees so that the focus could remain on the access to information issues and interests at play. The respondent stated:

> At the moment there is still room for discussion around what those [access] interests are. If the process was to go before a tribunal that could make binding orders, that discussion about interests may not occur to the same degree. Any court type process becomes about time and money.[75]

The investigatory process may show promise for the reasons suggested by this respondent. Specifically, it is flexible and offers room for those subject to the Act to come to a negotiated solution which in the long term may lead to greater transparency, fairness and efficiency.

Overall, the empirical data generated from the survey suggests a strong preference for the investigatory approach amongst the participating access officials, though not necessarily a strong indication that the investigatory approach has been effective in fulfilling the four values underpinning an access to information regime. There are particularly problems with efficiency and effectiveness. The survey results indicate that systemic challenges persist in responding to access requests, including issues relating to timeliness. Furthermore, the data illustrates that the federal ATI complaint resolution system lacks the concrete step of bringing about department-based policies and practices which could serve to further a culture of transparency, promote timeliness, reduce the re-initiation of processes for similar requests, and avoid investigations altogether as they take up time and resources from the handling of other requests.

74 From survey responses, on file with author.

75 *Ibid.*

Conclusions

In this chapter, I have defined three ATI dispute resolution models: adjudicative, investigatory and mixed, and shown their interconnection with the adversarial, inquisitorial and ombuds traditions. I have examined ATI legislation across Canada and the powers of Canadian Information Commissioners to reach the conclusions that ATI dispute resolution models run along a spectrum. Finally, I have argued that instead of conceptually building on an ombuds paradigm which espouses a notion of a citizen's defender, it is more accurate to conceive of adjudicative Information Commissioners as independent accountability agencies.

With an understanding of these dispute resolution models, this chapter has turned to look at the current debate over replacing the investigatory access complaint resolution process associated with federal Information Commissioner with direct access to the adjudicative system of the Federal Court. In addition to approaching the debate theoretically, it has addressed the debate empirically to determine which of the two models may be more effective in fostering governmental transparency. Based both on theoretical analysis and the preliminary results of an ongoing empirical study, I suggest that an explicit education mandate would strengthen the federal Information Commissioner's ombuds oversight. With greater qualitative resources such as training and wider powers of outreach education and research, the Office of the Information Commissioner could play a significant role in contributing to the achievement of the aim of the access legislation – namely, engendering a stronger culture of transparency within the executive branch of government. The federal access to information complaint resolution regime could draw upon the positive elements of the investigatory process identified by respondents to the study, to ensure that the resolution of individual complaints leads to a longer-term, systemic impact on government handling of access requests. Investing a specific statutory educational mandate in the OIC to work with government departments, with a view to creating long-term policies that address timeliness and proactive transparency practices within their particular departments, would be beneficial to fostering a culture of transparency within government. The empirical data suggests that officials would be amenable to buying into the processes and results generated from an additional mandate of this nature provided that the OIC built on the collaborative elements it currently uses in its investigations. Beyond this, independent methods for fostering the strong leadership within government departments that a number of respondents have suggested is required to achieve a corporate culture of transparency should be simultaneously pursued. This chapter has provided an opportunity to contemplate the policy goals of one administrative regime and to reflect on how institutional design and administrative processes might ideally serve to further those goals.

Table 15.1 Access to Information Dispute Resolution in Canada – Commissioner Processes and Powers: Provinces

	AB[1]	BC[2]	MB[3]	NB[4]
Title of process	Inquiry	Inquiry	Investigation	Investigation
Conducted in public or private?	At Commissioner discretion – s 69(2)	At Commissioner discretion – s 56(2)	Private – s 52	At Commissioner discretion – s 70(2)
Parties entitled to make representations?	Yes – s 69(3)	Yes – s 56(3)	Yes – s 64(1)	Yes – s 71(1)
Parties entitled to access representations of others in the dispute?	No, but done as a practice	At Commissioner discretion – s 56(4)	No – s 64(1)	No – s 71(2)
Compel production of records?	Yes[13]	Yes – ss 56 and 44	Yes – s 50(2)	Yes[14] – s 70
Enter premises?	Yes[16]	Yes – ss 56 and 44	Yes – s 51	Yes – s 62
Summons appearances?	Yes[13]	Yes – ss 56 and 44	Yes[17]	Yes[14]
Compel testimony under oath/affirmation?	Yes[13]	Yes – ss 56 and 44	Yes[17]	Yes[14]
Order-making powers?	Yes	Yes	No	No
Recommendations?	No	No	Yes	Yes

Notes:

1 See *Freedom of Information and Protection of Privacy Act*, RSA 2000, c F-25.

2 See *Freedom of Information and Protection of Privacy Act*, RSBC 1996, c 165. See also the Commissioner's *Policies and Procedures* under FIPPA: http://www.oipc.bc.ca/search.aspx?SearchTerm=Policies%20and%20Procedures(May2009).pdf.

3 See *The Freedom of Information and Protection of Privacy Act*, CCSM . F175.

4 See *Right to Information and Protection of Privacy Act*, RSNB, R-10.6. Between 1978 and 2010, the New Brunswick Ombudsman was responsible for resolving access to information disputes in the province. Under the current statute, individuals have the option of going to court directly for some matters.

5 See *Access to Information and Protection of Privacy Act*, SNL 2002, c A-1.1.

6 See *Freedom of Information and Protection of Privacy Act*, SNS 1993, c 5.

7 See *Freedom of Information and Protection of Privacy Act*, RSO 1990, c F.31.

8 See *Freedom of Information and Protection of Privacy Act*, RSPEI 1988, c F-15.01.

9 *An Act respecting Access to documents held by public bodies and the Protection of personal information*, RSQ, c A-2.1.

10 *The Freedom of Information and Protection of Privacy Act*, SS 1990–91, c F-22.01.

11 See *Rules of Proof and Procedure before the Commission d'accès à l'information*, c A-2.1, r. 2, s 18.

Nfld & Lab.[5]	**NS**[6]	**ON**[7]	**PEI**[8]	**QC**[9]	**SK**[10]
Review	Review	Inquiry	Inquiry	Review	Review
At Commissioner discretion – s 47(2)	At Review Officer discretion – s 37(1)	At Commissioner discretion – s 52(3)	At Commissioner discretion – s 64(2)	Public[11]	Private – s 53(1)
Yes – s 47(1)	Yes – s 37(2)	Yes – s 52(13)	Yes – s 64(3)	Yes – s 140	Yes – s 53(2)
No – s 47(2)	At Commissioner discretion – s 37(3)(b)	No – s 52(13) but done as a practice[12]	No – s 64(3)	Yes – no restrictions in Act or Code of Procedure	No – s 53(3)
Yes – s 52	Yes – s 38	Yes – s 52(4)	Yes – s 53	Yes – as an adjunct to adversarial, oral, public hearing[15]	Yes – s 54(1)(a)
Yes – s 53	Yes – s 38	Yes – s 52(4)	Yes – s 53	No	Yes – s 54(1)(b)
Yes[18]	n/a	Yes – s 52(8)	Yes[19]	Yes – as an adjunct to adversarial, oral, public hearing[15]	Yes – s 54
Yes[18]	n/a	Yes – s 52(8)	Yes[19]	Yes – as an adjunct to adversarial, oral, public hearing[15]	Yes – s 54
No	No	Yes	Yes	Yes	No
Yes	Yes	No	No	No	Yes

12 See *Code of Procedure for appeals under the* Freedom of Information and Protection of Privacy Act *and the* Municipal Freedom of Information and Protection of Privacy Act: http://www.ipc.on.ca/images/Resources/code-e.pdf.

13 Power granted by the *Public Inquiries Act,* RSA 2000, c P-39, incorporated by reference under s 56(1) of the *Freedom of Information and Protection of Privacy Act,* RSA 2000, c F-25.

14 Power granted by the *Inquiries Act*, RSNB 2011, c 173, incorporated by reference under s 61 of the *Right to Information and Protection of Privacy Act*, SNB 2009, c R-10.6.

15 See *Rules of Proof and Procedure before the Commission d'accès à l'information*, c A-2.1, r. 2, ss 22–23.

16 Power granted by the *Public Inquiries Act,* RSA 2000, c P-39, incorporated by reference under s 56(1) of the *Freedom of Information and Protection of Privacy Act*, RSA 2000, c F-25. Power to enter and inspect premises is available only upon declaration of the Lieutenant Governor in Council.

17 Power granted by the *Manitoba Evidence Act*, CCSM c E150, s 88, incorporated by reference under s 50(1) of *The Freedom of Information and Protection of Privacy Act*, CCSM c F175.

18 Power granted by the *Public Inquiries Act, 2006*, SNL 2006, c P-38.1 incorporated by reference under s 52 of the *Access to Information and Protection of Privacy Act*, SNL 2002, c A-1.1.

19 Power granted by the *Public Inquiries Act*, RSPEI 1988, c P-31, incorporated by reference under s 53(1) of the *Access to Information and Protection of Privacy Act*, SNL 2002, c A-1.1.

Table 15.2 Access to Information Dispute Resolution in Canada – Commissioner Processes and Powers: Federal Government and Territories

	Fed. Gov.[1]	NWT[2]	NU[3]	YK[4]
Title of process	Investigation	Review	Review	Inquiry
Conducted in public or private?	Private – s 35(1)	Private – s 32(1)	Private – s 32(1)	At Commissioner discretion – s 52(2)
Parties entitled to make representations?	Yes – s 35(2)	Yes – s 32(2)	Yes – s 32(2)	Yes – s 52(3)
Parties entitled to access representations of others in the dispute?	No – s 35(2)	No – s 32(3)	No – s 32(3)	At Commissioner discretion – s 52(4)
Compel production of records?	Yes – s 36	Yes – s 34	Yes – s 34	Yes – s 53(1)
Enter premises?	Yes – s 36	Yes – s 34	No	Yes[5]
Summons appearances	Yes – s 36	Yes – s 34	No	Yes[5]
Compel testimony under oath/ affirmation?	Yes – s 36	Yes – s 34	No	Yes[5]
Order-making powers?	No	No	No	No
Recommendations?	Yes	Yes	Yes	Yes

Notes:

1 See *Access to Information Act*, RSC 1985, c A-1.

2 See *Access to Information and Protection of Privacy Act*, SNWT 1994, c 20.

3 See *Access to Information and Protection of Privacy Act*, SNWT (Nu) 1994, c 20. Interestingly, although the Nunavut statute is based on the Northwest Territories' access to information and privacy legislation, the provisions offering the most coercive investigative powers have been removed from the Nunavut legislation. This removal could be for a variety of reasons – for example, it might be that the powers were not being used, and therefore deemed unnecessary for a Commissioner to fulfill its role.

4 See *Access to Information and Protection of Privacy Act*, RSY 2002, c 1.

5 Power granted by the *Public Inquiries Act*, RSY 2002, c 177, incorporated by reference under s 53(1) of the *Access to Information and Protection of Privacy Act*, RSY 2002, c 1.

Chapter 16
The Evolution of the Idiosyncrasy of the Role of Ombudsman/Person in Canada

Nora Farrell

Introduction

While the overarching goal of an ombudsman/person[1] role wherever it is located is the pursuit of administrative fairness, the developmental paths and current implementation of ombuds functions in Canada demonstrate that this inquisitorial mode of dispute resolution differs dramatically in structure depending on when, by whom or what and how the role was established. This paper will illustrate how this unique mode of dispute resolution has evolved serendipitously rather than by design. By pointing out the differences and similarities from a historical as well as a contemporary perspective within what I consider to be the three primary categories of ombuds work, the idiosyncratic reality of ombudsing in Canada will be readily evident. Building on this unpredictable foundation, the subsequent discussion of the intriguing multiplicity of mandates and reporting relationships, which has resulted in a Canadian patchwork of ombuds activity, will demonstrate how administrative fairness can be achieved through the use of various types of ombuds models. Ultimately, this analysis reveals that an ombuds role can contribute to a high level of administrative fairness irrespective of how the ombuds role is founded (that is, by legislation or policy), as long as the prerequisites of independence, impartiality and a commitment to contributing to an ethos of fairness are explicit in its design and in its implementation. An unintended but direct result of this winding approach to the establishment of ombuds roles is easy access to inquisitorial expertise for the purpose of administrative fairness in many areas of Canadian public, private and not-for-profit sectors.

1 Throughout this book, the following terminology has been adopted, in order to promote gender neutrality while also respecting the names of ombuds institutions. The capitalized expression, "Ombudsman" has been used for specific names (for example, the Swedish Ombudsman, the Ombudsman of Ontario). The lowercase words "ombudsman", "ombudsperson" and "ombuds" have been used, as nouns and adjectives, to represent general institutions, with preference for the use of the gender-neutral forms of "ombudsperson" and "ombuds" wherever possible.

Historical Foundation of Idiosyncrasy

As neither a federal ombuds of general jurisdiction has been created in Canada nor does any regulatory or professional body have the authority to specify how an ombuds should be constructed, the type of ombuds role established and the nature of its inquisitorial powers is dependent upon what entity established it and its vision for how oversight for administrative fairness should be fulfilled and by whom. As a result, not only the historical precedents but the political or personal philosophies of the legislators and/or the organizational or industry leadership extant at the time of creation of the ombuds role may also be influential with respect to both form and function. The opposite approach was taken in New Zealand in 1975 (13 years after inception of the role) when the *Ombudsmen Act 1975* (N.Z.), 1975/9 (28A s. 1)[2] was revised to protect the use of the term of "Ombudsman" by requiring consent in writing from the Chief Ombudsman in advance of any non-governmental ombudsman service being established in that jurisdiction.[3] In support of some form of codification of essential ombuds characteristics, the Australian and New Zealand Ombudsman Association (ANOZA) has set out six criteria as being elemental to any entity that is described as an Ombudsman in Australia and New Zealand.[4] These criteria, shown in italicized font below, and as defined in the ANOZA policy statement include:

- *Independence* which is predicated on the expectation that the ombudsman role is established in such a fashion that the ombudsman is not subject to the direction of the organization or legislature which established it; the ombudsman entity, which operates on a not-for-profit basis, has fiscal and administrative independence and the right to make public reports and statements. In addition, the ombudsman must function so not to act or be seen to act as an advocate for particular organizations. It is also noted that the ombudsman must be appointed for a fixed term[5] with removal only being possible for misconduct or incapacity by virtue of a clearly articulated review process.

2 *Ombudsmen Act 1975* (NZ), 1975/9, s 28A.

3 *Ibid*, s (1).

4 The Australian and New Zealand Ombudsman Association (ANZOA), *Essential Criteria for Describing a Body as an Ombudsman* (February 2010), online: http://www.anzoa.com.au.

5 These requirements do not make reference to whether the requisite fixed term is renewable. In my view renewable terms create the potential for both the perception of and actual interference with the independence of the role. Also, in Canada, many hybrid and organizational Ombuds enjoy permanent appointments, similar to those enjoyed by judges, which can only be terminated on the basis of personal misconduct or malfeasance.

- *Jurisdiction* being explicitly defined in the legislation or policy or Charter founding the role which should include general oversight of administrative actions or omissions along with the ombudsman's ability to decide what is within jurisdiction unless a Court of Law decides otherwise.
- *Powers* which include the capacity to conduct investigations in response to individual complaints as well as systemic issues or the authority to initiate an investigation on an "own motion" basis. In addition, ombudsman powers must be such that those who are contacted are obliged to respond and provide access to all relevant records and information. The ombudsman must also have the sole authority to decide what type of process to use, such as conciliation or other means, when handling a complaint.[6]
- *Accessibility* which allows for a complainant to interact directly with the Ombudsman Office, at no financial cost, and for the ombudsman [rather than some other authority] having the sole authority to decide whether to investigate the complaint raised. Also, it is expected that the investigation will be undertaken in a private fashion and details will only be released in an annual report or for the benefit of the public generally.
- *Procedural fairness* must be incorporated into the investigative work of the ombudsman with emphasis being placed on the opportunity for anyone who could be negatively affected by the ombudsman's conclusions or recommendations to be provided with the occasion to respond before a final decision is made; the ombudsman's and staff actions must demonstrate a lack of bias, partiality or prejudgment and the ombudsman must deliver reasons to the complainant and the respondent for any conclusions reached and recommendations made.
- *Accountability* demonstrated through the publication of an annual report and the ombudsman being responsible to Parliament if established as a Parliamentary ombudsman or to an independent body of relevant representatives if established for an industry or company.

While these criteria were written to reflect ombuds roles in Australia and New Zealand they are readily evident in the proper construction of many Canadian ombuds roles,[7] both in the public and private sectors.

The New Zealand reference is particularly relevant to this discussion for another more fundamental reason: New Zealand was the first common law country government to create an ombudsman and it did so in 1962 following the

6 It is worthy of note that the commentary on this criterion does not make any reference to the power of recommendation given how prevalent that construction is for Ombuds located in both common and civil law jurisdictions.

7 As there has been no Canadian equivalent put forward by a Canadian Ombuds organization I am including these terms for benefit of establishing definitions for the discussion which follows.

Danish Ombudsman model of operation.[8] Shortly thereafter, the first Canadian ombuds roles established by legislation were created following the New Zealand approach and adopted the Danish Ombudsman model of operation. This decision is significant with respect to the shape of the Canadian ombuds role as the Danish model does not include any form of judicial oversight or prosecutorial power which are imbedded in the more frequently referenced Swedish model.[9] Canadian "early adopters" of the ombuds concept were exposed to the New Zealand experience when Sir Guy Powles, the first New Zealand Ombudsman, visited Canada in 1964 to speak at the annual general meeting of the Canadian Bar Association (CBA) which resulted in the CBA recommending the ombuds role be studied for application in provincial and federal jurisdictions.[10] As well, a Professor of Political Science, Dr. Karl Friedmann, who became the first Ombudsman for the province of British Columbia, described the New Zealand Ombudsman legislation as "… a nearly perfect statute."[11] However, interestingly enough, two years prior to the establishment of any ombuds role in Canada by legislation, in 1965, an ombudsman was established, (in fact, the first academic ombuds role in North America), at Simon Fraser University (SFU) in Vancouver by the Students' Association.[12] This role continues today, almost 50 years hence, with joint funding

8 Mary Seneviratne, *Ombudsmen Public Services and Administrative Justice* (U.K.: Butterworths Lexis Nexis, 2002) at 54.

9 Ulf Lundvik, *The Ombudsmen in the Provinces of Canada* (Edmonton: International Ombudsman Institute, 1981) at 5 [Lundvik]. It is worth noting that while the current four national Swedish Ombudsman have the authority to initiate prosecutions and review judicial decisions they do not use these powers. Specifically, while the Swedish (and Finnish) Ombudsman legislation allow for intervention in court proceedings even to the extent of contacting judges to acquire both substantive and procedural information on cases being reviewed, as well as having the authority to impose penalties for lack of cooperation, current Swedish Ombudsmen responsible for judicial oversight have voluntarily limited their reviews to matters of procedure in an effort to demonstrate respect for the independence of the judiciary. See Gabriel Kucsko-Stadlmayer, *European Ombudsman-Institutions: a comparative legal analysis regarding the multifaceted realisation of an idea* (Springer: Wien; New York, 2008) at 28 for a detailed discussion of this point.

10 Karl Friedmann, Proceedings of the Conference on Ombudsman "Let Justice be Seen to be Done" (Vancouver: British Columbia Human Rights Council, March 1970) at 10.

11 *Ibid.*

12 This information was presented verbally and supported by copies of printed documentation by Laurine Harrison (now deceased), former Ombudsperson at Simon Fraser University (SFU) at a mid-year meeting of the Association of Canadian College and University Ombudspersons in 2001 at Wilfrid Laurier University in Waterloo, Ontario. In 2012, the website for the current Simon Fraser University Ombudsperson indicates that the office has been in place for "… over forty years." Source: "Office of the Ombudsperson", Simon Fraser University, online: www.sfu.ca.

Interestingly enough, this information is contradicted by reference made in the obituary of the former first Principal of Concordia University, John O'Brien where Mr. O'Brien

from the two SFU Students' Associations and the University, with a committee of University-wide representatives selecting the appointee, and is the first instance of the meandering approach to the establishment of ombuds roles in Canada.

Notwithstanding the diversity which is readily apparent with respect to the various ombuds constructions, a useful starting point for the definition of a modern ombuds in Canada can be found in the description provided by Justice Brian Dickson of the Supreme Court of Canada in *British Columbia Development Corp. v Friedmann (Ombudsman)*.[13] In this judgment Justice Dickson provided a foundational definition for an ombudsman as part of his rationale for determining that the Ombudsman for British Columbia did indeed have jurisdiction over a provincial Crown Corporation:

> ...The Ombudsman represents society's response to these problems of potential abuse and of supervision. His unique characteristics render him capable of addressing many of the concerns left untouched by the traditional bureaucratic control devices. He is impartial. His services are free, and available to all. Because he often operates informally, his investigations do not impede the normal processes of government. Most importantly, his powers of investigation can bring to light cases of bureaucratic maladministration that would otherwise pass unnoticed. The Ombudsman "can bring the lamp of scrutiny to otherwise dark places, ever over the resistance of those who would draw the blinds": *Re Ombudsman Act* (1970), 72 W.W.R. 176 (Alta. S.C.), per Milvain C.J., at pp. 192–93. On the other hand, he may find the complaint groundless, not a rare occurrence, in which even his impartial and independent report, absolving the public authority, may well serve to enhance the morale and restore the self-confidence of the public employees impugned. In short, the powers granted to the Ombudsman allow him to address administrative problems that the courts, the legislature and the executive cannot effectively resolve.[14]

While this description was written to describe the role of a classical, provincial ombudsman established by legislation, with oversight of governmental administration only, in my view the principles described also apply to many ombuds

---

was credited for having established the first Ombudsman role in a university in North America at Concordia University in Montreal. Unfortunately no specific date for the office being put in place is provided. Source: Philip Fine, "Administrator Negotiated Merger that Created Concordia University", *The Globe and Mail* (24 January 2012), online: http://www.globeandmail.com. Ultimately, it may be that both institutions are accurate in their claim of "first Ombudsman" in that SFU was likely the first Ombudsman role established within a Canadian university solely by a student association and Concordia is likely the first University to have directed the establishment of an Ombuds of general jurisdiction for the institution as a whole.

13 *British Columbia Development Corp. v Friedmann (Ombudsman)*, [1984] 2 SCR 447 [*British Columbia Development Corp.*].

14 *Ibid* at 461.

roles created via policy, terms of reference, Order-in-Council or even executive fiat within both the private and public sectors. Similarly, if the investigation reference is removed, the characteristics delineated by Justice Dickson also apply to organizational ombuds roles in the public and private sectors.

In light of the foregoing discussion it is worthwhile to know that Canadian ombuds scholar, Donald C. Rowat held the view that ombuds roles not founded by legislation should be described as "internal Ombudsmen."[15] While I support the importance of distinguishing the type of ombuds roles that have been established in a wide variety of different locations in many different ways, so as to ensure that users know what to expect when they approach them, I believe the use of "internal Ombudsman" may incorrectly convey the notion that this type ombuds is less independent than it actually is. For example, due to the culture of the organization and the organization's respect for the independence of the role, it is not unusual for the standard criteria for the establishment of the ombuds role as articulated by ANOZA earlier, to be the found within terms of reference or charter or policy which founds the ombuds role. As a result of a strong foundation of this nature coupled with the ombuds' personal credibility, while the role may not be configured so as to be as structurally independent as a legislated ombuds, the incumbent may be perceived as operating at the same level, by virtue of her demonstrated capacity to "speak truth to power."

The aforementioned Australian and New Zealand Ombudsman Association has also weighed in on this debate by stating that it is oxymoronic or contradictory to use such a term as "internal ombudsman" as this terminology indicates that the ombudsman is actually directed by an industrial organization or governmental official.[16] In Canada, even a cursory review of the annual and special reports disseminated in the public domain by various ombuds not established by legislation will demonstrate the high degree of independence and impartiality of those roles. As a result, I would also argue that the use of the descriptor of "internal" in concert with ombuds is not appropriate in Canada either as it clashes not only with the traditional understanding of and the commonly stated expectations for independence and impartiality but also the reality of Canadian ombuds practice. As a result, in my view the identification of the type of ombuds role should be based on an examination of not only on how it was established and the powers that it has in place but also on how it is implemented.

In summary, following on the "Dicksonian" tradition, Canadian ombuds roles typically have the following characteristics in common:

---

15 Donald C Rowat, "The American Distortion of the Ombudsman Concept and Its Influence on Canada" (2007) 50 Canadian Public Administration 42 at 50.

16 Australian and New Zealand Ombudsman Association (ANZOA), Media Release, "Essential Criteria for Describing a Body as an Ombudsman" (18 May 2010), online: http://www.anzoa.com.au.

- an inquisitorial rather than an adversarial frame work[17] for dispute resolution;[18]
- the power of recommendation only for conclusions reached;
- informality (the ombuds role is on the informal side of the dispute resolution continuum which typically ranges from formal court based adjudication on one side to individual negotiation on the other);
- accessibility (services widely advertised, easy to use and no fees charged);
- confidentiality;
- ombuds adherence to the principles of natural justice and administrative fairness in conducting their own work and assessing the work of others;
- impartiality, and
- independence (administrative, financial and ability to determine own operational policies, procedures and timelines).

However, the distinctiveness of ombuds roles in Canada can be seen in the diversity of mandates and reporting relationships for all manner of Ombuds Offices in Canada which will be described in detail in the next section.

Notwithstanding the diversity of structures, it is possible to categorize ombuds roles using a three-part typology, that I contend represents most accurately the ombuds landscape in Canada. I am positing that such a categorization is both necessary and instructive for two primary reasons: Firstly, as has been observed by Gregory Levine, over the last thirty years the establishment of ombuds roles has been increasing rapidly "... with an array of Ombuds types emerging in the private and public sectors. By and large these entities are organizational or executive Ombudsmen rather than parliamentary Ombudsman, though there has been an increase in specialty Ombudsmen of various types whose offices are parliamentary in nature."[19] Given this expansion and as the bulk of the Canadian ombuds research has been focused on statutorily established roles, it is important to give expression to the broader spectrum of ombuds activity. Secondly, given the increasing volume of ombuds roles being established, in a variety of ways, such a categorization will assist both complainants and respondents, as well as members

17 A practical example of the non-adversarial character of the role was provided by the Ombudsman for Ontario who recently took umbrage with a number of city councilors who refused to meet with his investigators without legal counsel present, by stating that "my investigations are not adversarial in nature, but fact-finding exercises" in explaining why there was no need or requirement for legal counsel to be present. See Richard J Brennan "Ombudsman Slams Sudbury Council for Lack of Co-operation in Investigation", *The Toronto Star* (3 October 2012), online: www.thestar.com.

18 See the Introduction to this collection for an explanation of the parameters of an inquisitorial process.

19 Gregory J Levine "The Ombudsman Plan in Twenty-First Century Canada" in Stewart Hyson, ed, *Provincial and Territorial Ombudsman Offices in Canada* (Toronto: University of Toronto Press, 2009) at 300 [Hyson].

of the public generally and those who study ombuds activities, with a reasonable expectation of what to anticipate when encountering a particular type of ombuds.

The tri-partite typology I am proposing includes the following models:

- *The legislative, classical or parliamentary ombuds*[20] (legislative) which is established by statute with strong powers of investigation and operates at arm's length from the establishing entity due to a high degree of structural independence and a requirement for impartiality and confidentiality;
- *The hybrid*[21] *ombuds* (hybrid) which does not have a legislative base but has the power of investigation, some degree of structural independence and a requirement for impartiality and confidentiality authorized by Charter, Terms of Reference, Order in Council or policy;
- *The organizational ombuds* (organizational) which does not have a legislative base and relies primarily on discussion, facilitation and mediation for assisting with the resolution of individual complaints, coupled with the responsibility for analyzing trends and providing recommendations. Policy or terms of reference require impartiality and confidentiality along with the provision of *de facto* forms of independence.

---

20 Please note that I am restricting the use of the term "Ombuds/man/person" for this discussion to those bodies which do not have powers of prosecution or enforcement and do not serve a regulatory or disciplinary function consistent with the foundational principles of the Danish Ombudsman model as originally established in Canada. The reader may be interested to know that Ulf Lundvik, former Chief Parliamentary Ombudsman, Sweden, described the Commissioner of Official Languages, the Privacy Commissioner and the Correctional Investigator as "... specialized Ombudsman-like offices ..." in Lundvik, *supra* note 9 at 13.

21 Linda C Reif, a Canadian legal scholar, who has written extensively on the practice of legislative Ombuds has used the term "hybrid" to define legislative Ombuds who are responsible for reviewing complaints of human rights violations in addition to maladministration. See Linda Reif, Mary Marshall & Charles Ferris, eds, *The Ombudsman: Diversity and Development* (Edmonton: International Ombudsman Institute, 1993) and Linda C Reif, *The Ombudsman, Good Governance and the International Human Rights System* (Leiden; Boston: Martinus Nijhoff Publishers, 2004). I have chosen to use the term "hybrid" as well but have defined it differently as I think it is reasonable to consider any role that has maintained many of the characteristics of the original version as well as adding on different ones, such as Ombuds no longer being exclusively established by legislation for oversight of governmental administration and operating in a more informal manner the majority of the time, as a "hybrid." Restricting its use only to Ombuds who have oversight of government administrative activity and who also handle human rights complaints would be very limiting. Please note that "hybrid" in this instance is not intended to mean that the hybrid role is the offspring of the legislative model and the organizational model. Rather, the hybrid model was well established in Canada before the organizational model came into use.

Structure of Current Ombuds Roles

Legislative Ombuds which are Established by Statute which Provide for Strong Powers of Investigation and Access to all Records

To begin, the classical, legislative or parliamentary ombuds[22] is established by statute and operates at arm's length from the establishing entity. It has a high degree of structural independence and a requirement for impartiality as well as having the authority and responsibility to maintain confidentiality. In addition, the legislative ombuds has strong powers of investigation and the ability to determine what procedures and dispute resolution techniques it will use in implementing its mandate. Ultimately, when a determination is made that a complaint is valid, conclusions and recommendations are made rather than a binding directive being issued.

In addition, it is important to recognize that a variety of supplementary mandates have been provided to some of the ombuds of general jurisdiction established via statute in Canada. This contributes to the complexity associated with providing a concise, easily understandable definition of the uniquely named ombuds role. The idiosyncratic approaches taken by the provincial and territorial legislatures which established these roles are illustrative of the customized construction of some governmental ombuds roles even within this very specific frame of reference for ombuds activity, that is, the ombuds role established by legislation. For instance, in 1967 both the Alberta Ombudsman and New Brunswick Ombudsman were created[23] with responsibility for general governmental administrative oversight. However, as result of additional legislative activity, the Ombudsman for New Brunswick took on a multiplicity of mandates. For instance, until April 2011 this Ombudsman was also the Child and Youth Advocate;[24] and had the responsibility to review decisions made by government with respect to the protection of personal

---

22 Please note that when I am describing Ombuds established by legislation the entities which are included are those bodies which do not have power of prosecution or enforcement and do not serve a regulatory, disciplinary or compliance function consistent with the foundational principles of the Danish Ombudsman model as originally established in Canada.

23 Frank Stacey, *Ombudsmen Compared* (Oxford: Clarendon Press, 1978) at 51 [Stacey]. Stacey observed in his worldwide study of Ombuds roles published in 1978 that in North America, Canadian jurisdictions had demonstrated the greatest zeal for establishing Ombuds offices overall. It is noteworthy that Joe Loran, current Deputy Ombudsman for the province of Alberta indicated in a speech on June 6, 2012 in Edmonton, Alberta at the Association of Canadian College and University Ombudspersons Conference that when the Alberta Ombudsman role was established there were only ten Ombudsman roles in existence worldwide.

24 See the *Child and Youth Advocate Act*, SNB 2007, c C-2.7. In other jurisdictions, this function is typically a stand-alone entity.

information[25] until an Access to Information and Privacy Commissioner was recently established. The New Brunswick Ombudsman is also responsible for complaints related to the provincial archives[26] and is empowered to review civil service employee appointments.[27] Next, in 1968 the Le Protecteur du Citoyen/ Québec Ombudsman was enacted[28] and in 2001 the mandate of the Health and Social Services Ombudsman was incorporated into that of the Protecteur du Citoyen.[29] In 1969 the Nova Scotia Ombudsman[30] and the Manitoba Ombudsman[31] were established. However, while the Manitoba Ombudsman was originally established with responsibility for administrative oversight of general jurisdiction only, from 1988 to 1997 the Office also became responsible for complaints related to the implementation of the *Freedom of Information Act* M.1988.[32] As of 1997, responsibility for complaints related to the administration of the *Personal Health Information Act*, M.1997 and the *Freedom of Information and Protection of Privacy Act*, M.1997[33] followed. In 1973 the Saskatchewan Ombudsman[34] was established followed by the Ontario Ombudsman in 1975[35] with the most restricted mandate of any ombuds of general jurisdiction in Canada as is evidenced in the following comparative chart prepared by the current Ombudsman for Ontario[36] as part of his lobbying efforts to expand his jurisdiction to include municipalities, universities, social services and hospitals (MUSH). The following chart also demonstrates at a granular level, both the differences and similarities in the provincial and territorial ombuds of general jurisdiction mandates generally.

In 1975, the same year that the Ombudsman for Ontario was created, the Newfoundland and Labrador Parliamentary Commissioner was finally established after the underlying legislation being passed in 1970[37] with broad jurisdiction

25 See *Right to Information Act*, SNB 1978, c R-10.3 as repealed by *Right to Information and Protection of Privacy Act*, SNB 2009, c R-10.6, s 99(1) and the *Protection of Personal Information Act*, SNB 1998, c P-19.1 as repealed by *Right to Information and Protection of Privacy Act*, SNB 2009, c R-10.6, s 98(1) and Hyson, *supra* note 19 at 106.

26 See *Archives Act*, SNB 1977, c A-11.1.

27 See *Civil Service Act*, SNB 1984, c C-5.1.

28 Stacey, *supra* note 23.

29 *Le Protecteur du citoyen* / The Québec Ombudsman, "History", online: http://www.protecteurducitoyen.qc.ca/en/the-quebec-ombudsman/history/index.html.

30 Stacey, *supra* note 23 at 45. For a short period of time in the 1990s the Nova Scotia Ombudsman was also required to serve as the Human Rights Commissioner due to fiscal woes.

31 *Ibid.*

32 Hyson, *supra* note 25 at 83.

33 The function of oversight of Freedom of Information and Protection of Privacy legislation is performed by separate Commissioners in other provinces.

34 Stacey, *supra* note 23 at 51.

35 *Ibid.*

36 Ombudsman Ontario, "The Push for Mush" (7 June 2011), online: http://www.ombudsman.on.ca.

37 Stacey, *supra* note 23 at 45.

Table 16.1 Areas of Oversight for Legislated Ombuds of General Jurisdiction in Canada

Province/Territory Ombuds	Boards of Education	Child Protection Services	Public Hospitals	Nursing Homes/ Long Term Care (LTC) Facilities	Municipalities	Police Complaints Review Mechanisms	Universities
Alberta	No	Yes	Yes[1]	Yes[2]	No	Yes	No
British Columbia	Yes	Yes	Yes[3]	Yes	Yes	No	Yes
Manitoba	No	Yes	Yes	Yes	Yes	Yes[4]	No
New Brunswick	Yes	Yes[5]	Yes[6]	No	Yes	Yes[7]	No
Newfoundland & Labrador	Yes	Yes	Yes	Yes	No	Yes	Yes
Nova Scotia	Yes	Yes	Yes	Yes	Yes	Yes	No
Ontario	No	No	No	No	No[8]	No	No
Québec	No	Yes[9]	Yes	Yes	No	Yes	No
Saskatchewan	No	Yes	Yes	Yes	No	Yes	No
Yukon	Yes	Yes	Yes	Yes	By reference[10]	No[11]	No

Please note that this chart is configured somewhat differently than the original entitled "The Push for Mush",[12] in that the jurisdictions are ordered alphabetically for ease of reading and acronyms have been used in the footnotes rather than repeating the name of the province or territory in full.

1 The AB Ombudsman has jurisdiction to investigate complaints about the patient concerns resolution processes of hospitals.

2 The AB Ombudsman has jurisdiction to investigate complaints about the patient concerns resolution processes of LTC facilities and nursing homes.

3 The BC Ombudsperson has jurisdiction over regional health boards and regional hospital districts.

4 The MB Ombudsman's jurisdiction over police, which are municipal, flows from her jurisdiction over municipalities. The Ombudsman also has jurisdiction over the Law Enforcement Agency (LERA) which is part of the Justice Department.

5 The NB Ombudsman is prevented from investigating a matter that is or has been investigated or reviewed by the Office of the Child and Youth Advocate. The NB Ombudsman is also the Child and Youth Advocate.

6 The NB Ombudsman has jurisdiction over Regional Health Authorities, which operate, own and dispense all services in hospitals.

7 The NB Ombudsman has jurisdiction over the NB Police Commission. The Commission is not included in the Schedule to The Ombudsman Act, but the Ombudsman has a working agreement with the Commission allowing them to review Commission files.

8 The Ombudsman can investigate some municipal closed meetings.

9 *Le Protecteur du citoyen* has some jurisdiction over administrative procedural matters relating to child protection services provided for by the directo*rs of youth protection.*

10 A municipality or Yukon First Nation government may at any time refer a matter to the Ombudsman for investigation and report.

11 The only police force operating in the Yukon is the RCMP, a federal body.

12 Ombudsman Ontario; see *supra* note 36.

that included universities, social services and hospitals but not municipalities. However, in 1990 after such a strong beginning, the Newfoundland and Labrador government de-commissioned the Office due to a change in political philosophy. The rationale for the repealing of the *Ombudsman Act* was the then Premier's belief that the Ombudsman Office was an unnecessary expense as in his view all of the Cabinet Ministers and Members of the House of Assembly (MHA) had actually demonstrated the ability to act as ombudsman for their constituents and interestingly, he posited they had done so far more effectively than the legislated ombudsman in place at the time.[38] This is a view that runs counter to the importance of the non-partisan and independent foundation of an ombuds role. In addition, the Premier's rationale calls into question how realistic it would be that all of the MHA's representing the citizens of the province of Newfoundland and Labrador would also come equipped with the skills needed for conducting investigations and assisting with the early resolution of complaints which are required for the effective implementation of the ombuds role. This turn of events in Newfoundland and Labrador is also a good demonstration of how even a well-constructed ombuds role established by statute, with a high degree of structural independence, can be eliminated by a majority government as the spirit moves it.[39] Subsequently, in 2002, the role was re-established under the name of the Citizens' Representative for Newfoundland and Labrador and a second responsibility was added via the *House of Assembly Accountability, Integrity and Administration Act* that provides for the Citizens' Representative to investigate gross mismanagement within the confines of the House of Assembly (the legislature).[40] Interestingly, the Citizens' Representative requested in 2010, after consultation with public representatives, his own staff and citizens of the province, that the Legislative Assembly change the name from "Citizens' Representative" to "Ombudsman" so the role of the Office would be more accurately identified.[41] To date, this change has not been made.

---

38 Bradley Moss, "Expedition Sailors: The Ombudsman in Newfoundland and Labrador" in Stewart Hyson, ed, *Provincial and Territorial Ombudsman Offices in Canada* (Toronto: University of Toronto Press, 2009) 126 at 128.

39 There was opposition to repealing of the Newfoundland and Labrador Ombudsman Act by academic leaders, such as Donald Rowat, political scientist of Carleton University, and by practitioners, such as Stephen Owen (then President of the International Ombudsman Institute) who saw the move as anti-democratic. Peter Boswell of Memorial University described the Premier's initiative more dramatically as "repugnant", "odious", "shameful and reprehensible." See *ibid* at 129.

40 Office of the Citizens' Representative, "Review of the Governing Legislation of the Office of the Citizens' Representative" (March 2010) at 3, online: http://www.citizensrep.nl.ca/pdfs/OCR-LegislativeReview.pdf.

41 *Ibid* at 4.

In 1977 the British Columbia Ombudsman for general governmental administrative oversight was created.[42] Lastly, the most recent addition to the governmental ombuds of general jurisdiction was established by statute in 1996 as the Yukon Territory Ombudsman. However, in this instance the part-time role was designed to be dual purpose and included the responsibility of the Information and Privacy Commissioner as well.[43] Presumably this approach was taken given the small population size of the jurisdiction, which was identified as 27,797 in 1991 and 30,776 in 1996.[44]

As there are hundreds of hybrid and organizational ombuds roles in Canada, the scope of this paper is not sufficient to provide a similar survey of the historical evolution of some of these roles. Rather, I will provide a few examples organized under the categories of "hybrid" and "organizational" to round out the panorama of Canadian ombuds activity.[45]

Hybrid Ombuds

These are established by policy, terms of reference, memorandum of understanding or charter which provide for the authority to investigate and access to all records:

- the majority of University and College ombuds[46]

---

42 Patrick J Smith "Fairness Inc.: Administrative Justice in B.C. – The Ombudsman Office at Thirty" in Stewart Hyson, ed, *Provincial and Territorial Ombudsman Offices in Canada* (Toronto: University of Toronto Press, 2009) 53 at 53. Please note that, as of 2009, the role is now officially recognized via legislative amendment as the British Columbia Ombudsperson in The Ombudsperson Act, RSBC 1996, c. 340.

43 *The Ombudsman Act*, SY 1995, c 17, was made effective in 1996 and the *Access to Information and Protection of Privacy Act*, RSY 2002, c 1, came into force on July 1, 1996.

44 Statistics Canada, "Population, Urban and Rural, by Province and Territory (Yukon)", online: http://statcan.gc.ca.

45 SA Bokhari estimated there were 200 Ombuds in corporations; 100 Ombudsman established in colleges and universities; 36 in newspapers in North America as of 2004 in "A Comparative Study of Ombudsman Office in Australia, Pakistan and U.K. Evolution, Efficacy and Challenge", online: www.policy.hu.

46 Examples of the structural independence of the Ombuds role established in higher education settings can be seen in the following examples: The Carleton University Ombudsperson role was established via a University Senate by-law in 1971; many Ombuds roles are constructed such that a committee of community stake holders representing students, faculty and administration hire the Ombuds (for example, University of Victoria, Camson College, University of Western Ontario, Ryerson University, University of Calgary, Alqonquin College, University of British Columbia); and funding for the role is equally shared by both student unions/societies and administration (for example, University of Victoria, University of Western Ontario, McMaster University, Camosun College, Algonquin College, Simon Fraser University, Carleton University). Also, a number of Ombuds report to the overarching governing body of the University, such as the University of Toronto Ombudsperson and Concordia University Ombudsperson. Links to the websites

- the majority of Canadian Bank ombuds who respond to complaints from customers and the over-arching ombudsman for Banking Services and Investments (OBSI)[47]
- media ombuds roles (for example, Canada Broadcasting Corporation[48] and Radio-Canada)[49]
- Crown Corporations, (for example, Canada Post Corporation Ombudsman)[50]
- Federal governmental ombuds, (for example, National Defence and Canadian Forces Ombudsman,[51] Taxpayers' Ombudsman,[52] Office of the Federal Ombudsman for Victims of Crime)[53]
- Not-for-Profit Organizations, (for example, some Community Care Access Centres in Ontario,[54] The Canadian Ski Patrol 790 (Ontario Division)).

Organizational Ombuds

These are established by policy, terms of reference, memorandum of agreement without the authority to investigate but often have access to all records:

- Corporations (for example, *Protectrice de la personne*/Corporate Ombudsman for Hydro-Québec, employees of the majority of Canadian banks; VIA Rail);
- Not-for-profit organizations (for example, Canadian Franchise Association Ombudsman);[55]

---

of all university and college Ombuds who are members of the Association of Canadian University and College Ombudsperson (ACCUO) are available online: http://www.uwo.ca/ombuds/accuo_aoucc/english/membership_websites.html.

47 The participating firms and the mandate for OBSI are available online: http://www.obsi.ca/UI/ParticipatingFirms/ParticipatingFirms.aspx.

48 CBC, "The Office of the Ombudsman", online: http://www.cbc.ca/ombudsman.

49 Radio Canada, "L'ombudsman de Radio-Canada", online: http://blogues.radio-canada.ca/ombudsman.

50 Canada Post, "Canada Post Ombudsman", online: http://www.canadapost.ca.

51 National Defence and Canadian Forces Ombudsman, "The National Defence and Canadian Forces Ombudsman", online: http://www.ombudsman.forces.gc.ca/index-eng.asp.

52 Taxpayers' Ombudsman, "Canadian Taxpayers' Ombudsman", online: http://www.oto-boc.gc.ca/menu-eng.html.

53 Office of the Federal Ombudsman for Victims of Crime, "Office of the Federal Ombudsman for Victims of Crime", online: http://www.victimsfirst.gc.ca.

54 Community Care Access Centre, "Community Care Access Centre, Toronto Central", online: http://www.ccac-ont.ca.

55 Canadian Franchise Association, "Franchise Ombudsman Program", online: http://www.cfa.ca.

- Some federal government departments which handle employee complaints (for example, Health Canada,[56] Heritage Canada[57]);
- Some law societies in Canada, specifically Alberta, British Columbia, Saskatchewan and Manitoba[58] set up Equity Ombudsperson roles which have been designed to assist lawyers, support staff and law students to address harassment and discrimination they have experienced in their workplaces, that is, within law firms. In addition, the Manitoba Law Society Equity Ombudsperson also has the mandate to speak with clients of law firms who believe they have suffered harassment or discrimination.
- Ombudsman, *Commission Scolaire de Montréal*[59] (French Language School Board in Montreal).

Using this tri-partite typology as an underpinning I will provide examples of how ombuds execute their inquisitorial functions and how other related activities contribute to their effectiveness in fulfilling their mandates for the pursuit of administrative fairness.

Characteristics of the Inquisitorial Nature of Ombuds Processes

The nature of the inquisitorial process has been defined elsewhere in this collection.[60] Therefore, I wish to focus on the following elements of the inquisitorial process: powers of investigation, own motion/initiative investigations, individual investigations and fairness criteria as key aspects of legislative and hybrid ombuds roles wherever they are located. Please be aware that while the organizational ombuds is not empowered to investigate complaints it is nonetheless expected to make recommendations on how to address systemic issues that are revealed through the nature of individual complaints brought to its attention along with the insights gained through the ombuds' unique "bird's eye view" of the organization. In order to delineate how ombuds' inquisitorial capacities are actually implemented I will provide in-depth explanations of the investigative

56 Health Canada, "Internal Ombudsman Service", online: http://www.hc-sc.gc.ca. This role was created in 2003.

57 "Ombudsman Office of Values and Ethics", Organizational Chart for the Department of Canadian Heritage, online: http://www.pch.gc.ca.

58 The Law Society of Alberta, "Equity Ombudsperson", online: http://www.ab.ca; The Law Society of British Columbia, "The Equity Ombudsperson", online: http://www.lawsociety.bc.ca; The Law Society of Saskatchewan, "Equity/Diversity Policies, Ombudsperson", online: http://wwwlawsociety.sk.ca; The Law Society of Manitoba, "Equity Ombudsperson", online: http://www.lawsociety.mb.ca.

59 Commission Scolaire de Montréal, "Commission Scolaire de Montréal (Ombudsman)", online: http://www.csdm.qc.ca/GlobalResources/TestNotFound/Structure/Ombudsman.aspx.

60 Please see the Introduction to this collection.

approaches and methodologies used by various ombuds in relation to each of the applicable categories of ombuds roles. The presentation of this material in this fashion will also demonstrate how the independence and impartiality expected of the hybrid and organizational ombuds' roles, along with the hybrid ombuds inquisitorial powers, coupled with their responsibility to opine and report on how to address systemic problems clearly differentiates these two types of ombuds roles from an in-house administrator or external mediator or facilitator who may also be tasked with assisting with the resolution of individual complaints. Prior to discussing the differences and similarities, I will address the possibility that some may believe that only an ombuds established by statute and who reports only to the legislature is capable of conducting truly independent and impartial investigations. The data provided below will clearly demonstrate that this is not the case as all manner of hybrid ombuds have "terms of reference" or "charters" that articulate their independence via various structural provisions as well as the strength of their investigative mandates and the requirement for organizational personnel to provide timely and complete access to all relevant information as identified solely by the ombuds. The notion that a hybrid ombuds is not able to operate on an independent and impartial basis as she does not have a legislated mandate is contradicted by the examples that follow as well as the panoply of annual reports written by many hybrid ombuds which are readily available in the public domain. Similarly, an organizational ombuds is also well equipped to bring fairness issues to the attention of the establishing body, without fear of reprisal, by virtue of the manner in which the terms of reference for the role are written and the individual appointee's ethical commitments.

Powers of Investigation

The legislative model

The *Ombudsman Act,* R.S.O. 1990 (the *Act*), most recently amended in 2006, defines the function of the Ontario Ombudsman in Section 14 (1) as:

> The function of the Ombudsman is to investigate any decision or recommendation made or any act done or omitted in the course of the administration of a governmental organization and affecting any person or body of persons in his, her or its personal capacity.[61]

After completing an investigation, the *Act* declares that the Ombudsman will then determine whether the act or omission being scrutinized:

61 *Ombudsman Act*, RSO 2006, c 35, Schedule C, s 14 (1) [Ombudsman Act (Ontario)]. Please note that the other provincial and territorial Ombuds of general jurisdiction have comparable enabling legislation with respect to investigative powers.

> a) appears to have been contrary to law, b) was unreasonable, unjust, oppressive, or improperly discriminatory … c) was based wholly or partly on a mistake of law; or was wrong.[62]

However, prior to forming a final opinion that is adverse to a governmental organization or employee, the Ombudsman is required to provide tentative conclusions and recommendations to the head of the Ministry for the subject matter of the complaint so that the Ministry can respond to the evidence assembled and the conclusions drawn from it. At this point, depending on the nature of the representations made by the Ministry or governmental agent, the Ombudsman may then decide to withdraw the report, do additional investigation, amend or refine the conclusions and/or change or maintain the conclusions, observations and recommendations as originally stated. Once the Ombudsman has made a final determination that a governmental agency has made administrative errors or omissions that need to be rectified for fairness to prevail, a final report detailing the rationale for the decision or the recommendation pursuant to Section 21 (3) is issued along with the requisite recommendation(s) for correcting the area(s) identified. This report will be sent to the governmental organization involved and the Minister responsible for that entity. The robust powers made available for publicly identifying unfairness are evident in the legislative authority provided by Section 21 (4) of the *Act* whereby the Ombudsman may forward a report to the Premier of the province and then the members of the legislature if within a reasonable period of time no action is taken by the government agency which the Ombudsman considers to be adequate and appropriate to the situation.

Another unique characteristic of the legislative ombudsman role is that she typically has vigorous powers for compelling testimony and the production of records in order to fulfill her investigative mandate. For example, in the Ontario *Act* it is forcefully stated that the Ombudsman may summon and examine under oath any complainant, government employee or any other person who is able to provide information related to the matter being investigated. Similarly, under Section 25 of the *Act*, the Ombudsman is empowered to enter any premises occupied by any governmental organization for the purposes of inspection and for conducting an investigation. In addition, it is an offence under Section 27 of the *Act* that any person who without lawful rationale intentionally "… obstructs, hinders or resists …"[63] the Ombudsman or (any other person empowered to do so by the *Act*). My understanding and experience is that these powers are rarely used but their sheer existence demonstrates the degree of strength inherent in the legislative ombudsman's investigatory powers. In addition to these powers, the Ontario Ombudsman has also established and published procedures for when he may notify the public about issues he is investigating in order to encourage more witnesses to provide information or simply because the subject of the investigation

62 *Ombudsman Act* (Ontario), *supra* note 61, Schedule C, s. 21 (1).

63 *Ibid*, s 27(a).

is so compelling it is believed that it is in the public interest for that information to be disseminated.[64]

In addition, in an equally forceful manner, the Ontario Ombudsman legislation via Section 24 (1) prohibits any legal action being taken against the Ombudsman or his or her staff for any action taken or report made in fulfilling the function of the Office unless it is done in bad faith. Similarly, except if a person is being tried for perjury, as stated in Section 19 (6), none of the information acquired by the Ombudsman during the course of conducting an inquiry or an investigation can be used in court proceedings for any purpose.

Finally, ombudsman legislation for Ontario and the majority[65] of other legislative Offices allows for the ombuds to initiate investigations on her "own motion" on a proactive basis as opposed to being limited to taking up only those issues that are brought to her attention by complainants. These types of investigations often result in a "special" report being issued on a specific area of government activity. While special reports are issued at the discretion of the ombuds, each legislative ombudsman is required to report annually on the work undertaken by her Office and to submit that report to the Speaker of the House who will then bring it to the attention of the Legislature.

The hybrid model

Academic ombuds situated in institutions of higher education typically have the power to investigate explicitly stated in their terms of reference. For example, the University of Ottawa Ombudsperson Terms of Reference which were approved by both the Senate and Board of Governors detail the Ombudsperson's powers in this fashion:

> 5.1. The Ombudsperson shall have the power to investigate any University-related complaint. All investigations shall be carried out in a fair manner and allow all persons implicated to respond to allegations made against them. The Ombudsperson may decide which modes of intervention, as defined in section 6, are the most appropriate in the circumstances.
> 5.2. The Ombudsperson shall have access, subject to applicable laws and policies relating to confidentiality and protection of privacy, to all files, records, reports, documents and information needed to fulfil the functions of the Ombudsperson.
>
> Requests by the Ombudsperson for information shall be handled in a mutually convenient and expeditious manner by all members of the University community.[66]

---

64 Ombudsman Ontario, "Procedures Under the Ombudsman Act", online: http://www.ombudsman.on.ca.

65 For example, the Yukon Territory Ombudsman legislation does not allow for investigations to be initiated other than via the lodging of an individual complaint.

66 The University of Ottawa Ombudsperson, "Terms of Reference", online: http://web5.uottawa.ca/admingov/ombuds-terms.html.

Similarly Bank Ombudsman who respond to client complaints also have investigative authority. For example, the Canadian Imperial Bank of Commerce states that if a customer is not able to resolve a concern with a local branch or office or the central "customer care" service, the client can bring the concern to the attention of the Ombudsman for "… an independent and thorough investigation."[67] In the same way, the mandate for the TD Bank Financial Group Ombudsman includes the authority to "… conduct a thorough and impartial investigation of all of the issues relating to our customers' concerns",[68] as well as being identified as an intermediary between individual and small business clients and TD Bank and its subsidiaries. A useful example of the type of issues a Bank Ombudsman may review can be found in the BMO Ombudsman's 2011 annual report posted on its website. In this instance, it is noted that, in 13% of the cases reviewed, compensation was offered to the complainant as a means of resolving the complaint fairly.[69] In addition, the majority of Bank Ombudsman websites indicate that customers who are not satisfied with their interaction with a particular bank ombudsman can escalate their complaint to the attention of the Ombudsman for Banking Services and Investments (OBSI).[70]

Another example of the strength of the hybrid ombuds' investigative capacity can be found in the Canadian Broadcasting Corporation's (CBC) Ombudsman. Its statement of principles indicate that: "The Ombudsman is completely independent of CBC program staff and management, reporting directly to the President of the CBC and, through the President to the Corporation's Board of Directors."[71] This reporting configuration could suggest that this role falls into the organizational ombuds category. However, other components of the CBC Ombudsman's mandate indicate otherwise. For example, it is mandated that this ombudsman will evaluate whether a piece of journalism or a broadcast complained about did or did not violate the CBC requirement that all journalistic activity must demonstrate accuracy, integrity and fairness. In addition, reference is made to the responsibility for fact-finding as part of the ombudsman's review process. As well, this ombuds role provides explicitly for the ability for the ombudsman to publish reports on specific cases that he has determined to be particularly noteworthy or consequential not only within the CBC and to the complainant(s) but to the general public as well. Many examples of the controversial matters handled by the ombudsman and the opinions he has rendered are publicly available at the ombudsman's website via his

67 CIBC, "Ombudsman's Office, Our Role and Mandate", online: http://www.cibc.com/ca.

68 TD, "Office of the Ombudsman, What is the Mandate, What is the Role of the Ombudsman", online: http://www.td.com.

69 BMO, "BMO Office of the Ombudsman Annual Report 2011" online: http://www.bmo.com/pdf/Ombudsman_Annual_Report_2011_EN.pdf.

70 For more information on this organization, see online: http://www.obsi.ca.

71 CBC, "The Office of the Ombudsman", online: http://www.ombudsman.cbc.radio-canada.ca/en/.

blog, website posts and annual reports.[72] This hybrid ombuds' published materials demonstrate that even without a statutory mandate he has not been curtailed from criticizing the actions taken by journalists employed by the body that funds his Office.

The organizational model of ombudsing does not have the power of investigation but is expected to report on the types of issues that are brought to its attention and make recommendations where appropriate. Interestingly enough, while organizational ombuds are not empowered to conduct investigations, they may choose to make inquiries about issues raised with them and typically organizational employees are required to respond to ombuds in a timely manner and to provide all relevant information.

Own Motion/Own Initiative Investigations

The legislative model

As noted earlier, many ombuds have the authority to launch investigations on their own motion or initiative. For example, In Newfoundland and Labrador, the Citizens' Representative (Barry Lewis) released a report in 2007 which made five recommendations for significant improvements for the care and treatment of female inmates along with mechanisms for increased access to justice for those held in geographically isolated parts of the province. The genesis of this investigation is noteworthy as it was sparked when Mr. Lewis read media reports about a female inmate who was forced to remain naked in her cell for a number of days due to concerns about her mental health.[73] Subsequently, in 2009 Mr. Lewis issued a press release[74] congratulating the government for allocating two million dollars for the construction of a facility for women and children in Happy Valley-Goose Bay. It is striking that Mr. Lewis comments in his investigative report that "Our office has never received a complaint from a female offender from Labrador."[75] If it were not for his ability to carry out an investigation on his own initiative, based on becoming aware of an issue rather than only being able to respond to complaints raised with him, the needs of this vulnerable population may not have been addressed. By way of methodology, this five month investigation beginning in February 2007 with the final report being released in June 2007, was launched

72 CBC, "Complaint Reviews", "Blog (2012)", "Resources" (and go to "Annual Reports"), online: http://www.ombudsman.cbc.radio-canada.ca/en/.

73 Office of the Citizens' Representative Province of Newfoundland and Labrador, *A Report of Facilities and Support For Female Offenders from Labrador Alone Among the Few* by Barry Lewis (June 2007) at 1, online: http://www.citizensrep.nl.ca 1 [Lewis].

74 Office of the Citizens' Representative for Newfoundland and Labrador, News Release/Communiqué, "Office of the Citizens' Representative – Commentary on Recent Infrastructure Spending Announcement" (19 February 2009), online: http://www.releases.gov.nl.ca.

75 Lewis, *supra* note 73 at 4.

on the basis of written notice of the intent to investigate the availability of facilities and support services for female offenders in Labrador to the Departments of Justice and Health and Community Services and a regional health authority. As the investigation progressed, notice of intent to investigate the same matter was provided to another regional health authority and the Legal Aid Commission. In addition, meetings were held with or submissions were received from current and ex-offenders, various Status of Women councils, relevant government bodies and not-for-profit organizations. In addition, 1,100 pages of text (including Court and Corrections and Community Services reports and United Nations standards) as well as photographic materials were analyzed by the three Investigators and one Senior Investigator who conducted the investigation. In addition, two trips were made from the Citizens' Representative's urban Office in St. John's, Newfoundland to various locations in Labrador. As is the norm with ombuds investigations a detailed investigative plan was prepared prior to the start of the investigation and amended as the investigation progressed.[76]

In another jurisdiction, it is worthy of note that over the past six years, as of Spring 2011 the Ombudsman for Ontario, André Marin has conducted 27 Special Operations Response Team (SORT) investigations.[77] This type of investigation is undertaken when the issues under review are complex, sensitive and serious in nature and of interest to many people; when an informal resolution is unlikely; and/or when the implications of the issues raised or observed are potentially far-reaching and systemic.[78] Typically, a team of investigators is brought together for the express purpose of completing in-depth reviews in an expeditious manner. Frequently, interviews with witnesses are audio taped and then transcribed to ensure accuracy. The topics of Mr. Marin's reports range from parents being required to give up custody of their children with special needs in order for them to be eligible for appropriate forms of residential care, to critiquing the governmental restrictions on the use of Avastin, a cancer treatment drug, to the lack of transparency of property assessment methods.[79] Mr. Marin's investigation of the origin and subsequent communication of the controversial security regulation (Regulation 233/10) passed by the province prior to the G20 summit held in Toronto in June 2010 which resulted in his report entitled "Caught in the Act" deserves more in-depth attention given the innovative investigative techniques employed. The investigative focus was the involvement of the Ministry of Community Safety and Correctional Services in the origin of Regulation 233/10

76 Lewis, *supra* note 73 at 5, 6.

77 Ombudsman Ontario, "SORT Investigations", online: http://www.ombudsman.on.ca.

78 Ombudsman Ontario, "Special Ombudsman Response Team", online: http://www.ombudsman.on.ca.

79 *Ibid.*

and the communication of it to police, media and the public.[80] For this investigation seven investigators and two early resolution officers rolled out their investigation in the usual fashion by conducting structured interviews; reviewing text provided by the Ministry; researching what had taken place at summit meetings that had been hosted elsewhere; visited physical locations and spoke with individuals in the area.[81] The innovation can be seen in their use of social media like YouTube, blogs, podcasts and Facebook to gather additional information. Using this approach the investigators were able to identify in excess of 5000 videos related to the G20 activities. In addition, the Ombudsman communicated with individuals via Twitter to ask them to contact his Office if they had information relevant to the issues being investigated.[82] The range of materials acquired and witness accounts received demonstrated how traditional investigative approaches can be enhanced by the use of social media.

Another example of how an ombuds investigation can be conducted is found in the work of Le Protecteur du citoyen/Ombudsman for Québec (Raymonde Saint-Germain) who in October 2009 tabled a report with the National Assembly on her investigation of the quality of government services for children with pervasive developmental disorders (PDDs) in October of 2009. In this instance the methodology used was a survey approach whereby one survey was distributed to 150 parents of children with PDDs and another survey was distributed to 13 local bodies responsible for handling complaints from rehabilitation centres for people with intellectual disabilities and developmental disorders.[83] In addition, 167 people including parents, practitioners and those responsible for managing services participated in interviews or focus groups. This approach was taken so as to be able to examine and document the experience of parents seeking services for their children from the point of first indicators of concern to the time the child was seven years of age or had completed the first grade. In this instance the three ministries and their agencies that are responsible for providing support, funding and care for children with PDDs accepted all 21 recommendations that resulted from Le Protecteur du Citoyen/Ombudsman's investigation.[84]

---

80 Ombudsman Ontario, *Investigation into The Ministry of Community Safety and Correctional Services' conduct in relation to Ontario Regulation 233/10 under the Public Works Protection Act ("Caught in the Act")* by André Marin (December 2010), online: http://www.ombudsman.on.ca.

81 *Ibid* at 39.

82 *Ibid* at 40.

83 Le Protecteur du Citoyen, *Looking Towards Greater Continuity in Service Delivery, Approaches and Human Relations: Special Ombudsman's Report on Government Services for Children with Pervasive Developmental Disorders* by Raymonde Saint-Germain (October 2009), online: http://protecteurducitoyen.qc.ca at 7–8.

84 Le Protecteur du Citoyen, Press Release, "Quebec Ombudsman's Report on Government Services for Children with PDDs: Looking Toward Greater Continuity in Delivery of Services, Approaches, and Human Relations" (8 October 2009), online:

The hybrid model

Hybrid ombuds[85] may also have the authority to initiate investigations on their own motion. For example, The Charter for the Fair Practices Commissioner at B (1) (b) states: "The Fair Practices Commissioner may, on his or her own initiative, investigate, identify and make recommendations on systemic issues within the WSIB."[86] By way of background, The Fair Practices Commission was established in 2003 to investigate complaints from employers and injured workers regarding the Workers Safety and Insurance Board (WSIB) in Ontario [an injured workers' compensation scheme]. It is instructive to see how this hybrid ombuds role used its "own initiative" authority. Initially in 2006 the decision was made to undertake a system-wide investigation into the processes used for making decisions about claims based on occupational diseases as in some instances the adjudication process was taking more than six months to complete.[87] This lengthy, six-month time frame had generated complaints about the emotional and financial consequences of this waiting period as well as the lack of communication as to what was happening with the injured workers' cases. The methodology followed was that written notice was provided to the President of the WSIB indicating the investigation would focus on organizational performance rather than individual staff performance in the areas of decision-making processes, communication and timeliness. The Commissioner's office identified a sample of statistically valid claims that were still in process after six months had elapsed to determine if the complaints being received were indicative of a wide spread problem. In addition, the Commission staff reviewed statistics and data on the claims in the sample as well the information obtained from conducting a random file review; and discussed the reports on file as well as interviewing the staff and managerial personnel in the Occupational Disease Unit. The Commission staff also met with

---

http://www.protecteurducitoyen.qc.ca/fileadmin/medias/pdf/communiques/en/TED_PressRelease.pdf.

85 Many academic Ombuds have this power established in their terms of reference. For example, the Terms of Reference for the Ryerson University Ombudsperson state: "Investigations may also begin on the independent initiative of the Ombudsperson in respect of anyone of the above entitled to make a complaint." See Terms of Reference for the Office of the Ombudsperson online at http://www.ryerson.ca/ombuds. This characteristic is also found in the "Sample Clauses" developed and posted by the Association of Canadian College and University Ombudspersons Association (ACCUO): "To investigate, at the request of any student of the University, or upon the Ombudsperson's own motion, (my emphasis) any grievances that may arise against the University or its boards, committees, academic or administrative departments, etc. or against anyone employed by the University exercising authority." See the full list of Sample Clauses online: http://www.uwo.ca/ombuds/accuo_aoucc/english/resources_sample_clauses.html.

86 Fair Practices Commission, "Fair Practices Commission Charter Document" (2007), online: http://www.fairpractices.on.ca.

87 Fair Practices Commission, *Annual Report for 2006–2007* at 8, online: http://www.fairpractices.on.ca [Fair Practices Commission].

other stakeholders, such as some union representatives and the Directors of the Offices of the Worker Advisor and Employer Advisor whose offices are in place to provide advice and support to employers and injured workers respectively. This seven-month investigation was concluded with a final report being issued after the WSIB President provided her written response to the Commissioner's preliminary findings and resultant recommendations.[88] In brief, the Commissioner (Laura Bradbury) concluded that the time frame for decision-making was too long and that the impact of the resultant delay on injured workers had to be given more consideration within the WSIB's model of adjudication.[89] Ten recommendations were made which were accepted in full by the WSIB in 2007 and which by 2008 had resulted in increased staff resources; a new comprehensive data base which allows for easier tracking of data; a pilot project being initiated which included two specialized back log teams to deal with claims over six months old; new means for measuring accountability; new training resources; as well as a model for delivery of service in a customized manner.[90]

A very important aspect of this investigation and many that are conducted by ombuds in all sectors is the commitment to and authority for follow-up on the fulfillment of accepted recommendations. In this situation, the Commissioner received bi-monthly reports on the progress made over the following year and met regularly with leadership from within the Occupational Disease Services Division to further inquire about progress made. In 2008, two years after initiating her investigation, the Commissioner indicated in a summary report that as a result of the steps taken by the WSIB that the complaints to her office about occupational disease claims had been reduced by almost half and that the back log of cases held by WSIB that were more than six months old had decreased substantially.[91] Three more years later in April of 2011, the Commissioner stated in her annual report that the number of complaints in the area of occupational disease claims has been reduced by 75% and there is no backlog.[92] These data demonstrate how an own motion investigation conducted by a hybrid ombuds had a profoundly positive effect on the injured workers whose claims are now being processed in a more customized and timely manner. In addition, the staff of WSIB have benefited from training and the introduction of a new model for service delivery which has increased their capacity to handle occupational disease claims in a timely and effective manner. It is also worthy of emphasis that the foregoing description of this hybrid Ombuds' execution of her investigative mandate, which was put in

88 Fair Practices Commission, *supra* note 87 at 9.

89 *Ibid.*

90 Fair Practices Commission, *Fair Practices Commission 2008 Annual Report* at 5-6, online: http://fairpractices.on.ca.

91 *Ibid.*

92 Conversation with Laura Bradbury, Fair Practices Commissioner on April 25, 2011.

place by the agency's Board of Directors, demonstrates how similar its style of operation is to work undertaken by statutorily established ombuds roles.

Another area in which ombuds are active that flows from their inquisitorial activities is trends analysis of complaints and inquiries. The result of this analysis may be an own motion investigation on a particular issue that continues to grow in size and/or seriousness or in the dissemination of progress reports coupled with recommendations for work still to be done. An example of a five year trends analysis undertaken by the Ombudsperson for the University of Victoria (Martine Conway) was highlighted in her 2010 annual report in which she made observations on what had happened in response to systemic issues raised in her previous reports over the past five year period.[93] In this analysis the Ombudsperson commented on the difficulty students with disabilities have (particularly those with disabilities which are not visible) obtaining academic concessions and recommended specific training for dealing with accommodations generally and as well as for those disabilities which were not as readily obvious. It was also recommended that priority be given to publicizing the options available for seeking academic concessions. In addition, the Ombudsperson recommended that a more preventative approach be taken to reminding instructors about proper implementation of grading procedures. In this review the Ombudsperson also acknowledged appreciation for the University ensuring students had electronic access to unofficial transcripts. This kind of trends analysis is informed by the complaints received, inquiries made and investigations undertaken, and is a regular part of ombuds activity.

While ombuds practicing in the organizational model do not have the authority to conduct own-motion investigations they are able to address concerns they have observed directly. Specifically, it is stated in the IOA Standards of Practice under the heading of Independence: "The Ombudsman exercises sole discretion over whether or how to act regarding an individual's concern, a trend or concerns of multiple individuals over time. The Ombudsman may also initiate action on a concern identified through the Ombudsman's direct observation."[94]

Individual Investigations

The legislative model

It is also important to acknowledge that thousands of individual investigations are conducted throughout the course of a year which can also result in life changing outcomes for complainants. For example, the Ombudsman for Saskatchewan determined through an investigation that an individual should be reimbursed for the $59,000 he spent paying for medical treatment he received in the U.S. related

---

93 Martine Conway, *Because Fairness Matters: The Ombudsperson Report*, vol 14:1 (March 2011) at 4, online: http://www.uvss.uvic.ca.

94 International Ombudsman Association, "Standards of Practice" online: http://www.ombudsassociation.org.

to the removal of a brain tumor.[95] This complainant sought medical assistance in the U.S. as he had not been able to obtain a definitive diagnosis as to his condition in his consultations with various Saskatchewan physicians. While the Ombudsman indicated the criteria used by the government to assess the claim were valid, and it was not reasonable for this individual to expect a response to his request for coverage so quickly (for example, one day in advance of the prescribed surgery), he was still recommending the costs be reimbursed by the government. The Ombudsman's rationale for doing so was that the government had communicated its decision to deny the complainant's request for payment (as the treatment he sought was available in Saskatchewan), via fax to his home and a voice mail message when the governmental staff were well aware that the complainant was not at home as he had notified them that he had traveled to the U.S. expressly for the purpose of seeking medical treatment. In this instance, the administrators of this program did not accept the Ombudsman's recommendation. However, the Minister responsible for this department, overturned this decision and indicated the payment would be made as he accepted the Ombudsman's rationale as being reasonable given the communication difficulties and the special circumstances.[96] This type of individual investigation is conducted quickly and involves the review of relevant legislation, policy and procedure as well as interviews with key personnel.

An investigation undertaken by the Ombudsman for the Yukon Territory in 2010 as a result of several complaints from individuals also had profoundly positive individual and systemic benefits. As a result of the investigation of these individual complaints the Ombudsman (Tracy-Ann McPhee) found that a regularly scheduled territorial health care insurance survey, which had been conducted twice a year for many years was carried out in such a fashion that the government breached its own legislation, that is *The Statistics Act*,[97] by collecting and sharing personal information in a manner that was not consistent with the legislation and by advising the 5113 recipients of the survey that if they did not complete the "voluntary" survey their health insurance could be cancelled.[98] While it was recognized by the Ombudsman that the government's effort to collect information was well intentioned, served useful purposes, and that the same

---

95 Ombudsman Saskatchewan, *Recommendations 2010: Third Quarter Report Update* (July–September 2010) at 2–3, online: http://www.ombudsman.sk.ca.

96 "Out-of-country Health Bill to Be Paid: Minister, Cost of Removing Brain Tumor Missed by Sask. Doctors Will Be Covered", *CBC News* (3 February 2011) online: http://www.cbc.ca/news.

97 *Statistics Act*, SY 2003, c 27.

98 Yukon Ombudsman, *Report after Investigation Ombudsman Act section 31(2) December 6, 2010: Re: Complaints to the Ombudsman – Health Care Insurance Survey Authorities: Health and Social Services; and Yukon Bureau of Statistics* by Tracey-Ann McPhee at 1, online: http://www.ombudsman.yk.ca [Yukon Ombudsman, Health Care Report].

wording had been used for previous surveys, her concern was that the approach taken was contrary to its own law. It was also noted by the Ombudsman that the government was not appreciating the import of its actions when it indicated that "… only a small group of people …"[99] were inconvenienced by having their health care insurance cancelled and then reinstated. In response, the government was advised by the Ombudsman that the use of a threat to encourage cooperation with this data collection effort when the legislation did not allow for such action was unacceptable. The government accepted the Ombudsman's recommendations for the proper conduct of future surveys and for communicating with those residents whose health care insurance coverage was cancelled on how to have the coverage reinstated on a retroactive basis.[100] In this legislative regime the *Ombudsman Act*[101] provides a comparable methodology to that cited earlier in that it requires the Ombudsman to give notice of her intent to investigate a matter to the relevant authority and have unfettered access to facilities, files and personnel. She also has the responsibility to advise the authority whose work is being investigated if her investigation results may be of an adverse nature before she finalizes her report so that the authority has the opportunity to make submissions verbally or in writing prior to the final report being issued.

The hybrid model

An example of an investigation undertaken on the basis of an individual complaint is captured in a case reported on by the Ombudsperson (Hervé Depow) for Algonquin College in Ottawa, Ontario in 2008/2009. In this instance an investigation was undertaken in response to a student's complaint that her professor had not graded her fairly.[102] Initially the Ombudsperson encouraged the student to familiarize herself with the policy governing her situation and then to meet with her professor so as to better understand why she had received a zero for an assignment. A meeting was held and as the student remained dissatisfied she formally appealed the grade of zero. The appeal was not successful and the student believed the review process was handled unfairly so she asked the Ombudsman to investigate. The Ombudsman met with the Chair of the Committee which had heard the student's appeal and reviewed the process followed and the material submitted by both the professor and the student. Through the Ombudsperson's review of the professor's submission it became apparent that the Professor was not complying with the directive in place for how any changes to the previously circulated information on evaluation of assignments was to be conducted. As a result, the Ombudsperson recommended that the Appeal Committee which had originally denied the student's appeal be reconvened to review the complaint

99 Yukon Ombudsman, Health Care Report, *supra* note 98 at 3.

100 *Ibid* at 4.

101 *Ombudsman Act*, RSY 2002, c 163.

102 Algonquin College Office of the Ombudsman, *Office of the Ombudsperson Annual Report 2008 to 2009*, case 5 at 7–8, online: http://www.algonquincollege.com.

taking into account the course outline, the directions for completing assignments, the evaluation criteria for the assignment in question and how the Professor had determined the mark for this particular student. The Committee reconvened and the Ombudsperson was invited to attend and meet with the Professor. Subsequently, the Professor agreed to review the grade assigned (which resulted in the grade moving from a zero to a passing grade) and to review his evaluation methods in relation to the College's directives on this subject. Through this investigation an individual unfairness was corrected and the likelihood of a comparable problem occurring again was reduced. It is important to recognize that the methodology used in this case is common to a hybrid ombuds approach for an individual matter whereby notice to investigate is generally provided verbally rather than in writing and the conclusions and recommendations are often issued verbally as well. In addition, the investigation is completed in a short time period rather than extending over weeks and months.

Further demonstration of the impact of the hybrid ombuds' investigative capacity with respect to individual complaints is evident through the statistics provided by the Ombudsman for Banking Services and Investments. It is noteworthy that in 2010 the recommendations made by the Ombudsman for Banking Services and Investments (OBSI) after an investigation had been completed, coupled with the monetary compensation that arose from facilitation by OBSI staff with member banks, resulted in financial compensation of approximately three and half million dollars. For this particular time frame, complaints were supported in 29% of the cases reviewed.[103] Also, it is worth emphasizing that OBSI was evaluated in 2011 by an external body, The Navigator Company, and was accorded high praise for its accessibility, transparency and fairness.[104]

The ombuds operating in the organizational model does not have the power to undertake investigations of individual complaints. Typically, the kinds of complaints which require investigation are referred to various Offices of compliance within the organization which are in place to ensure the organization acts in accordance with both organizational policy (Human Resources Offices) and various pieces of legislation (Equity, Whistle-Blower, Health and Safety and Anti-Discrimination Offices). However, organizational ombuds may make inquiries as they see fit about complaints that are brought to their attention or that they have observed.

Fairness criteria

When conducting investigations and determining outcomes it is common for both legislative and hybrid ombuds to use standard administrative fairness criteria to

103 Ombudsman for Banking Services and Investments, *OBSI 2010 Annual Report* at 48, online: http://www.obsi.ca.

104 Ombudsman for Banking Services and Investments, *Ombudsman for Banking Services and Investments 2011 Independent Review* at 7–8, online: http://www.obsi.ca [OBSI Review].

determine whether or not a matter has been handled fairly. Within the legislative model the Ombudsperson for British Columbia has posted the "Fairness Checklist"[105] to clarify what criteria she takes into account in the following areas: communication, facilities and services, decision procedures, appeal, review and complaint procedures, organizational issues and agency review and planning.

It must also be recognized that in the course of investigation it may be found that the governmental agency or institution has not made an error and the ombuds has determined that the decision complained about has been made fairly. While these decisions do not receive the same amount of media attention as the reports which indicate that a department or agency is rife with serious administrative errors or illegalities, acknowledgments of effective administration are routinely found in the annual reports of all types of ombuds and as noted by Justice Dickson in *British Columbia Development Corp*[106] can boost the morale of government administrators.[107] Interestingly enough, some ombuds include compliments to government personnel who have done their work particularly well in their annual reports. The Ombudsman for New Brunswick has gone a considerable step beyond clearing those impugned of unfair actions to providing awards of excellence for exemplary civil service based on the following criteria:

> … providing exceptional responsiveness and co-operation during the complaint-resolution process; consistently demonstrating the values of administrative fairness and accountability; demonstrating leadership in informal problem-solving and helping ensure the efficient resolution of complaints; and encouraging the application of systemic and system-wide problem-solving.[108]

The individuals selected were then acknowledged publicly for their work via ceremony and in print in Mr. Richard's 2009/2010 annual report. Interestingly enough, no mention is made of how the Office will deal with complaints which arise at a later date related to these award winners' actions or omissions.

Early Resolution Techniques

Legislative model

It is also important to note that in addition to in-depth investigative activity, all legislative and hybrid ombudsman offices receive thousands of complaints annually that are not investigated. In many cases the issues brought forward may not fall within jurisdiction or mandate, so the callers would be referred elsewhere. In some cases the issues raised would be premature, in that there is an adequate

---

105 BC Ombudsperson, "Fairness Checklist", online: http://www.ombudsman.bc.ca.

106 *British Columbia Development Corp.*, *supra* note 13.

107 *Ibid* at 461.

108 Ombudsman New Brunswick, *Annual Report 2009/2010 Ombudsman New Brunswick* at 11, online: http://www.gnb.ca.

remedy or appeal process that has not yet been used by the caller. In those instances the caller is advised that he must make use of these processes prior to bringing a complaint to the ombudsman/person.

In addition, for those complaints that do fall into jurisdiction, there may be no need to initiate an investigation. In actuality, the vast majority of complaints received by both legislative and hybrid ombuds in Canada are handled via early resolution techniques which include: inquiries for the purpose of clarification; shuttle diplomacy, mediation and conflict coaching. Stephen Owen, former Ombudsman for the Province of British Columbia, who addressed the importance of expanding upon the traditional investigative approach opined:

> In keeping with the general principle that it is the proper role of an ombudsman office to strive for the mutually acceptable resolution of a problem rather than necessarily finding a fault or absence of it, the office should attempt to provide informal mediation services wherever such an approach may be productive. This approach not only tends to result in greater satisfaction among all parties, but frequently provides a more rapid resolution than a full investigation oriented towards a finding of right or wrong.[109]

Some current legislative ombuds have adopted the same posture. For example the Ombudsman for Saskatchewan (Kevin Fenwick) noted on the cover of his 2006 annual report:

- We are Fair, Independent, Impartial
- What we do: **Negotiate**, Investigate, **Mediate** (bold text is my emphasis)
- Has Government Been Fair?[110]

This kind of public declaration of the use of early resolution activities alongside of the traditional investigative approach demonstrates the import attached to early resolution activities. It is also instructive to look at the reports of other legislative Ombuds Offices for evidence of the prevalence of the use of a non-investigative approach: a) in the 2009/2010 annual report of the Ombudsman for Ontario it is stated that of the 13,894 complaints handled, 780 were resolved with the Office's assistance and 5,206 were handled via "inquiry made/referral given/resolution facilitated";[111] b) the City of Toronto Ombudsman noted in her 2009/2010 annual

---

109 Stephen Owen, "The Ombudsman: Essential Elements & Common Challenges" in Linda C Reif, ed, *The International Ombudsman Anthology: Selected Writings from the International Ombudsman Institute* (Cambridge, Massachusetts: Kluwer Law International, 1999) at 55.

110 Ombudsman Saskatchewan, *Annual Report 2006*, online: http://www.ombudsman.sk.ca.

111 Ombudsman Ontario, *Annual Report 2009/2010* at 76, online: http://www.ombudsman.on.ca at 76.

report that of the 1,562 complaints received, 1,525 were dealt with using "early resolution" techniques; 9 cases were investigated and 2 investigations were still in progress.[112]

Hybrid model

The prevalence of the use of early resolution techniques can be found in the 2009/10 Annual Report of the University of Western Ontario Ombudsperson whereby it is reported that out of 373 concerns raised the majority (249 cases or 67%) were handled via the provision of advice. The 25 cases that involved the intervention of the ombuds staff included mediation, facilitation, shuttle diplomacy as well as information gathering and case reviews.[113] The 2010 annual report for the Ombudsperson for Simon Fraser University who also has the capacity to investigate when appropriate to do so, demonstrates that a large percentage of the 302 cases were also handled using early resolution techniques, such as direct and indirect mediation, provision of advice, coaching and seeking clarification.[114]

Organizational model

The daily fare of organizational ombuds is the resolution of complaints only through provision of advice and referral, mediation, shuttle diplomacy and coaching. For example, the Corporate Ombudsman/*Protectrice de la personne* for Hydro-Québec indicated in her 2009 Annual Report, which is publicly accessible via the Corporation's website, that of 148 cases settled, 15 had been mediated by the Ombudsman; 28 by the provision of advice or counsel and 21 by referral to the appropriate authority.[115] In this time period, complaints were raised in five broad categories – namely, discrimination, harassment, positions, status and miscellaneous. As a result of her discussions and interventions, the Corporate Ombudsman/*Protectrice de la personne* (Justine Sentenne) made two philosophical recommendations on how the corporation could ensure a strong emphasis on ethics continued within the company and suggested an increased focus on human dignity and respect for improving the work atmosphere. She also recommended the establishment of standards and guidelines for the efficient use of voice mail. In addition, praise was given to the corporation for its compassionate approach to accommodating employees who also serve as care-givers in demanding family situations and she expressed hope that the underlying value of compassion would be maintained in the future.

---

112 Office of the Ombudsman City of Toronto, *Annual Report 2010* at 34, online: http://ombudstoronto.ca.

113 Office of the Ombudsperson, University of Western Ontario, *2009/2010 Office of the Ombudsperson Annual Report* at 3, online: http://www.uwo.ca.

114 Simon Fraser, University Office of the Ombudsperson, *2010 Annual Report* at 4, online: http://www.sfu.ca.

115 Ombudsman, Hydro Quebec, *Report of the Activities of the Corporate Ombudsman 2009 Hydro-Québec* at 3, online: http://www.hydroquebec.com.

In summary, the inquisitorial process as implemented within the legislative and hybrid ombuds roles in Canada includes the following:

- provision of written or verbal notice of intent to investigate;
- in-depth investigative planning;
- expert level of investigative skill;
- authority to collect all relevant data without interference or restriction;
- ability to conduct interviews with all relevant personnel and witnesses;
- the responsibility to provide the organization or agency which may be adversely affected by conclusions and recommendations with the opportunity to review findings, tentative conclusions and recommendations before the final report is issued;
- the authority to determine when complaints should be investigated and in what manner; and
- the responsibility to make inquiries and conduct investigations, in a confidential, independent and impartial manner, as unobtrusively as possible so as not to interfere with the normal work of the administrative or corporate body.

In the organizational ombuds model, while inquisitorial powers have not been mandated, through effective listening and careful questioning the ombuds is well positioned to assist complainants with the determination and prioritization of their concerns and the generation and evaluation of options for going forward. In instances where the ombuds deems it is appropriate to make an inquiry the same expertise in listening and gathering information is used to facilitate problem solving by the parties in order to resolve the matter in dispute. In addition, organizational ombuds may also make recommendations to the CEO or a Board of Directors which are given considerable attention as a result of the ombuds' independent stature and well-informed analysis of trends observed.

As an ombuds can only implement its inquisitorial powers for the pursuit of administrative fairness for all concerned if its existence is well known and easily accessed, two additional criteria are characteristic of all ombuds roles in Canada regardless of where they fit in the aforementioned typology of practice.

Accessibility

A key defining characteristic of an ombuds role, which is by definition an alternative to the traditional dispute resolution system, should be the ease with which its services can be accessed and used. In order for an ombuds office to be effective, knowledge of its existence and how it functions should be wide spread. Hence many ombuds roles in all models of practice place great emphasis on reaching out to potential complainants through educational campaigns using all manner of public relations and marketing programs. For instance, the Ombudsman for the City of Montréal has created her Office's website so that the ombuds' mandate is described in 14 languages. For those potential complainants who have difficulty reading, a "simplified text" a.k.a. "plain language version" of the Office's mandate and operating procedures is available as well as a description of the office's role being provided in an audio/visual format.[116] Considerable attention is also paid by many ombuds to ensuring complainants are able to make use of ombuds' services easily once they have determined they will put forward a complaint. For example, staff or interpreters are able to communicate in a variety of languages (in the 2009 Ombudsman for Banking Services and Investments (OBSI) annual report it was reported that the OBSI staff are able to handle inquiries by communicating in 170 different languages);[117] complaints may be submitted via email or telephone; meetings are arranged to accommodate those for whom traditional office hours, child or elder care responsibilities or locations are a barrier, etc. As a result of a high level of accessibility individuals who believe they have been treated unfairly have the opportunity to acquire expert dispute resolution assistance at no cost to themselves, other than the time they invest in submitting and discussing their concern or complaint.

Similarly, there is very little benefit to having strong powers of investigation and highly skilled dispute resolution specialists if potential users do not know what the ombuds can do and how the service may be beneficial. As a result, the emphasis placed on providing education about the work of an Ombudsman can be seen in a 2009/2010 annual report where the Nova Scotia Ombudsman reported that his office had increased by 51% the number of individuals it had connected with through its outreach work. It was noted that reaching youth in residential and custodial facilities as well as seniors in residential care facilities had been a particular focus and that future efforts would include adult offenders as well.[118] This Office's various communication strategies are specifically targeted to meet the Ombudsman's educational goal of increasing citizens' accessibility in order to make use of the Office and for clarifying its role and mandate.[119]

Education for Potential Respondents and Problem Solvers

Well before a complaint is brought to the attention of a service provider or administrative decision-maker, ombuds from all models often offer orientation sessions to personnel in the agencies, organizations or corporations who may be responding to their queries in the future, on how their role and function is translated into specific operating procedures. In addition, the Ombudsman for Saskatchewan has pursued a preventative approach through an in-depth educational vector by developing a program known as the "Fine Art of Fairness"

116 Ombudsman de/of Montréal, online: http://ville.montreal.qc.ca.

117 OBSI Review, *supra* note 104 at 20.

118 Nova Scotia Office of the Ombudsman, *Annual Accountability Report for the Fiscal Year 2009–2010* (13 July 2010) at 17–18, online: Nova Scotia http://www.gov.ns.ca.

119 *Ibid* at 17.

complete with a comprehensive workbook entitled *A Guide for Fair Practice.*[120] This training program is delivered around the province to government staff on a regular basis. In the same trajectory, a detailed resource entitled *Practice Essentials for Administrative Tribunals*[121] was also published in 2009. In a similar vein, the Ombudsman for Manitoba issued a training manual entitled "*Understanding Fairness: A Handbook on Fairness for Manitoba Municipal Leaders.*"[122] A comparable approach has been used by the Ombudsperson for Students at the University of British Columbia, who operates as a hybrid model, whereby a "Fairness Checklist for Decision Makers" has been put forward to identify best practices in twelve different aspects of "procedural fairness."[123] These kinds of preventative approaches are an important adjunct to ombuds' inquisitorial approach to dispute resolution as they have the potential to reduce complaints and increase fair decision-making substantially.

While it is readily evident that there is considerable diversity in how Canadian ombuds have been established and structured across all three models of practice and how the resultant inquisitorial mandates are fulfilled, the distinctiveness which has resulted is not necessarily an obstacle to the delivery of effective ombuds services. In fact, the idiosyncrasy of ombuds service construction and delivery has allowed for the vertical and horizontal expansion of ombuds services into many important areas of Canadian endeavour, thus contributing to the democratization of many jurisdictions, agencies and organizations by contributing to fair decision-making in a timely manner in a wide variety of environments.

---

120 Ombudsman Saskatchewan, "A Guide of Fair Practice", online: http://www.ombudsman.sk.ca.

121 Ombudsman Saskatchewan, "Practice Essentials for Administrative Tribunals", online: http://www.ombudsman.sk.ca.

122 Manitoba Ombudsman, "Understanding FAIRNESS: A Handbook on Fairness for Manitoba Municipal Leaders", online: http://www.ombudsman.mb.ca.

123 Office of the Ombudsperson for Students, "Fairness Toolkit: Fairness Checklist for Decision Makers" (June 2010), online: http://ombudsoffice.ubc.ca.

Chapter 17
Evolving Capacities: The British Columbia Representative for Children and Youth as a Hybrid Model of Oversight

Mary Liston*

Introduction

Institutional design in the modern state increasingly incorporates features from both adversarial and inquisitorial models indicating considerable convergence.[1] This chapter examines the hybrid model provided by British Columbia's Representative for Children and Youth (RCY) and argues that the RCY offers important institutional insights regarding the effectiveness of these types of investigative bodies found across Canada as well as internationally. The paper also examines the evolution of procedural justice in this substantive policy area. I will argue that the hybrid model – at least with respect to children – illustrates how procedural fairness serves substantive rights. To show this, the paper does not engage in the substantive areas of family, health, education welfare or criminal policy and their accompanying areas of law but, rather, how the institutional shift

* I would like to thank Jeremy Berland (Deputy Representative and Associate Deputy of Monitoring, Research, Evaluation and Audit, Office of the Representative for Children and Youth), Laverne Jacobs, Marcia Valiante, and the anonymous reviewer for critical and constructive feedback on this chapter. I would also like to thank the conference organizers – Sasha Baglay and Laverne Jacobs – and conference participants for stimulating discussions and commentary.

1 Voluminous discussion regarding the precise meaning of the words "adversarial" and "inquisitorial" exists. For the purposes of this paper, I will maintain the common law understanding of adversarial and use inquisitorial in the more open-ended sense of an investigative model not premised on bipolar relations and with an active public official at the head who has a duty to investigate the facts and develop the issues. On the key differences between adversarial and inquisitorial processes, see the "Introduction" in this volume. For discussion of the adversarial–non adversarial debate, see Chapter 2 in Australian Law Reform Commission, *Review of the Federal Civil Justice System*, Discussion Paper 62 (Sydney 1999), online: Australasian Legal Information Institute, http://www.austlii.edu.au/au/other/alrc/publications/dp/62/); A Jolowicz, "Adversarial and Inquisitorial Models of Civil Procedure" (2003) 52:2 International and Comparative Law Quarterly 281–295; and Arie Freiberg, "Post-Adversarial and Post-Inquisitorial Justice: Transcending Traditional Penological Paradigms" (2010), online: http://papers.ssrn.com/sol3/papers.cfm?abstract_id=1609468.

to a hybrid model indicates a kind of praxis in which the institution's powers and functions as well as the rights of the vulnerable persons they affect have broadened and deepened. This enlargement of capacity is reciprocal, having been driven by internal domestic legal reform, changes in attitudes and norms with respect to children's autonomy, rights and dignity, and the increasingly direct influence of international norms such as those found in Articles 3[2] and 12[3] of the 1990 United Nations *Convention on the Rights of the Child* (CRC).[4]

Before examining the development and features of the Office of the Representative for Children and Youth, the chapter will first provide an attenuated history of the governance of children and earlier institutional models of state protection of child welfare. The BCRCY will be contrasted with these earlier models in section III to show its hybrid nature as well as its institutional strengths and vulnerabilities. The final section will then consider the BCRCY in an international context in order to situate it comparatively amongst other countries' children's representatives. A comparative angle discloses that the general trend in

---

2 Article 3 provides that:

1. In all actions concerning children, whether undertaken by public or private social welfare institutions, courts of law, administrative authorities or legislative bodies, the best interests of the child shall be a primary consideration.

2. States Parties undertake to ensure the child such protection and care as is necessary for his or her well-being, taking into account the rights and duties of his or her parents, legal guardians, or other individuals legally responsible for him or her, and, to this end, shall take all appropriate legislative and administrative measures.

3. States Parties shall ensure that the institutions, services and facilities responsible for the care or protection of children shall conform with the standards established by competent authorities, particularly in the areas of safety, health, in the number and suitability of their staff, as well as competent supervision.

3 Article 12 provides that:

1. States Parties shall assure to the child who is capable of forming his or her own views the right to express those views freely in all matters affecting the child, the views of the child being given due weight in accordance with the age and maturity of the child.

2. For this purpose, the child shall in particular be provided the opportunity to be heard in any judicial and administrative proceedings affecting the child, either directly, or through a representative or an appropriate body, in a manner consistent with the procedural rules of national law.

4 *Convention on the Rights of the Child*, Can. T.S. 1992 No. 3 [CRC]. Canada signed the Convention in 1990. Parliament and nearly all of the provinces initially approved it and the CRC was ratified in 1991. Alberta, which later endorsed the Convention in 1999, did not support the CRC because it argued that the rights contained in the document undermined parental authority. The CRC has not been automatically incorporated into domestic legislation due to Canada's federal structure. Nevertheless, Canada is obliged to conform, the Convention can indirectly influence policy and laws, and some provinces have taken steps to implement or incorporate the principles in specific statutes.

Western countries has been to create independent and stand-alone bodies, such as the BCRCY, with a specialized focus on children.

A Short Evolutionary Story

In order to see how the creation of the BCRCY marks a significant change from traditional approaches to child welfare and the accompanying institutional architecture, I will first provide a short genealogy encapsulating the historical development of different approaches to children's rights as well as norm change regarding children's rights in Western societies.

From Victorian Mores to Social Welfare

In many Western jurisdictions during the early twentieth century, a public official or single bureau was charged with protecting neglected or otherwise vulnerable children only when parents were deemed incapable or negligent.[5] The accompanying policy framework relegated responsibility for children to the private sphere for care unless they were abandoned, significantly endangered, neglected, or impoverished.[6] Churches provided the civil society complement to state care. Family matters not resolved in the private sphere, depending on family resources, entered the legal system only in extreme cases of child abuse, children's death, or divorce. As passive, voiceless objects of parental or state control, children were neither seen nor heard.

---

5 The United States government created a comprehensive federal agency devoted to children's rights – the Children's Bureau – in 1912. It lasted until the 1940s when the Truman Administration reorganized aspects of the federal system and the Children's Bureau lost most of its regulatory authority to larger agencies, becoming a small office limited to investigation and reporting. The complexities of federal–state relations in U.S. constitutionalism ensure that a national function will be very difficult to re-create due to disagreements about the proper extent of state or federal authority over family law. For more on this history, see Kriste Lindenmeyer, *A Right to Childhood: The U.S. Children's Bureau and Child Welfare, 1912–1946* (Urbana: University of Illinois Press, 1997). On the difficulties created by federalism, see Anne C Dailey, "Federalism and Families", (1995) 143 U Pa L Rev 1787 and also Ann Laquer Estin, "Sharing Governance: Family Law in Congress and the States" (2009) 18 Cornell JL & Pub Pol'y, online: http://papers.ssrn.com/sol3/papers.cfm?abstract_id=1131404.

6 Child welfare has been a government responsibility in British Columbia since 1919. For specific treatment of the early history of child welfare in British Columbia, see Christopher Walmsley & Diane Purvey, eds, *Child and Family Welfare in British Columbia: A History* (Calgary: Detselig Enterprises, 2005). See also R Brian Howe, "Implementing Children's Rights in a Federal State: The Case of Canada's Child Protection System" (2001) 9 International Journal of Children's Rights 361 at 362–3 [Howe].

The alternately paternalistic and *laissez-faire* Victorian model shifted with the development of the welfare state. Charged with multiple responsibilities for child welfare and embracing a new human rights culture, post-World War II states initiated a slew of reforms aimed at children in general as well as children-at-risk due to challenges posed by their families or particular religious or cultural communities. In most Western countries, humanitarian concerns, principles of compassion and benevolence, and the sentimentalization of childhood provided the ethical motivation for the development of modern institutions of child welfare.[7] As Viviana Zelizer persuasively argues, American culture shifted – morally, economically, and politically – to view children as economically "useless", but morally priceless.[8] Children's representation and participation in the justice system, however, did not shift as radically from the original common law legal baseline where they were designated chattels or property. They remained disadvantaged by adversarial legal processes premised on adult norms and persons that did not treat them as full legal persons who could claim rights along with the fulfilment of duties. Indeed, children were generally considered incompetent, incapacitated and dependent.[9]

The Unadulterated Adversarial Model: Lawyer Advocates

Lawyers traditionally acted on behalf of children when welfare, protection and family cases entered the court system. For common law jurisdictions, the earliest model was a court-appointed lawyer or guardian *ad litem* who represented a child in wardship, guardianship, child protection, and access and custody cases. Studies from Australia, New Zealand and the United States that have analyzed the effectiveness of lawyer advocates in representing children convey enormous

---

7 For an overview of this history, see the "Introduction" in Mona Gleason et al, eds, *Lost Kids: Vulnerable Children and Youth in Twentieth-Century Canada and the United States* (Vancouver: UBC Press, 2010) [*Lost Kids*]. For a similar history, but one that draws out the implications for the treatment of the child as a legal subject, see Daiva Stasiulis, "The Active Child Citizen: Lessons from Canadian Policy and the Children's Movement" (2002) 6:4 Citizenship Studies [Stasiulis].

8 Viviana Zelizer, *Pricing the Priceless Child: The Changing Social Value of Children* (New York: Basic Books, 1985). Risks to children, historically minimized by adults, became a cause for collective concern and a measure of the advancement of society in the American Progressive Era (roughly 1896 to 1920). Zelizer discusses the broad cultural shift whereby adults expressed empathic commitments to children though modern education, health, insurance, and labour policies and programs.

9 For a pithy summation of these problems, see JM Herlihy, "Dealing with Child Abuse: Adversarial versus Investigative Systems" (1992) 24:1 Australian Journal of Forensic Sciences 16 [Herlihy]. Herlihy focuses on historically recurring problems in child abuse cases in which children could be compelled to give evidence. See also Alison Cleland, "Legal Solutions for Children: Comparing Scots Law with Other Jurisdictions" (1995) 10 Scottish Affairs 6.

dissatisfaction with this model from many participating actors.[10] Systemic criticisms condemned how a common law system treated children as passive and inferior legal subjects, and emphasized how lawyers failed to listen properly to familial concerns, treat children with respect, and properly solicit their views. Children's reactions to the adversarial family law system are perhaps best captured in the words of one young interviewee: "Well, no offence, but I don't really think adults listen to us and they just want to think what they think, especially if the kid is younger. And I think the kids should be listened to as well as adults. I think they should be treated the way an adult is treated and be allowed to have their say."[11] These studies disclosed that lawyers often did not speak to or physically meet with the children they were charged with representing. Moreover, though lawyers were considered generally effective advocates in courts, they were shown to lack the expertise and focus that individuals solely devoted to considering children's interests and representing their wishes possess. In many cases, a clear tension existed in the lawyer's dual role as a person who was simultaneously acting for the court while also serving children's interests. With busy practices and large caseloads, lawyer advocates often lacked the time and energy to provide supports to children who experienced trauma and bewilderment in the court system because they were placed in adversarial relations with family members and/or governmental agencies. Studies measuring children's satisfaction with models of representation rank lawyer-only systems poorly.[12] Failing to act comprehensively and compassionately and playing only short-term, temporary roles in children's lives, the lawyer-advocate model was shown to fall quite short.[13]

The extension of legal rights to children and the statutory direction for legal actors to consider the best interests of the child in decision have not constituted an adequate remedy for the deficiencies of the adversarial model.[14] One critic of the adversarial system maintains that for the adversarial system to become

10 See Andy Bilson & Sue White, "Representing Children's Views and Best Interests in Court: An International Comparison" (2005) 14 Child Abuse Review 220 at 230–1 [Bilson and White].

11 This quote is from the Report of the Columbus Pilot study of case management and the adversarial family law system by the Family Court of Western Australia. Interviews with a variety of affected persons, including children, were conducted as part of the study. See Lisbeth T Pike & Paul T Murphy, "Invisible Parties: Listening to Children – A Social Science Perspective" (Paper presented at the Australian Family Law Conference, 24 October 2006) at 12, online: http://www.familycourt.wa.gov.au/_files/FLC%20Paper%20Oct06.pdf.

12 *Ibid* at 235.

13 For further discussion on this point, please see Chapter 14 by Jula Hughes which examines the challenges for traumatized victims testifying in adversarial systems.

14 For a vigorous critique of how the best interests principle has been interpreted and applied by judges in custody decision in the legal system, see Cindy L Baldassi, Susan B Boyd & Fiona Kelly, "Losing the Child in Child-Centred Legal Processes" in *Lost Kids*, *supra* note 7 at 192–212.

more flexible and meet the needs of children would "involve a change of such magnitude that it could weaken the very fabric …".[15] A fundamental overhaul of the adversarial system appears to be a non-starter, but the institutional consequence of this reality has been non-uniform incremental attempts at reform across a number of jurisdictions. Adversarial legal culture remains resistant to change and continues to permeate other models in common law countries.[16]

The Adulterated Adversarial Model: State and Volunteer Advocates

Generalized dissatisfaction with the adversarial system and lawyer-advocates produced a slate of alternative models from the 1970s on which modified the adversarial system to make use of investigative methodology and more comprehensive approaches to children's cases. The challenging and multiple needs of children resulted in the creation of expert bodies whose primary function was child advocacy or, alternatively, alternative dispute resolution processes. The use of these bodies was, until recently, the orthodox model in Canada and in other common law jurisdictions. Led by Ontario and Alberta, child advocacy offices became a preferred reform choice in Canada.[17] On the continuum of models, the Office of the Child and Youth Advocate (OCYA) in Alberta hearkens back to these early efforts to manage child welfare through an independent agency that acts as a check and a balance on government decision-making affecting young people and is primarily devoted to the amplification of child and youth voices, greater participation, and championing for child and youth rights (see Tables 17.1 and 17.2).

The OCYA functions as a delegate of the provincial Ministry of Children and Youth Services. The OCYA is accountable to, and receives its funding from, the Ministry and is therefore neither stand-alone nor independent. Nevertheless, it is expert in its specialized focus on children and youth. The OCYA's core functions remain traditional individual advocacy for vulnerable children and the

15 Herlihy, *supra* note 9 at 18.

16 In an early article, Carrie Menkel-Meadow analyzed the co-opting tendencies of adversarial lawyers – their attitudes and practices – when participating in alternative dispute resolutions systems. See Carrie Menkel, " 'Pursuing Settlement in an Adversary Culture: A Tale of Innovation Co-opted' or 'The Law of ADR'" (1991) 19:1 Fla St U L Rev 1. In her contribution to this collection (see Chapter 2), Robin Creyke discusses contemporary difficulties in shaking the adversarial culture within the context of hearings in Australian administrative tribunals that have been statutorily designated as "inquisitorial." In the Canadian context, see British Columbia, Ministry of Attorney General Justice Services Branch, *Legal Culture* (23 February 2005) at 1-18, online: http://www.ag.gov.bc.ca/justice-reform-initiatives/publications/pdf/LegalCulture.pdf.

17 Further information on Ontario's history and new model can be found in Paul C Whitehead et al, *A New Model for Child and Youth Advocacy in Ontario: Report prepared for the Ministry of Children and Youth Services* (2004), online: http://provincialadvocate.on.ca/documents/en/Final_Report_Eng.pdf.

investigation of complaints from adults and children regarding the provision of government services. It is one step removed from the lawyer-advocate model as evidenced by its responsibility for appointing legal counsel through its Legal Representation for Children and Youth services. It does not, unlike similar bodies in other jurisdictions, investigate children's deaths (See Table 17.2). The OCYA also does not undertake systemic reform efforts, attesting again to its main role as an *internal* advocacy system.[18] The primary audience for the Alberta office, then, is the Alberta provincial government.

A further step along the continuum brings us to the American model of citizen volunteers as guardians *ad litem* (see Table 17.3). In this model, state agencies recruit, train, and manage volunteer representatives from a variety of backgrounds – social workers, lawyers, and "ordinary" citizens – to act as court-appointed special advocates. Independent representation of abused and neglected children is their chief function, rather than legal services, and the shift to trained citizen volunteers reduces costs, especially when compared to the cost of using lawyer-advocates. Studies of citizen volunteers conclude that this model excels at providing effective and efficient representation, especially when volunteers work in tandem with lawyers to effectuate the best interests of vulnerable children.[19] Nevertheless, this model is both resource intensive due to the constant training of volunteers and exceptional in that perhaps no other country in the world embraces a tradition of volunteerism (instead of relying on the state) as the United States does. Finally, despite reliance on volunteer advocates in what appears to be a more radical system, these child representatives are subject to pressures to professionalize in order to best represent children's interests.[20] Voluntary citizen review boards and volunteer citizen guardians depend on quality appointments, a requirement which means that volunteers may have to undergo training in a variety of complex child development and welfare areas, including legal, in order to make competent judgements about a child's best interests.

18 Howe speculates that the OCYA differs from other models in Canada – indeed lags – because the more conservative and libertarian political culture of Alberta places greater emphasis on the privacy and autonomy of the family. Howe, *supra* note 6 at 362.

19 Bilson and White, *supra* note 10 at 229.

20 For a discussion of several of the strengths and weaknesses of citizen volunteers, see Mark Hardin, "A Comparison of Administrative, Citizen and Judicial Review" (1985) 7 Children and Youth Services Review 161.

Table 17.1 Oversight Models of Child Protection and Welfare Services – Comparison across Canada: Structure

	British Columbia	Alberta	Saskatchewan	Manitoba	Ontario
Name	Representative for Children and Youth	Office of the Child and Youth Advocate	Child's Advocate Office	Office of the Children's Advocate	Office of the Provincial Advocate for Children and Youth
Enabling Act	• Representative for Children & Youth Act (2006)	• Child, Youth & Family Enhancement Act (2000) • Protection of Sexually Exploited Children Act (2000)	• Ombudsman & Children's Advocate Act (1978)	• Child & Family Services Act (2003) • Adoption Act (2003)	• Provincial Advocate for & Children Youth Act (2007) • Child & Family Services Act (1990)
Standalone	✓	× Ministry of Children and Youth Services	✓	✓	✓
Independent	✓	×	✓	✓	✓
Terms of Office	• 5 years • Renewable for 2nd 5-year term	• 5 year non-renewable term	• 5 years • Renewable for 2nd 5-year term	• 3 years • Renewable for 2nd 3-year term	• 5 years • Renewable for 2nd 5-year term
Accountable to Legislative Assembly	✓ Select Standing Committee on Children & Youth	× Ministry of Children and Youth Services	✓ Directly	✓ Directly	✓ Directly
Funding from Legislative Assembly	✓	× Ministry of Children and Youth Services	✓	✓	✓
Recent budget	2009–10 = $6,991,519 2010–11 = $6,937,099	2009–10 = $7,233,000 2010–11 = $7,330,000	2009–10 = $1,621,000 2010–11 = $1,697,000	2009–10 = $2,384,000 2010–11 = $2,468,000	2009–10 = $6,100,000 2010–11 = $5,370,509
Specialized or exclusive focus on youth & children	✓	✓	✓	✓	✓

Note: × = does not have indicated feature ✓ = has indicated feature ×/✓ = indicates transition underway.

Quebec	New Brunswick	Nova Scotia	Newfoundland & Labrador	Yukon
Commission des droits de la personne et des droits de la jeunesse	New Brunswick Child and Youth Advocate	Office of the Ombudsman	Office of the Child and Youth Advocate	Office of the Child and Youth Advocate
• Quebec Charter of Rights & Freedoms (1975) • Youth Protection Act (1977)	• Child & Youth Advocate Act (2007)	• Ombudsman Act (1989)	• Child & Youth Advocate Act (2002)	• Child & Youth Advocate Act (2009)
✗ Child and Youth Division	✓ Decoupled from Ombudsman's Office in 2011	✗ Youth and Senior Services Division	✓	✓
✓	✓	✓	✓	✓
–	• Between 5 and 10 years • Non-renewable	• 5 years • Renewable (unspecified)	• 6 years • Renewable for 2nd 6-year term	• 5 years • Renewable for 2nd 5-year term
✓ Commission reports directly	✓ Directly	✓ Through the Ombudsman	✓ Directly	✓ Directly
✗ Ministry of Justice	✓	✓	✓	✓
– 2010–11 = $1,547,000	2009–10 = $1,679,000 2010–11 = $1,729,200	2009–10 = $1,658,000 2010–11 = $1,649,000	2009–10 = $1,128,700 2010–11 = $1,277,200	2009–10 = $211,000 2010–11 = $433,000
✗	✓	✗	✓	✓

Table 17.2 Oversight Models of Child Protection and Welfare Services – Comparison across Canada: Functions and Powers

	British Columbia	Alberta	Saskatchewan	Manitoba	Ontario
Name	Representative for Children and Youth	Office of the Child and Youth Advocate	Child's Advocate Office	Office of the Children's Advocate	Office of the Provincial Advocate for Children and Youth
Individual/case advocacy	✓	✓	✓	✓	✓
Systemic advocacy	✓	×	✓	✓	✓
Policy advocacy/ recommendation	✓	✓	✓	✓	✓
Public reports	✓	✓ via Minister	✓	✓	✓
Receive complaints	✓	✓	✓	✓	✓
Investigate complaints/ systemic matters	✓	✓	✓	✓	✓
Access to information	✓ Right to information (s.10)	×	×	✓	×
Subpoena power	✓	×	×	×	×
Investigate deaths	✓	×	✓	✓	✓
Legal counsel	×	✓ Appoints	×	×	×
Consultation processes	✓	×/✓ Underway	✓	✓	✓
Child welfare	✓	×	✓	✓	✓
Child and Youth Protection	✓	✓	✓	✓	✓
Public education	✓	×	✓	✓	✓
Informed by UNCRC principles	✓	✓	✓ Child and Youth First Principles	✓ Best interests	✓
UNCRC as direct influence	×	×	×	×	✓ Section 2(3)

Quebec	New Brunswick	Nova Scotia	Newfoundland & Labrador	Yukon
Commission des droits de la personne et des droits de la jeunesse	New Brunswick Child and Youth Advocate	Office of the Ombudsman	Office of the Child and Youth Advocate	Office of the Child and Youth Advocate
✓	✓	✓	✓	✓
✓	✓	✓	✓	✓
✓	✓	✓	✓	✓
✓	✓	✓	✓	✓
✓	✓	✓	✓	✓
✓	✓	✓	✓	✓
✓ via Minister	✓	✓	×	✓ Right to information (s.23(1))
✓	×	×	✓	×
×	×	×	×	×
×	×	×	×	×
✓	×	✓	✓	✓
✓	×	✓	✓	✓
✓	✓	✓	✓	✓
✓	✓	✓	✓	✓
✓	×	✓	×	✓
×	×	×	×	✓ Section 17(1)(b)

Table 17.3 International Models of Children's Representatives[1]

	British Columbia	United States[2]	United Kingdom[3]
Model	Independent, stand-alone agency accountable to Parliament	Panels of volunteers	Independent agency accountable to Parliament
Legal actors	Representative for Children and Youth is a Legislative Officer	Agencies recruit, train, manage volunteers (attorneys, social workers, citizen volunteers)	Children's Commissioners • England (2004) • Scotland (2003) • Wales (2000) • Northern Ireland (2003)
Legal framework	Specialized statutory regime blends inquisitorial and adversarial features but does not provide legal representation	ADR model which interacts with the courts but does not provide legal representation	Individual complaints heard in Wales & Northern Ireland; role in England is to promote rather than safeguard rights
Role of child	Participatory, represented, consulted	Represented, consulted	Participatory, represented, consulted
Convention Art. 3: best interests of the child	Indirectly through systemic advocacy	Primary	Shall have regard to or must regard relevant provision in England, Wales, Northern Ireland; mandatory in Scotland
Convention Art. 12: ensure procedural rights and enhanced representation	Indirectly by ensuring child's views/wishes are effectively & systematically represented	Duties ranked with best interests taking priority over enhanced representation & participation	Shall have regard to or must regard relevant provision

Notes:

1 Modified and expanded table from Andy Bilson & Sue White, "Representing Children's Views and Best Interests in Court: An International Comparison" (2005) 14 Child Abuse Review 220.

2 Note that only the United States and Somalia have not ratified the *Convention on the Rights of the Child*.

3 Until 2004, England's model was an independent government agency that employed guardians ad litem in conjunction with legal representation. Scotland employed a panel of guardians as its model where local authorities recruited and administered lists of guardians ("Safeguarders") who did not provide legal representation.

New Zealand	Germany	France	Norway
Independent Crown agency	National association of guardians *ad litem*	Special judicial system	Ombudsman (1981)
Children's Commissioner (2003)	Voluntary membership	Judge trained in child rights	Appointed by the king
Specialized statutory regime blends inquisitorial and adversarial features but does not provide legal representation	Self-regulating within national standards but limited accountability and no state control	Operates within the inquisitorial legal model	Operates within the ombudsman model with respect to public and private institutions but not family disputes
Participatory, represented, consulted	Participatory, less represented, consulted	Child has participatory right to express views directly to the judge	Represented, consulted, less participatory
Legislation incorporates principle	Co-equal with Art. 12	Carries less weight than Art. 12	Fully implements the CRC
Legislation incorporates principle	Effectuate child's will, opinion, rights to participation and self-determination	Legislation incorporates Art. 12	Fully implements the CRC

Specialized and Hybrid Ombuds[21]

Instead of the adulterated adversarial model, a different institutional remedy emerged as a common form in Canada: the ombudsman.[22] The virtues of the ombuds model in the child welfare context are a significant contrast to the Alberta model discussed above: greater independence and autonomy; greater accountability to the public due to the connection with the provincial legislature; specialized focus on children and youth; and, enhanced efforts at implementing policy recommendations and systemic reform.[23] These bodies conform to the "classic" functions of an ombuds by resolving citizen–government disputes through listening, investigating, weighing facts, and providing remedies to resolve the dispute. But, they are also specialized ombuds with jurisdiction over a particular policy area or subject matter. Lastly, those offices which are informed by rights (for example, civil and political, social cultural, human and collective) and international principles as part of their mandate can be considered "hybrid" ombuds.[24]

Ten children's advocacy offices currently exist in Canada, each defined by their provincial enabling statutes (see Table 17.1).[25] Table 17.1 shows that all are independent agencies, except for Alberta whose Office is contained within the

---

21 Throughout this book, the following terminology has been adopted, in order to promote gender neutrality while also respecting the names of ombuds institutions. The capitalized expression, "Ombudsman" has been used for specific names (for example, the Swedish Ombudsman, the Ombudsman of Ontario). The lowercase words "ombudsman", "ombudsperson" and "ombuds" have been used, as nouns and adjectives, to represent general institutions, with preference for the use of the gender-neutral forms of "ombudsperson" and "ombuds" wherever possible.

22 Norway established the first Ombudsman for Children in 1981. For an overview of types of ombuds, see Mary A Marshall & Linda C Reif, "The Ombudsman: Maladministration and Alternative Dispute Resolution" (1995) 34 Alta L Rev 215 [Marshall and Reif].

23 The provinces of Nova Scotia and New Brunswick delegated responsibility for children and youth to their ombuds offices as part of their general mandate or, in some cases, as a specialized function. Nova Scotia's Office of the Ombudsman, for example, has a Youth and Senior Services Division. In 2011, New Brunswick separated the Child and Youth Advocate from the Ombudsman; previously, they were merged in one office. Saskatchewan, while using one statute to enable both the Ombudsman and the Children's Advocate, nevertheless created a stand-alone Child's Advocate Office.

24 Marshall and Reif, *supra* note 22 at 231–4. See also Linda C Reif, "Building Democratic Institutions: The Role of National Human Rights Institutions in Good Governance and Human Rights Protection" (2000) 13 Harv Hum Rts J 1.

25 For further information on other provincial jurisdictions, see Robin MacLean & R Brian Howe, *Brief Report on Canadian Provincial Children and Youth Advocacy Offices: Highlights of Functions and Recent Activities* (August 2009), online: http://www.cbu.ca/crc/sites/cbu.ca.crc/files/images/Brief_report_on_Canadian_provincial_children_and_youth_advocacy_offices.pdf. Many people in the territory of Nunavut would also like to see an independent Child's Advocate established. See "Nunavut Child's Advocate Needs

Ministry of Children and Youth Services, and can therefore decide matters with relative freedom from the interference or influence of the executive branch of government.[26] The hallmarks of independence vary, but most of these offices have a significant degree of independence from the executive branch, are accountable to the provincial legislative assembly, exercise considerable statutory powers under their enabling acts, have greater security of tenure under their terms of office as well as operational autonomy, and possess more secure funding since their monies come from their provincial legislatures and not the executive branch. Most are stand-alone agencies focussing on a single policy area created through a special statute and are primarily devoted to child welfare. All of these offices hear complaints or issues raised by children, youth, or adults on behalf of children and youth, and are charged with investigative powers that can be used to engage in individual and systemic advocacy. Individual advocacy in response to complaints or concerns remains a core function. All offices respond to the voice of children, but some are more active in seeking and engaging children's voices. Most of the offices recommend policy changes to governments and engage in broad publicity and education efforts.

Québec offers another variation on the ombuds model. Its *Commission des droits de la personne et des droits de la jeunesse* is a specialized administrative agency which also houses a tribunal and is governed by a provincial Charter of Rights and Freedoms. The Commission acts like a conventional human rights agency, but with a specialized child and youth division. Similar to the ombuds model, the Commission reports to the provincial legislature. However, it also shares with Alberta a lack of independence in that it receives its funding from the provincial Ministry of Justice and is therefore subject to greater executive influence and control.

Each of these types of ombuds approximates an inquisitorial model that enquires into truth by engagement in a greater responsibility for fact and policy determination, possesses broad recommendatory powers, and shifts various burdens and responsibilities from the parties or the lawyer-advocate to the relevant independent authority. And, though each provincial body differs in scope and mandate, the institutional landscape is becoming less of a patchwork with Alberta standing as a clear outlier.[27]

Autonomy: Minister", *CBC News* (21 August 2009) online: CBC News http://www.cbc.ca/news/canada/north/story/2009/08/21/nunavut-child-advocate.html.

26 In this section I rely on Laverne Jacobs' concise overview of the concept of independence of administrative agencies in Canadian public law. See Laverne Jacobs, "Caught between Judicial Paradigms and the Administrative State's Pastiche: 'Tribunal' Independence, Impartiality, and Bias" in Colleen Flood & Lorne Sossin, eds, *Administrative Law in Context: A New Casebook*, 2d ed (Toronto: Emond-Montgomery, 2012) 233.

27 It is worth noting that federal jurisdictions such as Australia and Canada do not have a Children's Representative at the national level. Federal systems undoubtedly complicate the implementation of children's rights due to a lack of intergovernmental consultation

The Hybrid Model: B.C.'s Representative for Children and Youth

This section will first briefly set out the most recent history leading to the creation of the RCYBC – a history that includes the shift from traditional adversarial processes, two public inquiries, a conventional child and youth advocate, a children's commissioner, and an internal officer within the home ministry.[28] I will then analyze the structure and functions of the RCYBC in terms of innovative institutional design. Lastly, the section considers some challenges and problems that have arisen for this new model.

The Birth of a New Model[29]

The creation of the first Child, Youth, and Family Advocate in 1995 resulted from several key political moments within a lengthy period of institutional turmoil and political acrimony. First, the 1980s saw substantive change in the delivery of child

---

and coordination and can result in the creation of a patchwork leading to the arbitrary treatment of children across a national policy. See Howe, *supra* note 6 on the difficulties of implementing children's rights in a federal state such as Canada's where child protection, and other necessary constitutional heads of power, rest with the provinces. In 2003, the UN Committee on the Rights of the Child recommended that Canada establish an Ombudsman's office at the federal level that would be responsible for children's rights (online: http://www.unhchr.ch/tbs/doc.nsf/898586b1dc7b4043c1256a450044f331/995a15056ca61d16c1256df000310995/$FILE/G0344648.pdf). Until recently, Australia mirrored Canada in having either a Commissioner or a Guardian in every State and Territory to represent children and youth. Each of their roles differs according to their enabling legislation. But, in February 2013, the Australian government announced the appointment of Megan Mitchell as Australia's first Children's Commissioner at the national level for a five-year term. The Commissioner will be based within the Australian Human Rights Commission which had proposed the creation of the national Commissioner in 2010. Mitchell is formerly the New South Wales Commissioner for Children and Young People. See Australian Human Rights Commission, "Inaugural Children's Commissioner Appointed" (25 February 2013) online: http://www.humanrights.gov.au/news/stories/inaugural-children-s-commissioner-appointed.

28 For a thorough presentation of the historical context, see Michele McBride, *Report on Child Advocacy and Complaint Resolution Process* (Victoria, BC: Children and Youth Review, 2006) [McBride].

29 Consistent with the genealogy set out at the beginning of this chapter, child protection in B.C. began with the guardianship model for orphaned or neglected children as wards of the state and delivered through children's aid societies (the *Infants Act*, 1901). This was replaced by a model of social and child protection services (the *Protection of Children Act*, 1939), which then changed to a system of regional and community service delivery (*Community Resources Board Act*, 1974). Prior to the reforms which are the focus of this chapter, it morphed into an integrated system of social services, though one which was criticized for failing to recognize children's rights and for not providing a child advocate role (the *Family and Child Service Act*, 1981). McBride, *supra* note 28 at 5.

services with the enactment of the first piece of child protection legislation since 1939,[30] combined with deep budget cuts and reorganization of the government office devoted to delivering child welfare programs.[31] Economic and political turbulence resulted in a change of government in 1991 from the conservative Social Credit Party to the social democratic New Democratic Party (NDP). The NDP government vowed to reform the delivery of child welfare and protection services. They engaged in a broad public consultation exercise which resulted in the issue of two reports by the Ministry of Social Services, the first focusing on the views from non-Aboriginal communities regarding child welfare reform,[32] and the second focusing on Aboriginal communities in B.C.[33] Shortly after the second report, the province was rocked by the neglect, abuse and death of 5-year-old Matthew Vaudreuil in 1992 at the hands of his mother, with the media bolstering outrage by providing detailed reports on how the existing child protection services had mishandled his case. In response to these reports, the Minister of Social Services delivered new legislation – the *Child, Family and Community Services Act* ("CFCSA") – which promised a value shift in service delivery based on a model of least intrusion to families.[34] Though the provincial legislature passed the CFCSA in 1994, it did not come into force until 1996 in order to allow time for the development of new policies and procedures. The provincial government also created a public inquiry in 1994, charged with examining the circumstances leading to Matthew's 1992 death, with the aim of restoring public confidence in the child protection system. This became known as the Gove Inquiry and was headed by Mr. Justice Thomas Gove, a provincial court judge.[35]

After eighteen months of investigation and research, Mr. Justice Gove issued his report in 1995 recommending changes to B.C.'s child protection system as well as the creation of several new institutions: a new Ministry of Children and Family Development which consolidated several existing but then separate services under one institutional umbrella; the first Child, Youth and Family Advocate who would provide services for children and families having difficulties with the new ministry;

---

30 The *Family Child Service Act* (1981) was enacted in response to the Royal Commission on Family and Children's Law (1974–75), but failed to incorporate many of the important recommendations that the Commission made.

31 From 1983 to 1988, child protection services faced substantial reductions in the staff, contracting out, and a reorganization that removed a variety of services from the single office – then the Ministry of Social Services – to separate offices managing different aspects of child welfare and protection.

32 *Making Changes: A Place to Start* (Victoria, BC: Ministry of Social Services, 1992).

33 *Liberating Our Children, Liberating Our Nations* (Victoria, BC: Ministry of Social Services, 1992).

34 RSBC 1996, c 46.

35 British Columbia, Ministry of the Attorney General, *Report of the Gove Inquiry into Child Protection in British Columbia*, 3 vols (Victoria, BC: Queen's Printer for British Columbia, 1995).

and, a Children's Commission to review child deaths and to provide oversight of the new ministry. The overall policy direction shifted toward removing children from their homes instead of providing assistance to stay together – a major break from the family preservation model that had inspired the CFCSA. In institutional terms, then, B.C. moved away from the family-centred model that was commonly employed in Europe and which was premised on providing substantial resources for family support.[36] The CFCSA came into force after the Gove Report, but it was accompanied by new regulation and practices that reflected the move away from the family support model, resulting in an increase in the number of children in government care.[37] At the same time, community-based providers such as women's centres faced government cuts or closure, making the situation worse for those children in care.

This institutional architecture operated until 2001 when a new Liberal government looked at the various agencies involved in child protection as part of a Core Services Review. In addition to the three agencies created in 1995 and discussed above, the Coroners Service, provincial Ombudsman, and Public Guardian and Trustee also provided child-related services. In order to trim expenses and cut duplication, the government rationalized services by creating a new Child and Youth Officer who would replace both the Advocate and the Commissioner and act as the main oversight body. The Coroner would take on a new child death review function (one more limited than the Children's Commission), while the Ombudsman would continue to monitor general fairness issues. At the same time, the government engaged in large-scale budget cuts as well as a shift towards regional provision of services in anticipation of a devolved regional governance model.

But in 2004, individuals in the child protection system turned to the former Ombudsman, the former Advocate for Children, Youth and Families, and the former Children's Commissioner to ask them to communicate widespread concerns to the Premier about the impact of budget cuts on vulnerable children and the lack of accountability in the Ministry. After a letter from the three former public officials to the Premier elicited no response, they released their letter to the public in 2005. Very shortly after this letter garnered significant publicity, two Aboriginal infants in the foster care program managed by the Ministry died and their deaths became linked with the issues raised in the letter.[38] Public and media

---

36 Howe, *supra* note 6 at 371.

37 From 1979 to 1993, the number of children in care decreased from 9,000 to approximately 6,000 but from 1994 to 1999 the numbers increased from 6,000 to 10,000. See Darcie Bennett & Lobat Sadrehashemi, *Broken Promises: Parents Speak about B.C.'s Child Welfare System* (Vancouver, BC: Pivot Legal Society, 2008) at 16–17.

38 In 2005 Sherry Charlie, a 19-month-old Aboriginal girl placed in a kinship care agreement, was murdered while in the care of her uncle. In 2002, Chasidy Whitford, who was 2, was murdered by her father while the family was receiving child protection services. In both cases, the Liberal government was accused of sacrificing children to cost-saving

scrutiny resulted in the disclosure that no internal reviews of earlier suspicious child deaths and the two current deaths had occurred. The new Coroner's Service did not provide the same intensive death reviews as had the earlier Children's Commission and the Ministry itself did not release several internal reviews of the problems to the public. These failings of accountability and transparency, as well as the resulting public opprobrium, compelled the Minister of Children and Family Development to appoint the Honourable Ted Hughes, a retired judge, to engage in an independent review of the child protection system in 2005: the Hughes Inquiry.

The Hughes Inquiry examined advocacy for children and youth, oversight of the government's performance in protecting and providing services in B.C., and the systems for reporting and review of child deaths and how much they furthered public accountability. At the time of the Hughes Inquiry, the Ministry had gone through nine ministers in ten years, including eight deputy ministers and seven directors of child welfare. The Ministry, Hughes concluded, had implemented a policy shift to keep children at home, but without the social supports and staff training due to budget cuts.[39] At the same time, the provincial government pulled back some functions to the centre from the regions while concurrently preparing the ground for the eventual devolution of child welfare services to the control of Aboriginal authorities. As Justice Hughes wrote, each of these changes on its own posed formidable challenges, but together they "created a climate of instability and confusion" which ultimately frustrated the ability of the Ministry to protect vulnerable children and support families in crisis and need.

After four and a half months of research, public consultation, file review and data gathering, Justice Hughes submitted his final report in April 2006.[40] The report contained the results of his review and set of 62 recommendations to improve child protection and child welfare in British Columbia. One of his key recommendations was the creation of a new, independent body to oversee the child welfare system: the Representative for Children and Youth.

---

because children placed in these type of kinship arrangements were not counted as "children in care" and therefore their family providers received less government support compared to regular foster care providers.

39 Judge Hughes noted that this shift undid the earlier Gove-initiated policy direction, concluding that the earlier shift was misguided but had its basis partly in social workers' fears that they would be held responsible for children left in homes where they might be harmed. Indeed, a notorious case in Ontario involving the starvation death of an infant – Jordan Heikamp – resulted in a social worker being charged with criminal negligence for failing to intervene and protect him from his mother. The new policy direction therefore prioritized child protection over family preservation.

40 EN Hughes, *BC Children and Youth Review: An Independent Review of BC's Child Protection System* (7 April 2006) at 4, online: Ministry of Children and Family Development http://www.mcf.gov.bc.ca/bcchildprotection/pdf/BC_Children_and_Youth_Review_Report_FINAL_April_4.pdf.

Family Resemblances

By implementing a largely ombuds institutional model that kept some features of the adversarial system in the context of the oversight of child protection and welfare services, British Columbia proved to be an early provincial innovator.[41] The *Representative for Children and Youth Act*, enacted in May 2006, quickly followed on the heels of the Hughes Report.[42] Table 17.1 presents the following key features of the RCY: the RCY is a legislative officer, has the powers of a commissioner of inquiry, retains many of the functions of an ombuds, and possesses the structural independence of a provincial auditor general.

As an officer of the provincial legislature, the RCY must provide annual reports to the legislature via the Select Standing Committee on Children and Youth and it receives its funding from the legislative assembly.[43] To be appointed, the RCY must receive unanimous recommendation by a special committee of the legislative committee and then approval by resolution in the legislative assembly.[44] The term of office is for five years and is renewable for a second five-year term only.[45] It requires a two-thirds or more vote in the legislature to remove the RCY for cause or incapacity, though he or she may also be suspended from office with or without salary according to the same terms.[46] The office of the RCY has an almost $7 million annual budget which goes some distance to funding both investigative and consultative efforts. Table 17.1 shows that British Columbia, Alberta and Ontario are consistently the highest spenders on child welfare services and together comprise three of the four largest provinces in terms of general population. They are also the top three provinces in terms of numbers of Aboriginal persons resident.[47] Manitoba, on the other hand, was the highest spender per capita on child welfare services from 1992 to 1999, and it has the fourth highest Aboriginal population out of all the Canadian provinces and territories.[48]

41 The model for the RCY was influenced by concurrent developments in Ontario which resulted in the Office of the Provincial Advocate for Children and Youth (see Table 17.1).

42 *Representative for Children and Youth Act*, SBC 2006, c 29 [RCYA]. Though passed in May 2006, the Act itself came into force over three phases: 1) the enabling of administrative functions in November 2006; 2) the enabling of the advocacy and monitoring functions in March 2007; and 3) the enabling of the critical injury and death review and investigative functions.

43 *Ibid*, s 17(1).

44 *Ibid*, s 2(1).

45 *Ibid*, s 2(3) and (4).

46 *Ibid*, s 4(2).

47 The 2006 Census of Population is the source for these statistics as well as more detailed demographics, online: Statistics Canada http://www12.statcan.ca/census-recensement/2006/index-eng.cfm.

48 Howe, *supra* note 6 at 374. Despite its different model, one that is about limited intervention and not about family services and children's rights, Alberta provides the most funds.

Consistent with the investigative model, the Act permits the RCY to establish multidisciplinary teams in order to assist with reviews and investigations in child deaths and critical injuries.[49] These reviews and investigations do not replace parallel criminal investigations, and the RCY must wait until the completion of a criminal or other investigation by a public body.[50] Failure of persons to answer questions or cooperate may result in the RCY applying to the B.C. Supreme Court for an order to comply and, if non-cooperation continues, the RCY can initiate contempt proceedings in court.[51]

Other features of the RCY clearly parallel the practical problem-solving and investigatory role of an ombuds who can choose to act formally or informally, flexibly and efficiently. The RCY is charged with engaging in systemic and policy advocacy[52] and embraces stakeholder and public outreach as well as public education about children's rights and government and parental duties. Since the statutory definition of "child" is a person under 19 years of age, the scope of the RCY's child stakeholder concerns is quite broad.[53] Notably, in addition to the monitoring, reviewing, and auditing functions, the RCY is empowered to engage in significant research efforts.

The RCY possesses the discretionary initiative to investigate matters of import and can then submit Special Reports to the legislative assembly containing policy recommendations and information about governmental compliance with previous recommendations. The Speaker must lay these reports before the assembly and the standing committee as soon as possible.[54] These investigations, however, are not solely directed at uncovering the "truth" underlying individual cases, but try to ascertain the causes of systemic failures and then recommend measures that will successfully prevent children's critical injuries and deaths in the future. This statutory intention expresses an aim to overcome the fragmentation of information and dispersal of responsibility in various organizations thus ensuring greater accountability. The underlying ethos is one directed towards problem solving, is not confrontational but is consultative, and incorporates elements of restorative justice over forms of retributive justice.

Though it does have a clear advocacy role, RCY does not engage in formal advocacy in courts or before tribunals, thereby eliminating the earlier lawyerly forms of advocacy. The RCY has no statutory power to act as legal counsel.[55]

---

49 RCYA, *supra* note 42, s 15.

50 *Ibid*, s 13. Or, in some cases, until one year after the critical injury or death of the child – whichever comes earlier.

51 *Ibid*, s 14 and 14.1.

52 *Ibid*, s 6.

53 *Ibid*, s 1. "Youth" has a more limited definition: a person who is above the age of 16 but under 19.

54 *Ibid*, s 20.

55 *Ibid*, s 9. Nevertheless, the RCY also does have subpoena powers such as those possessed by child advocates in Nova Scotia, Saskatchewan and the Yukon.

So, while the RCY is not adversarial in the sense of providing or acting as legal counsel, the RCY does serve a more adversarial and confrontational function in the investigation review of children's critical injuries and deaths – a responsibility carried over from the earlier provincial model and one which operates in tandem with the Coroner's Office. Moreover, the RCY is tasked with preserving the individual autonomy of children in relation to family and state intrusion or control as legal counsel might do in dispute resolution processes. But the underlying child-centred approach focuses more on facilitating intervention than finding fault. A key function is to ensure that children no longer feel underrepresented, lack voice, and are disadvantaged by information asymmetries which adult decision-makers control and benefit from.

The appointment of Mary Ellen Turpel-Lafond as the first RCY also *indirectly* incorporates aspects of the adversarial system. Turpel-Lafond is a lawyer, a legal academic, and is currently on leave from the Saskatchewan Provincial Court where she is a judge, having been appointed in 1998. She has also worked as a criminal law judge in youth and adult court. She has a lengthy history of involvement in projects relating to access to justice, judicial independence, sexually exploited children and youth, and children and youth with disabilities including those who suffer from foetal alcohol disorder. It has long been noted that in the Canadian public law order, inquisitorial initiatives such as commissions and public inquiries are often headed by retired or acting judges.[56] While not adversarial on the surface, then, the role morality and rights advocacy endemic to the common law adversarial system is blended with the inquisitorial model through the appointments process. Such a blending, however, is clearly contingent on the types of persons who are selected for the position as an ongoing commitment, and future RCYs may not always have this legal background.

Close to half of the children in care in B.C. are Aboriginal, with a similar pattern existing across the country. In provinces with significant Aboriginal populations – including B.C. – children's representatives also incorporate a particularized focus on the circumstances of Aboriginal children. The selection of Turpel-Lafond illustrates this point well since she is an active member of the Muskeg Lake Cree Nation in Saskatchewan.[57] Her early life mirrors the experience of many of the children she represents – growing up in a poor home that was also afflicted by alcoholism and violence. Her background significantly underscores the policy shift that the RCY as in institution represents: the principle of family autonomy no

56 For an excellent overview of public inquiries in Canada, see Peter Carver, "Getting the Story Out: Accountability and the Law of Public Inquiries" in Colleen Flood & Lorne Sossin, eds, *Administrative Law in Context: A New Casebook*, 2d ed (Toronto: Emond Montgomery, 2012) 541.

57 She published a book on the history of the Muskeg Lake Cree Nation that was short-listed for a 2005 Saskatchewan Book Award. Turpel-Lafond says that she wrote the book for her children. See Mary Ellen Turpel-Lafond, *Maskeko-sakahikanihk: 100 years for a Saskatchewan First Nation* (Saskatoon: Houghton-Boston, 2005).

longer is balanced equally against the best interests of the child but, rather, the best interests will be weighted more heavily than family autonomy. This policy shift is most clearly recognized in British Columbia, Ontario and New Brunswick.[58] Each of these jurisdictions engaged in major reform after the tragic deaths of Aboriginal children. In jurisdictions with substantial Aboriginal populations, the best interests of the child will likely be supported by the principle of respecting different cultural and local community practices. The CFCSA, for example, explicitly requires the preservation of an Aboriginal child's cultural identity to be part of the determination of best interests by a director of adoption or a provincial court. In B.C., the "best interests" framework – understood as either a legal principle or a legal test – was subject to major debate over whether it was culturally and class specific, and therefore would be inappropriately applied to Aboriginal families. The outcome of these debates resulted in this modified best interests principle.[59]

The last notable feature of the RCY attests to the role of the office in furthering democratic and rule of law objectives. The enabling statute contains a powerful provision guaranteeing a "right to information." This right, which will be discussed in more detail in the following subsection, gives the RCY the power to access any information in the control of a public body (other than an officer of the legislature) or director that the RCY herself deems necessary to exercise his or her statutory powers, functions and duties.[60] Importantly, the public body or director *must* disclose this information despite confidentiality or privilege claims (other than solicitor–client privilege).[61]

Turpel-Lafond has used her statutory powers and mandate effectively.[62] Her earlier calls for the reinstatement of the position of director for child welfare met with success in 2011.[63] This position was axed in 2008, but Turpel-Lafond called

58 For an example of this shift in the weight given to governing principles, see New Brunswick's *Family Services Ac*t, SNB 1980, c F-2.2.

59 See, for example, s 52 of the *Law and Equity Act*, RSBC 1996, c 253: "52(1) In proceedings involving the guardianship, custody, access to or maintenance of a child the court must consider the best interests of the child. (2) Subsection (1) does not apply in proceedings under the *Child, Family and Community Service Act* except as provided in that Act."

60 RCYA, *supra* note 42, s 10(2).

61 *Ibid*, s 10(3) and (4). The *RCYA* is also subject to s.51 of the provincial *Evidence Act* relating to restrictions with respect to health care evidence.

62 Progress, however, has not been smooth and the RCY has repeatedly criticized the Ministry of Children and Family Development for failing, after more than five years, to implement more than half of Justice Hughes' 62 recommendations. See Representative for Children and Youth, News Release, "Missed Opportunities in Progress on Hughes Recommendations: A Symptom of Bigger Ministry Problems" (29 November 2010), online: http://www.rcybc.ca/Images/PDFs/News%20Releases/Hughes%20Rpt%20NR%20 Final%20.pdf.

63 See "B.C. Appoints Child Welfare Director", *CBC News* (31 March 2011) online: CBC News http://www.cbc.ca/news/canada/british-columbia/story/2011/03/31/bc-child-welfare-hughes.html.

for a new director after her January 2011 inquiry into the death of 21 infants in B.C. in order to provide more accountability into infant deaths and ensure that standards in child welfare practices are complied with. In October 2011, a special committee of the legislative assembly was struck to consider the re-appointment of Turpel-Lafond to her second term as required by section 2 of the RCYA. This special committee unanimously recommended her reappointment, which took effect in November 2011.[64]

Challenges to Independence and Judicial Review's Protective Potential

As we have seen, the BCRCY combines several functions: high-level advocacy on behalf of children, youth and their families; sophisticated policy development and systemic advocacy; review and investigation of deaths and critical injuries of children and youth receiving government services; and, auditing, monitoring, and reporting. Not only does the RCY represent a polyjural model of decision-making, it also serves a multidisciplinary coordination function across government departments. Lastly, it promotes open government and public accountability in a collaborative manner with other public bodies.

Challenges to the independence of the RCY take many forms, some obvious while others are more novel. Independent public institutions generally face threats to their independence in three ways: statutory reforms to reduce jurisdiction and powers; executive control of the appointments process; and budget cuts. Though financial support appears steady in B.C., economic downturns can easily result in substantial cuts to even well-regarded bodies.[65] And, as explained above, although the appointments process for the RCY is more rigorous and constrained than conventional processes of appointment in the administrative state through the use of executive discretion, the integrity of a public body significantly depends on the quality of the persons leading and staffing it.

Lastly, the RCY has faced a recent challenge to its powers and structural independence through an attempt at legislative reform. In April 2010 the provincial Liberal government, under then Premier Gordon Campbell, introduced legislation specifically aimed at not only restricting the ability of the RCY to access cabinet

64 For the official press release, see: Legislative Assembly Province of British Columbia, Press Release, "B.C. Representative for Children and Youth Reappointed for a Second Term" (15 November 2011) online: Legislative Assembly of British Columbia http://www.leg.bc.ca/cmt/39thparl/session-4/rfcay/media/mediaReleases/HTML/Rel-RFCAY-39-4-BCRepForChildrenAndYouthReappointedForSecondTerm-2011-NOV-15.htm.

65 In 2007, the RCY won the public battle to have her budget increased by an all-party finance committee: "Children's Watchdog Gets Full Budget Hike", *The Globe and Mail* (15 December 2007) online: http://www.theglobeandmail.com/news/national/childrens-watchdog-gets-full-budget-hike/article1367187/. Many motivated stakeholder groups in B.C. are committed to scrutinizing the provincial government in order to ensure optimal interaction with the RCY.

documents, but doing so retroactively.[66] The government asserted that cabinet privilege protected this information while Turpel-Lafond countered that "It's very important in my role to have a look at the system behind the curtain, if you like, and then very carefully report to the public to say, 'Here's an issue, here's what happened, here are some reasonable suggestions for improvement in the future.'… I'm in a pickle."[67] She maintained that she had access to cabinet documents in the past and that she, as a judge, was well aware of her duties not to violate privacy issues or disclose sensitive information to the public. The proposed bill was included in a miscellaneous package of unrelated legislation, leading to charges that the government was attempting reform by stealth tactics.

The RCY challenged the Office of the Premier and the Ministry of Children and Family Development (MCFD) in court seeking to enforce her right to information and disclosure of documents she needed in the course of her formal audit of the then "Child in the Home of a Relative" Program.[68] In May 2010, the B.C. Supreme Court determined that the provincial legislature did not intend that the s.20 legislative remedy contained in the RCYA should preclude the RCY's access to court in order to obtain a remedy for statutory breaches of s.10. In her judgment, Madame Justice Griffin suggested that the envisioned legislative remedy would be a report from the RCY containing a complaint that the Speaker would then present to the legislative assembly and the Select Standing Committee on Children and Youth. The assembly could, if it wanted to, compel persons to appear before it with the required documents. The legislative assembly would then have to determine

---

66 Bill 20, *Miscellaneous Statutes Amendment Act* (No. 3), 2nd Sess, 39th Parl, British Columbia, 2010, c 21. Section 36 originally provided that:

> Section 10 of the *Representative for Children and Youth Act*, S.B.C. 2006, c. 29, is amended
>
> (a) by repealing subsection (1) and substituting the following:
>
> (1) In this section:
>
> "committee" includes a committee designated under section 12 (5) of the *Freedom of Information and Protection of Privacy Act*;
>
> "officer of the Legislature" has the same meaning as in the *Freedom of Information and Protection of Privacy Act*, but does not include the representative, and
>
> (b) by adding the following subsection:
>
> (2.1) Subsection (2) does not apply with respect to information that would reveal the substance of deliberations of the Executive Council or any of its committees, including any advice, recommendations, policy considerations or draft legislation or regulations submitted or prepared for submission to the Executive Council or any of its committees.

67 New Legislation Will 'Cripple' B.C.'s Representative", *The Globe and Mail* (30 April 2010) online: http://www.theglobeandmail.com/news/british-columbia/new-legislation-will-cripple-bcs-childrens-representative/article1367247/.

68 *Representative for Children and Youth v British Columbia (Children and Family Development)*, 2010 BCSC 697. Of the approximately 4500 children in the program at the time, almost 50 per cent were Aboriginal.

whether the necessary information fell within a proper s.10 demand, and whether there had been non-compliance with that demand. She further noted that this process would likely require a determination of a claim concerning solicitor–client privilege, a function that normally lies outside the purview of a legislature and, because of this, the legislative remedy might prove inadequate or ineffective. But, on her interpretation of the statutory scheme, the legislature had in fact contemplated this potential problem. Section 23(5) contained clear legislative intent that the legislature never intended to "oust the courts" so that there was only a legislative remedy if the RCY was faced with a party refusing to comply with the RCYA.[69] Citing the principle of the rule of law as a justification for remedying this potential gap in a statutory scheme aiming to constrain arbitrary executive action, Madame Justice Griffin declared:

> The rule of law is a fundamental premise of our legal and democratic system. It means that no one is immune from law or excluded from the benefit of the law. For this reason, the notion that anyone, especially persons holding high public office, can breach their statutory duties without being accountable to a court of law is a highly exceptional proposition.[70]

She observed that the only documents specifically excluded from the duty to disclose in the statute are those covered by solicitor–client, not cabinet privilege, and that this could not have been a legislative oversight.[71] Lastly, if executive actors were concerned about the potential use of the documents by the RCY as they claimed, they too could seek either the prerogative remedy of prohibition in court which would constrain the RCY's conduct to her statutory confines, or a declaration clarifying the meaning of the confidentiality provisions in the RCYA that would relate to the information the government was obliged to produce. Justice Griffin concluded that the RCY had a right to the information, that the MCFD and the Office of the Premier breached their statutory duty, and therefore the RCY was entitled to the remedy of mandamus ordering the production of the documents. Justice Griffin articulated in her judgment what Justice Hughes initially argued in his report: that the goal of the RCY is to restore public confidence, depoliticize

69 Section 23(5) of the RCYA reads:

> The representative and a person appointed, employed or retained by the representative under section 7(1) or (4) or 15 must not give or be compelled to give evidence in a court or in proceedings of a judicial nature in respect of any matter coming to their knowledge in the exercise of powers and the performance of functions and duties under this Act, except
>
> (a) to enforce the representative's powers of review and investigation,
>
> (b) to enforce compliance with this Act, or
>
> (c) with respect to a trial of a person for perjury.

70 *Ibid* at para 74.

71 *Ibid* at paras 91–92.

child welfare issues, and provide a strong system of accountability. The right to information supported these goals. The offending section was removed from Bill 20 before it became enacted as law in June 2010.

Following Justice Griffin's decision, the RCY and the MCFD signed an Advocacy Protocol in 2011 aiming to, among many items, clarify their roles, commit to coordination and reciprocal respect, remove barriers to the RCY's functioning, and re-affirm the RCY's right to information in a timely manner.[72] Though the protocol provides another confirmation of how dynamic this model of accountability has become, it also serves as a reminder of executive efforts to remove a powerful public law right. The next stage of development will be the mandatory five-year comprehensive review under section 30 of the RCYA which requires the Select Standing Committee on Children and Youth to determine, among other statutory matters, whether the Representative's functions as described in section 6, are still required. The review will be completed in 2012.

Bodies such as the RCY are vulnerable to reform efforts when majority governments disagree with actions and criticisms and can put their displeasure into legislative effect. When this happens, the RCY's case stands as an example of how the adversarial legal system has the potential to protect a vulnerable investigative body. A broader institutional perspective affirms the complementary role that adversarial courts can play though judicial review, by acting as a necessary check on executive power and providing essential support for democratic and rule of law forms of accountability.[73] This does not mean, however, that the form of accountability served by the offices like the RCY will or need become more "legalized" or "judicialized."

"The Child is Father of the Man": International Kinship[74]

While a full examination is not possible in the confines of this paper, I will conclude by highlighting the convergence of norms around children's rights and institutional models in Western legal orders.

---

72 Representative for Children and Youth, *Advocacy Protocol between the Ministry of Children and Family Development and the Representative of Children and Youth* (4 April 2011), online: http://www.mcf.gov.bc.ca/child_protection/pdf/rcy_advocacy_protocol.pdf.

73 For a similar argument on the need for a range of functionally-complementary institutions providing a diversity of accountability approaches, see Mark Elliott, "Ombudsmen, Tribunals, Inquiries: Re-Fashioning Accountability Beyond the Courts", University of Cambridge Faculty of Law Research Paper No. 21/2012 (August 22, 2012), online: http://ssrn.com/abstract=2133879.

74 From William Wordsworth, "My heart leaps up when I behold" which is the epigraph to *Ode: Intimation of Immortality*.

International Relations

The last twenty years have seen substantial changes regarding the strength of children's rights – Western societies exhibit far less ambivalence about their importance – and the influence of the CRC domestically. Situating the RCY in the international landscape (see Table 17.3), we can see the growing right of children to participate in formal decision-making, to be listened to, and to be heard in various proceedings that affect their lives. Many jurisdictions clearly refer to the CRC in enabling legislation or incorporate particular principles to guide judicial interpretation, inform general standards and soft law, and constrain administrative action in order to conform to international norms. Even without incorporation in dualist legal systems, increased porosity is evident.[75] In monist jurisdictions, the CRC clearly has direct influence. The prevailing ethos is child-centred and child-inclusive with an emphasis on participatory rights that embody substantive guarantees of procedural fairness and recognize the equal moral status of children.

Table 17.3 confirms that the general trend in Western countries regarding the most effective institutional model has been to create independent and stand-alone bodies with a specialized focus on children. Systemic reform in Canada includes the recent strengthening of functions and independence of offices in Ontario and British Columbia by decoupling child advocacy from ombuds functions. Since the 1990s, states and territories in Australia have created children's commissioners. New Zealand created its Children's Commissioner in 2003. Lastly, Europe has seen the expansion of children's ombuds since Norway created the first Ombudsman for Children in 1981 with the United Kingdom providing some of the latest developments.[76]

Evolving Capacities

It is not hard to conclude that the elevation of children's moral worth has had a concomitant bolstering of the powers of public bodies charged with taking their views, rights and interests into account and facilitating their voice and will. The

75 For an early argument on the permeability of international norms in domestic law, see Stephen J Toope, "The Convention on the Rights of the Child: Implications for Canada" in M Freeman, ed, *Children's Rights: A Comparative Perspective* (Aldershot: Dartmouth Publishing, 1996).

76 For a list of members of the European Network of Ombudspersons for Children, see http://www.crin.org/enoc/members/index.asp. The European Network of Ombudspersons for Children (ENOC) is a not-for-profit association of independent children's rights institutions, established in Norway in 1997. Latin American also has many ombuds with children's rights units or staff dedicated to defending children's rights. For an earlier comprehensive overview of international developments, see Linda C Reif, "The Ombudsman for Children: Human Rights Protection and Promotion" in *The Ombudsman, Good Governance and the International Human Rights* System (Boston: Martinus Nijhoff Publishers, 2004).

value shift in cultural norms influences the representational and advocacy capacities of these institutions that must embody this new perspective. As Daiva Stasiulis argues, "Rather than view children as 'pre-citizens', or as silent, invisible, passive objects of parental and/or state control … children are cast as full human beings, invested with agency, integrity and decision-making capacities."[77] Guarantees of procedure fairness like those found in Articles 3 and 12 of the CRC give real effect to the substantive moral commitments confirming the dignity of child citizens. Nevertheless, an eye to historical development and recent innovation serves to remind that procedures, representation, and decision-making frameworks can, inadvertently and when badly designed, make the vulnerable even more vulnerable.

As a novel hybrid model, the BCRCY combines strong and systemic advocacy on behalf of children, youth and their families, many of whom are Aboriginal; sophisticated policy development; the review and investigation of deaths and critical injuries of children and youth receiving government services; auditing, monitoring, and reporting; and a multidisciplinary coordination function across government departments. Lastly, it promotes open government and public accountability in a collaborative manner with other public bodies. Though I have argued that a hybrid institutional model such as the RCY is a positive development, like other statutorily created bodies it is vulnerable to executive pressure and legal change. In the face of an attempt by the executive branch to curtail power and independence through statutory reform, the effectiveness of the RCY's democratic accountability function was vindicated by judicial enforcement of the right to information. The legal model of accountability therefore complemented the ombuds and the inquisitorial forms. But despite this optimal result, this case study therefore poses the recurring question of whose interests are being served at what costs regardless of the label or model chosen.

77 Stasiulis, *supra* note 7 at 508–9.

Index

For Product Safety Concerns and Information please contact our EU representative GPSR@taylorandfrancis.com
Taylor & Francis Verlag GmbH, Kaufingerstraße 24, 80331 München, Germany

www.ingramcontent.com/pod-product-compliance
Ingram Content Group UK Ltd.
Pitfield, Milton Keynes, MK11 3LW, UK
UKHW022007180926
475701UK00003B/236

9780367601317